Three Faces of Autumn

Three Faces of Autumn

Poetry, Prose, Translations

A Charles Guenther Retrospective

❧

First in a Projected Series

MID-AMERICA MASTERS

from

THE MID-AMERICA PRESS, INC.

Three Faces of Autumn

Poetry, Prose, Translations

A Charles Guenther Retrospective

EDITED AND WITH AN INTRODUCTION
BY
ROBERT C. JONES

෭ THE MID-AMERICA PRESS, INC.

THE MID-AMERICA PRESS, INC.,
P.O. Box 575
Warrensburg, Missouri 64093-0575

Copyright © 2006 by Charles Guenther

Charles Guenther's photo by Nancy T. Jones

ISBN 0-910479-28-3

To Esther and my family

for their love and encouragement

INTRODUCTION

"Even in a world which tends to be imitative, regimented and standardized, each poet is his own definition of poet, his own conscience, his own value, held in abeyance perhaps for a more solicitous appraisal by a generation later than his own."

Thus Charles Guenther, on the "definition of poet," in 1973, when he was awarded the Order of Merit of the Italian Republic, in the rank of Knight Commander, in recognition of his translations of Italian poetry—among them, poems of the late Nobel Prize winner Salvatore Quasimodo—and his "long and valuable work permeating two cultures."

Born in St. Louis, Missouri, April 29, 1920, Charles Guenther began writing poetry when he was 15, a student at Kirkwood High School. It was the beginning of a task still in progress: the task of defining himself as "poet."

In high school, he devoted hours in the library to reading poetry—especially European poetry, in translation at first and later in the original language. He learned French in school and started doing his own translations, writing out the literal English and then polishing it. From there, he moved into Italian, buying copies of Petrarch and Dante, reading the words, looking them up in a dictionary and writing the definitions in the margins. "It's hard to say why I started. Why does a person smoke or why does a person bowl?" He nods his head. "In a great poem, there is something magic, a haunting spirit. It's so rare that you keep looking for it."

He graduated from high school at 17 and went to work at the *St. Louis Star Times,* on the 5 a.m. to 2 p.m. shift as a copy boy. "It was the best experience a writer could have," he remembers, "because newspaper people—then, anyway—were a special and temperamental breed. It exposed you to the human comedy." He also enrolled in Jefferson College in St. Louis, where he edited the school paper. It was there that his first published translation appeared: a sonnet from the French of 16th century poet Joachim du Bellay. "I vowed I'd stop translating at 25—but never did stop. The challenge of poetry in other languages than English is so persistent that any poet who knows other languages ought to work in them to improve his own poetry."

In 1938 he left the *Star-Times* to enroll in Harris Teachers College where his courses included French, Spanish and extracurricular Greek. After graduation (AA, 1940) he passed exams for, and accepted several jobs for, the State of Missouri. In 1942-43 he worked for the U.S. Department of Labor and the Army Corps of Engineers; and in 1943 he transferred to the Army Air Corps (now U.S. Air Force) as a library technician heading a research unit at the agency later known as the Aeronautical Chart & Information Center (ACIC).

He remained at ACIC for 32 years, until 1974. There, after Federal exams, he was promoted to professional positions as a translator and librarian; and later (with off-duty studies at Saint Louis University) to geographer and supervisory cartographer. His translation duties had included geographic treatises and airport bulletins ("Not as interesting as translating poetry," he says, "but matters critically important to flight safety—the status of airports, radio frequencies, lighting and runways— which had to be printed and distributed as quickly as possible."). In the evening, after 1952, he taught writing courses, and continued writing and translating poetry. He corresponded with poets, writers and editors throughout the world and sent manuscripts to magazines: in the U.S., France, Italy, Greece, Japan, Australia, Africa . . . . His poems and translations appeared in more than 300 different journals and dozens of anthologies.

And in the midst of his "second job" of writing poems and translating poems, on April 12, 1953, with a review of Saint-John Perse's *Winds*, he began five extraordinary decades as a freelance writer for the *St. Louis Post-Dispatch*. "When that first review appeared," he remembers, "I considered reviewing a 'civic honor.' I still do." Readers found him to be "the rare reviewer who could recognize quality wherever it presented itself, and who loved the fresh and the new if it was good." When he retired as a reviewer, in December 2003, Book Editor Jane Henderson noted: "The *Post-Dispatch* gave Guenther a wider readership than many poets have. But Charles Guenther gave the *Post-Dispatch* a breadth of knowledge and experience that will be impossible to replace."

Meanwhile, he was active in library and writers' organizations; and he taught or directed workshops at writers' conferences in the U.S. during vacations. With his wife Esther, he also hosted gatherings for local and visiting poets.

In 1975, having received a BA and MA from Webster College in 1973 and 1975, he retired from government service to complete doctoral courses at Saint Louis University and pursue a career in teaching. He was appointed, in 1976, as Midwest Regional vice-president of the Poetry Society of America, succeeding poet John G. Neihardt (1881-1973); and until 1990, he organized the first PSA-Midwest conferences held in St. Louis. He also taught in Missouri and Kansas poets-in-the-schools programs; and, intermittently, English and French at a half-dozen colleges in Missouri and Illinois. In 1979, Southern Illinois University at Edwardsville awarded him the honorary degree of Doctor of Humane Letters.

Since his early recognition by a few critics, Charles Guenther has established his place among prominent American translators. In 1972 he read and recorded his poetry for the Archive of Recorded Poetry and Literature at the Library of Congress. Besides his contributions to literary magazines and anthologies, he has published a dozen books of poems and translations and, in 1976, edited an anthology, *American Women Poets*. He has received a number of awards: the James Joyce Award (1974) and the Witter Bynner Translation grant (1979) from the Poetry Society of America; the French American Bicentennial Medal (1976); the St. Louis and Missouri Arts Awards (2001), and in 2002, the Emmanuel Roblès International Award in Poetry.

This Charles Guenther retrospective of poems, prose and translations is significant: not only because it is (as T. S. Eliot has said of Ezra Pound's criticism) the writing of a poet about poetry, but because it is the writing of "poet"—as Charles Guenther, in his task of seventy years and more, has defined "poet"—writing about writing. The work assembled here reminds us, as Charles Guenther himself has reminded us: "Recognition by one's peers—with a prize or the opportunity to judge others' work at a national or international level—is appreciated. But recognition is vain and fleeting. It is the work, not the prize or the honor, that matters most. The work endures."

A NOTE ON THE TEXT

This retrospective collection includes Charles Guenther's selections of his poetry, critical reviews and essays, and translations, 1937 – 2004.

In all cases, the texts have been supplied and approved by the author.

In all cases of reviews or other essays published in scholarly periodicals, as well as material previously unpublished, the copy texts are those that have, before publication here, been supervised by the author.

When writing for the *St. Louis Post-Dispatch* and the *St. Louis Globe-Democrat*, Charles Guenther employed the *Post-Dispatch*, and the *Globe-Democrat*, house styles of punctuation and spelling; during his five decades of newspaper publication, those house styles varied widely, and frequently the author did not correct proof. With Charles Guenther's approval, the style has been made to conform to modern usage—practices involving ellipses, periods after abbreviated titles, the position of quotation marks, the use of italics, and punctuation after set-off quotations from poems which end sentences.

Robert C. Jones
Warrensburg, Missouri

ACKNOWLEDGMENTS

Some poems and translations in this selection are previously unpublished. Many others have appeared, sometimes in earlier versions, in *Phrase/Paraphrase* (Iowa City: The Prairie Press, 1970), *The Hippopotamus, Selected Translations, 1948-1985* (Kansas City, Missouri: BkMk Press, 1986) and *Moving the Seasons* (Kansas City, Missouri: BkMk Press, 1994). Acknowledgment is made to the following journals and periodicals in which the remaining poems and translations have appeared:

> *The American Poetry Review, Askance, Athene, Chelsea, Choice, Driftwind, Focus/Midwest, The Formalist, International Anthology (Athens), The Kansas Magazine, Light, The Literary Review, Luna, The Mid-America Poetry Review, Midland Poetry Review, The Midwest Quarterly, Nevertheless Press, New Directions, New Letters, The New Yorker, The Observer, Palisade, Partisan Review, Il Pensiero, Poet Lore, Poetry, Poetry Fund Journal, Quarterly Review of Literature, Quartet, River Styx, St. Louis Post-Dispatch, The Sparrow, Steppenwolf, The University Review, Webster Review, Weid, Western Humanities Review.*

Although extensive efforts have been made to communicate with all who hold copyrights in the material in this volume, it is possible that the efforts, for a variety of reasons, have not succeeded. If such instances have occurred, the Editor states that any errors brought to his attention will be corrected in later editions of this book.

*

The author expressly thanks Dr. Robert C. Jones, who initially proposed this book. Dr. Jones's considerable efforts over several years in its compilation and publication—and reflecting his own experience as poet, editor and teacher—are deeply appreciated. Special thanks are due also to Nancy T. Jones for her arduous, scholarly editing assistance, including the preparation of the indexes to this volume.

CONTENTS

I. Poetry

1937 – 2004

Most of the poems included here appeared in literary magazines since the early 1940s and were reprinted in two collections: *Phrase/Paraphrase, Poems* (Iowa City: The Prairie Press, 1970) and *Moving the Seasons: Selected Poems* (Kansas City, Missouri: BkMk Press, 1994).

Not included are nearly all the poems written from the mid-1930s into the 1940s. These pieces, mostly exercises in form (ballades, triolets, quatrains and sonnets on topical, whimsical and patriotic themes), were published in college and little literary magazines and journals with work by other poets of that era, including George Abbé, August Derleth, William Carlos Williams and others. Among the magazines were *Driftwind* (Vermont), *Palisade* (Iowa), and *Poet Lore* (then in Boston).

The poems are arranged in approximate chronological order of composition and/or publication (from Early Poems to New and Selected Poems). Finally, the selection, Light Verse, is a small sampling of many such pieces (limericks and parodies) written over seven decades.

Early Poems

"The Porcelain Pagoda" (p. 5) and "Aia" (p. 6) are two poems representative of my earliest work. "The Porcelain Pagoda" was published in *Palisade: The Magazine of Poetry,* Volume II, No. 4, Winter, 1943—my first publication outside of campus journals. I felt especially honored because, in the same issue, only a few pages away, appeared William Carlos Williams's poem, "The Gentle Negress."

"Aia," unpublished until now, I preserved and pasted on the flyleaf of my copy of Homer's *The Odyssey.*

The Porcelain Pagoda

(For the religious martyrs of China)

Men sailing down the stream
look at the tiles, intact:
no more a lighted beam:
all was ransacked.

Rows of its idols were
broken and burned: within,
dusts, no incenses.
                                    Here
yellow leaves spin,

whirling upon the floor,
swirling, exposing old
bits of a lama's lore:
only the bold

pray, but their cult must go
deep in a mountain room
only a few may know,
temple and tomb.

In the black lakka leaves,
on the slim lakka bough,
lonely the wild bird grieves,
moans alone now.

Seasons and seasons go:
no sound of gong or chime:
Who curbs the river's flow
curbs only time.

[1937]

Aia

This island is still washed with spray and brine
Though it is not the same as when one strolled
Its fields and sandy beach (if it's true-told),
Lured to enchanted caves to drink and dine
On roasted boar and sweet Pramnian wine
While sailors entertained him as they lolled
Their bearded heads above goblets of gold
And Circe flung crisp acorns to her swine.

Sometime far off, when men still fight and sing
And Troy is almost a forgotten word
On tongues that need a tune or something brighter,
We shall hear one song always vibrating—
Yet there'll be other music to be heard
And other dawns, rose-fingered, even lighter.

[1938]

Helen at the Gate

"So now we'll be in better circumstances,"
The old Trojan muttered, watching Helen leave,
"But don't bear any grudges, men, or grieve;
Just pardon her. See, she pays us with sweet glances.
For cities gain when they put aside their lances,
And after the blood it's better to forgive
(I speak as a man, not as a conservative).
Thank God she's gone, the Greeks stop their advances."

Good counselor, they laugh at you, the younger
Impulsive boys moved to believe that there is
Some vestige of glory in the sword and scepter,
Their eager pulses quick with battle hunger
That beat and bled for Helen and for Paris.
Oh Menelaus always should have kept her!

[c. 1942]

"Tenson" was written about 1947 or earlier, when I was immersed in reading the troubadours. The poet and scholar Guy Davenport considered this one of my better poems—for he appreciated the story references embedded in its terse lines. The poem's "aura" is strictly medieval, but the final refrain may be found in English Renaissance songs.

A CHARLES GUENTHER RETROSPECTIVE
Poetry: Early Poems

Tenson
(with commentary)

> *Poeta, volontieri*
> *Parlerei a quei due che 'nseme vanno.*
> —Inferno V

> *J'étais obscur au simple populaire;*
> *Mais on dit aujourd'hui que je suis au contraire.*
> —Ronsard

Take a straight song Shun
circuit diluted wine
See the immodest sun
yield the strongest line—

Giraut who would forbear
poetry of the dark
dropped such a remark
adding upon the clear

—Sleep or be understood
Raimbaut you claim too hard
applause of the multitude
rime's only reward

But Raimbaut interposed
("virtuoso of form"
to whom legend supposed
Beatrix was warm)

—What if my song's not
thrown to the ends of the earth
is there any sot
can judge it what it's worth

No abundant dish
is ever delicate
Giraut—Damn me if you wish
I've salt on my plate

THREE FACES OF AUTUMN
Poetry, Prose, Translations

. . .

As Marcellus Giraut
overweeningly
indiscreet let go
praise of the Maccabees

though "a count's equal"
provoked a reprimand
from her he courted and
saw her buckler turn
                          The sequel

to Bernart the scullion for
he had loved Agnes
                          Caught
by the viscount he sought
tutelage of Eleanore

Guillem de Cabestanh
the countess Seremonde
loved ate his heart atoned
(relics at Perpignan)

And knave Guillem to whom
with mysterious pride
a trobairitz replied
All Provence knew the doom

of heretic chatelains
(but think of indigo-
eyed Lucinda's profane
commanded fandango)

Sing sing the prince of Blaye
sing Rousillon who ran
ruefully
                Dan dan
dan deridan deridan dei

[c. 1947]

10

For a Friend Unjustly Maligned

A Job struck by infinite
pain will manifest
his grief and only fears it
won't faze us in the least.
When we see his plight,
the open sores, the bed of pains,
we'd better get used to the sight:
a man suffers and complains.

While he's hurt and still endures
incredible agonies,
plagues without cures,
we've seen patience exceed his:
he groused about his tortures.
You knew much worse than these.

[c. 1947]

"Triptych . . ." is fact and fantasy. It was written on the Meramec
Community College campus, in Kirkwood. The campus, once the site of
St. Joseph's College (a Catholic seminary) had been a wooded farmland
where cattle roamed and grazed. My friends and I ice-skated on the pond
there in winter. The poem is also an exercise, written in T.S. Eliot's "three
voices of poetry."

Triptych Written at a Myra Cohn Livingston Lecture

1

Among the oaks dead or dying, one
rattles in the winter sky where a man, a runner
remembers its green in the woods, or under its sleep
as a skater, where its branches now
are frozen, black swallows over a vanished pond.

2

What if I were this dead or dying
oak, rattling in the winter sky? ... A man
must remember his green, a runner
in the woods, with the grass or the crisp
leaves underfoot; but now I'm only
this frozen limb where the black
swallows alight over the vanished pond.

3

You are this dead or dying oak, a man
rattling in the winter sky but remembering
the green of the woods with grass or autumn leaves
underfoot; and when the oak slept you skated
here where you stand frozen now, limbs,
black swallows over a vanished pond.

[c. 1957]

Ste. Genevieve: Memorial Cemetery

The children find a game among the stones,
Searching for dates on them under the heavy trees;
Oak, pine and dark-fruited mulberries
Whose roots embrace and are nourished by the bones
Of the Vallés and the Roziers and the Linns.
A holiday. The town has sealed itself from the heat
Or gravitates to a park across the street,
Just within view, where a carnival begins

With a crash of popular music: visible lives
Divisible. Here by the spider and the mold
Children stop to eat mulberries. Blue and gold,
The day presents its trophies. The bee thrives.
The seasons' wheel gyrates and disappears
And memory withers from memorable acts,
Stripped to pairs of inconsequential facts
Sunk in a tended lawn for the pioneers.

You aren't mine, gentle people, except through the womb
Of Eve: infants, couples who took your vows
Together, but I love your coolness in the boughs.
Seasons are shadows whose continuum
Is to die. But how life flourishes there
For the silent, invisible, indivisible dead
In a corner of shade we think uninhabited,
Since no swan cries in this monumental air.

[1959]

New
and
Selected Poems

Six Picassos, One Ernst

The Acrobats (PICASSO)

A fat man A frail boy
He heavy in wisdom He light in sin
Struck a rose and blue
Attitude on a box

Did this horned man
Procreate
That sky-haired nude
Innocence
Thin as it is
And will the red creature hold
For all plainly to see
The clear flesh in his grasp
And spoil it by his will?

Still Life with Skull and Leeks (PICASSO)

With its own smell
Of decay long gone
This skull
Grins at the living
Pitcher   The leeks
Lying unaired
By the locked window give
A new energy of death
To this cheekless

THREE FACES OF AUTUMN
Poetry, Prose, Translations

Dora Maar: Three Portraits (PICASSO)

The cow the bull
The vegetable

Bare flesh strong
Nostrils and water-
melon breast
The last
Red and green striped
Torso and glad
Face depressed

Two Figures (PICASSO)

Inscrutably
Weary and depressed
With secrets
Of love and poverty

They sit (unable
Perhaps even to buy
One drink one pipeful)
Blue and blue against blue

And stay
Far into morning
Until the cafe closes
And they must build their own fire

A CHARLES GUENTHER RETROSPECTIVE
Poetry: New and Selected Poems

Clarinet Player (PICASSO)

Green notes sounded
Downdraft in a
Slimy well
          Drawn
A deep song

But I'm in that well
Those mossy blocks
Aren't real   Over me
There's a yellow mouth
Of a man who fingers
The keys
          And beckons
Consummate music

The Mirror (PICASSO)

Her glass repeats
Face to face
Full
Profiled
Belly and breasts
Ovally
Doubled
The glass with her
Foretelling age
In gray
Blue purple
But the womb
Is green

THREE FACES OF AUTUMN
Poetry, Prose, Translations

Portrait (MAX ERNST)

More flesh than eyes
Blue flesh
Volleys of motion
Her body ordered
As a bird stretched
In mist

And the print
Of bottle and bouquet

Buds of laughing and
Eyes quenched
In a wall of day

[c. 1962]

Twelve Pettisongs

Schooner (FEININGER)

Flowing umber
topsail in precise
angles cleaving
blue and yellow

Loners (PAUL KLEE)

Only two
but not together
rather
walking alone into the dark
blue to the vivid sun

Birdcatcher (PAUL KLEE)

O the plumes
pink blue green
orange yellow brown
in a setting
of blood

Naked (MODIGLIANI)

Oval
shoulders broad
hips
red purple black
fleshed lips

THREE FACES OF AUTUMN
Poetry, Prose, Translations

Girl (MODIGLIANI)

Four-letter words:
look   wish   love   girl

Mother/Child (PICASSO)

Rosy brown mother
chestnut child
                    Was Jesus
white?

Pierrot (PICASSO)

How the frail white-
costumed flesh in black
hat and pumps
quarrels with the dark
red green and brown
for dominion

Vase /Flowers (PICASSO)

Can the flowers be more beautiful
than the vase
apparent in permanence
as a flashing swallow
blooms?

Bathers (RENOIR)

Shimmering raw
fawn-fleshed
trio

A CHARLES GUENTHER RETROSPECTIVE
Poetry: New and Selected Poems

Clown (RENOIR)

My flesh
as clown:
pink and blue
joy among animals
clawing the sawdust

Boy (RUBENS)

Pouting flushed
plump with dreams
still the encumbered
flesh of his mother

Sunflowers (VAN GOGH)

Corps of yellow
green-yellow
brown
green
An attack of sunflowers

[1962]

In the early 1960s the St. Louis Bicentennial (or Visitors) Commission asked me to "write a poem" for the dedication ceremony planned for the Old Post Office. I didn't realize (or care) that they probably wanted a short piece. The poem deals with the entry of the 50 states into the Union (in chronological order), with a kind of prologue and postlude. The Commission had ordered flags of all 50 states, which were to be hoisted by 50 Girl Scouts around the Post Office after dedication speeches (and my poem?) by politicians and city fathers. Although the poem was not read, I attended the ceremony. It was a bitterly cold, windy February day. When I saw the Girl Scouts, shivering in smart but flimsy uniforms, one Scout to each flag, my heart went out to them as they awaited the end of the verbose oratory. I was glad, also, my long poem had *not* been read; a whole generation of Girl Scouts might have remembered me with rancour.

A CHARLES GUENTHER RETROSPECTIVE
Poetry: New and Selected Poems

USA /50

"America is alone: many together"—A. MacLeish

1

What winds blown from old countries carried west
Eric, Lief (Eric's son) and all the rest,
Captains and navigators from Moguer,
Outcasts, conquistadores to spoil the flower
Of the New World! Vinland to Peru,
Fruit of the Indies filled their caravels:

It was a paradise—Ponce de Leon's—
Palms, flamingoes, flying fish, the sun
Shafting the swamps.
                    It was De Soto's too:
Beautiful as a cane box full of pearls,
Espiritu Santo to the Apalachi,
North and west, Tocaste, Napateca,
Blue butterflies, plumed warriors in canoes,
Tokens of love: Mochila, Macanoche.

Come, bearded rider, sleep in the belly of the stream:
The peel-fish take you, the barbel and the bream.

2

Sails slackened on the shoals:
                    Virginia!
White cranes flew up to the high cedars,
Granganimo, the copper-capped, the king
Of bows and arrows, jungle villages strode
Lands of blue grapes and mortar-beaten corn;
And smoke was sucked from the embers of burned weeds.

Pasonagessit revelry: Priapus
And Proteus in the host of Merry Mount,
Morton and his Maypole and his beer-

Mad bacchanalians gamboling on the green;
And Cotton Mather's wonders: witches in a field
Drunk with diabolical sacraments,
Shrieks of all tormented by invisible hands
And miraculous visions. Salem trials.

So the raven flag, the castle and the lion
Rose, lily banners, the orange white and blue
Hauled up the Half Moon in from Amsterdam,
And the red cross on white, white cross on blue,
The Union Jack, the English Meteor flew;
Pine trees and rattlesnakes, Colonial rebels
Cut out the cantons on the village square:

And Franklin played with lightning and the French.
Washington shaped a land out of Valley Forge.

3

There are two New Englands, north and south:
Maine, Vermont, New Hampshire form the one,
Connecticut, Rhode Island, Massachusetts,
The other.
   Colors of all seasons: the salt
Marshes, maples on the inland hills
In autumn, the long-shadowed winter,
Yellow spring and the heavy fruit and shade
Of summer: cranberries and marble,
Red cherry limbs, the lusty Merrimac
Draining the stingy soil out of New England.

West of New England, the fingers of placid lakes;
There's Troy and Rome, Utica, Syracuse,
Niagara, broken bottomland, Lily Dale,
Millerite, Chautauqua, Shaker, Shinnecock,
Land of Yankee Doodle and Rip Van,
Vassar, island of fire, sing sing New York!

Newcastle, Kent and Sussex, Delaware
Of duco lucite dacron cellophane—names

A CHARLES GUENTHER RETROSPECTIVE
Poetry: New and Selected Poems

Milled by the willows on the Brandywine,
Clan of the admirable admiral.

Pennsylvania, America's friend:
Pittsburgh Gettysburg Hershey's chocolate bars
Ingots and blooms, electric boats and bears,
Germantown, Chestnut Hill and Seven Stars.

New Jersey, island of the Delaware—
Passaic Paterson Hudson's Palisades—
Slave of two cities bursts like a rose.

Empire state of the South, of rococola,
Coosa and Tallapoosa. Georgia booze
Grows hair on Brasstown Bald. Drink Coca-Cola

In Maryland east on Chesapeake Bay
The Chester Choptank Nanticoke Pocomoke rivers
Roll red and yellow. West to Wills Mountain,
The Appalachian Ridge; Antietam Creek
And Conococheague wind south to the Potomac;
Great Cumberland, the Piedmont, Sugar Loaf—
All testimonials to Baltimore.

South Carolina: sectional
Lowland and upland, hinterland and salt
Palmetto beaches, herons and hemlocks.

North Carolina: intellectual
Of Black and Blue Ridge Mountains, Hairy Bear,
Dismal Swamp, sound of the Albemarle.

Virginia, bright Virginia: daring Byrds
And brilliant Glass, apple aristocrat.

West Virginia, little Switzerland,
Charleston on the Kanawha, Koppers, raw
Star of synthetics, Wheeling of steel.

4

Maine and Vermont, mountain and maple.

From the Yadkin to Kentucky Daniel Boone
Opened the wilderness into Tennessee:

White Oak and Chickamauga, Tennessee
Is ridge and river, scarp and rolling plain,
Reelfoot, Cumberland, Big Monday mules.

Bluegrass and moonshine, possum and raccoon:
Heaven is Kentucky. Pennyrile and knobs.

Porcelain and peonies, an empire within
An empire, of Napoleon, Greasy Ridge,
Timken roller bearings, nuts and bolts,
Derricks and cranes, Buckeye wheelbarrows:
Ohio's deeper boom runs everywhere.

Indiana chimneys and yellow corn:
Hoosierland—sand, soil and light.

Oxbow and bayou, loblollies oaks
Cotton and indigo, azaleas, Rose
Of Mississippi, Natchez in decay.

Alabama: Tuskegee's trees,
Chickasaws Choctaws Creeks and Cherokees,
Coosa, Raccoon and Lookout, Little mountains.

Herculean Illinois and the dinosaur
Of cities: King of the Bombers Schemer Bugs
And thugs—Urbana Rockford Elgin Bloom-
ington East St. Louis Chicagoans
Hinky Dink, Bathhouse John and Scarface Al.

Detroit men with the millimeter gauge
Are Michigan's fishermen. River Rouge,
Willow Run, mercurial juggernauts.

A CHARLES GUENTHER RETROSPECTIVE
Poetry: New and Selected Poems

Manitowok, Sheboygan, melting pot
Of Germans Poles Norwegians Swiss and Danes:
Oshkosh Kenosha Neehah Green Bay—craft
Of Kraft and Kleenex, Borden's Badger State.

5

Missouri, little Dixie state of the saints
(Louis Charles Joseph François Genevieve)
Boonslick and Ozark, Taum Sauk, Pilot Knob.

St. Louis rose on timber, brick and stone,
Bellefontaine south to Carondelet,
Grew to the west, setting of steel and glass,
Seed of all settlement, womb of the West.

Louisiana: Creole and Cajun,
Noblesse of Negro, corn and Carnival.

Sweet Home and Hot Springs, chinchillas, Lake
Hamilton, melons of Hope, diamonds, strawberries, Ozarks and orchids—Arkansas.

Strawland oatland cornbelt Iowa hogs
("Corn makes 'em fat, it's oats that make 'em grow")

Port of Duluth, sea-fronting, swollen blue
Country of Astor, Sieur du Lhut, the Sioux,
The Chippewa, tamarack twist of the gray Mesabi,
Glaciers and gladioli, purple ore.

Heart of America Kansas, people of the south
Wind, out of New England and the South,
They came with Beecher's Bibles, buffalo
Hunters preachers abolitionists came,
Nation of Carry and Curry bleeding, one
Track of the Osage, Pike's Route, Oregon,
Lem Blanchard and the jayhawk yellow as the sun-
flower, yellow as corn and Turkey wheat.

29

And out of Nebraska William Jennings Bryan
Came, out of flat water country, railroad land
Of dusty Omaha, cornhusker city of men.

Colorado cradled potash padishahs,
Barons of sugar-beets, margraves of mines.
Big Thompson and Blue River, Gunnison
Tunnel through the Divide, irrigate
And make the prairie bloom, O columbine!

North Dakota, flickertail, inflamed
Whirlpool of semolina flour and wheat,
Sentinel Butte and Killdeer, Cannonball.

South Dakota, heart and soul of the great
Plain of the world: Bad Lands Black Hills Sioux Falls
Red and White Rivers Rushmore Borglum busts
Spearfish and Owl, chukar partridges.

Montana—it's "bigger than Italy"—
Of Wheelers dealers Anacondas and Hel-
ena's hot afternoons
                    Golcondas bawdy Butte
Custer Copperopolis and the Scratch-
Gravel Mountains, Molly Muck-a-Chuck
And Buttermilk Jim, Black Eagle, Hungry Horse
Sunburst gazoonis sapphires in the mud.

Down to the land of trails, the Oregon
Mormon Bridger's Bozeman Overland
Here where the rivers rise and flow to the west
And south: the Snake, North Platte and Yellowstone,
Rectangular Wyoming. O Jackson Hole!

Oklahoma: Five Civilized Tribes
By whom all things were given, even the land.

6

Florida: Big Cypress, Apalachicola,
Okeechobee and Okefenokee,

The circus, the citrus and the Seminole.

7

The Spaniards brought hide, hoofs and horns, longhorns,
Then shorthorns, hornless Anguses ran the range,
Santa Gertrudis, Texas strawberries.

(New Mexico's where Mr. Coronado
Ate corn-on-the-cob and bears have corkscrew tails
So they can sit without sliding into Texas.)

8

Rogue and Coquille, Burnt, Powder — rivers run
The Snake-edged state of the beaver Oregon
Of Klamath, Mount Mazama's Crater Lake.

Seattle to Spokane, the slopes of wheat,
Copper and fawn, emerald tumbleweeds,
Wenatehee red-cheeked apples, Walla Walla,
Rainier, Olympus, coulees and cascades.

Sandpoint to Pocatello, Idaho falls:
Moscow to Paris, Bear and Bitter Root
Lo Lo Clearwater Craters of the Moon.

9

California had men to match her mountains:
Cortez, Juan Rodriguez Cabrillo searched
For seven golden cities never found;
Fremont, Tom Larkin, Sutter and King (James)
Civilized a land of barbarous names:
Hangtown Puke Ravine Hell's Delight
Gouge Eye Brandy Gulch Petticoat Slide.

Deseret Utah and the living God,
Driven to the desert, Mormon pioneers,
The twelve apostles lean and bearded gray.

Naughty Nevada: Reno Tonopah
Towns of roulette and faro, slot machines

31

Lost Wages
                O bonanza! Comstock Lode

Arizona: Pimas, Penitentes,
The risen phoenix, tombstone epitaph.

10

Jump off to Juneau, sniff the Klondike air.
Chilkat   Kodiak   Katmai fumaroles
Barrow to Ketchikan, Aleutian chain,
Triangle of islands, panhandle, plateau;
Bering to Yukon, sedimented gold,
Salmon and spruce, walrus and wolverine,
Offshoots, Aleuts, Alaskan Eskimos!

11

Hilo to Honolulu and Niihau,
Green plains of Kaneohe, mynah birds
Chirp in the flame trees, banyans, coconuts:
Hawaii is aloha, holiday,
Head of a diamond, heart of a pearl.

12

Now men go weightless, fixed by the same star
That guided the mariner out of San Lucar,
And separate from the land, the forgotten land;
Blind to the rising headlands, the soft rain
Falling on the savannahs, the singing wind-
gaps in the Alleghenies, the long sundown
Hung high in the dusty plains, spikes of flame,
Snowplants in the Sierras and the black
Sands of Kalapana, the prairies choked with sand:

Remember the land, remember the land.

[c. 1962]

E. E. C.*

E.E. would have given us
the roof of his treehouse
(the better to see the
      " s   k   y ")

let no one trespass there
to take from his Nature
for man-ready rifles
make man-loving neighbors

No painter of unmyths
he knew realistic
alias "anecdotal"
was NOT legal tender

nor was nonobjective
alias "abstract"
both MIScalled "art"
(two sides of the same coin)

the man of good humor
of tulips and chimneys
whose art was a question
of being alive

looked forward to back
a most meaningful birth
until a red tide
freed a miraculous flood

  * *"Thank you for asking if I want my name in lower case:
no, I do not."*—Letter, January 17, 1958.

[1963]

33

THREE FACES OF AUTUMN
Poetry, Prose, Translations

Snow Country

In my mind there's a white country
with white trees
and black running brooks
and ponds stiff with reeds.
I take my sled again and go coasting
down the same hill where as boys
we went bellybusting, body piled
on body, breath on neck, eyes
stinging watery in the frosted air.

It was faster faster faster
we'd race and yell, urging the slope, coaxing momentum
like a runaway horse,
until—if we were lucky—the slowing sled careened
and we'd somersault shouting in heaps
through a snowbank, then arise
walking snowmen.

But now the hill is shorter and less steep
and the wind nips even through insulated clothes
and burns the ears and nose;
foot-flexed the sluggish runners ride
surfaces packed by cleated wheels
and not the least
riot enlivens this orderly winter.

What was the excitement of it? Each,
afterwards around the fire, with flaring cheeks
and warming the other. Nothing else.
Nothing? I remember now the steel tracks
and the lingering scream of a train in the icy night.
Down there was a second hill,
forbidden, where none of us ever coasted.
Now is the time to try it.

[1964]

Birdcatcher

A flight bending
the reeds of
easy ponds seeks
asylum in the
cold horizon.

Under the noisy
flock a birdcatcher
trumpets but a
farther distance
calls them, an inner
wind torments them,
they weave unknowing
the tightest net
where feathers disappear,
from first to last
the sky lifts at
their isosceles
advance: a breathlessness
of birds.

[1965]

"Arch," written about the time the Gateway Arch was completed, was one of many pattern poems I wrote when the Concrete poem became popular. Actually, the "concrete" or pattern poem dates back several thousand years, and carries through English Renaissance poetry and the European Dadaist and Surrealist poetry. It took me three different typewriters of differing type sizes to make the "arch" pattern; until now, the poem has been printed only once in that pattern, in *The Observer* (Southern Illinois University at Edwardsville) in a "sampling" of poems, in May 1979. I had submitted the poem to the *St. Louis Post-Dispatch* for possible use, but the art editor, George McCue, sent it back to me with an apologetic note saying that he'd like to use it, but feared there'd be a printers' strike if it were sent to the composing room.

ARCH

```
              your      rose
           Eero but  a hero's
          are gone O  window on
            brocades  a court  of
             busts &    freedom
             of gray     falling
             palaces      or ris-
             draped        ing Elk-
            purple-         coated
            liered           Lewis &
           chande-           Clark's
           & gold             little
          silver              town—
         Gaslit                palisa-
         clang!                 ded &
        & went                  river-
        tooted                  facing
        hooted                  turned
        trains                  around
        air and                 to west
        to blue                 meeting
        ward in-                mirror-
        soot up-                ing the
        whirled                 married
        packets                 streams
        puffing                 Jacob's
       water as                 Manuel's
       from the                 (O sage
       cut ice                  traders)
       ter cold                 fortunes
      or in win-                rocketing
      riverbank                 Risen out
      uncobbled                 of flames
      the muddy                 or plague
      furs over                 you flour-
     flour and                  ished and
     and hauled                 grew Belle-
     afternoons                 fontaine &
     hot summer                 south into
     labored on                 Carondelet
     Levee men                  and west a
     log cabins                 jewel-park
     Pain Court                 shimmering
     Auguste of                 structures
     O Pierre O                 So proudly
     now to all                 open your
     stone open                 steel gate
     Founder of                 St. Louis!
```

I've always considered "Escalator" a "Language" poem, in the style (or one of the styles) of the West Coast Language poets. But it also has "Minimalist" aspects. I first read it at a writers' conference, and it had a popular, if brief, circulation. At the request of the University of Nevada I sent an editor there an audio tape of the poem which was later sent and played at various universities and on WBAI radio in New York. The last I heard of it, it was at the University of Wisconsin. I might note that "Escalator" was not written as (or intended as) an anti-war poem, but has other, humanitarian interpretations.

Escalator

Except in the title this poem uses the 100-word computer
vocabulary of minimals proposed in "Semantic Message
Detection for Machine Translation, Using an Interlingua,"
by Margaret Masterman of the Cambridge Language Research
Unit (Paper 36, National Physical Laboratory, Teddington,
Middlesex, England).

1

Where	do you want	to go? *I ask*
To change	*you answer*	to re-form re-
see re-	do re-	hear re-
feel re-	smell re-	dream re-
mate re-	BE	

Don't	talk that	stuff
And re-	cover more	have more
You	can't buy	air
True but	if I	part from
this thing	I like	life If
I don't I	feel bad	and can't
laugh		

2

If	I must	see this
life if	I must	go up
and come	down	I want
to know	how you	and I
feel how	air and	world
come to	be and	spread

I want	to know	hard and
soft whole	and	part yes
I want	to know	this when
where and	this where	when and
how Not	one good	guess and
many	Answer,	man

3

Laugh, man	taste eat	feel pain
hot cold	smell life	soft life
see life	see wet	life
s p r e a d	plants and	beasts
mate	and	dream

Think	don't fight	talk this
thing that	thing and	hear more
buy and sell	give give give	and talk
cover up less	name cause	and change
and talk and	talk and talk	and pray

Whole worlds	pair up	and count
down	Round and	round
round and	round and	round you
go world	No answer	
No answer?		
Talk, man		

4

Good law	and	bad law
You can	have no	law See?
Go law go	bang	part
in pain	Please	must I fight?

I must but	I don't	want to

Yes I must	fight for this	good law

I answer	in kind	I answer bang

You answer	*bang*
I answer	*bang bang*

You answer	BANG BANG
I answer	BANG BANG BANG

You answer   BANG BANG   BANG BANG

I answer   BANG BANG   BANG BANG BANG

You answer   BANG BANG BANG BANG BANG BANG

I answer

BANG

world

please

[c. 1965]

Elements

I think
all circles
gathering the world,
I gather earth
air   fire   water

and in the beginning

discover a fifth
element
arching over and
moving
the seasons

[1966]

Three Faces of Autumn

I

Now sunfire stains
the tupelos
and the shadows
in trapeziums
off the haybarns
straggle and gather
by rocks and birches
where the crickets'
still-fast whirr
cries against the closed
season

II

Harvest-heart
of autumn, vegetable
feast, harrowed
earth free
of horse and ox,
limbs released
of leaves except the still
green lilac and the red
rowanberry where
the waxwings pillage
and the pileated
woodpecker
taps the rotted
trunk

III

Irreducible
bones, boughs;
the wind dries after
the rain-drums; a flight,
geese over the first
hard glaze
and the hillside's
cry of the loon
while the chill
yellow light
dies

[c. 1966]

A CHARLES GUENTHER RETROSPECTIVE
Poetry: New and Selected Poems

Beginnings

The past is gone, the future hasn't come,
the present slips away: do we depend
on nothing? Nothing answers, for it is dumb
and nothing has no beginning and no end.
For the time has come when the suffering of the root
becomes the root of suffering and the tree
of wisdom, bare of its customary fruit,
loses its image of abundancy.

And the time has come when the reason for desire
is tempered and the desire for reason
explodes from ashes into continuous fire
of light and heat against the severe season,
and in the meditation of the flame,
beyond the one sensation that it warms,
we perceive the function of its dancing game
and recognize the clarity of its forms;

until the time has come when the change of light
yields to the light of change, music of space
played in the half dark of an elusive night
of alternate despair and silent grace,
seeming to drown the time when the rest of being
ends and being at rest suddenly draws near,
when the sight of birds vanishes and the bird of seeing
flies away somewhere else, away from here.

[1973]

THREE FACES OF AUTUMN
Poetry, Prose, Translations

Missouri Woods

Post oak, white oak, black oak, Ozark rails,
shake roofs and fences split with maul and froe:
remember the timberland, the vanished trails.

Laid, lapped and paneled, propped or locked with nails,
the zigzag fences stretching row on row—
post oak, white oak, black oak, Ozark rails.

Tables and staves and dishes, pitch-lined pails
curled from a blade and fashioned long ago,
remember the timberland, the vanished trails.

Cradles and coffins, rafts loaded with bales,
bolts, blocks and pickets, handles for hammer and hoe;
post oak, white oak, black oak, Ozark rails,

logs hollowed for john boats, poles for paddles and sails—
their stubble and stumps poke up the crusted snow.
(Remember the timberland, the vanished trails?)

The blown out nest, the branch that cracks and falls
are lost from the land where only the birds know.
Post oak, white oak, black oak, Ozark rails:
remember the timberland, the vanished trails.

[1974]

A CHARLES GUENTHER RETROSPECTIVE
Poetry: New and Selected Poems

The Chase

The hare and the tortoise,
the hound and the fox,

they have in common
a fading ratio.

Yet, to lumber after a fine hare,
to lope after a sleek fox!

But the hard hills,
the mischief of winter!

Not even a ribbon
consoles; the race

an hallucination
of radiant encounters.

Only when we gather
the highest figs

from the highest branches
do we notice the stars,

and we ask what happened
to make the lightning

vanish, without remembering
when the chase is ended

the prize we wanted
or the one that mattered.

[1978]

47

Good Neighbor

The only time I spoke to Albert Walker
he was slumped in his car with a crumpled ten-dollar bill

between his legs. His chin was on his chest,
arms at his sides, eyes closed, and I knew right away

he was sleeping; but I knocked on the closed window.
"Are you all right?" But he didn't answer,

and then I saw the beer cans on the floor
behind the seat and I knew he had passed out.

I ran in the house and called the police
three times in ten minutes. I called the police

and asked for an ambulance. When the police came
I gave them a coat hanger to open the door

and it took ten minutes to open the locked door
and the fumes rushed out. It was a hot morning.

They shook his body and it was stiff; and I knew
he had been dead since yesterday afternoon

in plain sight on a busy boulevard,
counting his day's receipts. There might have been more

to all this than the curious neighbors knew,
magnetized in a horde around the five

police cars, the van, the ambulance and the hearse.
As the mailman said the next day, "It might have been worse,

he might have suffered." But why was he there
on the passenger side, sealed in so hot and still?

The only time I spoke to Albert Walker
he was slumped in his car with a crumpled ten-dollar bill.

[1981]

Birdkeeper

Birds birds . . . "Mister, do you keep birds?"
a passing boy had asked, and I might have answered,
"No, birds keep me." That was closer to the truth,
though we can't say we've given each other life,
but since I kept so many birds alive,
our lives together, they owed me the life
of these lines; I hadn't praised or reproached them,
or feared or punished them in ancestral ways
of superstition and strange amulets,
only indulged them beyond what nature meant
for them: the crippled mockingbird that flew
to greet us, alighted, suspended a frozen claw
and always took three raisins from our palm,
the catbird that took an uninvited seat
on our shoulders; sparrows, fat pure-blooded heirs
of pairs set free in Pennsylvania
or brought into St. Louis by Henry Shaw
that spawned into these fantastic chattering hordes
but kept the manners of gentlefolk; and jays,
crows, mourning doves, an occasional hawk.
                                        For you
a passing boy once asked, "Do you keep birds,
mister?" Spontaneous answer, "No,
they hold me prisoner!" But he'd have walked away
puzzled. Now like the hours and days I gave them
they've disappeared into a late winter sun.

[c. 1983]

"Union Station," a sestina written for the 90th anniversary of the station, deals mostly with the early history of the Station area—that is, with Chouteau's Pond (the "pool") which occupied Mill Creek Valley for nearly 100 years, before the land was drained and railroad tracks were laid through the Valley. The poem took about three months of research.

Union Station

Only the swallows circling these cones of silence
Make this their hostel now. Their invisible track
Circumscribes a valley where ancient springs
Flowed from the western hills before the air
Droned with wheels by the dam and the artificial pool
In the mills that stood near the gorge where Rock Creek ends.

How the face of the valley changes! One thing ends,
Replaced by another with intervals of silence:
Once there was a prairie with scrub oak, an occasional pool
Where buffalo grazed and drank, their rumbling track
Mistaken for thunder shook the morning air.
Flushing out every creature that flies or springs.

Yet who knows how many thousands of springs
The same scenario plays before it ends,
How many upheavals of earth and air
Hold no recollection in postludes of silence;
Only a beetle perhaps, inscribing its track
Patiently, returns to the edge of an obscure pool.

And here the Osage camped where the bed of the pool
Lay, settlers came for the pure springs
And the black earth, mountain men left to track
Deer and beaver from where the Missouri ends
Up to its headwaters in the lands of silence,
And boatmen labored and danced to some old French air.

THREE FACES OF AUTUMN
Poetry, Prose, Translations

Under cedars and cottonwoods, ghosts in the moonlit air,
Lovers pressed on the grass by the glassy pool
(Where have they gone? Only a winter silence
Lies with the faded stones by the vanished springs).
The valley reclaimed, the pond was drained to the ends
Of its arms and coves to lay the parallel track,

Nineteen miles of tentacular steel track!
Gray stones and Spanish tiles, spires in the air,
Rose over the roundhouse where the landscape ends,
Apex and terminus once of a human pool
That swarmed to the coupled cars with the well-oiled springs,
Where rolling stock stands here rusting in silence.

In the lace of a trestle and track, a sunken pool,
Honeysuckle hangs in the air: a new life springs
Until everything ends once more in the music of silence.

[1984]

A CHARLES GUENTHER RETROSPECTIVE
Poetry: New and Selected Poems

Three Sisters

i. Sara Pondering

(on Sara Teasdale and Vachel Lindsay)

Maybe it was some power in him you feared
as he went about trading his rhymes for sustenance,
an unbroken bronco whose exuberance
broke at last when his hope and fortune disappeared,

or maybe it was the fiery evangelist
in him, the visionary hustler of empty schemes,
or the carnival prophet hawking impractical dreams
or the missionary poet, the ragtime rhapsodist?

—all these perhaps.

                As we'd mistrust some wild
dark of the woods or an unknown deep of the sea,
your taming spirit couldn't be reconciled

to the eagle in him you admired flying free
into the sun where together alike are lost
your August rain and his November frost.

[1984]

53

THREE FACES OF AUTUMN
Poetry, Prose, Translations

ii. Remembering Marianne

(on letters from Marianne Moore, April 1962)

When I asked if the house I'd lived in was your same
childhood home and described it: the long antique
veranda, 1840s, cisterns, frame
now stuccoed yellow and tiled, where a stony little creek

trickled through a wild orchard of red plums
and a field of dewberries—you didn't say.
                                        (Still
our separate worlds were linked by the chromosomes,
as you called them, of each clustered syllable.)

Those years I took circuitous roads to truth,
ignored your hints, suggested even doing a "feature"
on you, but patiently you'd shrug and sluff

it off, saying, "I'm not important enough,"
adding, "Eliot is ideal."

                    We'll forget the architecture,
but I know I tasted those wild plums of your youth.

[1986]

A CHARLES GUENTHER RETROSPECTIVE
Poetry: New and Selected Poems

iii. Conjuring H.D.: A Year with Richard

(on Hilda Doolittle and Richard Aldington)

They say there is no hope / to conjure you
(How curious to read your lines at the rim
of a sonnet)
               Yet in a beech that shudders through
its leaves you were trembling and still to him:

a blossom shaken by the wind, a swirl
of startled sparrows flushed, an autumn mist
lingering in the woods or a lonely curl
of smoke in an evening dark as amethyst

—you were all these.
                  For when the spirit sum-
mons spirit, how to tell its strange embrace?
Is the reflection truth? Is it the cold

face of a lotus pool or is it the face
of flesh?
          No matter the image, young or old,
you have become in these. Now you've become.

[1987]

As a boy of seven, with a sister, when we lived at 3729 North Euclid, I played with Al Lewis's children when he lived around the corner. Al Lewis taught me to rope (and spin a lariat), ride, crack a bullwhip, and other cowboy tricks that he had learned as a wrangler (at age 15 or so) for Buffalo Bill and Pawnee Bill's Wild West Show (or circus, as he called it). Like my father and uncles, Al served in World War I; he had left home to join the circus around 1910. Once he gave me his boots (a cowboy's pride!), size 6—but my prematurely long feet couldn't squeeze into them. I leave to the reader the strange and improbable conduct of a cow pony.

Little Sorrel

—For Al Lewis

I'll never forget when I cut him out of the string,
bridled him in the corral, led him out
to the rig, dropped the saddle, wrapped the cinch
ring on his belly, gentle old cow-
horse, wooled him around a bit, gave him
a few light kicks in the paunch then swung aboard;
well-reined, he could turn on a dime and we range-
branded all morning and he didn't roll an eye.

So I took him in to water him and leaned
to slap his neck when he watched me like a hawk.
Kinky old plug, he snuffed and suddenly
dropped an ear, crow-hopped, humped, then pitched and pitched;
I pulled all the leather I could but we broke in two
and I dragged him back to camp with dirty hands.

[c. 1986]

Beau

—dead of feline leukemia

Named for general Beau-
regard the handsome one

with great triangular jaw
black bushy tail

and pure white breast and throat
you commanded a home for a year

imperious as a khan
knowing what pharaohs knew

nursed for two fortnights
as if our own lives hung

on the balance of your breath
we fought the vile disease

that violated your blood
and burned away your youth

You came in our winter lives
and died on the edge of spring.

[1984]

Eugene and Roswell

*On a centennial visit to the boyhood home
of Eugene Field (1850 - 1895) in St. Louis*

The tall brick house on Broadway stands alone
but its stairs still echo the steps of the two boys
as they climbed to their room where the dimming lamplight shone
at bedtime over these long abandoned toys
(now propped in chairs or ranked in stiff display,
on floor or mantel, in fading paint or clothes),
commanded even then forever to stare and stay,
passing the long, still nights in a sentry pose.

Summers in Amherst and Vermont, and more,
the boys picked strawberries, tamed wild squirrels and toads
and found a whole new universe to explore,
or toted their creel and poles down dusty roads
to a shady bank where time and the waters went
in a world of innocence, peace, astonishment.

[1995]

Spring Catalog

When April comes I no longer can see the Arch
from my window as the elms and maples foliate
blocking the view and the earth begins to melt and march
out of winter's lockstep, or stirs once more to mate

by the rosebeds: squirrels, rabbits and everything
airborne: doves, jays, robins. Soon there will arrive
new hybrids to plant. Yet the taste of this cold spring
is bittersweet with the uncertainty of what's still alive.

If to believe that what lies dead will be deployed
in some dimension again, alive and growing
invisibly, or in white or brown or green,

is beyond our reason, yet surely if it isn't destroyed
it must be inviolate, like the pain and peace in knowing
that what we may see isn't what we have always seen.

[1995]

A Posthumous Visit With Anatole Bisk

—In memoriam: Alain Bosquet

I was reading the morning paper over breakfast
when suddenly I came across my own obituary,
just a few lines; and when I got over the shock,
I realized I possessed, as a nobody now,
the singular advantages of being nameless:
to be as nice or contemptuous as I please,
to wander anywhere and to love everyone;
it's certainly not unappealing to an old writer.

Then it occurred to me: why do I need to attend
my own funeral Friday? There will be lovely roses,
someone will sing and perhaps recite a poem,
and blissfully anonymous I shall be
still wary of a vain, hypocritical world,
and faceless somehow recognize true friends.

[2003]

Light Verse

Annual Report, 1944

In the annual report to policy holders
(O praise their prudent and proper Protectors)
the financial statement and Board of Directors
(O praise the rock they hold on their shoulders)
the tabulated analysis of death
benefits: the benefits for nephritis
apoplexy accidents appendicitis
accumulated reserves never called *wealth*

Mindful of the Company and its principles
we are aware of its farsighted solemn
trusteeship and that from year to year depends
not on the misplacement of some decimals
or the miscalculation of a column
but on solid faith our pittance of dividends

[1944]

"Attachments" derives partly from my fascination with the gear and technology of early space exploration during the Sputnik and Apollo era. A technical library I once directed received thousands of scientific and technical reports, of which a few were relevant to that library's mission. I recall one report describing "anti-gravity coveralls" (doubtless used in training astronauts)—and of course "artificial gravity" became another "contrivance" of space exploration.

Attachments

The idea of man in space is fascinating:
over the atmosphere, thinner in relation
to the earth than an appleskin, he arched
from reality into mystery,
free in his motion, weightless.
                              In his vertical thrust
he lost all adhesion and
became immobile, until he contrived
cabins of artificial gravity.
He missed, you see, his attachments, a primitive
need at once obsessed him to hold fast
to something, for he didn't know
if he could cling to anything beyond.

[1960]

Instant Sonnet

A colleague sent an order for a sonnet.
"Lucky devil!" you say. ("Poor ange-
l" is more like it.) But I've put three lines on it;
not only that, I've contrived a rhyme for "orange."
The secret's in doing the words one by one,
making it line by line, stave by stave,
and before you know it, it's already half done.
Add another line and you've finished the octave.

Enter the sestet with more confidence
and now we've only four more lines to go;
mold it spare, unpadded, give it sense,
then drain the couplet like honey poured slowly from a cup, its substance long extended,
for suddenly this living exercise is ended.

[c. 1963]

World of Fun

Everything's possible from the Johnson Smith
Catalog: everything's made easy with the electronic lie
and love detector, the police handcuffs you can snap
over the Hercules wristband and escape
if you wish by the secrets of 15 baffling tricks
revealed in the 24-page book; the cane will dance
for you, the key will bend, the skeleton
glow, the handkerchief burn with the secret thumb;
do the waterfall shuffle with the Electric Deck,
tell all with the de luxe fortune-telling Predicta Board;
get smart, learn while you sleep, develop a winning
personality, overcome your enemies & hidden fears
with the Seven Keys to Power used by ancient priests,
kings and mystics. Moneyback guarantee.

For 150 $$$ you can buy a gorilla
suit with a gory mask and cause howls of laughter.
Big Ear and Super Phones and the Pocket Electronic
Blackjack Computer: split stand draw
and automatic bust; or do some impossible thing
with the Pocket Miracle Scientific Walking Spring
(nothing to wind, walks lifelike in your hands!)
Fun from the sun with miniature solar cells,
a sun-powered beany from your plastic hat,
104 easy gadgets you can build!
Last Supper tablecloths, the de luxe bottle
cutter, the pocket Metal Detector & Money Finder
to make you rich! 3000 colorful Indian
beads, silver enamel, liquid gold.

Turn light into current; virtually unlimited
life. No batteries needed. Unlimited life.

[c. 1980]

When The Muse Deigns To Amuse

Review of *The Penguin Book of Limericks,* compiled and edited by E. O. Parrott (Viking).

St. Louis Post-Dispatch, September 12, 1986, p. C3.

When looking for verse to amuse,
Spurn sonnets and quaint clerihews;
    The rondeau, villanelle
    Won't do nearly as well
As the limerick. (Read what ensues.)

Some limericks—e.g., by E. Lear—
Seem blithe, light and bland to the ear;
    This reviewer's apologies,
    But some such anthologies
Aren't what they purport to appear.

For our tastes run from natty to tatty
(And some are incredibly catty)
    And as you may surmise
    What some writers devise
Is racy and raunchy and ratty.

But this volume compiled by E. Parrott
Is well organized and has merit.
    If your preference is based
    On adult readers' taste,
Then buy it—and cautiously share it.

It Could Be Verse

Review of *For Better or Verse, One Hundred
Original Limericks,* by Joel Herskowitz (Better/Verse).

St Louis Post-Dispatch, February 25, 1990, p. 5C.

A physician from Mass. (Framingham)
Penned these limericks—a bit of a "ham"—
　　Nearly all squeaky clean,
　　Not a trifle obscene,
With scarcely a "heck" or a "darn."

Now if some men were meant to write verse
They'd do it to fatten their purse,
　　For of all their proclivities
　　Such bardic activity's
No blessing, but often a curse.

A reviewer may tend to be spiteful
Or serious (with words like "insightful");
　　While perhaps not bestselling
　　With its puns and odd spelling,
Doctor J's verse is simply delightful.

(The book is available by mail from Better/ Verse, P.O. Box 482, South
Station, Mass. 01701.)

II. Prose

1953 – 2004

Until the 1950s I published very little prose—and most of that was in magazines: about poets, mostly those I'd translated. In early 1953, Howard Derrickson—then art critic and acting book editor of the *St. Louis Post-Dispatch*—brought me a copy of *Winds* by St.-John Perse to review. It was the beginning of my 50 years of writing for the *Post-Dispatch*. In addition, from 1972-1982, I wrote reviews simultaneously for the *St. Louis Globe-Democrat*. This section omits prose published during the decade 1942-1952 but includes a wide selection of work published from 1953 through 2004, nearly all of which has never appeared in book form.

Like Hemingway, I never considered critical reviewing (which I define as serious, evaluative reviewing for a relatively wide range of newspapers and magazines) as "journalism." Critical reviewing has a valid, important place in the writing of every period because it reflects how other work, written and performed, is accepted or rejected. A slow song may be quickened or drastically changed in orchestration and arrangement; a play may be severely edited or adapted or "modernized." But the written word, in its original text, remains as it has always been—in Chaucer, Dante, Milton, Shakespeare, Poe. Only our attitudes, sometimes influenced or mirrored by critics, change in every generation.

Derrickson once asked me if I had a "formula" for writing my reviews. I told him I hadn't, but might have added that I did have a method: Usually I did not write a word until I had done a great deal of ancillary reading on the subject (sometimes, during the early years, in as many as 40 to 50 books; later, in at least a half-dozen books) to be able to write with some modicum of perspective and authority. I felt that I wanted to "command" my subject before writing on it: to give a creative response to a writer's creative work; but I did not want to write for academia alone. In fact, after a book editor told me that my style was more appropriate for a literary magazine than for a newspaper, I have tried to write for a wider audience, in a simpler style—which is only good, communicable writing, anyway.

Critical Reviews and Essays

1953-1962

Grand vision in an epic by a French diplomat

In the preface to his earlier version of St.-John Perse's *Anabasis*, T. S. Eliot writes that it is better to read such a poem six times and dispense with an introduction.

This remark, which might be applied to almost any poem, is especially true of *Winds*, published 22 years after *Anabasis* and now available in an attractive bilingual edition.

Winds is the latest and most ambitious work of Perse (in real life Alexis St.-Léger Léger) who was born in the Antilles and educated in France. It is an epic of four cantos written in the recent tradition of French prose poetry—the song not of a 20-year-old adventurer, a Lautréamont or Rimbaud, but of a career diplomat now in his 60s.

His language is so modern that it is hard to realize Perse is not among the younger French poets. Some of his *Éloges* were written as early as 1904, and are also now available in English. It would perhaps be well for the reader to begin with the shorter poems of *Éloges* or *Exile*, which have more obvious connection with events in the poet's life.

The translator, Hugh Chisholm, gives a faithful rendering of *Winds*, the more admirable because Perse is not easy to translate. Hugo von Hofmannsthal called him "untranslatable," and Eliot faltered over some passages of *Anabasis* in spite of collaboration with Perse. The winds of this poem are nameless and timeless.

Except for certain allusions, as to America in the second canto and the conclusion, most of the sites, persons and events are set free in our imagination. A pleasing total effect of movement with subordinating images, as in a strange, fascinating rite, penetrates into our language.

St.-John Perse is a major poet because he can harness the silent, unyield-ing elements—*Snow*, *Rains* and now *Winds*—to a grand vision of decay and rebirth, expressed in extremely personal rhythms. But he remains his own best spokesman:

> ... These were very great winds over the land of
>   men—very great winds at work among us,
> Singing to us the horror of living, and singing to us
>   the honor of living. . .

> And, with the savage flutes of misfortune, leading us,
>   new men, to our new ways.

Review of *Winds*, by St.-John Perse, translated by Hugh Chisholm. (Bollingen Series 34, Pantheon Books).

St. Louis Post-Dispatch, April 12, 1953, p. 4C.

A CHARLES GUENTHER RETROSPECTIVE
Prose: Critical Reviews and Essays, 1953-1962

Eloquent scholarship

In the history of American poetry, Ezra Pound is perhaps foremost among the animators and innovators. With T. S. Eliot and Wallace Stevens, he is usually a point of departure for modern poetry after Whitman. But his immense reputation may perplex many readers who have only a limited acquaintance with his work.

One explanation is that much of his earlier verse and criticism has long been out of print or available only in scarce foreign editions. To amend this situation, New Directions (lately chided for taking "old directions") has published 11 books by or about Pound in recent years.

The latest is this volume of translations representing several styles and stages in his development from 1910 to 1920. It includes poems from the Italian, Provençal, Chinese and Anglo-Saxon, Japanese Noh plays and maxims from the modern French essayist Rémy de Gourmont.

After taking as his early models the Victorian translators (Rossetti was both "father and mother" to him), Pound began to practice his own style and identity in the songs of Guido Cavalcanti and the troubadour Arnaut Daniel. He tried to embody in a new English idiom "some trace of that power which implies the man." He completely assimilated the personality of other poets and the spirit of their times. The result was a kind of high-geared scholarship decried by some critics as pedantry.

But, to Pound, translating was more than a scholastic exercise, it became a discipline and a way of reworking his own ideas. Even so, he considered his work on the troubadours "a makeshift" and branched out into other languages. It is hard to choose the best of this selection. Even the Noh, or "noble" plays, most alien to our own culture, stand out for their stark, direct rendering. But the Chinese poems from "Cathay" are most popular and are rated with Pound's finest original work   A sample is this "Separation on the River Kiang" from the eighth century poet Rihaku:

> Ko-jin goes west from Kokaku-ro,
> The smoke-flowers are blurred over the river.
> His lone sail blots the far sky.
> And now I see only the river,
> The long Kiang, reaching heaven.

THREE FACES OF AUTUMN
Poems, Prose, Translations

From such simple verses, written nearly 40 years ago, to his recent *Analects of Confucius*, Pound has steadily become recognized as one of the great translators of our time.

Review of *The Translations of Ezra Pound* (New Directions).

St. Louis Post-Dispatch, November 30, 1953, p. 2E.

Doubts on opium theory

Coleridge's "Kubla Khan," like Wordsworth's "Daffodils" and Gray's "Elegy," ranks among the 10 most anthologized poems in our language. It has been called "the quintessential poem of romanticism," though its magical creation links it with no particular literary school.

"Kubla Khan" is also one of the most popular hunting grounds for critics, whether they share John Livingston Lowes's celebrated view that it is a beautiful but meaningless dream fragment, or believe the poem affords deep symbolic interpretations.

Miss Schneider fires her opening round by examining the ideas of Lowes and the psychological and symbolist critics, whom she later challenges with her findings.

She brings out modern medical evidence opposing the notion of "Kubla Khan" as a special "opium dream" and concludes that both Coleridge's and Thomas De Quincey's "dream" writing spring far more from "the coalescing of individual temperament with literary tradition" than from opium eating habits.

Here she also makes convincing comparisons of Coleridge's ideas with the theories of Erasmus Darwin, the eighteenth-century physiologist, who seems to have escaped the notice of other Coleridge scholars.

The rest of the book forms probably one of the most incisive critical studies written on "Kubla Khan." The author delves into the poem's sources, date and meaning with a great deal of reserve and few presuppositions.

Echoes are found mainly in Southey's poem, "Thalaba" (which, Miss Schneider picturesquely writes, was composed "as with a dump truck") and Walter Savage Landor's "Gebir."

Coleridge's poem has the texture of Milton, too, who haunted the Lake poets with cadences and sound patterns and provided many a romantic with elaborate hidden correspondences. Yet Miss Schneider points out the trouble of drawing parallels between these settings and "Kubla Khan" and the danger of mistaking a "generic likeness" for an "influence."

THREE FACES OF AUTUMN
Poems, Prose, Translations

Finally, she feels the coolness of the poem and of the poet himself, "dehumanized behind his mask of hair and eyes and magic circle," who created the vision of an unbuilt paradise.

The casual reader may skip the extensive notes and still enjoy this book. But the appendices, including one on Dorothy Wordsworth's drinking can, named "Kubla," are sprightly and, as much as the main text, certainly recommended for reading.

Review of *Coleridge, Opium and Kubla Khan*, by Elizabeth Schneider (University of Chicago Press).

St. Louis Post-Dispatch, January 19, 1954, p. 2B.

Eliot on Pound

In making this selection, T. S. Eliot aims to show that "Pound has said much about the art of writing . . . that is permanently valid and useful"; that "he said much that was peculiarly pertinent to the needs of the time at which it was written"; and that "he forced upon our attention not only individual authors, but whole areas of poetry, which no future criticism can afford to ignore."

To this end Eliot has culled material from four of Pound's books which are now almost unobtainable, and added other essays never before published in book form. He has sorted the essays under three headings: "The Art of Poetry," instructive writings with characteristic Poundian firmness; "The Tradition," excursions into authors from Homer to Henry James; and "Contemporaries," including evaluations of Yeats, Frost, W. C. Williams and Eliot himself.

The result is a pleasing unity of material in each group, although this unity is gained by sacrificing over-all chronological arrangement. One suspects, too, that Pound would not have made the same choices and grouping. He might have preferred to include only those writings having most practical value to young authors, and it is not likely that he would have omitted his vital essay on French poets which appeared originally in *The Little Review*.

Because the question of Pound's confinement will undoubtedly come to the minds of many readers, it might be well to point out that Eliot tactfully avoids the whole issue. In so doing, he gives silent assent to Pound's own statement that "one work of art is worth 40 prefaces and as many apologiae." Moreover, the issue is relevant only in a broad sense to the present selections. What is important is that Eliot succeeds admirably in his stated purpose. The *Literary Essays* are the best representative selection available. Together with the same publisher's recent *Translations* and inexpensive *Selected Poems*, they form a convenient approach to a study of Ezra Pound's impact on our literature.

Review of *Literary Essays of Ezra Pound*, edited with an introduction by T.S. Eliot (New Directions).

St. Louis Post-Dispatch, March 15, 1954, p. 2B.

THREE FACES OF AUTUMN
Poems, Prose, Translations

The poetic process

"The first effort of the poet," writes T. S. Eliot in this short, reflective essay, "should be to achieve clarity for himself, to assure himself that the poem is the right outcome of the process that has taken place." To avoid a maze of speculation, Eliot does not describe this process in detail but points out, to the writer accustomed to writing for himself, how difficult and fascinating is the craft of making speech for imaginary characters.

In an earlier essay on "Poetry and Drama," Eliot had stated that the writer of non-dramatic verse writes in terms of his own voice, that the question of communicating to the reader is not paramount. *The Three Voices of Poetry*, a lecture given in England last November, develops this idea and applies it to all forms of verse. Of the three voices he defines, the first voice is that of the poet talking to himself, the second is that of the poet addressing an audience and the third is that of the poet when he creates a dramatic character speaking in verse. Eliot maintains that in every poem, from the lyric or "meditative" to the epic and dramatic, more than one voice may be heard. The first and second voices are most often found together in non-dramatic works and are combined with the third voice in the drama. The division into three voices is a neat breakdown of the writer's creative purposes; almost too neat, we would feel, were it not that Eliot himself knows the limits of his theme. For he hints at the existence of a fourth voice, as in Browning, whose gift of dramatic monologue was practiced best outside of the theater. Browning, he adds, cannot bring his characters to life, to speak for themselves, in monologue form. They are really the poet talking to other people.

The Three Voices of Poetry is one of Eliot's most trenchant writings on poetic processes and has an effortless, informal style seldom found elsewhere in his work. Yet we hope that he will sometime go further into the problem of poetic obscurity, as an outgrowth of this and earlier lectures. Because it is easy to follow, this little work serves as a splendid introduction for readers not already acquainted with Eliot's prose.

Review of *The Three Voices of Poetry*, by T.S. Eliot (Cambridge University Press).

St. Louis Post-Dispatch, September 8, 1954, p. 2E.

A rose for Faulkner

Critical notice of William Faulkner is now in a third decade. It began with his series of sensational novels produced during 1929-1932, when he was at first censured for brooding on the past and leading a "cult of cruelty" in modern writing.

Even today he is haunted by complaints over his "gruesome gallery" of characters and his dense style. But the fury has largely subsided, leaving a residue of well-tempered judgment.

Instead of argument on what his work ought to be, there is acceptance of what it is. Critics now tend less to pick fault with the aloof Faulkner than to cudgel each other in the most scholarly way on such questions as his themes and techniques.

The present book, a reissue, went almost unnoticed when first published three years ago.

Following in the wake of Faulkner's recent best seller, *A Fable*, it gives important insights into his earlier writing and will likely reach a receptive audience. It consists of 16 selected essays arranged in four groups dealing with the region of Faulkner, his writing as a whole, his method and language and his individual works.

The essays are not a florilege of tributes, but penetrating studies of a figure who is considered by many Europeans to be America's greatest living writer.

All of the pieces were taken from leading literary magazines and, with one exception, date from 1939 to 1951. The book then is neither inclusive nor current. Faulkner enthusiasts will miss later articles, from R. W. B. Lewis's study of *The Bear* in *The Kenyon Review* (Autumn 1951) to R. W. Flint's "Faulkner as Elegist" in *The Hudson Review* (Summer 1954). And no attempt has been made to bring the introduction and bibliography up-to-date. Yet, what this book does contain is of permanent value.

There is Malcolm Cowley's introduction to *The Portable Faulkner*, praised by Robert Penn Warren as "one of the few things ever written on Faulkner which is not hagridden by prejudice"; there is Warren's own sweeping study of the novelist's achievement, Conrad Aiken's *Atlantic Monthly* article, which 15 years ago turned the tide of Faulkner criticism; and much more.

In the section on particular works, two of the most interesting essays, by Olga Vickery and Ray B. West Jr., are reprinted from *Perspective*, the St. Louis magazine noted for its showing in collections of best American stories.

Summing up, Faulkner's stock is still rising on the literary market and reflective readers will find this book a wise investment in enjoyment.

Review of *William Faulkner: Two Decades of Criticism*, edited by Frederick J. Hoffman and Olga W. Vickery (Michigan State College Press).

St. Louis Post-Dispatch, December 21, 1954, p. 2B.

A century of Walt Whitman

The popularity of Walt Whitman fell off in the late 1930s after a generation of Imagist and Federal poets had exploited his style. This reaction is still seen in the most popular textbook used today in teaching poetry in American colleges, a critical anthology bristling with scores of lesser poets but without a line from Whitman who sired them all.

In his own day, especially in his last years, Whitman was a paradox of honor and neglect. "I am destined to have an audience," he once said. "There is little sign of it now." Yet even before the Civil War, "Leaves" were scattered far abroad and many European critics hailed Whitman as the only authentic American singer.

More than 50 biographies have appeared on Whitman but he remains one of the most puzzling subjects to literary historians. His "self-puffery" left little room for biographers to add their own praises and from the outset he was an easy target for deflation and fanciful gossip. In 1905, for instance, Henry Bryan Binns invented a New Orleans romance about the poet, an episode taken up and embellished by later writers.

Yet, as the author points out in *The Solitary Singer*, not one fact has ever been found to support this story. Freighted with so many sources, a biographer must be not only honest but accurate. Author Allen belongs to the new school of biographers who hold that a scientific sifting of facts leads to the best appreciation of a subject. Here, with a good crust of history as on an unearthed coin, we see most of the poet's strengths and foibles.

On the obverse side are Whitman's devotion to family and friends, his steady rounds of hospitals to visit Civil War soldiers and the dogged vision which produced his great elegies and meditative poems. On the converse side are his total lack of critical judgment about his own verse and his fluctuating enthusiasms and opinions.

Throughout, Allen proves that a biography can be both factual and entertaining. No doubt the poet—himself an authority on "the biography famous"—would marvel at this heavily documented reconstruction of his life. After reading *The Solitary Singer* we are convinced that Whitman's masks were not hollow and that he has never really lost his place in the main stream of American writing.

Review of *The Solitary Singer: A Critical Biography of Walt Whitman*, by Gay Wilson Allen (The Macmillan Co.).

St. Louis Post-Dispatch, February 15, 1955, p. 2B.

A CHARLES GUENTHER RETROSPECTIVE
Prose: Critical Reviews and Essays, 1953-1962

The Classical revival

"Without the written heritage of Greece and Rome," R.R. Bolgar points out in this valuable study, "the world would have worn a different face. How that heritage was studied and eventually assimilated ranks therefore as one of the major problems of European history." In brief, this is Bolgar's thesis and he tackles the problem directly by tracing the whole classical revival which began about 700 A.D. and lasted until about 1700.

In its early period the revival was marked by reforms in the education and taste of the old Byzantine Empire and by a new interest in learning, as far west as Ireland. In the parade of figures of that time, one of the most interesting was the eleventh century sophist, Psellus, studious but unscrupulous, who tried to turn Byzantium into the spiritual heir of Athens and almost succeeded. A philosophy professor, he is best remembered for having restored the cult of Plato at a time when Aristotle held the field.

In the twelfth century the main interest of educators was for literature, and the teaching method aimed at lessening the influence of the pagan authors whose works were studied. Generally, Bolgar maintains, the writers of the Middle Ages "speak to us from an unfamiliar universe. Their voices sound across a gulf, discoursing on problems we do not share." This feeling of strangeness vanishes at once with the Renaissance. Yet one of Bolgar's main arguments is that we should not assume that the Middle Ages and the Renaissance were two distinct cultures. "The Renaissance way of life was not the result of a reorientation," he adds. "It was the result of a long and slow development which can be clearly traced in the preceding centuries."

Bolgar shows us how, early in the Renaissance, Petrarch and other scholars brought Greek and Roman works into vogue again and awakened Europe with the great impulse of humanism. But the humanists, he writes, did not adapt themselves to their time as well as the more intuitive men of the Middle Ages. Instead they had become "propagandists for the ancient texts" and hardly belonged to the Renaissance. "Humanism," he concludes ironically, "can be convicted of the atrocious crime of having a long history; but at the same time it stands in closest alliance with needs and impulses generated by the very trends which would destroy it."

Later, in the high Renaissance, the scholar-translator Erasmus is held up as a guide to the reader who wants to understand the humanist practice of imitation and its effect on creative writing. Bolgar praises Erasmus for his imagination, sympathy and mental grasp and unstintingly calls him "the greatest man we come across in the history of education."

In its scope and purpose, *The Classical Heritage* reminds us of Gilbert Highet's *The Classical Tradition*, published six years ago. While the latter book is more readable, even entertaining, many of its audience, including specialists in the humanities, will find this new work interesting for the broad issues and blunt questions the author discusses.

Review of *The Classical Heritage and its Beneficiaries*, by R.R. Bolgar (Cambridge University Press).

St. Louis Post-Dispatch, May 3, 1955, p. 2B.

Andalusian sketches

It seems incredible that *Platero and I*, a best-seller in the Spanish-speaking world for over 40 years, has not previously appeared in English translation. More incredible perhaps is that its author, the 1956 Nobel prize-winner in literature, is still scarcely known to Americans. Yet were it not for this little classic, his only famous prose work, Juan Ramón Jiménez would share the even greater obscurity of another Nobel prize poet, the late Gabriela Mistral.

Translated or authorized for translation into 10 languages, *Platero and I* has been compared with *Alice in Wonderland* in universal appeal. The complete work consists of 138 short prose sketches of the author's native village of Moguer, all loosely drawn together by the characters of the poet and his donkey Platero. Platero, whose name means "Silver," is pictured as "small, downy, smooth—so soft to the touch that one would think he were all cotton, that he had no bones. Only the jet mirrors of his eyes are hard as two beetles of dark crystal."

No amount of description can convey the charm of this book, its deceptive simplicity and colorful imagery. Conversational in tone, the sketches cover a wide range of subjects, scenes and events which, individually, are subordinate to the quiet lyricism and tenuous drama of the over-all work.

By fortunate coincidence, these two English versions have come out almost simultaneously. The Roach translation has the advantage of being complete while the Robertses' rendering, which had appeared in England before this American edition, lacks only 33 of the prose sketches. The books are similar in format, attractively printed and copiously illustrated with line drawings.

Compared textually, however, the translations are as different as one could expect in any prose work. The Roach rendering is more literal and more faithful to the original flavor than the other, which is crisply idiomatic (sometimes too crisp) but often more accurate. The situation is puzzling in that all the translators claim the Spanish poet's blessing of their work and his aid in clarifying details.

But most readers probably will not care whether a tree is called an oak or a walnut, or an instrument is described as a horn or a cymbal. It is enough to say that although both versions could stand much revision, they are adequately translated for enjoyable reading.

To know *Platero and I* is to know Andalusia, at least that Andalusia close to the author's childhood. Yet, for all the beauty and charm of this book, Jiménez's poems far surpass it in strength and subtlety of expression. Through his prose we are drawn to the poet Jiménez, while the best work of other great modern Spanish poets—Antonio Machado, Gerardo Diego and Vicente Aleixandre—remains to be introduced in translation.

Review of *Platero and I,* by Juan Ramón Jiménez. Translated by Eloise Roach (University of Texas Press). *Platero and I,* by Juan Ramón Jiménez. Translated by William and Mary Roberts (Duschnes).

St. Louis Post-Dispatch, December 1, 1957, p. 4C.

Poet to poet

A poet's letters to his creditors or some casual acquaintance are apt to
be pretty dull reading. But a poet's letters to responsive, talented
fellow-artists often furnish the most candid views of his life and work and
of the social and literary scene of his time. The Thomas-Watkins
correspondence, of which only the Thomas half is preserved, falls in the
latter class. It is one of the most important books by or about Thomas
issued since his death at 39 over four years ago. The significance of these
letters lies in their span, from April 1936 to December 1952, coinciding
with Thomas's great creative period. There is unfortunately one great gap
between 1948 and 1952 during which there was no correspondence except
two letters now lost. But Watkins helpfully and, we trust, accurately fills
in these lacunae with a lot of reminiscent commentary.

When the Thomas-Watkins team rubbed intellects the result was perhaps
not as sparkling as it was enlightening. Here we see Thomas in all his
lighthearted spontaneity, spouting his likes and dislikes, his extravagant
feelings and the trials of his poetic craft. We find that during the 30s
Thomas considered Yeats the greatest living poet, and that Hardy was his
favorite twentieth century poet. Among his contemporaries, he admired
Auden's wit and versatility but disliked his social themes.

There are sidelights, too, on Thomas's method of composition. Watkins,
who typed many of the Thomas poems, describes the latter as "a slow and
patient craftsman." He sometimes devoted a page or two of work-sheets
to a single line, gradually building up the poem, phrase by phrase. Yet,
despite such lavish care, Thomas always realized that his poems existed
only as a result of "divine accidents."

Finally there are interesting drafts of a number of poems, including "Poem
in October" and the powerful "Refusal to Mourn," scattered among the
letters. Comparing these early drafts with the final versions in the
Collected Poems, we see how rightly Thomas applied his artist's intuition
and became, like every great poet, his own severest critic.

Review of *Letters to Vernon Watkins by Dylan Thomas,* edited, with an
introduction, by Vernon Watkins (New Directions).

St. Louis Post-Dispatch, March 9, 1958, p. 4F.

Patriarch of poets

"Authentic poetry," Juan Ramón Jiménez has written, "is known by its profound emotion, by its full, deep tide, by its intuitive metaphysics." Recipient of the1956 Nobel Prize in literature, Jiménez has published verse for nearly 60 of his 76 years and has become one of the few authentic voices in Spanish poetry. Although best known as the author of *Platero and I* (once cursorily called his "odes to a donkey"), he has produced some 30 books of verse and a vast amount of prose in that time.

The *Selected Writings* cover the period from 1900 to 1956 and are the first representative choice of his work available in English. Significantly, they show Jiménez's attitude, shared by only a few great poets of our time, that the true creative life consists in a constant ascent towards perfection. The various stages of his development are nowhere better revealed to us than in this latest collection.

The early poems, like those of Yeats, are elegiac and imagistic. They contrast strongly with the later spiritual and intellectual style. At 22, Jiménez had already published four books of verse, mostly in the manner of the French Symbolists whose work influenced Spanish poetry at the turn of the century.

A group of 55 early poems bearing the stamp of Verlaine and Samain opens the *Selected Writings*. These are followed by 13 prose poems from *Platero and I.*

The rest of the book consists of prose and verse from the *Diary of a Newlywed Poet*, written in the United States during World War I: *Portraits of Writers and Artists*, short, deft sketches of such figures as poets Rubén Darío and Antonio Machado and composer Falla; lectures on society and poetry, published in English for the first time; and poems and essays written in America after Jiménez's exile during the Spanish Civil War. There is a final selection of 30 of some 3000 aphorisms written by Jiménez up to this time.

The translations by novelist and TV-playwright Hays are generally competent, literal and true to the poet's original expression. There are occasional errors ("fountain" for "mountain") and misinterpretations (the hybrid "*insombre*"rendered as "sleepless").

Some readers may wish the Spanish texts were included, since these have been hard to get from libraries and importers alike. But this unilingual edition gives us a more generous selection in English, into which much of Jiménez's imagery and insight transforms remarkably well.

Review of *Selected Writings of Juan* Ramón *Jiménez*, translated by H. R. Hays and edited with a preface by Eugenio Florit (Farrar, Straus and Cudahy).

St. Louis Post-Dispatch, April 10, 1958, p. 2B.

THREE FACES OF AUTUMN
Poems, Prose, Translations

Bohemia versus Academia, current trends in American poetry

What has happened to American poetry in the fifties? Has it transferred its headquarters from the New England salon to the West Coast saloon? To the observer of the American literary scene a striking and abrupt change seems to have occurred in the last few years. Poetry is divided more sharply than ever into two camps, the academic and the Bohemian. It has turned vocal again, accompanied by histrionics in the bistros.

Four years ago foreign critics noted that American literary taste had changed since the socially-conscious 1930s; that American society, now become mature and sophisticated, had a corresponding change in its cultural climate; that it was now possible for the American writer to honor purely literary values in a way that would have shocked the preceding generation.

As recently as last year Rolfe Humphries, in introducing his second series of *New Poems by American Poets* (Ballantine Books), described certain traits fashionable in mid-twentieth century verse. The new poems, he wrote, use a common idiom, are "rather consciously literary, very competently turned, showing considerable evidence of serious study of technique . . . , interested in observation almost to the point of catalogue, and withal rather noncommittal in spirit, not very reckless, just a bit chill."

This description was certainly accurate, at least as far as it applied to the work of such younger poets as Philip Booth, Donald Hall, Philip Murray, Louis Simpson and Richard Wilbur, and to verse published in leading quarterly reviews like *Hudson, Kenyon* and *Partisan.* Yet it did not at all fit the poetry appearing in such pyrotechnic magazines as *Origin* (Dorchester, Mass.), *Contact* (Toronto) and *Inferno* and *The Miscellaneous Man* (San Francisco). These and similar little reviews, founded between 1950 and 1954, printed and promoted early work by the then unknown younger beat generation poets as well as better quality verse by some older writers. Now mostly defunct, these magazines have been superseded by others with equally unique names like *Ark III, Combustion, Hearse ("A Vehicle Used to Convey the Dead"), Measure* and *Gallows.*

Although Kenneth Rexroth has claimed that "the interest in reciting poetry to jazz did originate in San Francisco" and that he originated it, there is

96

still some doubt about its beginnings. It might have started in New
Orleans. One avant-garde group there, The Climax Jazz Art and Pleasure
Society of Lower Bourbon Street, pioneered in this field and published
two "sessions" or issues of a sporadic organ, *Climax*, now suspended. The
circulation of this review is a tribute to the easy-going spirit of New
Orleans. It contrasts with the "friendly, interested environment" of San
Francisco where Customs authorities seized Allen Ginsberg's book *Howl*
and charged its publisher, Dr. Lawrence Ferlinghetti, with selling obscene
literature. In this, the most famous censorship case of our time,
Ferlinghetti was completely vindicated; but the national publicity that
followed enhanced his reputation and increased sales of *Howl* and other
City Lights publications.

Whatever its origins, the jazz-poetry performance unquestionably has been
given its strongest impetus by Rexroth and Ferlinghetti. Yet this is just the
latest refinement to one of man's oldest professions: swapping a song or
tale for a glass of ale. Since Homer and Petronius, and maybe on the
Sumerian plain, music and poetry and bars and bards have gone together
like poppies and corn—the plant, that is. Villon, too, recited his ballades in
Paris inns five centuries ago, and Jonson and Shakespeare declaimed in
the famous Mermaid Tavern. And in our century, how many a saloon
patron enjoyed tippling to Kipling!

Even the humblest poem is worthy of an audience, and, except to the poet,
it should not matter where that audience is gathered. While Ferlinghetti
has read his "Junk Man's Obbligato" in such cool watering spots as The
Cellar, Harvard poet Richard Wilbur, now teaching at Wesleyan
University (Conn.), has lectured at Pennsylvania's Industrial Research
Institute and discussed the problem of creative thinking in poetry with
business and industrial leaders. Most audiences, I believe, can readily
distinguish between the Bohemian and the academic poem. One would not
expect to hear, for example, Robert Lowell's "The Quaker Graveyard at
Nantucket" recited in a bistro. But some poems by academic poets, like
Karl Shapiro's "Cadillac," could easily accompany jazz anywhere.
The academic poets meanwhile are as active and ubiquitous as the neo-
Bohemians, but they favor presenting their work less spectacularly in the
scholarly publications. Among the bastions of Academia now are
Audience, The Schooner, The Kenyon Review, The Literary Review and
the *Sewanee, Western* and *Yale Reviews*.

It is interesting to note that one such journal, the *Quarterly Review of Literature*, devoted an entire recent issue to poetry by, and tributes to, Kenneth Rexroth. But the academic magazines have censorship problems, too. Recently the fairly conservative *Beloit Poetry Journal* at Beloit College (Wis.) lost its sponsorship for having printed a piece the school trustees considered objectionable. The attitude of these reviews toward the jazz-poetry movement was well expressed last spring by *Audience*, published in Cambridge, Mass. This impressive quarterly is an independent venture but has Harvard's 300-year-old tradition in its background and a battery of top-ranking poets and critics on its editorial and advisory boards. Commenting on the "anti-academic hipsters," *Audience* editors conceded that such a movement was inevitable since "modern poetry was becoming precious, arcane and professional." But, the editors added, "we hope that any interest that is agitated will be in literature itself, not in the fabulous hipsters."

Despite the attention San Francisco poets have received, there is a surprising lack of serious study and criticism of their works. The best younger talents have been confused with, and obscured by, minor "beatnik" characters while the major experienced poets—Ferlinghetti, Patchen, Rexroth—have attracted many followers to whom the pose is more important than the poem.

Yet I unhesitatingly consider Allen Ginsberg's *Howl* one of the five or six finest poems by a young American poet of the 1950s. Ginsberg, like his great symbolist and surrealist forebears, has an extraordinary depth of style and language and his work is written in the most authentic tradition of Baudelaire and Rimbaud.

As for the recitation of poetry to jazz, its validity as a performing act is undeniable. But basically poetry is neither composed to jazz nor improvised to jazz. Nor is the vocal performance of a poem necessary to its composition. Of utmost importance to the poet, always, is to avoid mediocrity in composition.

There will always be great audiences to appreciate and interpret great works, and there will always, we hope, be competent and sometimes great performers. Thus, unless the poet's performance whets and improves his talents or provides him a living, he might spend his time better in creative endeavor.

A CHARLES GUENTHER RETROSPECTIVE
Prose: Critical Reviews and Essays, 1953-1962

One justification sometimes given for the jazz-poetry recitation is that it brings poetry "back to the people." Yet only a small segment of people actually share in these recitals and understand or "feel" them. Most poets, I think, would prefer a non-captive audience, one willing to put forth effort to read or listen to their poetry—in books, on records or on radio or television. These are the true mass media.

Last July millions of American viewers had their first glimpse of a jazz-poetry performance when Kenneth Patchen read some of his own verse with the Chamber Jazz Sextet on the nationally televised *Stars of Jazz* program. (The poet and the sextet later performed at the Brussels world's fair.) The whole combo, for all its talent, seemed self-consciously out of its natural environment. But Patchen, a brilliant and outstanding poet, at least made one point clear to the American public. "The beat generation," he explained, "hasn't enough energy either to rock or to roll."

St. Louis Post-Dispatch, December 7, 1958, p. 2N.

Journeys into *Faust*: new studies of a classic

Many writers before and after Goethe, including in our time Stephen Benét, have woven a successful tale around the theme of a man losing his soul. *Faust*, first published 150 years ago, still stands out among these works, not for its disjointed plot but for the superb artistry of its style, characters and symbolism. As André Gide wrote, "Everything in it is saturated with life."

This German drama even has one advantage to us over comparable English classics like *Hamlet* or *Paradise Lost*: it may always be recast into a new translation which would not resemble a travesty of the original work.

Yet no first-rate verse translation of the complete *Faust* (Parts I and II) has appeared for nearly a century since that by Bayard Taylor whose talents seemed precisely suited to the task. In the preface to his version, Taylor held that the translator's job "is not simply mechanical: he must feel, and be guided by, a secondary inspiration."

Bertram Jessup's new rendering of Part I is justified by some passages of good natural dialogue. In other passages Jessup imitates the very style and vocabulary which make Taylor's work outmoded for modern readers. There are strange alternations of archaic and modern word forms ("thou" and "you," "doth" and "does," etc.), inversions and padding of lines. Jessup's translation of the song of the King of Thule and the final dialogue between Faust and Margaret are more fluent than Taylor's; but in other scenes, like the famous Walpurgis Night Intermezzo, Taylor's is more vigorous and readable. By comparing just these two versions, we see how fleeting that "secondary inspiration" can be in the most successful translators.

Stuart Atkins's study of *Faust*, like that by Alexander Gillies published last year (Macmillan), minimizes the play's biographical connections with Goethe's life. The only themes Atkins considers are what is said in *Faust* and the play's power as a poetic statement.

He discusses both Parts I and II and, like Gillies, sees *Faust* as a unified, closely knit work. By concentrating on the text itself, he shows that *Faust* is not "an unhappy mixture of character drama and allegorical pageantry"

100

but "one of the greatest secular poetic statements of how man searches for the meaning of life and of God."

Goethe once confided to his young friend Eckermann, "They come and ask me what idea I meant to embody, in my *Faust*; as if I knew myself and could inform them." Fortunately there are many devoted and brilliant interpretations, like this one by Atkins, to unfold for readers the universal human message of this work which is considered the poetic epitome of Goethe's experience.

Review of *Goethe's Faust: Part One*, translated by Bertram Jessup (Philosophical Library) and *Goethe's Faust: A Literary Analysis,* by Stuart Atkins (Harvard University Press).

St. Louis Post-Dispatch, July 20, 1958, p. 2B.

THREE FACES OF AUTUMN
Poems, Prose, Translations

E.E. Cummings at sixty-three

"Cummings," wrote the poet and critic Allen Tate, "is one of the most prolific poets of his generation and one of the half dozen best. His famous typographic distortions have put a great many readers off, but there is nothing very difficult about them for persons who are willing to give as much attention to poetry as to a tooth paste advertisement."

Recent winner of the 1957 Bollingen prize, one of the top three or four awards annually given to American poets, E. E. Cummings has been called "the terror of typesetters" and his poetry lightly compared to the ruins of a typecasting establishment. Yet after 35 years he has proven that experimental poetry can be good poetry and, moreover, that it can reach a large audience and be appreciated. The citation accompanying the Bollingen award, which carries a $1000 stipend, praised the poet's "gifts of natural wit and lyric imagination with which he has delighted so many for so long."

E(dward) E(stlin) Cummings was born in Cambridge, Mass., in 1894, the son of a Unitarian minister. He was "educated but not tamed" at Harvard, where he took a bachelor's degree in 1915 and an M.A. the next year. During the first World War he enlisted in the Norton Harjes Ambulance Corps and served in France. In 1917, through an official error, he was detained for three months at a French concentration camp at La Ferte-Mace, an experience which later produced his grim and powerful best-selling novel, *The Enormous Room* (1922). Cummings emerged from that war in the American army, thoroughly Frenchified and remembering more of the language than *quarante hommes et huit chevaux*. In fact he remained in Paris until 1924, just long enough to study painting, publish his novel and establish himself as one of the leading American avant-garde writers.

While many a poet has turned novelist, Cummings became a novelist turned poet. *The Enormous Room* at once placed him in the front rank of the young novelists back from the war such as Hemingway, Faulkner and John Dos Passos. Yet it was mainly as a poet that Dos Passos considered Cummings when reviewing that book in *The Dial* in 1922. "The man who invented Eskimo Pie," he complained, "made a million dollars ... but E. E. Cummings, whose verse has been appearing off and on for three years now, and whose experiments should not be more appalling . . . than the experiment of surrounding ice cream with a layer of chocolate . . . , has hardly made a dent in the doughy minds of our so-called poetry-lovers."

His first book of poems, *Tulips and Chimneys*, was published in New York in 1923. When he returned to America the next year his reputation was as great as T. S. Eliot's. Though somewhat younger, Cummings was popularly considered of the same generation as such other experimentalists as Ezra Pound, W. C. Williams, Marianne Moore and Wallace Stevens. ("In any case," Pound wrote him playfully, "remember I'm oldern you are.") In the late '20s Cummings became a close friend of Hart Crane, who was struck by his "prodigal and startling" sensibility. He published three more books of verse and a play. His poetry continued to appear in vigorous, if transient, literary magazines like *The Dial*, *Broom*, *S4N* and *The Transatlantic Review*. It was an exciting period to which the Cummings idiom, extravagant, daring and iconoclastic, was perfectly tuned.

For the next decade his popularity waned. He became an anachronism in an era of social consciousness. Still, he had adherents; among them was Pound, who wrote to publisher friends that Cummings had "70 poems that nobuddy loves"—"bright inimitable but with difficulty salable verses." In 1930, in an ultimate rebellious gesture, Cummings published a 63-page book with no title, a blank frontispiece and meaningless text and illustrations. The next year a book of his drawings and paintings appeared under the title *CIOPW*, signifying the first letter of each medium used: charcoal, ink, oil, pencil and water color. He kept producing poetry despite its acceptance by only the happy few: *W (Viva)* (1931), *No Thanks* (1935) and the first *Collected Poems* (1938). His other works of this period were *Tom* (1935), a ballad based on *Uncle Tom's Cabin,* and *Eimi* (1933), a journal of a trip to the Soviet Union. His more recent books of verse are *XAIPE* (1950) and *Poems: 1923-1954.*

In 1950 Cummings was honored by the Academy of American Poets fellowship of $5000 for "great achievement" over many years, to become, as Randall Jarrell wrote, "one more dean of American poets." In 1955 he received a special citation from the National Book Award committee. The outstanding qualities of Cummings's poetry are its proportion, inventiveness and variety. Hopkins and Mallarmé were the first modern poets to split the word, thereby giving poetry a new dimension. They were followed by more or less radical experimenters: Arno Holz, Apollinaire and the Dadaists such as Philippe Soupault. Yet, unlike the Dadaists, Cummings gives meaning to his poems and consciously invents new uses for words. In his poem "what a proud dreamhorse," for instance, he uses "beautiful" and "happens" as nouns; elsewhere he turns "am," "if" and "because" into nouns. Or he sometimes employs a noun like "april" as a verb. This technique forces the reader's mind into fresh analyses and demands careful study of the poetry. Here it is impractical, of course, to compare the Cummings product with a dentifrice ad.

It is also impossible to appraise the Cummings breadth of style by a few anthology pieces. Among the 600 poems in his latest collection one can probably find more to shock, delight, puzzle and move the reader than in the work of any living poet. The variety of moods—tender, raging, lofty, glad, grotesque and satiric—is extreme. The most surprising aspect of Cummings, as an individual and in his poetic art, is his pursuit of traditional values deeply rooted in New England transcendentalism. Beyond the mask of innovation he can use traditional forms but is not bound to them.

Today Cummings, at 63, is slight of build and keeps a youthful appearance. With his attractive wife Marion he spends the winters at his Greenwich Village studio and the summers on a 300-acre wooded farm at Silver Lake, N.H. In recent correspondence he informed this writer that he is "both painting and writing, as always" and has a book coming out next autumn to be entitled *95 Poems*.

Cummings's paintings, luminous and delightful as his poetry, have been exhibited at the American-British Art Centre and the Rochester Memorial Gallery. His most recent one-man art show was held last May at the University of Rochester. When I asked him if he would ever consider holding a joint exhibit of his poems and paintings, he answered, "No. Perhaps because I feel it might encourage the immemorial unmyth of 'a poet who is also a painter.'" At the same time, he feels that his painting complements his writing—"if I go without one or the other I miss it." Poet and/or painter, E. E. Cummings (or e. e. cummings if you like) has an intellectual integrity possessed by very few present-day artists. He has said simply, "Art is a question of being alive." Having infused new life into our language for two generations, he is still going strong.

St. Louis Post-Dispatch, March 30, 1958, p. 5C.

Old master, new style

On a recent lecture tour in Texas, T.S. Eliot commented on the "beat generation" poets by stating he expected to see their popularity wane. Considering their work as "a form of existentialism," he added: "I don't see why a whole generation should be so gloomy. There are a lot of things to be cheerful about." The "beat" or bistro bards of course represent the most modern phase in the perennial search for madder music and stronger wine. As such, they find greater affinity with the new rhythms of Kenneth Rexroth and Lawrence Ferlinghetti than with the older syncopations of *The Waste Land.* But time has not diminished Eliot's voice in matters of poetic taste, and as a poet and playwright he has reached an Olympian status comparable to that of Yeats 20 years ago.

Eliot's latest essays, *On Poetry and Poets*, were nearly all written in the last 20 years. They are marked by a clarity and quiet assurance not found in the earlier *Selected Essays*, first issued in 1932. The first part of the book concerns poetic principles. There he discusses poetry's social function, what constitutes "minor" poetry and a "classic," and he includes the famous essays on "The Frontiers of Criticism" and "The Three Voices of Poetry." In the second part of the book Eliot applies his principles to the work of specific poets from Virgil to Yeats, including Milton, Byron, Goethe and Kipling. The two essays on Milton, written at intervals of ten years, are among the most interesting. In the earlier essay Eliot suggested that Milton, though a great poet, had a "bad influence" on poetry which persists to our time. Milton, he wrote, lacked visual imagination; his gifts were "naturally aural." But in the more recent essay (1947) Eliot concludes that "poets are sufficiently liberated from Milton's reputation, to approach the study of his work without danger, and with profit to their poetry and to English language."

On Poetry and Poets enhances T. S. Eliot's position as one of the immediate founders of modern literary criticism. It reaffirms his power to raise critical inquiry to the level of creative expression. And it is his most important prose work in 25 years.

Review of *On Poetry and Poets*, by T.S. Eliot (Farrar, Straus and Cudahy).

St. Louis Post-Dispatch, June 16, 1958, p. 2B.

THREE FACES OF AUTUMN
Poems, Prose, Translations

Prince among the prophets

It was not unusual that Roger Caillois, in his *Poétique de St.-John Perse* (Gallimard, 1954), included a section of Perse's writings as a special supplement to his study of that poet. In doing this he expressed something of the frustration every reader feels who seeks a simple exegesis of Perse's work. A similar feeling had perhaps caused T. S. Eliot, twenty-five years earlier, to write of his own translation of *Anabase* that it is "better to read such a poem six times and dispense with a preface."

Amers (*Seamarks*) is the longest poem published to date by Alexis Saint-Léger Léger whose pseudonym, after the Roman Perseus, is as vague and evocative as his poetry. In scope and complexity this work surpasses even *Anabase* with its stately, land-locked movement. Like most of Perse's poems since *Éloges* (1911), *Seamarks* is distinguished by a great elemental theme developed in epic length and style with a complex of elusive references. As in *Pluies* (*Rains*), *Neiges* (*Snows*) and *Vents* (*Winds*), the broad theme of loss and renewal appears also in *Seamarks*, in which the sea is used in its traditional sense as a life-symbol.

Although parts of Wallace Fowlie's translation were published before in *Poetry, The Yale Review* and elsewhere, only this complete bilingual edition impressed this reviewer with the poem's total pattern and significance. The very title *Seamarks*, which might be awkwardly defined as "landmarks on the sea," precisely conveys the poet's meaning; it is at once specific and symbolic and sets the tone of the whole poem. The work consists of four major sections or movements. The first is a six-part Invocation beginning "And you, Seas . . . ," a grand overture with Whitmanesque touches, in which the poet summons

> . . . the Sea that came to us on the stone steps of the drama:
> With her Princes, her Regents, her Messengers clothed in
> pomp and metal, her great Actors their eyes gouged out and her
> Prophets chained together, her women Magicians stamping on
> wooden clogs, their mouths full of black clots, and her tributes
> of Virgins plodding in the furrows of the hymn,
> With her Shepherds, her Pirates, her Wet-nurses of infant
> kings, her old Nomads in exile and her Princesses of elegy, her
> tall silent Widows under illustrious ashes, her great Usurpers of
> thrones and Founders of distant colonies, her Prebendaries and

106

her Merchants, her great Concussionaries of provinces rich in tin, and her great travelling Sages mounted on rice-field buffaloes.

In the next section, a magnificently wrought nine-part Strophe, further symbolic characters emerge from the tall or low-lying cities to sing the sea's praises: a celestial navigator ("the Master of stars and navigation"), the Tragediennes, the Patrician Women, the Poetess, the girl prophet among the Priests, the Lovers and others who play lesser roles in the drama. In the long Chorus that follows, the sea is then celebrated in concert as the eternal sea of every name, having all attributes the poet can muster in his song. A brief Dedication concludes the poem. Altogether the translation shows a fine grasp of Perse's difficult style and a mastery of recreating, as far as faithful rendering will allow, the sumptuous melody, rhythms and imagery of the original.

St.-John Perse has probably come as close as any poet of our time to creating a new poetry which springs from the sources of history and spans all history. He can transform his own experience into vast universal symbols of exile, mutability and a thirst for infinity. Like a Schliemann digging through the debris of all civilizations, Perse views them all simultaneously, objectively, in terms of the future. His medium, the prose poem, has its rich traditions in Lautréamont and Rimbaud; yet he is more kindred to Claudel than either of these in his personal career and the dramatic aspects of his poetry. There is still a great difference between them, however: Claudel, even with his great spiritual metaphors, poetizes the concrete in person, place and time; Perse skirts the limits of the indefinite with a "vision stripped of all contingency."

Readers are naturally inclined to link elements in Perse's life with allusions in the poems. But in one of his most self-revealing documents, a letter to Roger Caillois dated January 26, 1953, Perse writes, "My work . . . has always evolved beyond space and time . . . it intends to avoid any historical or geographical reference . . . it intends to avoid any personal incident." The same letter deserves quoting further for its pertinence to *Seamarks*:

> Nothing seems to me, moreover, more surprising than to explain a "poet" always by "culture." Personally I'm greatly astonished to see favorable critics appraise the poems as a crystallization, since poetry to me is movement above all—

in its birth as well as in its growth and final release. The very philosophy of the "poet" seems to me the ability to recall to himself, fundamentally, the old elementary "Rheism" of ancient thought—like that of our pre-Socratics in the West. And his metrics too, which some attribute to rhetoric, lead only further to movement and the frequentation of movement in all its most unforeseeable living resources. Hence, for the poet, the importance of the Sea in everything.

It is just a half century since the first poems of *Éloges* began appearing in French reviews, and a quarter of a century since Marcel Raymond ranked *Anabase* with Valéry's *La Jeune Parque* as one of the two greatest poems written during and after the first world war. Now, at the age of seventy-one and after eighteen years of residence in the United States, Perse is unmistakably a major French poet.

Seamarks proves his steadiness and strengthens his position, a position American poets have long recognized, mainly by Eliot's *Anabasis*. It would be tempting to speculate that Wallace Fowlie's superb translation may be as influential on latter-century American poetry as, say, Macpherson's *Ossian* was on the Romantics. Whatever its ultimate influence, *Seamarks* is a work of remarkably sustained power and vision, "a chant of the sea as has never been chanted."

Review of *Seamarks*, by St.-John Perse. Bilingual edition, with translation by Wallace Fowlie (Bollingen Series LXVII. Pantheon Books).

Poetry, 93 (February 1959) pp. 332-335.

Langston Hughes's timeless voice

Poets today are no longer considered to be "born." They are made by the long discipline of graduate English courses. This is especially noticeable in poets under 40, whose work appears in increasing abundance in the best literary magazines. But if any poet can be said to have a mainly natural talent, that poet is Langston Hughes. The reason for this is that Hughes draws his inspiration not so much from books as from life around him and from his experience.

Hughes, now 57, is a native of Joplin, Mo. After finishing high school there he lived for a year in Mexico, studied a year at Columbia University, then worked his way to Europe where he spent almost a year in France, Italy and Spain. His first national publication was in *Crisis* magazine in 1921. In 1925 he won a prize given by *Opportunity* magazine for his poem "The Weary Blues." The next year he published his first book of verse under this title. After these achievements he was awarded a scholarship to Lincoln University, in Pennsylvania, where he graduated in 1929.

Since then Hughes has devoted his time to writing and lecturing, activities which have brought him several fellowships and other honors. He has published nearly 30 books in varied fields, including a cross section of his own work, *The Langston Hughes Reader* (1958).

The contents of his new *Selected Poems* were chosen by Hughes from seven earlier books and include some work never published before. The several hundred poems are grouped under 13 sections having titles like "Afro-American Fragments," "Shadow of the Blues," "Lament Over Love" and "Montage of a Dream Deferred." Altogether the collection is handsomely designed and printed.

Hughes is most successful in his poems and ballads which have a definite rhythm or beat; the free verse, written mostly in the '20s, has not worn so well. Whether or not he is the "original jazz poet," as Arna Bontemps has acclaimed him, he remains the most active lyricist of that category of jazz still known as the "blues." He was the first poet fully to exploit and appreciate the regular poetic pattern of the blues.

The best elements of Hughes's poetry are its clarity, its depth and authenticity of feeling, and its varied treatment of moods and themes. In

109

the conventional sense his technique is not outstanding, but his verse often carries a power lacking in verse by more fussy craftsmen. The poems here range from fast-moving conversational pieces to ballads on traditional topics. Hughes has a mystical strain, too; certain poems ("Cross," "Silhouette," "Genius Child") are reminiscent of Blake's *Songs of Experience*.

Underlying these *Selected Poems*, both "the grim and the glad," is a voice of pain and isolation, of a deeply felt contemporary anguish. "I am the American heartbreak," the poet writes; and the song of his "Night of the Four Songs Unsung" repeats like a *cante hondo* or lament: "Sorrow! Sorrow! Sorrow! Sorrow!" By whatever name it is known—"angoisse," "agonia" or the "blues"—the voice of this suffering spirit is true, timeless and universal.

Review of *Selected Poems of Langston Hughes*, illustrated with drawings by E. McKnight Kauffer (Alfred A. Knopf).

St. Louis Post-Dispatch, March 22, 1959, p. 4B.

A line of poets

Robert Lowell, aged 42 and of the perennially distinguished Lowell clan, can hardly be called "rather odd" like his forebears. ("Percy saw canals on Mars, Amy loved to smoke cigars," ran an old Harvard quip.) He has become in fact—like the non-partisan sons of deceased presidents—something of a symbol of an earlier, palmy era of Briand pacts and maroon Pierce Arrows. In *Life Studies*, which contains 23 poems and a long prose fragment, he exploits his family background fully. He even makes this background interesting by regarding it rather clinically and with unsparing honesty.

Four of the poems are historical and dramatic monologues and four others are epistles addressed to other writers. But mainly *Life Studies* is by a Lowell about the Lowells. Coming as it does in the wake of Horace Gregory's fine biography, *Amy Lowell: Portrait of the Poet in Her Time* (Nelson), *Life Studies* reveals what other Lowells thought of Amy, and is itself an important literary document.

Practically all the poems of Robert Lowell are full of objects and details rather than themes and ideas. In this respect they have a peculiar resemblance—though it is only superficial—to Amy Lowell's imagism. The strength of his poetry lies not in his ability to catalog everyday things and events in skillful verse, but in his subtle observations, his suggestion of meanings. This technique is more like Robert Frost's than Miss Lowell's. Above all, it is Robert Lowell's—for he is perhaps the best poet in an eminent line of poets.

Review of *Life Studies*, by Robert Lowell (Farrar, Straus and Cudahy).

St. Louis Post-Dispatch, July 21, 1959, p. 2B.

THREE FACES OF AUTUMN
Poems, Prose, Translations

Pound's mirror of memory

> If we never write anything save what is already understood, the field of understanding will never be extended. One demands the right, now and again to write for a few people with special interests and whose curiosity reaches into greater detail. —*Canto 96.*

Five years ago Ezra Pound remarked that his poetry wouldn't be understood for another 30 years. He said this without a trace of either regret or satisfaction; it was a practical prediction based on experience. For it was not until the early and middle 1950s, or some 30 years after their first appearance in1925, that the early *Cantos* were studied seriously in American universities.

The graduate seminar at Yale, *The Analyst* at Northwestern, the English Institute at Columbia, newsletters and researches at California—all of these, while rather uncoordinated, made up the first considerable Pound scholarship. Their efforts did more in three years to show the compositional logic of Pound's poetry than 30 previous years of speculative essays.

Meanwhile, after the Second World War, New Directions published or reissued an average of a book a year by Pound and made hard-to-get early works of the poet once more available.

The *Cantos* are undeniably Pound's most important work. To know them is to know the poet: his preoccupations with Agassiz, Frobenius, Del Mar, Gaudier and a host of other forgotten artists, scholars and thinkers. In language and structure these 14 new *Cantos* are as difficult to the ordinary intelligent reader as any of the preceding 95, but they lack the bitterness of the previous *Section: Rock Drill, Cantos 85-95.*

All of life and civilization, history through recorded time and the mirror of his memory are Pound's materials for his epic. If one grasps the language, including a half dozen foreign languages, there always remains the content, the separate and unified meanings of the poem to comprehend. Yet to dismiss the *Cantos* subjectively on various grounds is to deny oneself a share of perhaps the most complex and challenging poetic experience ever written. Very few poets are, or have ever been, as faithful and uncompromising in their art as Ezra Pound. One can only speculate

112

that if his poetry does reach a mass audience by 1985—the same size audience as, say, Eliot and Frost now have—Pound should have a whopping good centenary. That is, if civilization isn't like *1984*.

Review of *Thrones: 96-109 De Los Cantares*, by Ezra Pound (New Directions).

St. Louis Post-Dispatch, February 17, 1960, p. 2B.

THREE FACES OF AUTUMN
Poems, Prose, Translations

Unique anthology

Some books, like Helmut Hatzfeld's *Literature Through Art* (Oxford, 1952), have attempted a comparative study of art or music and literature. *Poets and the Past* is somewhat different. It is based on the premise that the various arts, though contingent, exist in their separate realms; their only relation is in the Past, "an inexorable riddle, an imagined abstraction which never fails to excite and draw the attention of the artist."

This unique anthology consists of 15 poems especially commissioned to accompany 19 photographs of pre-Columbian sculpture. The poets represented are Stanley Kunitz, Richard Wilbur, W. C. Williams, Louise Bogan, C. Day-Lewis and others equally well known.

Many readers may wonder if verse thus written to order, as it were, can be first-rate poetry. The answer is that some fine, even "great" poems have been written as a result of a patron's or publisher's request. The poems in this book, if not the best the poets have written, are consistently well-crafted. The sculpture, symbolizing as it does the ancient yet highly organized cultures and their decay, was apparently an exciting challenge to the poetic imagination.

The relationship between the poems and the plates is subtle and seldom explicit. Yet even the most explicit poems (by Jean Garrigue, Day-Lewis and Williams) show no straining after word and image. Lee Boltin's photos, with their wide-ranging tones, are beautifully reproduced.

Review of *Poets and the Past,* edited by Dore Ashton. Photographs by Lee Boltin (André Emroefich Gallery).

St. Louis Post-Dispatch, May 18, 1960, p. 4B.

Pasternak as a poet

Boris Pasternak, who died last week, was known in his homeland not as a novelist (for *Dr. Zhivago* has not been published there) but as a poet and particularly as a translator of Shakespeare's tragedies.

Thirty years ago Prince Mirsky called him "unquestionably the greatest living Russian poet" for his "freshness of perception and diction" and "tensity of lyrical emotion." It was mainly as a lyric poet, too, that the Royal Swedish Academy cited him when announcing the 1958 Nobel prizes.

Pasternak was fortunate to have many English and American translators.

Among them, besides the translators of these volumes, have been Babette Deutsch and the poet's sister, Lydia Pasternak-Slater. The abundance of translations has made it likely that at least one fairly accurate English version of many of his poems exists. Since most of us don't know Russian and don't have the Russian texts anyway, we must appreciate the translations for their effectiveness as English poetry.

Great poetry is elusive. To recast it from one language into another takes accuracy of interpretation, a mastery of poetic form and a feeling for both languages concerned. The translator must also be struck with, and want to communicate, the wonder of a great, strange poem. No translator consistently meets these standards. Thus, Messrs. Kayden and Reavey, Miss Deutsch and the rest have each sometimes rendered a poem better than anyone else.

The Kayden and Reavey books are nearly equal in scope. Mr. Kayden gives us 115 poems compared with Mr. Reavey's 103. Each volume has some selections not included in the other, and each covers Pasternak's poetry from *My Sister, Life* (1917) and *Themes and Variations* (1923) to verse written in the last two or three years.

Kayden's has a short, interesting introduction quoting a letter from Pasternak to the translator, and a section of notes on the poems. Reavey's has a longer introduction, plus three prose addresses by Pasternak and a bibliography. A section of 35 poems dated 1955-1959 is one of the high points of the Reavey collection.

THREE FACES OF AUTUMN
Poems, Prose, Translations

There is enough different material in these books to justify what at first may seem a duplication of publishing. There are noticeable differences, too, in the translations. Reavey has followed Pasternak's idea that "translations must have a closer connection with the original than is usually attempted." His literal versions, if perhaps more complete and accurate, are generally less spirited than Kayden's. He conveys the sense, and Kayden the essence, of Pasternak as a poet.

With crisp lines, simple rhythms and full rhyme, Kayden's renderings hold a slight edge over Reavey's as English verse. In his poems as in his novel, Pasternak effectively depicted the Russian landscape. His last poems were largely pastoral—with titles like "Summer in the Country," "Autumn Woods," "Ploughing Time" and "Hayricks"—and remind us a little of Robert Frost's verse.

The last poem in Kayden's book, "The Passing Storm," and "The Nobel Prize" in Reavey's volume, restate Pasternak's attitude of disengagement shared by Dr. Zhivago. Despite his use of Christian themes, which are pictorially, not mystically, developed, Pasternak was not a great Christian poet like the English and Spanish Christian mystical poets. Pasternak's attachment to Christianity was synonymous with a love for human freedom. He stirs our interest, or at least our curiosity, by adopting something of the Christian-Hebraic tradition, orphaned, alas, by Western writers who have unlimited freedom to express it.

Review of *Poems by Boris Pasternak*, translated by Eugene M. Kayden. (The University of Michigan Press), *The Poetry of Boris Pasternak*, translated and introduced by George Reavey (G.P. Putnam's Sons).

St. Louis Post-Dispatch, June 5, 1960, p. 4C.

116

The 1960 Nobel Laureate

St.-John Perse, winner of the 1960 Nobel Prize for literature, has been
recognized for over 30 years as one of the greatest poets of modern
France. Although American readers have had his books available in
superb bilingual editions, published since 1949 in the Bollingen Series,
Perse remains virtually unknown to the mass audience.

Even among poets who know his work well, he is still enigmatic in private
life.

Perse, whose real name is Alexis Léger, was born in the French West
Indies in 1887 and educated in France. Like the poet Paul Claudel, he had
a long career in the French diplomatic service, which he entered in 1914.
He served several years in China, attended the 1922 disarmament
conference in Washington, then returned to Paris to serve with Aristide
Briand. In 1932, at Briand's death, he was appointed Permanent Secretary
for Foreign Affairs. At the fall of France in 1940 he came to the United
States. For a short time he was a consultant on French literature at the
Library of Congress. He still lives in Washington.

As a poet, Perse is highly independent; he cannot be classed with any
school or movement, nor is his art visibly linked with that of any other
poet. One of his best critics, Roger Caillois, has written, "The work of St.-
John Perse appears in a superb solitude." Yet this doesn't preclude
comparing and describing his work. Like certain other important French
poets (René Char and Henri Michaux), Perse uses the form of prose-poetry
inherited from such nineteenth century writers as Lautréamont and
Rimbaud. In Perse's hands this form becomes both lyric and epic.

Perse is the unique master of the epic/ode, of long lyric metaphors which
synthesize all ages and cultures. The winds of his *Winds* (1946) are
nameless and timeless; in *Seamarks* (1957) the sea is "of every age and
every name." In this respect Perse's work is totally unlike Pound's *Cantos*,
for example, which are full of clues to persons, places and events.

Perse's poems are strikingly adaptable to translation. They usually deal
with some elemental theme (rain, snow, winds, the sea) and unfold vast,
mutable landscapes full of exotic, mysterious detail. Music, color and
rhythm come forth in evocative, ceremonious phrases. The "versets,"

which are usually longer than Claudel's, blend sound and meaning until, as Wallace Fowlie writes, "The poem seems to form and grow before one's eyes."

From his first book, *Éloges* (*Praises*), published 50 years ago, to his recent *Chronicle*, St.-John Perse has strengthened his position in modern poetry. Now he is ranked with the four or five major French poets of the past century, from Baudelaire to Valéry. In his *Letter on Jacques Rivière*, Perse once wrote, "My name doesn't belong to the literary world." But his verse will always stimulate and fascinate readers for its sonorous music, opulent imagery and magnificent vision.

St. Louis Post-Dispatch, November 6, 1960, p. 4B.

Villon updated

Though rarely acknowledged as such, François de Montcorbier, alias Villon, is perhaps the number one predecessor of the beat generation poets. About a dozen well-known English versions of his works have appeared in the last century. We may rightly ask if another translation is really necessary and whether this one has anything the others haven't. The simple answers, *no* and *yes*, need some explanation.

In the first place, most readers probably aren't interested in every line Villon wrote. One can get acquainted with this fifteenth-century poet by reading a few of his ballades and Wyndham Lewis's biography of him. Many early translations, like Rossetti's are still unexcelled. Even Swinburne, carried aloft on his own sibilants, could settle down in Villon's eight-syllable lines. Good recent translations include Robert Fitzgerald's "Ballade of the Hanged Men" and Hubert Creekmore's "Lament of the Lovely Helmet-dealer." All of the translations just mentioned are expertly done in English rhyme and meter.

Anthony Bonner's good idiomatic versions lack rhyme and meter. To turn ballades into free verse may at first seem unorthodox, just an easy way out of searching for ingenious rhymes to match the original poet's wit and imagery. But any effort Bonner has spared on technique has been spent on readability.

In a direct style and modern language, Villon's tartness, compassion and poignancy come through very well. From beginning to end, in *The Legacy, The Testament,* the miscellaneous verses and poems in slang, the Bonner rendition reads like a racy novel. Other material—the French texts, a bibliography, notes, and music to a rondeau—adds much to this book's value.

Whatever it lacks in poetic form, the Bonner translation restores a realism to Villon which many readers have not recognized in him before.

Review of *The Complete Works of François Villon*, translated with a biography and notes by Anthony Bonner (David McKay Company).

St. Louis Post-Dispatch, January 15, 1961, p. 4F.

THREE FACES OF AUTUMN
Poems, Prose, Translations

Changing tastes in poetry

Stanley Hyman has written one book of literary criticism, *The Armed Vision,* and edited another, *The Critical Performance,* which are small classics of modern critical writings.

The present volume falls somewhat below them in its length and the range of authors and works examined. Yet it does not fall below them in quality; it is, on the whole, a thorough, thoughtful and well organized work for the "four revolutions" it covers. The four revolutions in taste Hyman deals with are ancient Greek literature, English Neo-Classicism, English Romanticism and modern literature.

Hyman contends that when a critic makes a general statement about poetry, he has some particular poem in mind as a standard. Among the ancient Greeks, Aristotle and Longinus are the critics Hyman gives as examples. Both, he shows, esteemed Sophocles and disrespected Euripides, but for different reasons.

English Neo-Classicism is represented by Dryden (as critic) on Shakespeare (as poet). Next, the chapter on English Romanticism begins incongruously with a discussion of Pope's "The Rape of the Lock" and Samuel Johnson's criticism on Pope. Further in that chapter Hyman deals with a true Romantic, Wordsworth, and with Coleridge's criticism on that poet.

Here Hyman is particularly adept; he shows how Coleridge, in his *Biographia Literaria,* uses Wordsworth's poetry to create a taste by which Coleridge's own poetry, and all later Romantic poetry, may be enjoyed.

Under "Modern Literature" Hyman points out that Milton's "Paradise Lost" was the standard of taste for Victorian England. He then gives a resumé of that poem to prepare the reader for a discussion, which follows, of Matthew Arnold's essay on Milton.

Concluding *Poetry and Criticism,* Hyman gives a close reading of T. S. Eliot's "Sweeney Among the Nightingales." This poem, like "The Rape of the Lock," gives a wider significance than its trivial events would ordinarily justify. "Sweeney Among the Nightingales" deals with sordid events, not noble ones (and here Eliot contradicts Arnold).

Hyman shows convincingly that Eliot, in his critical essays, "created the taste by which he was to be enjoyed." These essays, he adds, made it possible for Eliot's poetry "to survive in the world of Milton and the mighty dead without conceding an inch." Such, Hyman concludes, is the true relation between poetry and criticism.

Review of *Poetry and Criticism: Four Revolutions in Literary Taste*, by Stanley Edgar Hyman (Atheneum).

St. Louis Post-Dispatch, September 22, 1961, p. 2B.

THREE FACES OF AUTUMN
Poems, Prose, Translations

What makes a poet

Once I was introduced to a young lady who informed me that she was a writer. Politely interested I asked, "What do you write?" "Oh, poetry and prose—mostly," she answered. I was fond of repeating this story until lately, when I told it to a friend of mine, an educator, and haughtily added, "Poetry and prose—mostly! What else is there?" And my friend replied, "Why music of course!"

I never met that young lady again. I might have inquired if she was also a writer of music. The important thing, though, was that this friendly squelch set me thinking again about the old and modern distinctions between prose and poetry, and the relations of music to poetry. We'll return presently to the differences between prose and poetry.

"What makes a poet"—this title is really a subterfuge, a catchall. I chose it because it's extremely flexible. It can apply to the poet and his qualifications. Or if we think of the phrase as having inverted construction, it can mean "What a poet creates" and apply to the poet's product. In either case we can only touch upon a subject of such scope at this time. These will be naive observations and comments which I hope may awaken or strengthen some interest in reading poetry.

In one of his early essays Mr. Pound wrote that you can spot the bad critic right away because he starts out by discussing the poet and not the poetry. Mr. Pound's autobiography, which precedes his *Selected Poems*, consists of two dozen lines of terse facts and statements. Most biographers are far less prudent and selective.

Unquestionably the work of a poet is more important to me than his life, however fascinating this may be. Still we should realize that the work is inseparably linked with the life. Sometimes a poem which seems, at first reading, superficial or imitative may be charged with new meanings if we have an accurate account of the poet's life. The life is relevant, and I heartily agree with Mr. Robert Graves when he says that a poet cannot write true poems and at the same time be heartless or insincere or grasping in his personal relations.

Just as biography-making has led some writers into strange by-ways, criticism has made prose writers out of men who set out to be poets. I use the term criticism here in its broadest sense, including the theory, history and evaluation of literature. In the last forty years we have passed through a baroque age of criticism. This is supported by figures on American book production.

In 1920, 409 books of poetry and drama were published compared with 423 in 1955. This was a yearly increase of only 14 books, but it represented a decrease from eight per cent of total book production in 1920 to four per cent in 1955. Forty years ago fewer books of criticism than of poetry were published; but by 1955, over one hundred more books of criticism than of poetry reached the booksellers' shelves. The production of criticism had more than doubled while poetry-making remained static. This age of criticism seems to have reached a climax in the mid-fifties when the clash between the New Critics and the Chicago Critics was most intense.

Criticism is characteristic of what Mr. Auden called, just 13 years ago, our Age of Anxiety. Here I should like to alter Mr. Auden's title a little, to refine it if possible to apply to the 1960s. I should like to consider this the age of apprehension, since apprehension implies many more things than anxiety: it includes the perception of our poets and imaginative writers, the opinion of our critics, and the fear and foreboding which Mr. Auden originally implied in his title.

Yet we may rightly complain that it is sometimes easier to find a book of criticism on a poet's work than to find a book of his poems.

The word poetry, as we know, comes from the Greek *poiein*, meaning to make. Only one modern writer, as far as I know, has used this word in its ancient sense. M. Jean Cocteau applies it to all of his works. He separates his production into categories called "poetry of the novel," "critical poetry," "poetry of the theater," "graphic poetry" and "poetry of the film."

The definition of a poet as a "maker" or "craftsman" of anything but verses has long ago slipped from the language. We usually think of a poet as someone who expresses himself imaginatively, esthetically, in a concentrated language which arouses powerful thoughts, ideas and emotions in us. Sometimes we give the name of "poet" to a musician, a sculptor, a painter, a boxer or a dancer; and we mean that their mode of expression—their melody and rhythm, their sense of form or color, or their motion—awakens some esthetic response in us.

Let us turn now to what makes a poem.

Aristotle once complained (*Poetics*): "Even when a treatise on medicine or natural science is brought out in verse, the name of poet is given by custom to the author; and yet Homer and Empedocles have nothing in common except the metre, so that it would be better to call the one poet, the other physicist rather than poet."

Let's think about this for a moment. Our idea of a poet has been associated with the *form* he uses rather than his language, style, the content of his verses. And only a few discerning readers and critics have given the name poetry to something not having the name of verse.

One reason for this partial blackout of our concept of poetry is that modern criticism has dealt more with lyrical than with dramatic and narrative poetry. Noteworthy exceptions are the great and continuing body of Shakespeare and Dante criticism. By modern criticism I mean from the Romantic period up to our time, from Coleridge on. Poe, in his "Philosophy of Composition," and Arnold in 'The Study of Poetry" have both left us an idea of poetry's fragmentation, of how short passages and specimens suffice to explain poetry for us.

Today the long verse narrative is scarce; the novel of course has replaced it.[1] Yet in relatively recent times, until the nineteenth century, any verse production entitled a "poem" was usually assumed to be a long narrative work. A writer didn't consider himself a poet until he wrote something in the Homeric tradition. Now we see the rare verse narrative advertised as "a novel in verse."

The great communicative forces of poetry are rhythm, music, imagery and meaning. The critic or analyst of a poem usually concerns himself with one or more of these forces. When his criticism or analysis fails, and it most often does fail in some respect, it is because he is unable to receive the full signal strength of each of these forces as transmitted by the poet.

That is, where these forces are transmitted to begin with, by a great poet. At the same time, the critic is to be commended for tuning in on the poet.

A CHARLES GUENTHER RETROSPECTIVE
Prose: Critical Reviews and Essays, 1953-1962

Even the highly trained critic—who may also be an accomplished poet—is ordinarily a specialist in one or two aspects of poetry, in one or two of those forces I mentioned.

I have spoken of those "communicative forces" as if they were all a poem consists of—a way of expression, a way of communication. But the poet's purpose in communicating and his motivation are also important. The aim and motivation (what used to be known as inspiration) make the difference between a piece of excellently wrought verse and a great poem.[2] I don't want to be caught up in superlatives here. (Too many critics are excessively shy of them.) But I'd like to make one more observation: that a great poem works a metastasis on the sensible reader. It transforms him; he is not the same person as before.

Poetry itself is protean. It takes many shapes and forms. A common fault of many of even our best poets is that they have limited their appreciation and emulation of poetry to one particular form, style or period. Poetry to me has gradually become an activity which doesn't require the discarding of something of value just because something new and different has come along. At the same time, we must continually re-evaluate poetry of the past and give it new meanings. As readers we must keep a balanced perspective. Before we praise or condemn a new poem or a new book of verse, we should honestly ask ourselves whether the work of certain poets of the past, whose work we have always admired, doesn't have similar faults and virtues.

In this process of evaluation the critic is immeasurably helpful to us. Often he is a specialist in one period or school of poetry. When his interest is limited primarily to one writer, however, his range of vision may be too narrow for us to rely on his judgment of many different poets, schools or periods. We must be wary, in short, of every critic (and poet as well) who stops "growing and becoming," as Arnold would say, and lapses into a "being and resting," or sitting on his laurels.

In his *Advancement of Learning* Bacon maintained that poetry can be "taken in two senses: in respect of words or matter." Bacon's distinction between prose and verse reaches the heart of much modern criticism, insofar as critics are preoccupied with citing the prosaic quality of certain verse or the poetic quality of, say, Thomas Wolfe's novels. But modern criticism is also concerned with the sense of words which Bacon writes

125

about. Some of our most competent literary theorists have dwelt upon *The Language of Poetry, The Structure of Complex Words, The Meaning of Meaning,* and so on. This concentration on words seems to have evolved during the first 30 years from a concentration on style which occupied literary theorists during the last 30 years of our century. As usual, the poets—Hopkins and Mallarmé particularly—were the precursors of this trend, this emphasis on the word.

The two literary theorists most influential on criticism and creative writing during the last generation have been Mr. Richards and Mr. Pound. Yet it is interesting to note their differences. In *The Meaning of Meaning* (1922) Mr. Richards introduced the distinction between the "referential" aspects of words and the "emotive" aspect. This distinction, as Mr. Cleanth Brooks noted, seemed to split in two not only the world of words but the universe itself, widening the gap between fact and fiction, science and poetry, thought and emotion. Mr. Pound in his *ABC of Reading* (1934) pointed out, however, that "you still charge words with meaning mainly in three ways, called phanopoeia, melopoeia, logopoeia. You use a word to throw a visual image on to the reader's imagination, or you charge it by sound, or you use groups of words to do this. Thirdly, you take the greater risk of using the word in some special relation to 'usage,' that is, to the kind of context in which the reader expects, or is accustomed, to find it." Miss Elizabeth Sewell in *The Structure of Poetry* takes practically the same view as Dr. Richards towards the function of language. She says that a poet's use of language varies between two extremes. The first is where the poet writes intuitively, the second is where he writes with acute intellectual inquiry. I'd like to add a third extreme, although it isn't practiced much any more. That is, where language is used neither intuitively nor intellectually but purely by chance selection. This is the "words from the box" method practiced by the Dadaists some 40 years ago. This method may sometimes produce a successful piece of writing or an interesting painting. But I doubt whether any great poem or painting, at least any which has come down to us, has ever been produced wholly by accident.

I remember the phenomenal Dr. Merrill Moore, the most prolific poet of our time and a prolific writer of medical articles as well. Several years ago I was partly to blame for fostering the legend that he wrote 100,000 sonnets, a legend he neither confirmed nor denied. (After his death in 1958 the number was more accurately given as 40,000.) Because of his prolificacy Dr. Moore, and not Miss Gertrude Stein, seems to me the archetype of the rapid-fire, intuitive poet.

Intuition, reason and chance. How pat and innocuous it would seem to say that these things—with the essential poem-maker and the essential language—make the poem. But the terms are too vague. They explain nothing, no poems in particular; they only suggest the most general approach to reading or creating a poem. We might as well say that experience, observation and learning are the basis of all poetry (as they are in a sense) or of all man's acts and creations for that matter. Father Hopkins has spelled out the elements of a good poem more specifically. A poem, he says in one of his letters, is made of a surprise of rhythms, a sense of beauty, a "rash-fresh" imagery.

The poet's function is, at most, to evoke ideas, not to create or to state them. "You don't make poems with ideas, you use words," Mallarmé once remarked to the painter Degas, who left some pleasant sonnets. The poet's spiritual experience propagates ideas and expression in other fields and in other creative forms than poetry: in philosophy, drama, fiction, painting, the dance. The poet is the instrument of this qualified experience. The deepest self, a sub-self, makes the poet; and the poem is the audible cry of this self—like the cry of the Pythian priestess who, breathing fire, panting, drunken, shrieked a kind of "holy language honored among men."

NOTES

[1] An interesting debate has been going on between Mr. Watt and Dr. Tillyard on whether the novel is a new form or merely an extension of the epic and tragedy.
[2] The poet Virginia Berry has pointed out to me that motivation and inspiration are indeed different, but that they may exist simultaneously and may be blended together in the making of a poem.

From an address given at Pius XII Memorial Library, St Louis University, April 3, 1960, at the opening of National Library Week.

Missouri Library Association Quarterly, Vol. XXII, No. 1, March 1961, pp. 2-6.

THREE FACES OF AUTUMN
Poems, Prose, Translations

Within the permissible

In 1944 Arthur Koestler wrote in the *Partisan Review* that "even the literary movements in Russia . . . have not spontaneously, organically grown, but were decreed at Party Congresses and by utterances of government spokesmen" and that such decrees applied to poetry, drama, architecture, films, historical research, and philosophy.

Westerners have long felt that the official Soviet attitude has stifled intellectual development. They are perplexed whenever an outstanding Russian writer does emerge, and are curious to know how and why. Now the Western press has aroused widespread interest in 29-year-old, Siberian-born Yevgeny Yevtushenko by publicizing his travels and recitals on three continents; but it has focused on his personality and largely ignored his poetry. To fill this gap, Penguin and Dutton have issued a small, English language selection of 22 poems translated by a student of Russian and a young Jesuit poet. The translations, in supple iambics, are extremely well done both rhythmically and idiomatically.

The poems date from 1952 to 1961 and are fairly representative. The translators wisely exclude Yevtushenko's more recent "party line" verses which have little literary merit. Yet, despite the superb translations, *Selected Poems* is of mixed quality, and in this respect resembles many books of British and American verse.

The minor poems are generally on love ("Waiting"), trivial experiences ("Encounter"), and party toadying ("Party Card"). Unlike his great predecessor Mayakovsky (1893-1930), who wrote matchless love lyrics, Yevtushenko often seems incapable of selfless love. In "Waiting," for instance, he writes (the italics are mine):

> *My* love will come
> will fling open her arms and
> fold *me* in them,
> will understand *my* fears,
> observe *my* changes . . .
> will take *my* head in her hands.

Other poems like "Colours" and "The Companion" show a similar egocentrism or dispassion.

The three longest poems, however, "Zima Junction," "On a Bicycle," and "Babiy Yar," reveal the best of Yevtushenko: his freshness, descriptive skill, and most intense emotion. "Babiy Yar" (1961) in a 62-line translation, is a bold if belated protest against the massacre of Jews at Kiev during World War II. But the most impressive poem by far is "Zima Junction," a long autobiographical narrative of about a thousand lines, in which the poet recounts his thoughts and experiences during a summer visit to his native town after an absence of some years.

Zima, near Lake Baikal, is where Yevtushenko's great-grandfather was exiled and "starved all through his life." But after several generations life improved a little for the peasants and the poet as a boy "scarcely had one single care in the world." Now poignantly he sees the town grown smaller because he walks with a longer stride. He reminds himself that he "came home for strength and for courage,/for the truth and truth's well-being." He glimpses that truth briefly in a series of bucolic episodes of masterly description reminiscent of the Provençal poet Mistral in "Mireille" or of such French poets as Verhaeren or Jammes. He goes fishing and berry-picking. But unfortunately life isn't all fishing and berrypicking; ideological questions rear their collective head. The fisherman, an old railway-man, calls the *komsomol* "so boring it was a pain" — a line no doubt offensive to the *komsomol* contributing to the poet's brief withdrawal from that organization. The fisherman describes his nephew, not yet 25 and on the Committee:

> He sits there, that green kid,
> steamed up, banging his
> bossy fist—he even walks in a different way.
> There's iron in his eyes; and
> as for speeches,
> it isn't words to get the business done,
> it's business only there for the sake of words.

Later Yevtushenko meets a happy barefoot boy who runs away from a collective farm; he talks with a disillusioned Moscow journalist about "those first one-sided certainties" and how today (then several months after Stalin's death) there is a "rumination of yesterday's silence,/and silence smothering yesterday's events." Toward the end of the poem are observations on love of much greater depth and maturity than in the shorter poems.

THREE FACES OF AUTUMN
Poems, Prose, Translations

Among the shorter poems, "Visit" (1953) seems to be a brief study for "Zima Junction." Other pieces—"People," "In Georgia," and "Schoolmaster"—are well worth reading. "Schoolmaster" strongly resembles Frost's poetry in style and theme.

For over five years Yevtushenko has been the subject of hostile and enthusiastic articles in such journals as *Neva*, *Novy Mir*, and *Literaturnaya Gazeta*. Yet he is not a poet of revolt. This selection shows nothing as bold as, say, Lawrence Ferlinghetti springs on American readers. Yevtushenko is outspokenly loyal: "Consider me a Communist!/My whole life tells you," he writes. More recently, in a poem titled "City in the Morning" (*Literaturnaya Gazeta*, July 17, 1962), he is more insistent: "I'm a Communist by my very nature./Communism bids me be angrier and angrier/at what stands in its way."

Libraries will need *Selected Poems* to meet a popular demand. But anyone interested in a truly defiant and angry Soviet poet should read A. S. Yesenin-Volpin's *A Leaf of Spring*, 31 poems and an essay, translated by George Reavey and published by Praeger last year (bilingual text, $3., 173 pp.). Yesenin-Volpin, recently arrested and imprisoned, writes, "There is no freedom of the press in Russia, but who can say that there is no freedom of thought." Yevtushenko, a conformist by comparison, has tested this freedom only as far as its popular limits.

Review of *Yevtushenko: Selected Poems*, Yevgeny Yevtushenko (E. P. Dutton & Co.).

Focus/Midwest, December 1962, pp. 22-23.

Critical Reviews and Essays

1963-1972

The haunting *duende*

The late Nobel prize-winner Juan Ramón Jiménez (1881-1958) has been called "the Debussy of modern Spanish poetry" for his delicate, subtle lyricism. Both artist and poet, he lived in his own private world, a world greatly influenced by his memories of pre-revolutionary Andalusia. His verse has the *duende*, as the Spanish say, an elusive, haunting spirit found in works of the greatest numbers of all the arts.

The 300 poems in this book were chosen by Miss Roach, with the assistance of Jiménez and his wife Zenobia, from some 2500 lyrics and represent a half century of the poet's significant creative periods. These periods extend through some 32 collections of verse by Jiménez, dating from his youth in Spain and France, his marriage to a Vassar graduate and, after the Spanish civil war, his residence in the United States and Puerto Rico.

Miss Roach prefaces the book with her recollections of a meeting with Jiménez, and Ricardo Gullón has contributed an interesting biographical introduction.

Like several previous Jiménez works in translation this volume lacks the Spanish texts which even now, six years after the Nobel award, are hard to get. The omission of original texts, a deficiency of many books of translated verse, cannot be blamed entirely on publishers, however. Few publishers break even on poetry without the added cost of issuing bilingual editions.

Miss Roach has struck a successful compromise by adding indices of both the Spanish and English titles and first lines. She has also arranged the poems chronologically under the titles of the original Spanish books.

These translations are somewhat less literal and with more interpolation than Miss Roach's version of Jiménez's *Platero and I* (1957). She has kept much of the rhythm and some of the rhyme and assonance of the Spanish without detracting from the poems' spirit and meaning. Sometimes she splits a word, carrying it over into another line, a

133

THREE FACES OF AUTUMN
Poetry, Prose, Translations

technique Jiménez also used. Only rarely does an awkward phrase (like "the stagecoach enters town by the large bridge") slip in among the thousands of translated lines.

The choice of poems is excellent on the whole; yet, curiously, it includes only one out of some 25 or more poems (mostly unpublished) which the Jiménez family has selected and privately distributed since the poet's death. This poem is "Uno" ("*Quiero dormir, esta noche*"), which Miss Roach has rendered as follows:

> I wish to sleep, this night
> that you lie dead; to sleep;
> sleep, sleep, parallel
> to your total sleep;
> to see if I reach you, thus!
>
> Sleep, dawn of the evening;
> source of the river, sleep;
> two days that may shine together
> in nothingness, two currents
> going, as one, to the end;
> two wholes, if this life be something,
> two nothings, if all is nothing. . . .
>
> I want to sleep your death.

Altogether Miss Roach's translations are crisply and beautifully done. Her book partly fills a need for more extensive translation of modern Spanish verse, including works by such poets as Vicente Aleixandre and Gerardo Diego.

Review of *Juan* Ramón *Jiménez: Three Hundred Poems, 1903-1953*, translated by Eloise Roach (University of Texas Press).

St. Louis Post-Dispatch, March 31, 1963, p. 4B.

A CHARLES GUENTHER RETROSPECTIVE
Prose: Critical Reviews and Essays, 1963-1972

A poet on poetry

"Since the age of fifteen," Robert Graves writes in *The White Goddess*, "poetry has been my ruling passion and I have never intentionally undertaken any task or formed any relationship that seemed inconsistent with poetic principles." Few writers have practiced such single-minded devotion to poetry as Graves or have been so consistent in their views on the art. For forty years, for instance, since publishing his study "On English Poetry" (1922) he has preached the differences between Apollonian or analytic poetry and Muse or inspired poetry. His election last year to the poetry chair at Oxford University gave him a further opportunity to vent his ideas and feelings on this subject and to declare himself, as usual, on the Muse's side.

In all six of these essays delivered at Oxford the old feud flares up again. It is an offshoot, or more accurately a refinement, of the old quarrel between "classic" and "romantic"—terms Graves uses subtly as a classical scholar who professes the "uncontrolled" romantic style. In the first two essays Graves champions "The Dedicated Poet" of emotional trance, John Skelton, and deflates "The Anti-Poet," Virgil, as a drudging opportunist. In the third essay, "The Personal Muse," he recounts the theme of "The White Goddess" and traces the origins of English love-poetry from Gaelic, Provençal, and Arabic sources. The other three pieces are rambling addresses on "Poetic Gold," a bitter comment on the awarding of "gold" medals of base material; "The Word Baraka," an Islamic term for lightning, which Graves transmutes into "blessedness," and "The Poet's Paradise," an account of Graves's experience of eating hallucigenic psilocybe mushrooms.

As in *The Crowning Privilege* (1956), Graves is tart, entertaining, and self-revealing in the *Oxford Addresses*. Yet one must read the *Collected Poems* (1961) of Graves to get a true insight into his sense of poetic values, to see the poet's strengths and defects. On the minus side Graves, despite all his mumbo jumbo on the Muse, hasn't written poems which make "the hairs stand on end" (Housman's practical razor test of a "true poem"). In a curious critique he calls Raleigh's "Walsinghame"—a ballad inferior to Keats's "La Belle Dame"—"the most compelling of all Muse poems in English." And while tilting at other poets he ignores their best Muse or "trance" poems: Yeats's "He Remembers Forgotten Beauty," for instance, and Pound's "The Alchemist."

135

THREE FACES OF AUTUMN
Poetry, Prose, Translations

As a scholar of poetic legends, however, he is one of the strongest influences of our time on certain young American and English poets. One wonders, indeed, what directions many young poets would take without Graves who not only pulls down the new idols of academicism, machinery, and commercialized entertainment but restores a purpose to poetry, a dignity to traditional myths, and mysteries.

Review of *Oxford Addresses on Poetry*, by Robert Graves (Doubleday and Co., Inc.).

Focus/Midwest, September 1963, p. 24.

A CHARLES GUENTHER RETROSPECTIVE
Prose: Critical Reviews and Essays, 1963-1972

Gallic influence: French poets and America

Back in 1951 Ezra Pound asked me if I had read some recent work of his in a certain quarterly. Involved at that time in translating new French poetry, I told him I had not; in fact, that I hadn't "kept up at all lately with new American poetry." Pound sniffed, stroked his mandarin beard, then quipped triumphantly: "Neither has the *Hudson Review*."

French poetry, like American, has its currency. Many poets come and go with and without fanfare. Only a few abide. Today, although some critics may argue otherwise, the impact of French verse on American and British, long evident in Pound and T. S. Eliot, continues. While W. B. Yeats wrote that young poets in his day were translating Verlaine and Verhaeren, American poets now translate poets like Senghor and Supervielle. Such interplay of cultures concerns more than "heritage." Actually, there is a current "exchange." In 1918, Pound could write with assurance that "America's part in contemporary culture is based chiefly upon two men familiar with Paris: Whistler and Henry James." This is no longer true.

Since then, the swift growth of communication (in all senses) has greatly broken down old cultural barriers. In the future, aided by newer electronic means of translation and transmission, we may well import ideas—and their vehicles of language, form and style—as readily as we now import Renaults and Volkswagens. A review of new work by five well-established French poets is given here. All except Jacques Dupin, who is 36, are in their forties and fifties. These few poets cannot represent the whole French literary scene; yet their verse, in the best modern traditions of Symbolism and Surrealism, has depth, vigor and originality.

The late Albert Camus wrote, "I consider René Char our greatest living poet." Char (b. 1907) has published over a dozen books of verse, plays and prose, excluding partial editions. His most important recent work, published last year by Gallimard is *La Parole en Archipel* (*The Word as an Archipelago*), a 162-page collection of verse composed between 1952 and 1960. It contains several major poems already translated and published in this country.

Char, indeed, has been paid the highest compliment, in an oblique way, by American writers—for not only has his verse appeared in translation in a score of stateside reviews and influenced poets like W. C. Williams and

Richard Willbur, but it has been plagiarized. The now defunct *Neo Magazine*, for instance, carried a poem titled "The Stranger," lifted from Char's "Compagnie de L'Ecolière," under another poet's by-line. Char's poetry is strongly affected by Heraclitean philosophy. Many of the 78 poems in *La Parole en Archipel* deal with the theme of death; for example, "The Escape," "In the Procession" and "The Raised Scythe."

From the last-named poem are these lines:

> When the herdsman of the dead pounds his stick,
> Dedicate my scattered color to summer . . . .
> From the wet fern to the feverish mimosa,
> From the old goner to the newcomer,
> Love's motion, subsiding, will tell you:
> "Except there, nowhere, misfortune is everywhere."

In a similar vein is "Eternity at Lourmarin," dedicated to Albert Camus. It touches on the death of Camus in a car accident and concludes,

> With the one we love we have stopped speaking, and it isn't silence. What is it then? We know, or think we know . . . . At the repressed moment when we question the whole importance of the riddle, grief suddenly sets in, the grief of one fellow for another, which this time the archer cannot pierce.

The president of the Republic of Senegal, Léopold Sédar Senghor (b. 1906) is one of the finest Negro poets of French expression. He is known for his verses written in a long-breathed, incantatory style like that of the late Paul Claudel. His best poems are long, or are composed in long cycles, and are very difficult to translate because they contain many unusual African terms and place-names. Yet Senghor's verse has universal qualities, as in these lines written for a *khalam*, a four-stringed guitar used to accompany odes and elegies:

> I don't know at what time it was, I always confuse childhood and
>   Eden,
> As I confuse Life and Death—a bridge of sweetness joins them ....
> My heart is a casket of precious wood, my head an old parchment
>   of Djenne.
> Sing only your lineage, that my memory may answer you.

A CHARLES GUENTHER RETROSPECTIVE
Prose: Critical Reviews and Essays, 1963-1972

> I don't know at what time it was, I always confuse past and
>   present,
> As I confuse Life and Death—a bridge of sweetness joins them.

Translated selections of President Senghor's poetry will appear in a half
dozen magazines in the United States, and in a recent letter he wrote that
Les Editions du Seuil (Paris) intends to publish his collected poems in a
single volume. Here is an extract from his poem "Negro Mask," dedicated
to Pablo Picasso:

> She sleeps and rests on the sand's purity.
> Koumba Tom sleeps. A green palm tree veils her hair's fever,
>   coppers her curved brow
> Her closed eyelids, twin basin and sealed fountains . . .
> O face just as God created you before the memory of ages
> Face of the world's dawn, don't open like a tender throat to stir my
>   flesh.
> I adore you, O Beauty, with my monochord gaze.

Pierre Emmanuel, born the same year (1916) as the American poet John
Ciardi, is one of the most prolific major living French poets. He spent his
early years in the United States and, like Senghor, was educated in France.
Since 1940 he has published some 30 books of verse and prose. Many of
his finest poems are written in loose alexandrine verse, in long cycles and
on religious themes: "Babel," "Jour de Colere" ("Day of Wrath") and
"Sodome." Emmanuel's latest books include *Evangéliaire* (1961) and *La
nouvelle naissance* (*The New Birth*), issued by Les Editions du Seuil.
From the latter volume, just published in September 1963, are these lines
from the poem "Nativity," appropriate at this season:

> True God and true man
> God delivered to men in that Man filled with God,
> Your first cry as a man is joined with the last sigh on the Cross ....
> The cry of the newborn is also the lark of our resurrection.
> You are born a man to sustain everything of man, crushed like dry
>   earth between our fingers. Like clay, we'll soak You in
>   Your blood. You'll lose heart and the will to be,
> God will pretend to withdraw his hand.
> So in our eyes of flesh He goes today in that stable where the final
>   surrender is foreshadowed.

THREE FACES OF AUTUMN
Poetry, Prose, Translations

Alain Bosquet (b. 1919) not only is a leading poet but has actively interpreted American verse to French audiences. He served in the French and American armies during World War II and became an American citizen in 1943. Recently he has translated and published anthologies of American and Canadian verse, and written ten essays on Emily Dickinson and Walt Whitman. Among Bosquet's own books are *Quel Royaume Oublié?* (*What Forgotten Kingdom?* 1955), *Premier Testament* (*First Testament*, 1957) and *Deuxième Testament* (*Second Testament*, 1959). A bilingual selection from these volumes is *Alain Bosquet: Selected Poems*, a paperback edition in the World Poets Series (New Directions).

This previously untranslated poem from *Quel Royaume Oublié?* (Mercure de France) shows Bosquet's fresh imagination, much admired by Conrad Aiken and other American poets:

> Every stone is an age: count them,
> then if the vine sleeps, wake it
> for a witness is needed at the horizon
> that the stranger stalks. Each shadow too
> attracts some male: an ocean
> which comes here despite our altitude.
> Dry that tear! It could become a poisonous animal;
> then our kingdom would take
> the road of scorn, and the mountains,
> tired of living, would bleed white.

Jacques Dupin, a close friend of Char, was born the same year (1927) as American poets W. S. Merwin and James Wright. His latest book, *Gravir* (*To Climb*) was published by Gallimard in August 1963. This is a 109-page collection of poems and prose aphorisms, all showing the strong influence of Char's style, themes and imagery. A good example is this piece titled "The Present of a Night," with its prophetic overtones of a last judgment:

> Was this rock, assailed by stars, with crevices from which leprosy in advance of praise had progressed beyond all measure—was it going to yield to the lazy cadence of the fountain of the dead? The ball was undone, the dancers transparent. Blood flowed, grass became deep. At dawn, in great secret, lovers' lips struck against a limitless dew.

Here, finally, is another short poem from *Gravir*, out of a suite titled "Saccades":

> Tongue of black bread and pure water,
> When a spade turns you over
> The sky goes into action.
> Our loving arms blacken,
> Our laboring arms are wreathed.
> Just the power
> Of our successive corpse
> And my library of pebbles
> Falling in the ravine.

St. Louis Post-Dispatch, December 1, 1963, p. 4K.

THREE FACES OF AUTUMN
Poetry, Prose, Translations

Frost's 'quality friend'

Louis Untermeyer once told me of his warm friendship with Robert Frost. Yet I did not realize the degree of warmth, the depth of intimacy of that friendship until I read this superb collection of letters. Reading it, I felt as if Mr. Untermeyer had personally turned over to me his whole file of Frost letters for a few days' perusal; and not only let me read the letters with great delight, but commented upon them every few minutes.

Such perhaps is the ideal experience of the reader of a volume of letters: to feel some acquaintance with one or more of the correspondents. Yet even from a purely literary viewpoint, the Frost letters, covering the period from 1915 to 1962, form a significant and lastingly engrossing document.

It is a massive assemblage of puns, *jeux d'esprit*, drafts of poems, comments on the current literary scene (especially on versifiers), and serious and practical discussion—all quite revealing to most of us who knew Frost only by his poetry or his occasional remarks to the press (e.g., on his trip to Russia) since he became a national dean and don of poetry under the Kennedy administration.

With all his cunning and punning, Frost was dealt some severe emotional blows over the years of these letters. The culmination of them, perhaps, was the death of his wife Elinor in 1939. Other tragedies beset him: the mental illness of his sister and one of his children, the death of a daughter from tuberculosis, and the suicide of his son Carol. Yet he withstood these losses stoically and continued to devote himself to writing verse, publishing his 22nd volume just before his death at the age of 89.

The most interesting letters are those on his craft and fellow-craftsmen. Some of the poems included have a kind of private imagery for Frost and Untermeyer; other poems, like an end-rhyme exercise titled "Trouble Rhyming," have a more general appeal.

Few of Frost's contemporaries in poetry escaped his incisive criticism. Not only the Imagists (Amy Lowell was a favorite target), but poets like Conrad Aiken, E. A. Robinson, Edgar Lee Masters and T. S. Eliot, who did not openly align themselves with Imagism (or "Amygism," as Pound put it). John Gould Fletcher got his praise. Vachel Lindsay, on the other hand, was the inspirer of Frost's only extended parody, titled "John L.

Sullivan Enters Heaven." Frost's interest in younger poets never flagged, and he met and befriended the young Russian Yevtushenko, among others, on his overseas tour in 1962.

Louis ("My Quality Friend") Untermeyer has made these letters live for readers by adding elucidating comments and notes. Some readers will miss the convenience of an index, but this is a small omission. Altogether, no comparable book of letters has appeared since Ezra Pound's *Letters* were published in 1950.

Review of *The Letters of Robert Frost to Louis Untermeyer*, with commentary by Louis Untermeyer (Holt, Rinehart and Winston).

The Cresset (Valparaiso University), January 1964, p. 25.

THREE FACES OF AUTUMN
Poetry, Prose, Translations

Five Leningrad poets

Until about ten years ago Russian poetry was not widely read in the
United States. The familiar, popular authors (Pushkin, Turgenev,
Dostoevski, Tolstoy) were known, mostly for their fiction and plays, and
they were names out of a past century and a vanished social order.
There were poets for those interested: Lermontov, and later Blok,
Mayakovsky, Anna Akhmatova, and of course Pasternak, whose *Poems of
Yury Zhivago* were appended to his best-seller. In the sixties two new
poets appeared and were lionized by Western audiences: Yevgeny
Yevtushenko and Andrei Voznesensky, both now considered "older" and
"very Moscow."

In Russia, poetry is an everyday experience, and today in Leningrad it is
more popular than any activity except sports—ahead of music, painting
and dancing. There are a hundred poetry groups and about 6,000 people
writing verse in Leningrad alone. Suzanne Massie, an editor and
journalist, has chosen and prefaced works of five of these Leningrad poets
who range in age from 32 to 41 years. *The Living Mirror* is a brilliant
surprise. It is no ordinary anthology but is really five separate small books
of selected poems, with English translations facing the Russian texts. Ms.
Massie adds a photo and a crisp word portrait of each poet, vignettes
which seem done with photographic powers of observation or total recall,
enhancing our understanding of the poets and their work. All five poets
represent a "transition generation" who have shared common experiences
since World War II. All have been soldiers, and worked in factories and
as ordinary laborers. Only one is a university graduate. Still, they are
individual poets, differing in their viewpoints and poetic methods.

Victor Sosnora (b. 1936) writes a wide range of verse from short symbolic
lyrics to dramatic narratives filled with Russian history and legend. The
lyrics may contain a simple simile as in "Roses," which "resemble people,
living just the same sunny, kind, brief life." Or they may be charged with
symbolism, as in "Letter":

> Oh, remember me in your garden where
> ants with red shields lived . . .
> remember me in your tears where
> the white nights are like shackles and where
> castles of blue uniforms will guard you every night.

A CHARLES GUENTHER RETROSPECTIVE
Prose: Critical Reviews and Essays, 1963-1972

Sosnora's symbolism is most evident in the six selections from "The Thirteen Owls"—the owl (like Pushkin's horseman) symbolizing authority. In "The Bronze Owl," Sosnora's

> Giant horses carry Russia along,
> squiggles of owlish dogma beneath,
> Byzantine owlish ikons beneath
> And a tiny, tin horse.

Gleb Gorbovsky (b. 1931) is the oldest of the group. He writes lyrics with short, frequently rhymed lines in a style resembling the late French symbolist Henri de Régnier, a poet still read more in Russia perhaps than in the West. Gorbovsky's style is direct, simple, often earthy:

> Stir up, like an ant hill
> The whole world of puzzles and problems . . . .
> Stir it up, poke it.
> Sit down on a tree stump—and watch.

Or tight, agitated:

> I am mined. A sign should be hung on my breast . . . .
> Do not touch! A splinter will cut you in two . . . .
> But now spring will come again,
> and my body will be torn to shreds!

Alexander Kushner (b. 1936) is a kind of poet's poet and is considered the most respected and established poet of his generation in Leningrad. He has published three books of verse since 1962 and is regarded as a "writing" poet rather than a singing or "reciting" poet. A former teacher, he now works only on verse translations and criticism. Kushner's verse is formal and symmetrical, mostly rhymed couplets, quatrains, sestets and octaves. Yet he is more than an academic traditionalist. His lines include clean, sharp images of contemporary Leningrad: "I close my eyes and see/ That city in which I live: /Yes, and a faraway roof, /The sun and the Neva's view . . . ."

Joseph Brodsky (b. 1940) is the youngest and the most controversial. Incredible as it seems to us, in 1963 he was sentenced to five years of forced labor in exile as a "semi-literary parasite," despite the expert

145

defense testimony of his fellow poets. In 1969 he was invited to several poetry congresses but was refused permission to leave Russia. (He has since been compelled to leave, and has planned to emigrate to the United States.) Perhaps poems like "A Halt in the Wilderness" (describing the state's destruction of a church), embarrassed the regime. The poem is one of several long descriptive narratives in the Brodsky selection, and it begins: "So few Greeks live in Leningrad today that we have razed a Greek church, to make space for a new concert hall, built in today's grim and unhappy style . . . ."

Also included is George L. Kline's masterful translation of Brodsky's curious pattern poem, "The Fountain," with lines of varying length resembling a fountain spray's rising and falling.

Largely self-taught, Brodsky has translated the English metaphysical poets, and has welded their style and language to his own Petersburg tradition. Altogether, he appears irrepressible, a poet of great energy and a fine craftsman. In the English tradition he might be compared with Shelley, Francis Thompson or Dylan Thomas.

Constantine Kuzminsky (also born in 1940) has worked as a jockey, a hydrologist and (like several others in this group) a geologist in Siberia. A prolific poet, he has written some experimental verse, but generally his style is disciplined and formal. He has translated Byron, and some of his poems are Byronic in style and have been set to music.

Kuzminsky's poems are often filled with Greek classical allusions and Russian history and legend. His long work-in-progress, "The Tower of Babylon," somewhat resembles Pound's "Cantos." It is ambitious, complex, and includes lines in other languages: old Slavonic, French, English, Latin and German.

Like Kushner and Sosnora, Kuzminsky has written a great deal of verbal music considered untranslatable. Yet the poetic versions done for *The Living Mirror* by Paul Roche and John Statathos, with George Kline, Ms. Massie and Max Hayward, are done with great skill and dedication.

As Kuzminsky has eloquently summarized the problems of translating Russian poetry: "Poetry is the concentrated beauty of a language. It is natural and . . . untranslatable, because if it loses its own country, it loses everything . . . there will come a time when poets will communicate not only with words, but with sounds."

Review of *The Living Mirror: Five Young Poets From Leningrad*, by Suzanne Massie (Doubleday).

St. Louis Globe-Democrat, December 30-31, 1972, p. 4E.

Critical Reviews and Essays

1973-1982

Neruda: 'No burning allegiances'

In his 69th year, Pablo Neruda (Neftali Ricardo Reyes) is one of the most durable poets of the Spanish language. His first book, *Crepusculario*, appeared just 50 years ago, and by the 1940s he was recognized as one of the best known names in Latin American poetry. He has now published 20 books of verse and his work has been translated into more than 80 languages. *New Poems* contains 59 poems chosen and translated from three recent volumes: *Los Manos del Día* (*Hands of the Day*), 1968; *Fin de Mundo* (*World's End*), 1969, and *Las Piedras del Cielo* (*Stones of the Sky*), 1970. It does not represent or mention his later books of verse: *Más Piedras del Cielo* (*More Stones of the Sky*), 1971, and *Geografía Infructuosa* (*Fruitless Geography*), 1972, both published by Editorial Losada, Buenos Aires.

Neruda is a Chilean diplomat who has held consular posts in the Far East, Europe and South America. He has also been active in Chilean politics and served as a senator during World War II. After Allende's election, Neruda was appointed ambassador to France.

It is tempting to compare Neruda with other poet-diplomats like Paul Claudel, St.-John Perse and Octavio Paz, but there are wide differences— religious, social and political as well as literary. The son of a railroad conductor, Neruda never had royalist sympathies. He regards himself as a loner: "In this free confraternity I've no burning allegiances. I was always a lone iron-monger," he reveals in his poem "Ars Poetica."

Ben Belitt's translations, facing the Spanish texts, are generally crisp and competent, though sometimes puzzling. For instance, in "Silence Packs Itself" he renders "Pedro" as "Pedro" instead of the Biblical "Peter" we presume it is. Although easier to translate than the hermetic poets like the Spaniard Vicente Aleixandre, Neruda offers a few pitfalls to his translators.

In his long introduction Belitt points out that Neruda cannot be "homogenized," as the Swedish Academicians tried to do in citing the poet for the 1971 Nobel Prize: "For poetry that, with the action of an elemental force, brings alive a continent's destiny and dreams." But it seems ill-fitting and pointless for Belitt to provoke, as he does, a quarrel with his fellow translator Robert Bly. (Even a Nobel laureate needs all the translators he can get!)

Both as poet and as politician, Neruda has much in common with W. B. Yeats, the Yeats of "Byzantium" and "Second Coming." This is evident in poems like "The Square in the Crystal" and in this poem, "Touching Topaz," quoted in full:

> Touching topaz, one is touched by the topaz: a bland fire awakens as grapes are awakened by wine. Before coming to be, the clear wine works in the stone: it seeks circulation, wants words, bears a mystical nutriment. It shares the human kiss of the skin; the power of that meeting, the stone and its human observer, blazes out in a headlong corolla; subsides, and reveals what it was: flesh and stone; in their solitudes: enemy entities.

This has the magic, the *duende* of Neruda's poetry.

Review of *New Poems (1968-1970),* by Pablo Neruda, translated and edited by Ben Belitt (Grove Press).

St. Louis Globe-Democrat, June 9-10, 1973, p. 4D.

A CHARLES GUENTHER RETROSPECTIVE
Prose: Critical Reviews and Essays, 1973-1982

Ezra Pound—mover, shaker, iconoclast

Soon after one of my visits with Ezra Pound more than twenty years ago, I was asked to talk about him extemporaneously at a St. Louis Poetry Center meeting. As a follower of Pound in "aesthetics" (he bantered with me about this) but non-partisan in politics, I was sensitive to his controversial reputation. For those not familiar with Pound, I wanted to describe his position in broad, innocuous terms, then proceed to discuss his early poetry, before the *Cantos*. So I began by saying that Pound was usually considered "right" (or "rightist") in his political views. Immediately a sweet diminutive lady in the back row sprang up and snapped, "Ezra Pound is NOT right—he's wrong!"

This was an unnerving lesson for me in communication, a sobering reminder that poets and their words and ways are often misunderstood. Readers who cannot understand Pound's poetry will certainly understand his prose, at least in the Cookson choice of essays. Whether as mover, shaker and iconoclast or as a critic with gentle reminiscences, Pound seldom minces words. When he does, his euphemism is intentional and often with a touch of humor.

Selected Prose 1909-1965 contains 66 pieces on a wide range of themes of special interest to anyone seeking keys to Pound's *Cantos*. The earliest essay, "What I Feel About Walt Whitman," is a terse, prophetic tribute ("I am immortal even as he is, yet with a lesser vitality"). Most of the remaining essays are concerned less with poetry and poets than with topics which preoccupied Pound in writing the *Cantos*: history, religion, culture and economics.

While disdaining avant-garde poets like Apollinaire, Pound nevertheless recognized certain artists—including Picasso and "the intellect inside it," Francis Picabia. Along with Picabia he admired Wyndham Lewis and Jean Cocteau as "lively minds meeting a common need of the period." He felt Picabia "could cut the barnicles off Picasso, Cocteau, Marinetti" but he considered contemporary philosophers (including Bertrand Russell) as heavy, insensitive dunderheads.

Selected Prose 1909-1965 is also valuable because it allows an impartial assessment of Pound's writings on coin, credit and economics; it clarifies his stand on World War II; and it shows the impact of Confucian

153

principles on Pound's thought. The section on "Civilization, Money and History" seems remarkably current, dealing with up-to-date problems. Three noteworthy essays are those on "Peace," "The City" and "ABC of Economics."

Pound's aim in all these essays is "not to persuade the reader to accept some private system of ideas on history," but to "make people think." Editor Cookson has culled four quotations which he believes summarize Pound's guiding beliefs in politics and economics: "(1) The republic . . . means, or ought to mean 'the public convenience.' (2) 'The right aim of law is to prevent coercion, either by force or by fraud.' (3) 'Sovereignty inheres in the power to issue money, or to distribute the power to buy (credit or money) whether you have the right to do so or not.' (4) 'Civilization depends on local control of purchasing power needed for local purposes.'"

Rather awkwardly Cookson also defends Pound against charges of anti-Semitism, reminding readers that the poet made more derogatory remarks about other nations and religions than the Semitic. Cookson adds that Pound, via radio, publicly defended "the small Jew" against Fascist per-secution.

Like most people in Italy, Pound was unaware of what the Nazis were doing and was deeply shaken by news of the atrocities. One would like to believe that Pound's statement in *The Guide to Kulchur* (1938) is more characteristic of him than any racially biased remark: "Race prejudice is a red herring. The tool of the man defeated intellectually, and of the cheap politician."

In his massive study, *The Pound Era*, Hugh Kenner appropriately gives more space to Pound's literary and economic interests than to political and racial issues. (The poet "seemed to talk of nothing but banks.") As for Germany and Italy, Pound barely noticed such matters as Hitler's obsession of eastward expansion and Mussolini's dreams of African empire—"so he and his critics talked past each other for decades."

With this magnificent biographical-critical work Kenner has come full circle in his longtime pursuit of Pound—starting with earlier books and essays on E. P. and on Pound's contemporaries Wyndham Lewis, James Joyce and T. S. Eliot. One of the sharpest younger critics during the

1950s, Kenner seems to have found his greatest challenges and enthusiasms in Pound's work.

Kenner separates Pound into three periods: roughly up to 1919, from
1919 to 1945, and from 1945 until the poet's death in 1972. Declaring
Pound's "Homage to Sextus Propertius" as "the great unknown poem of
our time," Kenner shows it to be "the fruit of a creative exasperation" the
poet never regained.

E. P.'s prophetic vision came to light many times in our dialogues and
correspondence. In the mid-fifties he mentioned and later wrote to me of
"the young Senator from Massachusetts" as a likely President of the
United States. Pound was among the few Americans to recognize the
stature of Missouri Senator Thomas Hart Benton and to mark the
centenary of Benton's two-volume work, *A Thirty Years' View, 1821-
1851*. (But he never wanted credit for this and he was always interested in
how Missouri honored Benton.) Pound also sparked a revival of interest in
the American naturalist Louis Agassiz and the explorer Leo Frobenius.

In 1955, Pound casually predicted to me that his work would enjoy a
revival "in thirty years"—realizing, I'm sure, that 1985 would mark the
centenary of his birth. This prediction seems very likely to come true,
since the Yale University Library just established, in October 1973, the
Center for the Study of Ezra Pound and His Contemporaries. His talented
daughter, Mary de Rachewiltz, a poet and translator, was recently named
Curator of the Ezra Pound Archive at that Center.

What Pound wrote in an obit for T. S. Eliot in *The Sewanee Review* (1966)
applies equally to himself: "Let him rest in peace. I can only repeat, but
with the urgency of 50 years ago: READ HIM."

Review of *Selected Prose, 1909-1965*, by Ezra Pound, edited by William
Cookson (New Directions) and *The Pound Era*, by Hugh Kenner
(University of California Press).

St. Louis Globe-Democrat, February 16-17, 1974, p. 12A.

155

THREE FACES OF AUTUMN
Poetry, Prose, Translations

Jean Wahl (1888-1974): A Reminiscence

It was over thirty years ago when I first contacted the French poet and existentialist philosopher Jean André Wahl. Some of his *Poems of the Prison and the Camp* had just appeared in a French-Canadian review and I had sent him English translations of them. Wahl, who was described as "A tiny man with a face like a benevolent hawk," was then living in South Hadley, Mass., and teaching at Mount Holyoke and Smith College.

Jean Wahl was the son of a professor of English. He was born in Marseilles but later lived and attended schools in Paris where he prepared for a teaching career. He taught steadily at various secondary schools and universities from 1914, when he was rejected for World War I military service, until after his appointment to a professorship at the Sorbonne in 1936.

After the German army entered Paris in June 1940, Wahl went to Mâcon, in the free zone of France, to join his parents and his brother. On receiving word that the Sorbonne was to continue as usual, he returned to Paris to teach a seminar on the German philosopher Martin Heidegger.

But the Germans eventually got wind of Wahl's anti-collaborationist sympathies and his Jewish background. In July 1941 they confined him in the notorious La Santé prison. From a guard he learned that he would remain there for two years, then would be sent to a concentration camp and shot.

Lacking writing materials at La Santé, Wahl wrote poems in his mind and tried to remember them. One day he received a parcel of books wrapped in brown paper. Using a needle, he scratched the poems he could recall on the brown paper. Several days later a fellow prisoner stealthily passed him a pencil stub. But when Wahl tried to decipher the needle marks, he found only one poem legible. This poem was "Evening in the Walls," a terse, powerful record of prisoners speaking to each other at night through the windows of their cells, sharing in the darkness their deepest thoughts, emotions and speculations on their fate:

> You are with me this evening, all my friends.
> I hear your voices in the dark, I see your faces.
> My power is made of all your little powers.
> And as I think of you I gather strength.

Just five weeks after entering La Santé, Wahl was transferred to the German concentration camp at Drancy, near Paris, which had 3500 inmates, all Jews. There he had freedom to read, write and lecture, but food and living conditions were even worse than at La Santé. Illness, especially dysentery, was rampant. Despite the many privations, Wahl wrote nearly a hundred poems during his two months of confinement at Drancy.

Meanwhile the Refugee Scholars Fund in New York was working to bring him to the United States. (That fund eventually brought over some 70 noted scholars of many fields and faiths, from many European nations.) Finally Wahl had a stroke of good fortune: the chief physician at Drancy, a Frenchman, added Wahl's name to a list of sick prisoners to be released. Wahl returned to Paris at once.

Three weeks later Wahl learned that the Germans had listed him as a "public enemy" to be shot on sight. By a series of dangerous underground maneuvers, suspenseful as a spy movie, he reached the free zone with the help of friends. There he stayed until June 1942, living in Mâcon and Lyon. He arrived in America that July and settled in Massachusetts where I got in touch with him.

During those war years Wahl sent me not only his own verse but also exciting new work by younger French poets, many of whom were exiled in North Africa. He sent me copies of *Fontaine*, France's leading literary review, which he helped to edit, then published in Algiers. This experience provided a lasting link for me between the work of an older generation of poets I had been reading, like Henri de Régnier and Paul Valéry, and the poetry of newer writers like Louis Aragon, Henri Michaux, René Char, Pierre Emmanuel and Alain Bosquet. The French poets who had influenced Pound and Eliot were set aside. Wahl gave me an immediacy I had never known, with French poets I had never met.

In return, I translated some of Wahl's poems and had them published in American magazines, including *The New Yorker* and the little literary monthly, *Driftwind*, published in Vermont. My last communique from him was a special delivery letter in which he told me elatedly of his plans to return to Paris, for the Allies had freed his beloved France.

Jean Wahl's death on June 19, 1974 (he was 86) does not signal the end of his thought and works. Wahl, who was a distant relative of Henri Bergson, surely had an impact on philosophers and philosophy in his time. In his singular ways he also influenced French and American poets and poetry. Somewhat less known than Jean-Paul Sartre (whom he once failed in a course at the Sorbonne), Wahl left a significant legacy of ideas in philosophy. Two of his books are still in print with American publishers. *Philosophies of Existence* (Schocken Books, 1969) is an introduction to the basic thought of the philosophers Kierkegaard, Heidegger, Jaspers, Marcel and Sartre. The other volume, *A Short History of Existentialism*, is available from two publishers, Citadel Press and Greenwood Press, and has been something of a bestseller in its field for twenty-five years.

The following is a translation of a poem from my collection in English of Wahl's poetry titled *Voices in the Dark: Poems of the Prison and the Camp*:

> A lean day in a convict's suit, a smell
> Heavy turn of keys that close the lock
> Brutal steps of the conqueror, his shouts and insults—
> Grinding my teeth with force I bore those sufferings.
> The step out in the corridor was a warning
> And the key closed upon a deaf despair.
> I lie down, but I've only the right to sit.
> I smile; the jailer then forbids that smile.
> Is my hair white now? I am feverish.
> I cannot count or see myself, but must
> Keep a few memories, a will, a faith
> And too, some images of hair and lips.

St. Louis Post-Dispatch, September 29, 1974, p. 3B.

Auden—dance and the drum

When W. H. Auden came to live in the United States in 1939, at the age of 32, he was the most famous British poet of his time and his writings were enthusiastically received by American publishers. In one sense he was already American. Some of his light poems and cabaret songs, like "Blues" and "Foxtrot from a Play," were full of American slang, and he appreciated such popular figures as Fred Astaire and Mae West.

Auden was able to write in the easy, colloquial style of Robert Frost and E. A. Robinson whom he had admired. But more important than Auden's facility for poetic mimicry and acting were the qualities of tension and paradox in his work. He seemed ridden with personal anxiety. With the publication of his postwar baroque eclogue *The Age of Anxiety* in 1948, he was regarded as a major voice of his time, just as T. S. Eliot had been regarded after *The Waste Land* appeared a generation earlier.

This new posthumous collection, *Thank You, Fog*, contains the last poems of Auden which he had already gathered in book form, with title and dedication, before his death in September 1973. If he had lived, he probably would have added enough poems to double the size of this 60-page book. As it stands, it contains the poems he had written after he left New York early in 1972 to return to his native England. It also contains two lyrics; written in 1963-64 for the musical comedy based on *Don Quixote* and Auden's last work for the stage, *The Entertainment of the Senses*, written in 1973 in collaboration with Chester Kallman.

In these last poems Auden is again revealed as a skilled, graceful poet, a formal craftsman who respected his art and its traditions. (He once boasted that he was not vain except about his knowledge of metre and his friends.) Time will establish whether he was, for example, the last major British or American poet who wrote sonnets. Yet poetic form was only a vehicle for him, following function, not preceding it. This is borne out particularly by "Ode to the Diencephalon" and "A Contrast," both written in Sapphic form, and "Unpredictable But Providential," in classic hexameters.

Auden is perhaps at his best expression in the terse epigrammatic stanzas of "Address to the Beasts" and "A Thanksgiving," in the deceptively light "Recitative By Death" and in the gentle "Nocturne." In "Address to the Beasts" he projects himself into the thoughts and senses of beasts with an

159

empathy rare among humans who still slaughter without feeling: "To you all scents are sacred—except our smell and those—we manufacture . . . . Of course, you have to take lives—to keep your own, but never—kill for applause." And if beasts cannot produce "a genius like Mozart" neither can they "plague the earth—with brilliant sillies like Hegel—or clever nasties like Hobbes."

In "A Thanksgiving" Auden catalogues many of his sources and influences, from Hardy and Thomas and Frost to Brecht, Horace and Goethe. There are also Kierkegaard, Williams and Lewis, who guided the poet "back to belief" after the "hair-raising things—that Hitler and Stalin were doing—forced me to think about God."

"Recitative By Death" is the "old" Auden of the thirties, but tougher, more mature. Here Death speaks: "Liberal my views upon religion and race;—Tax-posture, credit-rating, social ambition—Cut no ice with me. We shall meet face to face, . . . Westchester matron and Bowery bum,—Both shall dance with me when I rattle my drum."

Finally in the bucolic "Nocturne" the poet of faith and purpose ruminates and inquires: "Out there still the Innocence—that we somehow freaked out of—where can and ought are the same: . . . the way its fauna respect—the privacy of others.—How else shall mannerless minds—in ignorance imagine—the Mansion of Gentle Joy—it is our lot to look for,—where else weak wills find comfort—to dare the Dangerous Quest?"

American poets who met or knew Auden will not soon forget him. Most of the themes of *Thank You, Fog* are already known to his readers. To those readers his last poems will be a familiar delight; to other readers they will be a revelation.

Review of *Thank You, Fog: Last Poems*, by W. H. Auden (Random House).

St. Louis Globe-Democrat, November 23-24, 1974, p. 10A.

Gems of Spanish poetry

Since 1900 Spain has had its most vital resurgence of poetry in nearly 300 years. The Spanish Civil War briefly slowed that trend when some poets were exiled or kept in silence; but even then some of the finest work of such poets as García Lorca, Rafael Alberti and Miguel Hernández was produced. These three, and two dozen other top-ranking poets, are represented in this large new collection edited by poet and translator Hardie St. Martin. The Spanish texts appear on pages facing the English renderings by 22 American poets.

Fittingly, *Roots and Wings* opens with work by Miguel de Unamuno and Antonio Machado, the major poets of the Generation of 98 which brought new attitudes and a new expression to Spain. These two poets alone gave new life to Spanish writing. "Shake off this sadness, and recover your spirit," Unamuno wrote: ". . . the man who wants to live is the man in whom life is abundant." And Machado observed, "And all Spain,/in her dirty spangled party dress,/is still with, us: poor and weak and drunk; /but now from a bad wine: the blood of her wounds."

The next generation, sometimes known as "ultramodernist," is represented by ten poets, the most prominent of whom are Jorge Guillén, García Lorca, Vicente Aleixandre, Alberti and Hernandéz. Important lesser-known poets are also represented: León Felipe, Pedro Salinas, Gerardo Diego, Emilio Prados and Luis Cernuda. Cutting across these generations and somewhat apart from them is Juan Ramón Jiménez, who with Unamuno and Machado "blazed the paths that have led into all twentieth-century Spanish poetry," as St. Martin notes in his introduction. Among the post-Civil War poets featured are Luis Rosales, Gabriel Celaya, Blas de Otero and Carlos Bousoño. Ten other contemporary poets including Gloria Fuertes, Angél González, and Claudio Rodríguez complete the collection.

Because it covers a period of such rich production, this anthology is necessarily exclusive. Scores of other poets justifiably might have been included in *Roots and Wings*. Among the Generation of 98 alone, FranciscoVillaespesa, Manuel Machado, the dramatist Eduardo Marquina and the novelists Pérez de Ayala, Valle-Inclán and Pío Baroja, all of whom published verse, are left out. St. Martin acknowledges such omissions and adds, "I think it is important to experience the poem in

THREE FACES OF AUTUMN
Poetry, Prose, Translations

Spanish . . . . By insisting on a bilingual edition, I cut the space in half and consequently had to sacrifice some highly respected poets."

Perhaps the only poems this reviewer misses are some of the mystical poems of Dámaso Alonso, Leopoldo Panero and José María Valverde which might have given this volume an added dimension. Yet it is hard to fault a collection which is so finely edited and beautifully produced. St. Martin worked about ten years on this project; he has translated about 40 of the poems and the remaining translations were made by such poets as Robert Bly, W. S. Merwin, William Stafford and James Wright.

Roots and Wings is a kind of landmark volume which seems to do for the poets of Spain what Dudley Fitts's anthology did for Latin American poets 35 years ago. The collection fills a gap and brings the American public in touch again with a poetry greatly neglected until now. But the anthology marks an era, and it is important to realize that poetry continues to be written in Spain by dynamic young poets whom Machado exhorted long ago, in his poem "A Young Spain," to

> . . . go to your adventure
> clean and alive in the divine light,
> clear as a diamond, pure as a diamond.

Review of *Roots and Wings, Poetry from Spain, 1900-1975*,
edited by Hardie St. Martin (Harper & Row).

St. Louis Post-Dispatch, January 30, 1977, p. 4C.

One of James Joyce's many adversities

By present-day standards James Joyce would be a loser. Illness and personal tragedies marked his life. He had long periods of near-blindness and he was often unemployed. And his masterwork *Ulysses* was tied up in litigation for 12 years before it could be distributed in the United States. *James Joyce in Padua* relates to one of Joyce's many adversities; in 1912 he was denied a diploma for a teaching position in the Italian public schools, despite his brilliant success in the examinations for the position. (The reason given was that the Ministry of Education did not recognize Joyce's 1902 degree from the University of Dublin as equivalent with a degree from an Italian university.)

Nevertheless, out of that experience Joyce left two essays—bright, lively and concise—one on "The Centenary of Charles Dickens" and the other, written in Italian, on "The Universal Literary Influence of the Renaissance." These essays form the main part of this volume. A translation, commentary, notes, a bibliography and nine illustrations are added, making this a thorough and attractive little book despite its rather limited scope.

As one who has noticed a lucuna, from June 11, 1910, to August 19, 1912, in Stuart Gilbert's *Letters of James Joyce* (1957), I find Berrone's book a useful link between Joyce's earlier and later work. Berrone's recovery of the two missing essays from the University of Padua was the result of long, patient efforts. The fine, scholarly presentation of these essays (particularly the one on Dickens) shows us still another facet of Joyce's life and work.

Review of *James Joyce in Padua,* edited, translated and introduced by Louis Berrone (Random House).

St. Louis Post-Dispatch, January 1, 1978, p. 4C.

THREE FACES OF AUTUMN
Poetry, Prose, Translations

The poetry of Petrarch

The Italian Renaissance poet Francesco Petrarca (1304-1374) was more
than the maker of hundreds of songs and sonnets celebrating his love for a
beautiful young lady named Laura. With Dante and Boccaccio he was a
father of the Italian language and, through his perfection of the sonnet
form, the originator of a new school of poetry which quickly spread to
England, France and Spain.

Petrarch's "scattered rhymes" were left untitled and, as critic Theodor
Mommsen noted, lacked the organic unity of Dante's sonnets to Beatrice
in *La vita nuova* (The New Life). Petrarch, who first met Laura some 35
years after Dante's work appeared in 1292, owed much to Dante who, were
it not for his divine vision, was perhaps as much a Renaissance man as the
younger poet.

Although it is out of print, the standard English version of Petrarch is still
Petrarch: Sonnets and Songs, translated by Anna Maria Armi and
introduced by Mommsen, a 600-page work published 30 years ago. That
older work, like Mortimer's selection, is skillfully done in English rhyme
and meter with the Italian and English texts on facing pages.

While Mortimer translated just 46 poems, Ms. Armi translated all 366
poems, certainly a labor of rare dedication. Still, Mortimer's selection
contains enough of Petrarch's finest work to acquaint us with that poet's
themes, style and vision.

This new translation has the flavor of the poet's own idiom, and we can
easily see how Petrarch's imagery follows Dante's, as in these lines from
canzone 129:

> From thought to thought, from mountainside to mountain
> Love leads me on . . .
> Among high mountains and wild woods I find
> some kind of rest. . .
> Where a tall pine-tree or a hill gives shade
> sometimes I stop, and on the nearest stone
> my mind will draw her face. . .
> Often I've seen (who will believe me now?)
> on the green grass or in transparent water
> her living self.

Mortimer's *Petrarch* keeps the poet's elegance and strength. This selection with its introduction and notes is basic Petrarch done in extremely good taste.

Review of *Petrarch: Selected Poems*, translated into English by Anthony Mortimer (University of Alabama).

St. Louis Post-Dispatch, January 15, 1978, p. 4C.

THREE FACES OF AUTUMN
Poetry, Prose, Translations

Confessional poetry

One of the current trends of American poetry is to write "confessionally." But confessional poetry was written back in the Middle Ages, by Juan Ruiz and Villon among others, and in fact much lyric poetry since antiquity has been openly self-revealing. Still, many American poets have found new ways to write about themselves. Now that the trend is here, it was inevitable that critics would examine it in full-length studies. This book is one of those studies.

David Kalstone has chosen five varied temperaments "with an eye to contrast": Elizabeth Bishop, Robert Lowell, James Merrill, Adrienne Rich and John Ashbery, all of whom have a strong and developing sense of how poetry serves as autobiography.

Elizabeth Bishop, once "the most impersonal poet" of the group, increasingly reveals herself and her childhood memories while keeping her tough powers of observation. The late Robert Lowell made a sharper, more dramatic shift to the autobiographical with his *Life Studies* (Farrar, Straus), a memoir partly in verse, partly in prose.

James Merrill, on the other hand, "knew/That life was fiction in disguise" since his childhood, as he points out in his poem "Days of 1935." Poetry, he feels, has two natures; it is accountable both to daily life and to the "really inhuman depths" he occasionally explores.

Adrienne Rich too is strongly committed to autobiography. Yet while Merrill tries to free himself from the past, Rich works toward the future, toward change. Whenever she does look back on her old poetic self, it is to reassess that past, perhaps to heal a breach or to call for individual or social change. With a passionate intelligence she is often committed to noting her present feelings, "the pain of the moment" as Kalstone observes.

Finally, John Ashbery examines himself and his experience in unique ways. Disregarding objects, figures and key incidents, he writes autobiography in more abstract terms, with a sense of trying to gain access to his experience. Past and present are often discontinuous. He uses forms, like the sestina, but only as devices at "getting into remoter areas of consciousness." His verse is alternately light and serious, mystifying and demystifying. Yet he is honest about his contradictions, and he is one of the most penetrating critics of his own attempts to record his minute private feelings.

Kalstone, who previously wrote a study of Sir Philip Sidney, *Sidney's Poetry* (Harvard), reveals a wide latitude of appreciation in this new book. *Five Temperaments* is a fine, sensitively written introduction to the work of five significant poets of our time.

Review of *Five Temperaments*, by David Kalstone (Oxford University Press).

St. Louis Post-Dispatch, February 2, 1978, p. 3B.

THREE FACES OF AUTUMN
Poetry, Prose, Translations

Ear to fading rhythms

Of all American poets who took part in the Imagist movement from 1914 to 1917, John Gould Fletcher (1886-1950) was perhaps the "purest" practitioner.

His many early books, especially *Irradiations: Sand and Spray* (1915) and *Goblins and Pagodas* (1916), written in free verse and polyphonic prose, brought the most sensational new poetic rhythms to American readers since Whitman's *Leaves of Grass*. Fletcher's reputation survived a full generation, and in 1939 he won a Pulitzer Prize for his *Selected Poems*.

Like most other Imagists (especially, Pound, Hilda Doolittle and F. S. Flint) Fletcher was strongly independent of the movement as fostered by Amy Lowell. Amy and Ezra were his mentors and kind patrons during those early years. He was also a close friend of Conrad Aiken, whose verse Amy disliked, and he defended and sometimes even emulated Aiken's use of rhyme and meter.

Both Pound and Miss Lowell were successful in placing Fletcher's poems in magazines like Harriet Monroe's *Poetry*. His opinion of Pound in those early years is best summed up in this passage from a letter to Miss Monroe: "Ezra Pound, with whom I greatly disagree in artistic theory and practice, has the sense to know decent stuff when he sees it, and to say so. You ought to make him editor of your paper."

Since his death Fletcher has suffered neglect mainly because of his early connections with the Imagist movement. Today few readers know of Fletcher or read his verse. Thus, the best part of de Chasca's book is the second part dealing with Fletcher's theory and practice of Imagism, particularly the last chapter quoting many of Fletcher's poems. Yet the short poems and brief quotations lack the breathtaking range of the *Symphonies*, and one must inevitably return to Fletcher's books (if they can be found) or to old anthologies like Louis Untermeyer's.

A study like this on Fletcher has been long overdue. De Chasca's book has shortcomings, however. It contains a number of errors, typographical and factual. The index is incomplete. And, more important, the influence of the French symbolist poets on Fletcher, while mentioned, was far stronger than described. Even Amy Lowell recognized this influence when she followed Fletcher—not to mention Pound—in her book *Six French Poets* (1915).

Finally, the appearance of "Edward" Arlington Robinson on both pages 114 and 160, for instance, shakes our confidence in the author's background knowledge of the period covered. But despite these flaws, de Chasca's book has a dynamic, entertaining style. *John Gould Fletcher and Imagism* is not a full-scale critical biography, but it recaptures much of the spirit of the Imagist movement's exciting early years.

Review of *John Gould Fletcher and Imagism*, by Edmund S. de Chasca (University of Missouri Press).

St. Louis Post-Dispatch, February 12, 1978, p. 3B.

THREE FACES OF AUTUMN
Poetry, Prose, Translations

May Sarton: sensibility in art and life

"I shan't be hurt if you do not like these," May Sarton graciously wrote on sending me a sheaf of poems for use in an anthology several years ago. In thus expressing her own feelings, not only in her novels, poems and memoirs but in her daily correspondence, she also shows a sensibility toward others which has characterized her whole art and life.

Selected Poems of May Sarton is the second major book of verse by its author in recent years, the other being her *Collected Poems 1930-1973* (416 pages, Norton, $10) issued in 1974 and still in print. With almost any other poet one might question the need or rationale for this new book which is essentially an abridgement of the earlier collection. But there are good reasons.

For instance, the editors have arranged the poems thematically (not chronologically as they appeared before) into seven sections about imaginative art, love, solitude, nature and other subjects. Having heard May Sarton's verse read from pulpits and at conferences, I am convinced that she must be one of America's most quoted living poets. This new book, then, is quite useful to speakers who look for quotations from her to support and enliven their own ideas.

Now in full maturity, May Sarton has a brilliant, open mind and a young heart. She writes,

> I had been the woman
> With a camera eye
> Who notices everything
> And is always watched . . .
> Yes, I am alive.

Whether written in self-reflection or in observation, or both, her poems show a rare combination of abundance and self-discipline. In writing both formal and free verse, she is an adept practitioner of organic form—that is, the form always follows the function of her poetry. She does not, for instance, simply write sonnets; she writes poems, some of which happen to be in sonnet form. The editors' introduction to this book helps readers understand her uses of form and how the themes of art, love, solitude and nature are interlocked in her life and work.

As for the eight poems she sent for the anthology, I couldn't refuse any and published them all. For like many readers, I have long realized that May Sarton has found a perfect identity in poetry, and that poetry to her has a high purpose, as she writes in "My Sisters O My Sisters":

> To be through what we make more simply human,
> To come to the deep place where poet becomes woman,
> Where nothing has to be renounced or given over
> In the pure light that shines out from the lover,
> In the warm light that brings forth fruit and flower,
> And that great sanity, that sun, the feminine power.

Review of *Selected Poems of May Sarton,* edited with an introduction by Serena Sue Hilsinger and Lois Brynes (Norton).

St. Louis Post-Dispatch, September 26, 1978, p. 3C.

THREE FACES OF AUTUMN
Poetry, Prose, Translations

All things together move

"I don't think you'll amount to much as a poet," Mitchell Kennerley told John Hall Wheelock some 70 years ago when he urged the young poet to turn to writing novels. But long before his death last March at age 91, Wheelock had published a dozen books of verse and become one of the best loved and most honored American poets, winner of The Poetry Society of America's gold medal, the Bollingen Prize in Poetry and numerous other awards.

Wheelock by nature seemed to avoid the spectacular, and his life and work were anything but sensational. A friend of Sara Teasdale, who died in 1933, he once wrote sensitive, spiritual lyrics which she admired. He tended to be quiet and cogitative, and his style, reminiscent of Robert Hillyer's or Mark Van Doren's, was affirmative, dignified and musical. He favored the abstract in an age which touted the concrete and imagistic. Yet, while his poetry seemed occasionally out of tune with his time, Wheelock was anything but tired and conservative, as one literary historian has unjustly labeled him. "He was ever alert to the needs of younger poets in his counsel," his friend Charles Wagner wrote. As a senior editor at Scribner's for 46 years, Wheelock continually encouraged new poets, introducing Allen Tate, May Swenson, Louis Simpson, James Dickey and a score of others to the American public.

This Blessed Earth is a commemorative volume published on the 92nd anniversary of Wheelock's birth. A rather small collection, it contains just 27 poems, but half of these were written in recent years. While several of Wheelock's best known and most anthologized pieces ("Earth," "Triumph of Love," "This Quiet Dust") are omitted, the selection is beautifully balanced and in excellent taste. The section of earlier poems includes "The Holy Earth," with its blending of the natural and physical with the metaphysical world where "The wind breathes like a prayer" and "all things together move / To the one end." There is the exotic "Bonac," sensuous and musical (not unlike Coleridge's "Kubla Khan"), with its superb catalog of nature in an enchanted land "where grape and honeysuckle/ Tangle their vines, where the beach-plum in spring/ Snows all the inland dunes; bird-haunted land/Where youth still dwells forever." And other older poems abound, relating nature with life and death: "The Divine Insect," "Wood-Thrush," "The Gardener," "Herring-Gull," "Evening Contemplation" and "Unison."

172

These earlier poems, meticulously crafted, are among those which established his high reputation. But, amazingly, the style and quality of Wheelock's most recent poems showed no signs of diminishing. One of these is "Affirmation," a long, intricate meditation in which the poet steers gracefully and coherently through nearly 200 lines to a conclusive message of positive faith. "Address to Existence" is reminiscent of Matthew Arnold's "Dover Beach" in its style, but is a strong rebuttal to Arnold's philosophy. Several other recent poems, especially "Self-Counsel in Age," "This Pain" and "Intimations of Mortality," reveal a self-knowledge very few poets attain at any age.

Wheelock's poetry, as this posthumous volume shows, has strength and durability transcending the more innovative, ebullient work of many of his contemporaries. If his poems remind us of Wordsworth, Coleridge and Arnold instead of Pound and Eliot, that too is high praise. For poetry is forever pluralistic in its styles and themes. As for Wheelock, the testimony of his life in poetry is aptly condensed in his lines from "The Concert":

> . . . I came home to the Truth,
> Which had been mine—oh, might it ever be—
> When, in the marvellous morning of my youth,
> I walked this blessed earth,
> Watchful, in adoration and ecstasy.

Review of *This Blessed Earth, New and Selected Poems, 1927-1977*, by John Hall Wheelock (Scribner's).

St. Louis Post-Dispatch, August 27, 1978, p. 4D.

THREE FACES OF AUTUMN
Poetry, Prose, Translations

Poetry of acorn spirals and silences

Not since the Imagist era of 50 to 60 years ago have American women turned to poetry with such enthusiasm as today. But there is a difference. Despite the fine craftsmanship of the great figures earlier in the century (Millay, Teasdale and Wylie), today's poets have more power, range and openness than ever before.

Some observers may trace the present renaissance to the popular, tragic appeal of the late Sylvia Plath and Anne Sexton. But the roots go much deeper. Even in the early 1930s new attitudes of self-awareness and social protest, currently strong in poetry, were evident in Marianne Moore, Genevieve Taggard, the young Muriel Rukeyser and others. A new generation, too, had just then matured: Babette Deutsch, Louise Bogan, Léonie Adams and the brilliant Fugitive poet, Laura Riding, were among the most prominent names. In the 1940s a host of young poets appeared, including Elizabeth Bishop, Gwendolyn Brooks, Gene Derwood, Ruth Herschberger, Barbara Howes, Josephine Miles and May Sarton. In the 1950s and 1960s came Denise Levertov, May Swenson, Mona Van Duyn and Diane Wakoski.

Thus there was no abrupt reappearance of women, or even the "new" woman, in poetry, but rather a continuity, a gradual flowering.

A few recent books from large and small presses are described here. Several of these are outstanding works and will perhaps win major prizes. The other volumes represent at least an important stage in the development of the poets' work.

One thinks of Daisy Aldan as a word artist, in the same class perhaps as the late Anais Nin. In *Between High Tides* (Folder Editions), her fifteenth book, Ms. Aldan alternates between meticulous description of the outer world and minute self-examination. Her poems at times seem outwardly calm with an inner turbulence, and at other times tremulous on the surface but with underlying composure. Even the titles—"In A Frozen Moment," "I Am Moved By A Necessity From Within," "Vertical Is Our New Sight" —suggest the contemplative nature of this poet who startles us with the "artfully/designed acorn-spiral of Self" she reveals. Her background is broadly cosmopolitan, and her influences include G. M. Hopkins, Mallarmé and Apollinaire.

Dowry, poems by Janet N. Beeler (University of Missouri), is the 1978 winner of the Devins award for poetry. Ms. Beeler, too, has a strong self-awareness and she is able to project that self into other women of history and myth, such as Sappho and the medieval French poet Christine de Pisan. "Holy women," she calls them, quoting Rilke—women who "had found the means for Being within themselves." Taste, touch, smell and, above all, colorful imagery mark these poems; but the sensuousness is purposeful, not superficially descriptive. *Dowry* covers a wide spectrum of experience in a mature, even form and style.

Pond, by Gay Phillips (Release Press), contains 40 poems in a consistently spare, simple style. The book, apparently the author's first, is uneven in quality; but the best of the poems are slices of life, earthy little narratives spoken in halting, confessional lines. Other pieces, more whimsical, include fairy tales retold in capsule form—"Frog Prince," "Red Riding Hood" and others. "Goldilocks," for instance, with its fresh, surprise ending: the little bear dancing

> wanted
> her to stay
> so they would all know
> who was who.

The Collected Poems of Muriel Rukeyser (McGraw-Hill) is the capstone in the career of a major poet. As such, it cannot adequately be "abstracted" in a brief review. But we can touch upon its contents—a dozen books under a single cover. Ms. Rukeyser is the author of 14 books of poems, six books of prose and numerous translations and children's books. By age 25 she had already become perhaps the most exciting new poet on the American scene; she had just published her second book, *U.S. 1* (1938), following her earlier *Theory of Flight* (1935) with its long title poem and shorter verses written in the Auden-Spender style. Today Ms. Rukeyser remains one of the strongest and most versatile of American poets, and of course one of the most durable. Her strength of spirit, her commitment to freedom, and her full, rich lyric gift abound in *The Collected Poems*. Here is a sample, a poem titled "Then," from her recent volume *The Gates* (1976):

> When I am dead, even then,
> I will still love you, I will wait in these poems.

THREE FACES OF AUTUMN
Poetry, Prose, Translations

When I am dead, even then
I am still listening to you.
I will still be making poems for you out of silence;
silence will be falling into that silence,
it is building music.

This collection should, finally, bring her certain recognitions which she
has long deserved.

Another substantial work deserving major recognition is May Swenson's
New & Selected Things Taking Place (Atlantic-Little, Brown), an unusual
combination of new and selected poems. One of the most striking
elements of Ms. Swenson's poetry is form, and this volume establishes her
as perhaps the most versatile living poet in the use of free forms. Form
always seems to follow the function of her themes and images, in "shapes
of speculation," in strong visual metaphors. The imagery is often celestial:
solar or lunar. When earthly, it is often aquatic: rivers, lakes, seas, coves.
This collection of 63 new poems, with a generous selection from five
earlier books, is Ms. Swenson's finest to date.

Two other recent books, both in paperback, are *The Centre Holds* by
Fanny Ventadour (Editions Two Cities) and *Ciao Manhattan* by Rebecca
Wright (Telephone Books). Ms. Ventadour is both artist and poet and her
verse has appeared widely in magazines and anthologies. As one might
expect, color, line and perspective dominate her work. Yet she also makes
imaginative use of events, as in "A Dream of Trees on the Way to a Moon
Shot," a poem which bears comparison with some of Ms. Swenson's
poems on lunar themes. These bright, fresh poems show strong influences
of French surrealist poets like Apollinaire and Reverdy.

Rebecca Wright is a young, talented Missouri poet who recently made a
recording of her poetry for University of Missouri-St. Louis radio station
KWMU. As in her earlier book, *Brief Lives* (1974), *Ciao Manhattan* opens
with the title poem, a long, self-searching narrative in sweeping lines in
which past and present shift and mingle. Although the imagery is private,
even abstruse sometimes, the fast-moving language yields subtle
meanings, satisfying or disturbing. And despite, the occasional slackness
of the narrative, the poems have a consistent structure, beginning casually
and ending abruptly. Above all, Ms. Wright's poems have refreshing
exuberance.

A CHARLES GUENTHER RETROSPECTIVE
Prose: Critical Reviews and Essays, 1973-1982

Strong creative energy, in fact, marks the work of all these poets; for women today, whether as persons or as poets, are more freely expressive and less quiet and recessive. As Rebecca Wright observes:

> . . . there is all this joy
> and not knowing exactly where it comes from
> I look after each person or object, listen to each sound
> proposing it as a source, but after all
> the joy is still within me.

St. Louis Post-Dispatch, April 1, 1979, p. 4D.

THREE FACES OF AUTUMN
Poetry, Prose, Translations

Translation: a cross pollination of cultures

Literary translation used to be largely a pastime for the elite. Young self-made writers seldom practiced the craft. After World War II, which produced many "interpreters" (of words if not of cultures), there was a flowering of higher education and an increased need for world cultural exchange. A translation revival began.

Of course, many publishers like Boni and Knopf and J. Laughlin had long brought world writing to American audiences. Laughlin's New Directions (which Ezra Pound miscalled "No Directions" and other playful but unprintable things) took the lead in postwar translation, particularly from the French and Spanish. New Directions nurtured dozens of young translators like H. R. Hays, Delmore Schwartz, Roger Shattuck, William Jay Smith and Louise Varese.

By 1978, when the American Literary Translators Association was formed with more than 380 members, translation had come into its own.

Earlier translators and their struggles for recognition, however, are largely unknown or forgotten. And today the field is so crowded that one translator cannot "hog" a language or ask his colleagues (as Pound told others over a generation ago) to "work on the Greek and leave the Chinese to me." Yet, despite the competition, the young translator is now accepted and respected in the vanguard of world culture, and encounters few constraints.

Translations are among the most noteworthy and durable products of large and small presses alike. This is particularly true in the field of poetry which places special demands on the translator. The most recent posthumous book of Robert Lowell, for example, *The Oresteia of Aeschylus* (Farrar, Straus & Giroux), is more than a literary rendering. Lowell aimed at something beyond the elaborate precision of other translations of the Greek play. He tried, he said, "to trim, cut, and be direct enough to satisfy my own mind and at a first hearing the simple ears of a theater audience." In this he was eminently successful, although he seldom reaches the bold colloquial level of Pound's translation of another early play, Sophocles's *Women of Trachis* (New Directions). But Lowell's followers will find *The Oresteia* both a highly original re-creation and an exercise in which Lowell developed his own style. A related book, *Robert*

Lowell: Life and Art, by Steven Gould Axelrod (Princeton) is also recommended.

In recent years the Translation Center at Columbia University has encouraged translators by awarding generous fellowships for the study and translation of certain African, Oriental, East European and other lesser known languages. Partly because of these fellowships, new Hungarian, Polish, Romanian and Turkish writers are becoming better known to the West.

Bells in Winter, by the Polish writer Czesław Miłosz, translated by the author and Lillian Vallee (The Ecco Press) is one of several new books of Polish verse in English. Miłosz, 68, survived the Holocaust—which he predicted in his poems of the 1930s—and now teaches at Berkeley. *Bells in Winter* is both introspective and retrospective. The poems date back to 1936 and are embedded in modern European history. Stated simply, Miłosz's message is that man is incapable of grasping his experience, and his chances of understanding that experience diminish with the passage of time. This theme appears subtly in the poem "Encounter" in which the poet recalls a man gesturing at a passing rabbit, and observes that neither the man nor the animal is alive today. He concludes, "0 my love, where are they, where are they going/ The flash of a hand, streak of movement, rustle of pebbles. / I ask not out of sorrow, but in wonder."

Another noteworthy book of Polish verse is Zbigniew Herbert's *Selected Poems,* translated by John and Bogdana Carpenter (Oxford University Press), which received honorable mention in last year's Islands and Continents translation competition. The Islands and Continents Translation Award, a $1,000 annual prize, was established two years ago by the poet and translator Jonathan Cohen. Cohen has drafted several guidelines for evaluating translations of poetry. First, he asks, are the translations truly poetic? Next, does the translation open up a new door; that is, does it extend the range and capacity of our own speech, our own art and sensibility? And finally, is the translation of a previously translated poet radically new, or a meaningful improvement on what we already have?

This last criterion applies to Arthur Rimbaud's *Illuminations*, a new American translation by Bertrand Mathieu with a foreword and lithograph

179

THREE FACES OF AUTUMN
Poetry, Prose, Translations

by Henry Miller (BOA Editions). Since Rimbaud—like Baudelaire, Rilke and Pablo Neruda—has been translated so often, still another version of *Illuminations* may seem superfluous. But Mathieu's translation is more than justified by its breezy, uninhibited style. Mathieu certainly catches the spirit of Rimbaud more than any other translator. While he acknowledges and profits by earlier versions of *Illuminations*, including Louise Varese's (1946) and Wallace Fowlie's (1953)—both of which are generally more literal and accurate—he prefers a freer colloquial idiom. One important scholarly find has been overlooked, however, in this translation: Rimbaud's sources of the *Iluminations* in century-old French magazines as discovered by the American Robert Clive Roach. But this oversight does not reduce the fast, fresh pace of the translation.

A truly original and outstanding work is the latest Islands and Continents award-winner, *The Penguin Book of Zen Poetry*, edited and translated by Lucien Stryk and Takashi Ikemoto (The Swallow Press). Unlike many other Penguin volumes, this book is in hardback and is printed on fine paper with 14 complementary illustrations. Its major value, however, is in the text itself. Many of the poems have never before appeared in English. It contains hundreds of Japanese and Chinese poems, ranging from three-line haiku to ten-or 15-line vignettes, all rendered in spare, precise language. The poets extend from the twelfth century to the contemporary Japanese master, Shinkichi Takahashi (born 1901), who is represented by a separate section of about 49 poems.

Although relatively new, the Islands and Continents award probably carries more weight with translators than most such prizes, since poet-translators themselves finance the award through contributions and benefit readings. Its principal patrons include Jonathan Cohen and Robert Bly. Cohen, who lives in upstate New York, recently told a reporter, "I keep my thermostat at 55 degrees all winter to help pay for that prize!" That indeed is the kind of sacrifice which speaks a universal language.

St. Louis Post-Dispatch, May 13, 1979, p. 4C.

Lizard among the foliage

Although his poetry was long ago published in the United States, in H. R. Hays's 1947 translation, Bertolt Brecht (1898-1956) still is best known in this country as a playwright. The most gifted of postwar East German writers, Brecht was the librettist for Kurt Weill's *The Threepenny Opera*, which ran for six years; and he wrote several other plays which appeared on and off Broadway.

The *Diaries 1920-1922* foreshadow only Brecht's ability as a writer. They show none of the social and political radicalism which he embraced a few years later. Never perhaps a true proletarian, Brecht was the son of a well-to-do printing executive. He was spoiled as a youth, affected even in his caring moments, and (though he lived with many women) incapable of love.

"Why am I incapable of writing about people I love?" he asks himself. And he rightly answers, "One sees only objective facts."

As expected, then, the diaries exude snobbishness: he refers to "yokels," "niggers," "country bumpkins." Even a cafe violinist—maybe because he works for a living—is "a slimy fellow." There is none of the bleakness, or starvation, or inflation one associates with Germany after World War I. None of the stark melodrama of early Emil Jannings movies. Life was merely a sodden bore.

"It has taken to raining," he writes (1920); "we must look around for fresh ways of filling our time. Films and ballad-singing will see us through another half-moon, but after that we'll have to take off in some other direction; lizards among the autumn foliage in October."

But despite his seeming laziness, his lounge-lizardry, Brecht in these early diaries shows an ability to write well and a fine appreciation of other writers: Georg Buchner, G. K. Chesterton, Knut Hamsun, Hermann Hesse and many others.

And his vignettes of actors, especially of Charlie Chaplin in 1921, are superbly descriptive. The translation of this book is in crisp, colloquial English, and the editor has added a "cast of characters," an index and some 20 photos.

THREE FACES OF AUTUMN
Poetry, Prose, Translations

True proletarian or not, Brecht developed convictions and convinced the world, through his drama, that they were authentic. In his 44 plays, and in his poems spanning 44 years, he could project himself into others' sensations of pain, hunger, anger, exile and grief.

As he writes in the "Song of the Storm Trooper,"

> It was my brother, hunger
> Made us one I know
> And I am marching, marching
> With my own and brother's foe.

Review of *Bertolt Brecht: Diaries 1920-1922*, edited by Herta Ramthun, translated by John Willett (St. Martin's).

St. Louis Post-Dispatch, June 24, 1979, p. 3B.

On the origins and practice of poetry

This is a selection of 29 essays and manifestoes by 29 twentieth-century poets on the origins and practice of poetry.

The writers editor Reginald Gibbons chose are for the most part strong and authoritative. They include Boris Pasternak, Antonio Machado, René Char, Eugenio Montale, Marianne Moore, W. H. Auden and many more, representing many viewpoints and about a dozen countries or cultures.

Despite the international tone, American names predominate, for nearly half of the book is taken up by Americans from Wallace Stevens and Hart Crane to Wendell Berry and Gary Snyder. The ideas set forth cut across at least three generations, reminding us how close we are to a new century, another division of literature.

The foreign poets' essays are generally well chosen and give credence to the idea of the universality of poetic experience. But in several cases a stronger choice might have been made; for example, Paul Valéry's "Poetry and Abstract Thought" instead of his notebook ramblings. In addition, an essay by Nobel Prize poet Salvatore Quasimodo on "Poetry and Politics" might have been included to complement Auden's article. In the latter essay Auden deals with the opposing schools of Classicism and Romanticism which, he believes, signify "aristocratic" and "democratic."

Of the three essays by Spaniards, García Lorca's piece on the *duende*, written in 1930, should be required reading for all who appreciate arts in any form. To Lorca the *duende* (meaning a goblin or haunting spirit) was a mysterious power—of "black" sounds in music, for instance—which differs from angelic power or the power of the muse. The *duende* is particularly felt in music, dance and the spoken word.

Another excellent but little known piece is Wendell Berry's "The Specialization of Poetry," a scrupulous, even-handed analysis of interviews with eight modern poets including Galway Kinnell, William Matthews and Anne Sexton.

Berry makes a strong case for the continuance of form in poetry. "Why," he asks, "is it necessary for poets to believe, like salesmen, that the new inevitably must replace or destroy the old? . . . . Why cannot the critical

THREE FACES OF AUTUMN
Poetry, Prose, Translations

faculty, in poets and critics alike, undertake to see that the best of the new is grafted to the best of the old?"

Altogether Gibbons has assembled a motley and at times dazzling group of spokesmen in *The Poet's Work*. He has done a great service to poets in retrieving a number of hard-to-find or nearly forgotten works of special interest.

Review of *The Poet's Work*, edited by Reginald Gibbons (Houghton Mifflin).

St. Louis Post-Dispatch, September 4, 1979, p. 3B.

A CHARLES GUENTHER RETROSPECTIVE
Prose: Critical Reviews and Essays, 1973-1982

The world is a kaleidoscope

The poems of Richard Eberhart are evolutionary, not revolutionary, and perhaps this explains their durability. His latest book, *Ways of Light*, contains about 40 poems, mostly new, on themes long familiar to his readers: reminiscence, survival through change, and the wonders of the natural world.

There are reminders of poets long gone—Dante, Coleridge, Keats. But there are also more immediate memories of Eberhart's peers: Williams, Agee, the Sitwells, Ted Spencer and Robert Lowell. "We lived when words were like roses on bayonets," he writes in "Nostalgia for Edith Sitwell"; and elsewhere he recalls the appearance of endlessness "in the time that was whole and hardy." The poem he writes to Lowell has "slingshot words" meant for the Goliath of Death.

Poem after poem reflects a preoccupation with time and change, especially "Then and Now," "Time's Clickings," "Survivors" and "Autumn." To Eberhart the world is a kaleidoscope in which decades, like pieces, shift and fall into place and the world's energies have a stable instability. Eberhart's "Stopping a Kaleidoscope" bears comparison with Robert Frost's "Stopping by Woods on a Snowy Evening," if only to show the differing natures of the two poets, one cerebral, the other natural. "Sameness ever the same, ever changing," Eberhart writes,

> No ebb, no flow not subject to change,
> No changelessness in our consciousness
> Remaining . . . .

But the rational man in Eberhart cannot overlook nature.

Occasionally the intellect commands the poet, as when he calls the sky "The sensorium/ Of ineluctability." But more often he writes of nature's wildness: of a snowfall, winter squirrels, a fat spider, a swarm of gnats, the cry of a loon. Nature, he reveals, taught him to accept irrationality. In "Autumn," a remarkably fast-paced poem of fresh imagery, the poet concludes that

> It is time
> To put this house in order but fate will do it to us.

THREE FACES OF AUTUMN
Poetry, Prose, Translations

Still, he has known love, a magical, improbable god "that lights on mortals." He has known faith, too, he who "Had to destroy grief/ To resurrect belief," as he writes in "The Rose." And when, as in "Wet June," the poet is "pressed down by time toward the end/Of life," his silence will—— be "as deep as that of the flowers."

Review of *Ways of Light, Poems 1972-1980*, by Richard Eberhart (Oxford).

St. Louis Post-Dispatch, May 25, 1980, p. 4B.

Covering poetic wars

Thanks to the Romantic and more recent Surrealist movements, it is recognized that poems proceed from several levels of consciousness and reflect many attitudes. Robert Bly has long shown a multiple consciousness—of humanity, nature and the universe—in his own poems, particularly in his book, *Light Around the Body,* which won a National Book Award.

News of the Universe is Bly's remarkable six-part anthology of 150 poems and prose poems by 75 poets who represent many centuries and cultures. The theme of the book grows out of the old Classic vs. Romantic confrontation which traces back, in modern times, to the eighteenth century.

Bly develops his thesis formidably in his essays and meditations placed among the sections of poems.

The first section illustrates the "old position"—that nature is inferior to human reason, an attitude reflecting pre-nineteenth century ideas of such writers as Descartes, Lessing, Milton, Swift and Pope. The second section represents a development of the Hölderlin-Novalis-Goethe stream or tradition—the opening of a new position of sensitivity towards nature.

The Romantics began "feeling" nature, and more recent poets began "thinking" nature. Bly points out that "modern" poets—Eliot, Auden and Pound, for instance—often are ironic and not in the stream of nature. "We are aware of that tradition and admire it," he adds. But he feels we should also be aware of the old "non-human or non-ego energies" resurrected by Romantics like Blake, Keats and Nerval.

The last four sections of this anthology form one of the most remarkable selections put together in recent years. There are scores of poems adeptly chosen as touchstones between the world of plants and animals and the world of humans. It is one world, as Bly shows in such poems as Hesse's "Sometimes," Eberhart's "The Groundhog" and Wilbur's "Beasts." It is a world recognized over a century ago in Baudelaire's "Correspondences" (Bly's "Intimate Associations") and more recently in Ponge's "The End of Fall." Most of the translations, including versions of the Persian Sufi poet Rūmī, are done by Bly himself in a crisp modern idiom.

THREE FACES OF AUTUMN
Poetry, Prose, Translations

Robert Bly, as poet, translator and editor, has increasingly become a major force in American poetry. This fresh, bright collection reflects his wide, rich experience with poetry and poets of many ages and cultures including our own. *News of the Universe* is an appropriate coup for Sierra Club Books.

Review of *News of the Universe, Poems of Twofold Consciousness*, chosen and introduced by Robert Bly (Sierra Club Books).

St. Louis Post-Dispatch July 6, 1980, p. 4C.

Every little movement has its day

American readers have long been familiar with the work of English Movement writers like Kingsley Amis, Donald Davie, Elizabeth Jennings and Philip Larkin. But the history and aims of the Movement itself have been little-known and ill-defined. In this book Blake Morrison traces the Movement's origins, describes the class and culture of its members, shows their search for an audience and, finally, reveals the divisions which led to the decline of the Movement in the late 1950s.

Morrison's study is brilliantly researched and written. It concentrates on seven poets and novelists—the above four plus D. J. Enright, Thom Gunn and John Wain—and mentions scores of others in passing. It shows especially the divergent lines of Movement writers who could not seem to agree on anything, even on whether to write for a mass audience or a select audience. Movement writers were elitist in background but they tried, not always successfully, to identify with a postwar welfare-state Britain in which elitism and privilege were considered "ugly notions."

One thing is certain: Movement writers shunned the Modernist generation just before them. It is astonishing, for instance, to see how few of the 70 poets in Kenneth Rexroth's anthology, *New British Poets*, representing the late 1940s, are even mentioned by Morrison. The Movement shunned Pound, Eliot, Spender and their followers in favor of Hardy, Graves and William Empson. Empson was celebrated for his "greatness," and a refrain from his poem "Aubade" was widely imitated: "It seemed the best thing to be up and go." (Like the U.S. Beat Generation, Movement poets seemed to delight in being "on the go.")

Today many Movement writers continue in their distinct, and often distinguished, ways. But as a movement, alas, they came and went. Perhaps a line from Thom Gunn's "On the Move" best describes the ephemeral Movement: "A minute holds them, who have come to go."

Review of *The Movement: English Poetry and Fiction of the 1950s*, by Blake Morrison (Oxford).

St. Louis Post-Dispatch, July 27, 1980, p. 2G.

189

THREE FACES OF AUTUMN
Poetry, Prose, Translations

Poems that are in touch with the source

In an earlier book, *Journal of a Solitude* (1973), May Sarton showed an almost daily preoccupation with poetry. If she was not making poems, she felt that she should have been making them. One day she felt "set free, in touch with the deep source . . . where poetry lives." Another day she chided herself for filling the weekend with friends to prevent depression, knowing she "should have turned the corner" and written poems instead. In *Halfway to Silence*, containing about three dozen new poems, May Sarton writes of things natural and observed: geese, an oriole, a brook, a storm, trees and the seasons. She writes of characters and settings, real or imagined: "The Lady of the Lake," "Beggar, Queen, and Ghost," "Old Lovers at the Ballet." She writes of omens and returning myths; and she writes of emotions—jealousy, pain, fear, and mostly love.

Her poetry, let it be known, is not blatantly confessional or filled with strong social messages, but stresses craftsmanship: rhyme—soft or hard—meter, music and abundant imagery. Yet her poems have social meaning through the universality of her revealed self, a self not unlike our own selves. We find affinities with her. "I contain love as if it were a warhead," she writes in "Autumn Sonnets," and we recognize the supreme clarity of that love in her lines. In other poems, geese are a symbol of a woman's abandonment, pain is broad as a country, jealousy is a destructive flame, a tree is a "blessing of pure form that opens space." Basically, to May Sarton the poem is "a dialogue with the self," reflecting feeling, not thinking, as when she writes:

> My gentle earth is barren now, or nearly.
> Harden it well against the loss and change;
> Prepare to hold the fastness, since I know
> The open self must grow more harsh and strange
> Before it meets the softness of the snow.

Such simple but strong lines as these are indeed "a gift from powers beyond" the poet's will. *Halfway to Silence* is a powerful new testament of one of America's most widely known and loved poets.

Review of *Halfway to Silence, New Poems*, by May Sarton (Norton).

St. Louis Post-Dispatch, August 3, 1980, p. 4C.

A CHARLES GUENTHER RETROSPECTIVE
Prose: Critical Reviews and Essays, 1973-1982

Jarrell, Snyder on poems, poets

Relatively few distinguished American poets since T. S. Eliot and Ezra
Pound have been equally distinguished as critics. Babette Deutsch,
Randall Jarrell and Howard Nemerov are notable examples. Others like
Frost, Stevens and Cummings wrote few formal essays on their craft and
fellow craftsmen, although in some cases interviews, letters and memoirs
abound.

Randall Jarrell (1914-1965) was one of the best and brightest younger
poets and critics of his time. Although he won a National Book Award in
1961, he never got quite as much recognition as he deserved—partly
perhaps because he wrote in the shadow of the aging giants of modernism
who still lived and flourished: not only Eliot and Pound but also Moore,
Williams, Tate and others. *Kipling, Auden & Co.* contains nearly 70
essays and reviews that were published in literary journals over a 30-year
period to 1964. It is Jarrell's fourth book of criticism and follows another
posthumous collection, *The Third Book of Criticism*, which appeared in
1969.

During his lifetime Jarrell was instantly popular among an intense if
narrow audience. His earlier books, *Poetry and the Age* (1953) and
Selected Poems (1955) set the tone of his work and solidified his
reputation. Jarrell's main publishers then were Knopf and Atheneum, but
this latest Farrar, Straus book is superior to any of the trade books Jarrell
published during his life, and is in keeping with his reputation.

As for contents, some readers may find much of *Kipling, Auden & Co.*
uninteresting, especially the topical reviews and verse chronicles dealing
with minor and forgotten poets. But perusing this book is like going
through a flea market. Jarrell's wit and imagination give life to the
"objects" (the books he reviews), or at least a certain fusty charm to them.

The fact that the most powerful anthologists unaccountably ignored him
certainly salted his critical essays.

For instance, one old adversary, Oscar Williams (who omitted Jarrell from
the *Little Treasury* anthologies) is dealt with as follows: "Oscar
Williams's new book is pleasanter and a little quieter than his old, which
gave the impression of having been written on a typewriter by a

typewriter." And elsewhere Jarrell describes Karl Shapiro's "Trial of a Poet" as "a sort of bobby-soxer's 'Mauberley.'"

At his best, Jarrell was a spokesman of his age not unlike Matthew Arnold was a century ago. The eight or ten major essays in this book could stand alone as a collection, and it is good to have them out of dusty magazines. There is a particularly brilliant piece on André Malraux's book, *The Voices of Silence*. Other outstanding essays are "Love and Poetry," "Against Abstract Expressionism" and "The Taste of the Age."

In his relations with other poets Jarrell was at times caustic but never cruel or dishonest. Speaking for himself and perhaps others whom Jarrell reviewed, Karl Shapiro once said, "I felt as if I had been run over but not hurt." Maybe this resurrection of Jarrell's prose will serve as a touchstone for a new generation of readers and writers for whom "formal" and "essay," singly or combined, are words vanishing from the vocabulary.

Gary Snyder, who represents a new wave of poets and critics, begins his collection of talks and interviews with the year Jarrell's collection ends, 1964. Snyder is not so much a reader and critic as an observer and commentator. Like Robert Bly, Galway Kinnell and certain other recent poets, Snyder tends toward the mystical, archetypal and naturalistic. He pretends, or at least he impresses us, that he lacks a sense of organization and unity; thus, he allows this collection, *The Real Work*, to be edited and introduced by a patient, persistent scholar, William Scott McLean.
To some readers, perhaps, Snyder's attitude may seem a pose. He perceived a need, he says, to "de-educate" himself after college. That is, to "get back in touch with people, with ordinary things: with the body, with the dirt, with the dust, with anything you like, you know—the streets. The streets or the farm, whatever it is. Get away from books and from the elite sense of being bearers of Western culture."

Yet Snyder was too talented and too realistic (and perhaps too civilized) to decline a term as an official of the California Arts Council, or to spurn major literary awards and publications. (In defense of awards he writes, "They don't do any harm as long as they don't make you come to New York and have a dinner to get the prize.") Lest we judge him too harshly, however, we must realize that Snyder represents a reaction from the formal age of New Criticism of the 1950s. He looks back to the primitive in art and culture. The lessons he learned from Pound, Eliot and Yeats were lessons of life, not "literature." He is a "shoot from the sixties root" in poetics, politics, anthropology and biology, a self-styled "ethnobotanist." He is no mere outgrowth of the long-disappeared beat generation, but one of the more productive and enlightened members of that era.

If Snyder's mask appears simple, his approach to life and writing is not simplistic. He follows the strong tradition of social consciousness, of Whitman and Masters, just as Jarrell favored the Poe-Hart Crane tradition of formal craftsmanship. Snyder finds "inspiration" in Whitman, whom he considers "a good communal poet"; but Snyder is more sophisticated than Whitman (if we dare use that term about either poet), and far more realistic.

Much of Snyder's appeal lies in his fresh treatment of unusual themes— South Indian poetry and dance, for example. These themes may at first seem exotic and esoteric, but they are rooted in Snyder's wide-ranging experience. Above all is his will to survive. Having seen friends done in by booze and drugs, Snyder clearly prefers sobriety to self-destruction.

These talks and interviews show Snyder in a variety of evolving attitudes, all "real" at a given place and time. But ultimately the real Gary Snyder is the poet whose synthesized perception of the world, East and West, comes to us in symbols and sense-impressions. Some of his finest lines, as in an earlier book, *Myths and Texts* (1960), flow like cool water:

> One moves continually with the consciousness
> Of that other, totally alien, non-human:
> Humming inside like a taut drum,
> Carefully avoiding any direct thought of it,
> Attentive to the real world flesh and stone.

Review of *Kipling, Auden & Co., Essays and Reviews 1935-1964*, by Randall Jarrell (Farrar, Straus & Giroux) and *The Real Work, Interviews & Talks 1964-1979*, by Gary Snyder (New Directions).

St. Louis Post-Dispatch, August 10, 1980, p. 4F.

THREE FACES OF AUTUMN
Poetry, Prose, Translations

Elegance and artifice of Marianne Moore

"I am not important enough for a feature," Marianne Moore wrote me in April 1962, adding that "T. S. Eliot is ideal material."

It was then ten years before the death at age 85 of St. Louis-born Miss Moore and ten years after she had scored a "hat trick" by winning three major American poetry prizes in 1952: the Bollingen and Pulitzer Prizes and the National Book Award, all honoring her *Collected Poems*.

Having read most of Eliot's French sources, I felt almost too familiar with him, and I found Miss Moore's life and work more interesting in several ways. Above all, I admired the stylistic ingenuity of her poems and translations.

Unlike some poets, Miss Moore left a large body of comments on her work and her techniques. In 1919 she wrote to Pound: "Any verse that I have written has been an arrangement of stanzas, each stanza being an exact duplicate of every other stanza." Her early poem "The Fish" is one such tour de force. Yet she also insisted that she never planned a stanza. Instead, she said, "Words cluster together like chromosomes . . . I may influence an arrangement, or thin it, then try to have successful stanzas identical with the first." Her revisions were many as she tried to construct a coherent "architecture in print." The technique was successful even in the briefest poems like "Arthur Mitchell," addressed to the artist who danced the role of Puck in *A Midsummer Night's Dream*:

> Slim dragonfly
> too rapid for the eye
>   to cage—
> contagious gem of virtuosity—
> make visible, mentality.
> Your jewels of mobility
>   reveal
>   and veil
>   a peacock-tail.

With characteristic modesty, as in her correspondence with me, she also wrote: "I can see no reason for calling my work poetry except that there is no other category in which to put it. Anyone could do what I do, and I am, therefore, the more grateful that those whose judgment I trust should call it poetry."

Although noted for her concrete style, themes and imagery, Miss Moore could handle abstract subjects as well. She had never married but she wrote a poem titled simply "Marriage," filled with wisdom on "This institution,/perhaps one should say enterprise" which, she felt, required "all one's criminal ingenuity/to avoid!" A patchwork of about 30 quotes and references, this poem of 300 spare lines illustrates her style—her "hybrid method of composition" as she called it—as well as anything she wrote. "Marriage" is reprinted in *The Complete Poems*. It originally appeared as a chapbook in 1923, two years after her first book, *Poems*, had been published in London without her knowledge (actually "pirated") by her friends Bryher and H.D.

Moore's three awards in 1952 were but a few in a string of honors in her long career, the first being *The Dial* Award in 1924 for her second book, *Observations*. Her first poem was published much earlier, however, in the May 1915 *Egoist*, and thereafter her work appeared in such magazines as *Poetry*, *The Little Review*, *The Dial*, *Broom* and Alfred Kreymborg's *Others*—all eminent in their time. As editor of *The Dial* from 1926 until its demise in 1929, Miss Moore sought work with "individuality" and "intensity." She found such qualities in Hart Crane, whom she discovered and encouraged; Crane's poem "The Bridge" first appeared under her editorship.

From her earliest work to her last, Marianne Moore drew important critical attention, usually acclaim. By the late 1920s she had become a public personality. Critics found her style particularly suited to the concrete themes she chose, ranging from baseball (she was an avid fan of the Brooklyn Dodgers) to assorted creatures like birds, fish, mammals and reptiles. Meanwhile she defined her poems simply as "observations, experiments in rhythm, composition, and subject matter."

W. H. Auden at first "could not make head nor tail" of Moore's poems, but he later admired her "fastidiousness; the love of order and precision; the astringent, ironical sharpness." He enjoyed especially the fanciful, exotic creatures like "The Pangolin," an "armored animal—scale/lapping scale with spruce-cone regularity." But Randall Jarrell, who criticized Moore for her preoccupation with only "the nicer animals," might have eulogized instead the ants which the anteater pangolin devoured. Jarrell also wrote that her rhymes rejected "the firm kinesthetic confidence of the common English rhyme" and "force us to slow or stumble in our efforts to feel or even to find them." As for Moore's meter, Howard Nemerov once found it "very jittery"—a comment Moore herself understood, for she thought her poem "The Buffalo" had a "kind of pleasing, jerky progress" which readers might not appreciate.

But most others, readers and critics alike, were enthusiastic if somewhat puzzled by her poems. Louis Untermeyer, one of her most appreciative editors and critics, was fascinated by her "scissorlike method" of composition and admired her qualities of elegance and artifice combined with wit and whimsicality. Moore's, he wrote, was "a highly special poetry for specialized tastes," yet he felt that "no contemporary author is more original and less likely to be 'dated.'"

This latest edition of *The Complete Poems* has a few shortcomings. First, the book does not contain Miss Moore's total output. But more important is the fact that some of the poems are abridged. Her famous "Poetry," for instance, is reduced to only three lines:

> I, too, dislike it.
> Reading it, however, with a perfect contempt for it,
>   one discovers in
> it, after all, a place for the ' genuine.'

Fortunately, the original 29-line version is quoted in end-notes to the volume.

On the other hand, some pieces like "To a Prize Bird" are added which did not appear in *The Collected Poems* (1951). But only nine of the 241 "Fables" of LaFontaine which Moore translated and published in 1954 are included in *The Complete Poems*. The publishers justify the many omissions with a cryptic epigraph quotation from Miss Moore: "Omissions are not accidents." Despite its omissions, *The Complete Poems* of Marianne Moore is the best and most complete collection now available. It contains nearly 130 of Moore's finest poems along with 35 pages of her notes on those poems—enough for a good introduction to her work. It is work, after all, which T. S. Eliot called "part of the body of durable poetry written in our time."

When we think of Marianne Moore we are perhaps most often reminded of her war poem "In Distrust of Merits" which begins, "Strengthened to live, strengthened to die for medals and positioned victories?"—and ends,

> Beauty is everlasting
> and dust is for a time.

We are reminded, too, that there are many ways of celebrating poets, and that Miss Moore herself has been the subject of unique honors. In Brooklyn, as I recall, a group has planted and dedicated a tree in her memory every November on her birthday.

Although she loved her adopted city of Brooklyn where she lived from 1929 to 1965, Marianne Moore had an equal affection for the city of her birth. In another letter to me that spring of 1962, in which she detailed her family history in this area, she concluded, "I cannot think any city more cultured than St. Louis."

Review of *The Complete Poems of Marianne Moore* (Macmillan/Viking Press).

St. Louis Post-Dispatch, August 31, 1980, p. 4B.
Helicon Nine, No. 19 (1988) pp. 33-34.

Black poet's rich treasure

Sterling Brown is "a national treasure," writes Michael Harper in his preface to the first collected edition of Brown's poems.

It is especially fitting that Brown's book is one of five volumes in the 1980 National Poetry Series, along with books by Joseph Langland, Ronald Perry, Wendy Salinger and Roberta Spear.

Brown was born in 1901, and it is now nearly a half century since his first book of poems, *Southern Road*, appeared in 1932. He was recognized almost at once as one of the outstanding young black writers of his generation, with Claude McKay, Jean Toomer, Countee Cullen, Langston Hughes and others. As a longtime teacher at Howard University, critic, scholar and editor—*The Negro Caravan* (1941) and other works—Brown has been a mentor of thousands and a legend in his own time.

Brown's *Collected Poems* is unique in that it serves three purposes: first, as a long overdue gathering place of his poems; second, as a sourcebook of the many works by and about Brown, and finally as a tribute to Brown's quiet but powerful influence on three generations of writers.

Brown emerged at a time when Negro folklore and dialect poetry were still largely unappreciated or misunderstood. *The Collected Poems* shows Brown's rather astounding range—as humorist, social realist and serious poet—and his peerless sense of organic form. In this last aspect, form, Brown shows complete versatility. As an authority on jazz and a student of Eliot and Pound and the new poetry of Frost and Sandburg, he wrote free verse, folk ballads and formal sonnets with equal skill.

His folk characters like Slim Greer, Sister Lou and Sporting Beasley are as authentic and colorful as any characters out of E. A. Robinson or Edgar Lee Masters's "Spoon River," for example.

He wrote of classes, too, like "Harlem Street Walkers":

> Why do they walk so tragical
> Oh, never mind, when they are in
> The grateful grave, each whitened skull
> Will grin . . .

And finally, in formal poems like "Mill Mountain," Brown could work the lyrical magic of the best traditional English and American poets:

> . . . We have learned tonight
> That there are havens from all desperate seas,
> And every ruthless war rounds into peace.
> It seems to me that Love can be that peace . . .

Review of *The Collected Poems of Sterling A. Brown*, selected by Michael S. Harper (Harper & Row).

St. Louis Post-Dispatch, November 23, 1980, p. 4B.

THREE FACES OF AUTUMN
Poetry, Prose, Translations

Book shows vast range of Brecht's poetry

Bertolt Brecht (1898-1956) wrote more than forty plays and is best known as a dramatist. Much of his dramatic success, however, lay in the scores of clever, popular and eloquent lyrics and ballads in his plays.

Like certain other playwrights—Maxwell Anderson and Tennessee Williams, for instance—Brecht wrote and published verse piecemeal. In Brecht's case, many of his poems went unpublished during his lifetime.

But Brecht as a poet has not been unknown to American readers. In 1947 H. R. Hays published a 180-page bilingual *Selected Poems* of Brecht whose verse has also appeared in English in a host of anthologies. *Poems 1913-1956* at last brings into English the extent of Brecht's talent, his greatness.

Although the German texts are omitted, the book contains 450 pages of poems in translation arranged in 10 chronological sections. There are 200 additional pages of introduction, profuse and varied notes, an index (in German) and a list of the poems, and a memoir by H. R. Hays. Besides Hays, the 35 translators include such poets as Michael Hamburger, Muriel Rukeyser and Stephen Spender.

The poems are rendered mostly in simple, powerful and moving free verse, and sometimes quite well in rhyme and meter.

Some critics now rank Brecht with Rilke as one of the two or three major German poets of our century; but only time will tell whether his verse will hold its meaning for future readers. Certain qualities of both poets cannot be compared.

Of major importance is Brecht's vast range of form and tone, light to serious. In *Poems 1913-1956* we find a grand scale of devotional, lyric, narrative and satiric verse addressed to audiences of all ages.

Brecht had a unique skill in treating passing events as timeless and universal. American readers will recognize this especially in the section of American poems (1941-1947) when Brecht read and wrote in "the little garden at Santa Monica." There, among other things, he recalled the misdeeds of Hitler and wrote:

A CHARLES GUENTHER RETROSPECTIVE
Prose: Critical Reviews and Essays, 1973-1982

> That soon he will die and dying
> Will have outlived his fame, but even
> If he were to succeed in making this earth
> Uninhabitable, by
> Conquering it, no song
> In his honour could last.

Brecht's poems were not merely topical, but sensitively contemporary.

He could write as a peer of "The Old Man of Downing Street," of Charles Laughton and of Charlie Chaplin. In a poem, "Laughton's Belly," only a Brecht could recognize how "the great man Laughton performed his (belly) like a poem / For his edification and nobody's discomfort."

And more somberly, in "Letter to the Playwright Odets" he notes that in (Clifford) Odets's play *Paradise Lost* the families of the exploiters are destroyed at the end, and Brecht asks, "What do you mean by that?" Are the exploiters weakened, he continues,

> Or should you feel sorry for them?
> . . . do you now feel compassion
> For the man who has stuffed himself sick?

Affluent and successful, Brecht might have eased into a quiet, comfortable life, but he was continually preoccupied with crises, misfortunes, struggle and disorder. Despite his aristocratic background and pampered youth, he championed the poor and oppressed. Some might question the sincerity or force of his convictions on social issues; but there is no doubt of his eloquence, his power of persuading others on these issues:

> The storm that bends the birch trees
> Is held to be violent
> But how about the storm
> That bends the backs of the road-workers?

he asks in a poem "On Violence." We are reminded of Villon and Shelley, whose lives Brecht knew and whose work he translated. Brecht's roots in fact go back to Rome, Greece and Babylon, for there was no time and place he did not identify with. Nor was any creature or event, it seems, unworthy of his attention.

Although Brecht was of our time, oddly he had few counterparts in our time. Like the Belgian Verhaeren, he was a singer of the tentacular cities; and like W. H. Auden, a chronicler of crisis years. His end? Let him sing it himself in these lines from the poem, "His End":

> So that a moon might touch his death with glamour
> He left the town before the end was near . . .
> Towards midnight three continents went under
> Towards dawn America crumbled away
> So that when he died it was as if none of it had ever been
> Neither what he saw, nor what he did not see.

Review of *Poems 1913-1956*, by Bertolt Brecht, edited by Ralph Manheim and John Willett (Methuen).

St. Louis Globe-Democrat, October 18-19,1980, p. 6B.

Fresh and powerful rhymes

The old *Oxford Book of Light Verse* chosen by W. H. Auden over 40 years ago began with Chaucer and ended with the new English laureate John Betjeman. An entirely new selection, *The Oxford Book of Satirical Verse*, chosen by Geoffrey Grigson (Oxford), keeps the almost exclusively British flavor of Auden's anthology but has a bit more spice added. The fare ranges from John Skelton to Clive James (b. 1939). Many old favorites, such as Swift, Pope, Burns and Byron, are included along with poems by Shelley, Peacock, Max Beerbohm and others who did not appear among Auden's choices. Fittingly, Auden himself is well represented in this handsome new collection. Pound, Cummings and Hemingway are among the Americans included.

One of the best poetry collections of the year is *Voices Within the Ark: The Modern Jewish Poets,* an international anthology edited by Howard Schwartz and Anthony Rudolf (Avon). Unlike ordinary paperbacks, this is a large-format volume of more than 1,200 pages. More than 350 modern Jewish poets from over 40 nations are represented. All texts are English originals or in English translation. Altogether this is a superb chorus of "Voices."

While there are many books of love sonnets, one of the latest and best collections of sonnets on many themes including love, death, nature and isolation is *This Powerful Rhyme*, selected by Helen Plotz (Greenwillow Books). The choice ranges from early English examples by Wyatt, Spenser, Shakespeare, Donne and Milton to modern American sonnets by Richard Eberhart, Raymond Henri, Howard Nemerov and Muriel Rukeyser. Through fads and fashions, the sonnet—even in distorted forms—has always had its adherents. This beautifully bound, meticulously edited volume adds new lustre to the sonnet.

A fresh, unusual anthology is *News of the Universe: Poems of Twofold Consciousness*, chosen and introduced by Robert Bly (Sierra Club Books). It contains 150 poems and prose poems by 75 poets who represent many centuries and cultures. The theme of the collection grows out of the old Classic vs. Romantic confrontation which traces back, in modern times, to the eighteenth century. The modern poems are particularly well chosen as touchstones between the world of plants and animals and the world of humanity.

THREE FACES OF AUTUMN
Poetry, Prose, Translations

Few editors have dared to place the translator of a literary work above the original foreign-language author. In *The Oxford Book of Verse in English Translation* (Oxford), editor Charles Tomlinson does just that, stressing the creative aspects of translations by English and American poets from Gavin Douglas (1474-1522) to Michael Alexander (b.1941). Much of the work is from Greek, Latin and Hebrew sources, but some Germanic, Romantic and other languages are represented. Extracts from Fitzgerald's famous *Rubaiyat* are included, along with work by other fine translators of all periods of English and American culture. The Pounds (Ezra and his son Omar) are here with Dryden, Swift, Pope, Rossetti and scores of other names. Both poems and translators are well chosen.

Thousands of poets have written about New York City. Howard Moss, poetry editor of *The New Yorker*, has gathered about 200 of these poems by 130 poets in an anthology titled *New York: Poems* (Avon), a handsome paperback of 350 pages. Interestingly, many of the poets are not native New Yorkers; and some, like Jiménez and Lorca, are native Spaniards. British, Puerto Ricans and Midwesterners alike sing the city's praises. New York-born Howard Nemerov and English-born John Morris, both at Washington University, are among the poets represented.

By coincidence, two unusually fine collections of Roman poetry, ancient and modern, have appeared from university presses. They are *Roman Poetry: From the Republic to the Silver Age*, translated and introduced by Dorothea Wender (Southern Illinois), and *A Roman Collection*, edited and introduced by Miller Williams (University of Missouri). Americans "feel right at home with the Romans," Wender writes in her preface. Williams's volume supports this attitude with a variety of good pieces by the writing residents of the American Academy in Rome. Richard Wilbur's sestet "To the Etruscan Poets" summarizes the efforts of all writers, old and new, in the concluding lines:

> You strove to leave some line of verse behind
> Like a fresh track across a field of snow,
> Not reckoning that all could melt and go.

African poetry is no longer a primitive novelty to the world of literature. It is appreciated for its esthetic and social functions in African life and culture. *Leaf and Bone: African Praise-Poems*, an anthology with commentary by Judith Gleason (Viking), is an attractive selection. The lyrics and comments are organized into a dozen sections by types of "praise" to natural and social subjects. The final section, "Praise to the End" is of special interest, for it contains nothing but eight blank pages (by design or accident?). But the "Presence of Spirits" section is haunting, beautiful.

St. Louis Post-Dispatch, December 7, 1980, p. 6L.

THREE FACES OF AUTUMN
Poetry, Prose, Translations

Poetry: Warren was never better

Robert Penn Warren is one of those giant oaks in the forest of American letters. Born in Kentucky 75 years ago, he was educated at Vanderbilt, California and Oxford, and for 50 years taught English at a half dozen American universities. For over 40 years—several generations—the texts he wrote or edited, including *Understanding Poetry* and *Understanding Fiction,* done in collaboration with Cleanth Brooks, have affected the work of tens of thousands of writers. Perhaps he is the greatest single influence on American writing today. Along the way, Warren has published 34 books, including 10 novels and 13 volumes of poetry. He has garnered scores of honors, among them the National Medal for Literature, the National Book Award and three Pulitzer Prizes (one for fiction, two for poetry).

But aside from this clutter of awards, or perhaps in spite of them, Warren remains an incredibly fine poet. *Being Here*, a selection of about 50 poems dated 1977-1980, is wrought with the sure hand of a Landor or Yeats and compares favorably with anything he has ever published. *Being Here* contains five sections of poems and is arranged thematically, "with echoes, repetitions, and variations in feeling and tonality," as Warren explains in an afterword. That is, the themes are not monotonously clustered in separate sections but are artfully repeated throughout the book. Care in arrangement of poems, as Warren shows here, can enhance even the finest quality of composition. The thematic repetitions are haunting at times and seem cyclic, as in life; in fact, the structure of the book forms a kind of autobiographical narrative.

The narrative mode has always been one of Warren's strengths. He has an unusual ability to deal with persons, places and events on several planes, from multiple viewpoints. His book opens with the poem "Speleology," at once crisply descriptive and self-reflective with its lines,

> I must have been six when I first found the cave-mouth
> Under ledges moss-green, and moss-green the inner dark.
> Each summer I came, in twilight peered in...
>
> Years later, past dreams, I have lain
> In darkness and heard the depth of that unending song...
>
> And in darkness have even asked: Is this all? What is all?

This is followed by other poems on Warren's boyhood, then a poem on a
funeral and a long "Recollection in Upper Ontario, From Long Before."
The first section also contains poems on sleep and dream—"The
Moonlight's Dream" and "Platonic Drowse"—and these themes are
repeated in later sections in such poems as "Dreaming in Daylight,"
"Dream, Dump-heap and Civilization" and "Vision." In another poem,
"Better Than Counting Sheep," Warren reveals his formula for finding
elusive sleep. "Try to summon," he writes, "All those ever known who are
dead now, and soon / It will seem they are there in your room, not chairs
enough / For the party. . . . / Then you are, suddenly /Alone."

Warren can even take worn abstract topics, always difficult to deal with—
truth, for instance—and treat them with fresh honesty. In "Vision" he
writes,

> The vision will come—the Truth be revealed—but
> Not even its vaguest nature you know—ah, truth
> About what?. . .
> Can it be that the vision has, long back, already come—
> And you just didn't recognize it?

And more tersely, in a poem titled "Truth":

> Truth is what you cannot tell.
> Truth is for the grave.
> Truth is only the flowing shadow cast
> By the wind-tossed elm . . . .

As with all poets whose gift is mainly narrative, Warren has prosaic
lapses. But a poet cannot often recount an event and sing about it at the
same time without straining for artificiality. Warren strains only for
compression, the hard, cryptic phrase. Yet he sometimes releases
unexpected melody:

> . . . the past is de-fogged
> And old foot tracks of folly show fleetingly clear before
> Rationalization again descends, as from seaward.

Time and the seasons, wildlife and the harvests, and the poet's travels
form the bases of other poems. There is a strong recurrent lunar theme,
too, in poems like "The Moonlight's Dream," "August Moon," "On into

the Night" and, at the close of the book, "Night Walking" in which the poet encounters his son "silent, face up / To the moon" and admonishes him:

> At any rate, you must swear never,
> Not even in secret, the utmost, to be ashamed
> To have lifted bare arms to that icy
> Blaze and redeeming white light of the world.

Readers familiar with Warren's earlier ballads, or his shorter narratives and lyrics like "Revelation," "Pursuit" and "End of Season," will find many of these new poems comparably powerful and durable. Yes, Robert Penn Warren is an oak like those "Bearded Oaks" he wrote about in a poem nearly 40 years ago, when he mused:

> We live in time, so little time
> And we learn all so painfully
> That we may spare this hour's term
> To practice for eternity.

Review of *Being Here: Poetry 1977-1980*, by Robert Penn Warren, (Random House).

St. Louis Globe-Democrat, December 27-28, 1980, p. 6E.

The Frost-Cox letters

Books on Robert Frost continue to blossom. But as this new account shows, readers who believe there is little left to learn about Frost may be surprised. The friendship between Frost and Sidney Cox, who taught at Dartmouth, lasted from 1911 until Cox's death in 1952 at age 62. That friendship is examined in detail objectively for the first time.

As Frost devotees know, Cox wrote the early biography, *A Swinger of Birches,* which Alice Cox had published five years after her husband's death. Now 18 years after Frost's death we have in this new volume the surviving Frost-Cox correspondence, which includes nearly 50 previously unpublished Frost letters. Unfortunately, some of the Cox letters are lost. Frost considered Cox a "great teacher" but ironically admitted, "I wish I had kept some of the great letters he wrote me but I am no curator of letters or anything else."

Nevertheless, this collection of correspondence, finely woven with commentary by William Evans, shows how deep-rooted, frank and enduring the friendship was. Frost truly liked Cox and needed his support, for Cox was a good listener and a good companion. As for Cox, he found in Frost (who was once a teacher himself) rare insight and understanding. As Alice later wrote, Sidney "might have done more good writing if he had not burned himself up with his teaching, and his teaching came first with him." Like many a "great teacher," Cox was disappointed at not being promoted; in searching for a new position, he secured a recommendation from Frost.

Of course there were trials and misunderstandings. One test of the friendship occurred in 1926-27, when a publisher asked Frost—who already had six honorary degrees and a Pulitzer Prize—to name a biographer. Instead of naming Cox, who considered himself Frost's Boswell, Frost invited Gorham Munson to write the biography. Still, Cox supported Munson and gave him a lively account of the poet which Munson used in his book (1927). This experience made Cox work harder in the race to be Frost's biographer, and two years later his own book, *Robert Frost: Original "Ordinary Man"* appeared.

Frost, an intensely private person, did not want Cox "thrusting in," and perhaps felt he had been too revealing in conversation to let Cox be his biographer. But when the friendship became strained, Frost felt neglected and the warm relationship resumed. Frost's manner, his mask, was abrupt and gruff as usual while Cox remained kind, generous and loyal.

Frost had only two other friends, Louis Untermeyer and John Bartlett, with whom he corresponded voluminously throughout his life. The Frost-Cox letters show an important new facet, if not a new dimension to the lives of both men. Frost put it best perhaps: "Our intimacy was a curious blend of differences that if properly handled might prove an almost literary curiosity."

Review of *Robert Frost and Sidney Cox: Forty Years of Friendship*, by William R. Evans (University Press of New England).

St. Louis Post-Dispatch, July 5, 1981, p. 4F.

Judging a poem is like judging a rose

Serious poetry practically never hits the best-seller lists. But to their credit, many major trade publishers and university presses continue to underwrite poets and to issue new titles. One reason perhaps is that more good poetry is being written now than at any time in American history; but this is a safe assumption when we consider population gains and the growth of higher education.

Still, not all critics agree. Reviewing a well-known popular anthology recently, Richard Kostelanetz observed, with dismay, that that collection represented the "garbage death" of our culture. The anthology, purporting to include the best American poetry from all regions, was "simply undistinguished." Most of the poems he found "prosy in language and loose in form, with weak line breaks and mundane subject matter. . . In lieu of poetic language and poetic tropes, the book is filled with poetic attitudinizing—the authorial voice making the kinds of comments that we associate not with accountants or used-car dealers but with the profession of poetry." And he quotes convincing examples.

Because no two tastes will always agree, the reader must acquire and develop his own taste. In some respects judging a poem is not unlike judging a rose. Most important is form, whether traditional or free, suitable to the theme ("variety" in a rose). Important, too, are imagery (color), freshness (substance) and strong, supportive language (the "stem and foliage" of a rose). Finally there is balance and length (size) and a right stage of "bloom"—that is, a poem neither too obvious nor too abstruse. Some readers will recognize right away the *duende* or magic of the poem, just as the trained rose judge will notice the overall inflorescence of a given variety of hybrid tea. Perhaps the comparison is far-fetched, but among the books described here, there is surely something to please nearly everyone.

Few American poets today are more consistently formal than John Ashbery. His latest book, *Shadow Train* (Viking), contains 50 poems of 16 lines each. Yet these poems are not, as his publicity states, "of identical length," for within his chosen form of four quatrains Ashbery varies the metrical patterns and line lengths considerably. Although many of the poems look alike page after page, they are "organically" formed of differing substances: observations, experiences, objects, events. Ashbery deals with the "deeper outside" things, with "the truth inside meaning." He writes below the surfaces of life, wondrously, as an observer of our world who is submerged in another.

George Barlow defines "Gumbo" as the "food of the spirits." His new book, *Gumbo* (Doubleday) is a slice of Americana, mostly West Coast places, types and happenings. We can't be indifferent to Barlow's style; either we relate and respond to it or we don't. Although many of the pieces are private jottings to friends, others like "American Plethora" (a put-on of the McDonald's menu) are easily understood. The best poems are a long "Eulogy" and portraits titled "Titta" and "Main Man Gone," all strong and poignant.

William Pitt Root considers himself a westerner, "happiest living near an ocean or a desert." This fact is important, for in his latest book, *Reasons for Going It on Foot* (Atheneum), Root is preoccupied with water-land imagery. There is "land over a blue idea /of godliness," "a forked twig running /at the speed of water," and a god who "is light dissolving/stones sea and each horizon." The style is light and easy, sensuous and eloquent. Root's poetry has "pure" language in free form. The blending of themes— European, Native American and Oriental—is unique and appealing.

Daryl Hine, an editor and translator, has long been admired as a poet's poet. His work is saturated with a unique mixture of the traditional "stuff" of poetry: Greek, French and English themes and references, for instance. His skill in constructing a poem dominates in such pieces as "Linear A," based on the Greek alphabet. Hine's new *Selected Poems* (Atheneum) is an elegant show case of work by a very fine craftsman.

Heather McHugh's third book of verse, *A World of Difference* (Houghton Mifflin), is a kind of capsule commentary on our times. McHugh delves into life with fresh, breezy immediacy. In "Elemental," for instance, she writes, "I want to last one more winter,/live in this austerity and learn /the elements responsible /for weeping, burning, /burying and song." This is a strange, strong and exciting book.

What a rarity! *The Booth Interstate*, poems by Thomas Rabbitt (Knopf), is a book of sonnets. Or rather, to purists, it is a collection of 14-liners which have occasional hard and soft rhymes with loosely woven meter. There are single sonnets and sequences, including a pair on poets Hart Crane and

A CHARLES GUENTHER RETROSPECTIVE
Prose: Critical Reviews and Essays, 1973-1982

John Berryman, who are among Rabbitt's influences. The settings are
varied: New England, the South, Russia and Poland. Rabbitt has a fine gift
for narrative, tightly spun in these short poems. The range and tone are
startling, from idyllic to violent, from hauntingly imaginative to realistic.

Radcliffe Squires has a gift for taking the obvious world around us and
showing us new dimensions we have never seen before. In a word, he may
be called a "metaphysical" poet. Instead of the idea of a soul inhabiting a
body, for example, he writes of "a body inhabiting a soul." The gardens he
describes in *Gardens of the World* (Louisiana State) are but one section of
nine poems in his latest book. There are 30 other poems on themes ranging
from ancient Greece to the modern American West.

David Wagoner, novelist and poet, writes some of his best narratives in his
poetry. Each of his poems, it seems, tells a story in taut, precise language.
Yet his descriptive power is found even in short quatrains like "For a Bird-
watcher" who is perceived as "invisible, a part of the landscape /Among
the singers over and under earth." Wagoner's new poems, *Landfall*
(Atlantic-Little, Brown), cover almost every aspect of nature—sea, sky,
fire, and his own garden where the buds of a root-bound rosebush "Open
and close the eyes of summer."

St. Louis Post-Dispatch, August 9, 1981, p. 4B.

THREE FACES OF AUTUMN
Poetry, Prose, Translations

Collection puts poet's work in perspective

Sylvia Plath will always be viewed from two extremes of fact and legend. There are two ways of reading her: with Romantic, intuitive feeling or with total sympathetic detachment. It is best, perhaps, to blend these ways, for she poses special problems.

How, for instance, can one identify with a brilliant, elegant young poet who in the fullness of success took her own life?

The answer is not in identifying with her but in patiently assimilating the poems with mature contemplation. *The Collected Poems*, long overdue, are the starting point, for the poet's work must be seen as a whole of three or four parts. This is what Miss Plath's husband, Ted Hughes, has done in editing the collection. The edition contains a numbered sequence of all 224 poems Miss Plath wrote after 1956 along with 50 (juvenilia) written before that year.

Hughes's presentation of Miss Plath is done with exceedingly fine taste. He focuses not on his own role in her life but on her poetry and its chronology and development. In a surprisingly brief five-page introduction he reveals Miss Plath as a precise, finical writer who never scrapped any of her efforts. Instead, she worked every poem into some final form suitable to her.

Hughes observes: "Her attitude to her verse was artisan-like; if she couldn't get a table out of the material, she was quite happy to get a chair, or even a toy. The end product for her was not so much a successful poem, as something that had temporarily exhausted her ingenuity." Thus, *The Collected Poems* contains not only what juvenilia she saved, but all poems she wrote after 1956.

The first phase of Miss Plath's work consists of more than 200 poems written before 1956. Hughes chose 50 of these poems that seem, at their best, "as distinctive and as finished" as her later work. He arranged these pieces in an appendix and added a complete list, alphabetized by title, of all the early poems with dates of composition. He also adds 22 pages of notes on the later poems. The second phase, as defined by Hughes, dates from early 1956 to late 1960 and is represented here by about 127 poems. The third and last phase extends from September 1960 (when Plath started dating her typescripts) to her final poems, "Balloons" and "Edge," both written on Feb. 5, 1963, less than a week before her death.

Sylvia Plath's genius lay not only in her dogged, fussy habits of composition but in her ability to play more roles more intensely than almost any other poet of her time. Her poems have personal and projected dramas, inner symbols and imagery, distinctive sound and substance, and unique form and texture. Even the early poems, which Hughes calls "inspired highjinks, but frequently quite a bit more," show an exciting talent. There's nothing wrong with reading Miss Plath with feeling only, for the excitement generated by intuitive discovery. One can at least relate to her, if not identify with her. But one can relate better perhaps to a pain-wracked Keats (as I did at 17) or a storm-tossed Shelley—or even the brave rheumatic Diane Wakoski.

The reader must be aware that Miss Plath entered her own poems in an infraconfessional and messianic way that makes most other "confessional" poetry seem bland by comparison. Beginning one poem with the title "I Am Vertical," she continues:

> But I would rather be horizontal.
> I am not a tree with my root in the soil
> Sucking up minerals and motherly love
> So that each March I may gleam into leaf . . .

A year and a half later this idea grew in the cryptic poem "Ariel," written on her 30th birthday, Oct. 27, 1962, less than four months before she took her own life early one morning:

> And I
> Am the arrow,
> The dew that flies
> Suicidal, at one with the drive
> Into the red
> Eye, the cauldron of morning.

Review of *The Collected Poems,* by Sylvia Plath (Harper and Row).

St. Louis Globe-Democrat, January 23-24, 1982 p. 4B.

THREE FACES OF AUTUMN
Poetry, Prose, Translations

Skills honed on verses

Nearly every eminent prose writer also has written verse—Thomas Wolfe, Ernest Hemingway, Willa Cather, James T. Farrell. Some, like Thomas Hardy, D. H. Lawrence and Tennessee Williams, have written strong, memorable lines. For other writers versecraft may be a rhetorical exercise or just a warm-up for more important works of fiction or drama.

The poems of William Faulkner, John Updike and E. B. White now are available in fine, well-edited volumes. Faulkner's book, introduced by Joseph Blotner, includes a dozen "Mississippi Poems," which first appeared in a very limited edition two years ago. (That earlier edition consisted of facsimile typescripts of the poems, reproduced from the collection of Louis D. Brodsky.) These poems, with an accompanying essay on "Verse, Old and Nascent" by Faulkner, are dated October 1924. To these is added a group of 16 sonnets titled "Helen: A Courtship," dated June-September 1925.

Faulkner was more imitative in his verse than in his novels. The poems have many classical images (even fauns and nymphs) drawn from Victorian poets like Swinburne and from the French Symbolists. Such images appear in the sonnets written to Helen Baird, who was 21 in 1925 and on whom Faulkner modelled the character Pat Robyn in his early novel *Mosquitoes*. The "Mississippi Poems" have fewer classical references and deal mostly with nature and the seasons. Most of Faulkner's poems have a golden serenity one associates with an idealized antebellum South.

John Updike's and E. B. White's verse, on the other hand, is brash, light, topical and funny—and sometimes serious. While Updike is best known as a novelist, four of his 25 books are verse and his awards include a 1959 Guggenheim Fellowship for poetry. *The Carpentered Hen*, which Knopf has reissued as a "present" to Updike on his fiftieth birthday this year, was actually his first book, published 25 years ago. Most of these poems originally appeared in the *New Yorker* magazine where Updike worked on the staff from 1955 to 1957.

In his new foreword to this book Updike acknowledges his debt to a host of light versifiers from F. P. Adams and Ogden Nash to E. B. White and Phyllis McGinley. Although most of his later poetry (all in print with

216

Knopf) is more serious, Updike admits that light verse gave him an "aesthetic bliss" as keen as any he ever experienced. *The Carpentered Hen* holds its age well. Except for a few dated references (to some movie stars, for instance), the poems are fresh and appealing. Some readers may consider pieces like "Poetess" and "To an Usherette" sexist, but no topic or purpose of such light verse is to be taken too seriously.

E. B. White in prefacing his *Poems and Sketches* shows a healthy respect for poetry, which he defines as "what is memorable." Poetry to him is moving and mysterious. As for his sketches, he uses the word as an "umbrella" for everything that is not a poem. About half of this book is verse; the other half consists of articles and stories, mostly very short pieces, some of which appeared in the *New Yorker*.

Like his fellow *New Yorker* writer James Thurber, with whom he once collaborated, White considered almost no subject sacred or taboo. His interests ranged over every aspect of life. It is almost superfluous to mention White's influence, through his 20 books and many magazine articles, on American letters and tastes. It easily can be said of the *Poems and Sketches* that there must be something fundamentally wrong with any reader of the English language who cannot find something delightful in this book.

Faulkner's poems have a rare literary and scholarly appeal. The many photos in *Helen: A Courtship*, and especially the 100-page essay by Carvel Collins, add much interest to the book for Faulkner fans. Updike's and White's volumes have a general appeal, as much as their other books. Faulkner, Updike and White all have known the forms and techniques of poetry, and used them well. Their knowledge and practice of verse improved their sense of language and rhythm—and added strong new dimensions to their prose.

Review of *Helen: A Courtship* and *Mississippi Poems*, by William Faulkner (Tulane/Yoknapatawpha), *The Carpentered Hen and Other Tame Creatures*, by John Updike (Knopf) and *Poems and Sketches of E.B. White* (Harper and Row).

St. Louis Post-Dispatch, May 2, 1982, p. 4F.

THREE FACES OF AUTUMN
Poetry, Prose, Translations

Finding the rare, right words for poetry

The French expression *le mot juste* implies much more than "the right word." It contains the idea of the precise word for which no other word or synonym exists. Yet many French words, like English words, have so many variant meanings that it is almost impossible to translate them. How useful it would be, especially for reviewers, to produce a precise word that also accurately describes the many facets of a book under consideration.

This would be invaluable when dealing with poetry, which challenges the reviewer in several ways. First, even in a long review it is impossible to cover every poem in a book. So there are some gaps; only what the reviewer likes or dislikes or understands is stressed. Nor can a reviewer convey adequately in prose the "spirit" of a single poem or of the total book. But the reviewer tries.

To illustrate the problem, here are seven recently published and notable books of American poetry with seven key words I'd use to describe them.

Elizabeth Bartlett's word is "ingenious." In her book, *Memory Is No Stranger* (Ohio University) she continues writing in her unique form of the 12-tone poem, inspired by composer Arnold Schönberg's 12-tone scale. Each of the poems has 12 lines—six couplets of 12 syllables each. The form lends itself well to various uses as rhymed or free verse, in single lyrics, in multi-part poems, and even in narrative sequences. Ms. Bartlett handles the form gracefully and sensitively. This is smooth, undulant and often brilliant poetry.

But "undulant" is a word reserved for Marvin Bell, whose life literally flows through his poetry. His book, *These Green-Going-to-Yellow* (Atheneum), is not "confessional" in tone, but Bell is personally involved in each of the 31 poems, even in the narratives. Bell's lines are hard, direct and almost prosy at times. But the scenes and episodes—whether of Africa, Italy, the South Seas, New York City or Iowa—carry subtle messages. From the core of his own experience he relates "the strange case of humanity, / whose suffering goes on and on."

Robert Bly is more "meditative" in his new book, *The Man in the Black Coat Turns* (Dial) than in his earlier works. These poems deal mostly with male grief and with relations between fathers and sons, topics seldom covered in American poetry. The grief underlies and permeates such poems as "Mourning Pablo Neruda," "The Grief of Men" and "Kennedy's Inauguration." Bonds between father and son are treated in "The Prodigal Son," "My Father's Wedding 1924" and in the poet's lines to his ten-year-old son Noah. Bly's poetry is strong, gentle and penetrating.

David Ignatow too has written of a paternal relationship in his poem titled "Father and Son," among his new poems in *Whisper to the Earth* (Atlantic/Little, Brown). But the "relationship" is grim and unreal, and the episode is deadly. A mugger hugs the poet around the throat and demands money. "Is this my son," the poet muses, "this tall, husky young man who is extracting the bills from the fold and now returning the wallet?" They are strangers, but an uncanny bond exists between them. Ignatow is "perceptive." He probes the depths of persons, creatures and objects—even an apple, a leaf, a stone, an insect.

Philip Levine's poems, *One for the Rose* (Atheneum), are extraordinarily "vibrant" in many senses of the word—resonant, virile and vital, for instance. His style is like Bell's, flat and casual, sometimes called "projective." There is one personal episode after another, recounted mostly in segments of 30 to 60 lines. The smooth, running description whets the reader's interest and curiosity. There is a broad range of themes, from commonplace memories of childhood to imaginary voyages of the spirit.

Louis Simpson's poetry alternates from personal to impersonal. The slices of life he serves the reader are all genuine or "veritable" (his key word). His book, *Caviare at the Funeral* (Franklin Watts), is largely narrative, dealing with events from World War II Europe to present-day America. As a change of pace, one poem, "Profession of Faith" contains a revealing credo:

> As a writer I imagine, characters,
> giving them definite features
> and bodies, a color of hair.
> I imagine what they feel
> and, finally make them speak.
> Increasingly I have come to believe
> that the things we imagine
> are not amusements, they are real.

THREE FACES OF AUTUMN
Poetry, Prose, Translations

Finally, Robert Penn Warren in his collection, *Rumor Verified: Poems 1979-1980* (Random House), proves again what an American stalwart he is. "Substantial" is the word for him, in all its manifold meanings including steady, solid, sensible and even (in a creative sense) opulent. But beyond the structure of the man and his poetry, or perhaps in that structure, is a metaphysical strength sorely needed in our time. Warren has a grand concept of what makes a poem, yet he is not at all grandiose. Rather, he finds reality and eternity in small things like blowing dandelion fuzz and the crackling of pond-ice. No review can convey the beauty and power of this poetry.

Indeed, these capsule reviews have consumed scores of adjectives. And each of the key words also describes, in some degree, all the other books. For poetry is wondrously open-ended. Just as every poet continuously defines himself in his work, so too is every poem its own unique definition of the craft. In a word, this is poetry.

St. Louis Post Dispatch, June 6, 1982, p. 4E.

Lives behind the lines of poetry

The philosopher Alfred Whitehead reminds us that ideas are more important than people and events—but oh, how fascinating it is to read gossip about the lives and doings of others!

Eileen Simpson's recollections are crisp and detailed; at times they seem a virtual soap opera about an entire American literary generation just passed. Yet they serve a positive aim in humanizing one poet who, ten years after his death by suicide, now tends to be forgotten.

Mrs. Simpson married the late John Berryman (1914-1972) in October, 1942. Until their divorce 15 years later, she shared the strange, unpredictable intensity of his life while developing her own career as a psychotherapist and author.

The title *Poets in Their Youth* (adapted from a line by Wordsworth) may be misleading. The book is much more than the title implies, for the author describes a wide circle of poets, novelists, critics and philosophers. Many of these were well into their vocations of writing and teaching when the memoir begins, about 1941.

There are vignettes of Mark Van Doren, Allen Tate, Edmund Wilson, Saul Bellow, Ezra Pound, T. S. Eliot and many others.

But the main characters are the Berrymans' contemporaries, born during and just before World War I. The list reads like a necrology of some of the finest poets of that generation. Dylan Thomas (1914-1953) was the first of the group to die. Ten years later Ted Roethke (1908-1963) died; he was followed by Randall Jarrell (1914-1965), Richard Blackmur (1904-1965) and Delmore Schwartz (1913-1966). The last to die, following Berryman himself, was Robert Lowell (1917-1977). These writers were among the closest friends of the Berrymans.

Of equal influence in their lives were novelists, including wives of some of the poets: Caroline Gordon (Mrs.Tate), Mary McCarthy (Mrs. Wilson), Jean Stafford and Elizabeth Hardwick (Lowell's wives), and Elizabeth Pollet (Mrs. Schwartz).

Poets in Their Youth is a book of revelations. A few glimpses:

THREE FACES OF AUTUMN
Poetry, Prose, Translations

•Simpson likened the "PR boys" (co-founders of *Partisan Review*) to "clever little faces above Buster Brown collars"; and later to "a cross between Rabbinical scholars and bookies, who argued and shouted at one another in a smoke-filled office littered with manuscripts."

• Van Doren (who was best man at the Berrymans' wedding) was a particularly strong influence on John; praise from him, and from Schwartz, Tate and Blackmur "mattered most" as Berryman wrote his finest poems ("Dream Songs" and "Homage to Mistress Bradstreet").

• The arguments between John and his mother following his father's suicide left Eileen "a helpless observer," exasperated with both.

• While John smoked three packs a day and drank heavily, Randall (Jarrell) "didn't drink or smoke, disapproved of gossip and sexual innuendoes in conversation, and had no tolerance for small talk—didn't even know what small talk was."

• The Philip Rahvs's cat was "scary" and suspected of being "a snoop and a spy." It eavesdropped on conversation, then "slunk off to its room to record what had been said." Natalie, seeing Eileen's uneasiness, took the pet in her lap and stroked it—"Which led Philip to expound, in his rich Lithuanian accent, a theory he had: A woman who says she wants a child would, if she understood herself better, realize that what she really wanted was a cat."

• Delmore (Schwartz), the intriguer, had hinted to Lowell that Jean Stafford "was interested in another man (himself perhaps?)" whereupon Lowell socked him. "The fistfight that ensued brought the Ellery Street winter to a dramatic close, and explained the coolness between the two men."

• Berryman was so apprehensive about the reviews of his first book (*The Dispossessed*) that he had Eileen read and digest them for him. John was also "capable of not answering the telephone no matter how persistent the ring, or not opening the mail no matter how attractive the envelopes."

A mixture of truth and good taste, humanizing substances, seems to be the stuff of *Poets in Their Youth*. For whatever reasons, Simpson deals sparely with John's poems, leaving their criticism to others. Other recent books, especially on Blackmur and Lowell, give a more complete account of the life and work of writers who influenced Berryman. But Simpson's memoir has warmth, humor and precision; it is essential reading for anyone interested in Berryman, the man and his poetry.

Review of *Poets in Their Youth, A Memoir*, by Eileen Simpson (Random House).

St. Louis Post-Dispatch, July 18, 1982, p. 4E.

Critical Reviews and Essays

1983-1992

Pasolini, an Italian legend

> Life and literature: Pasolini bound them tightly together to the
> point of confusing them, to the point that they canceled each other
> out, and then, by a miracle, were reborn from their ashes entirely
> distinct, each with its own appearance, or were sublimated into a
> utopia similar to a negative theology.

So writes Enzo Siciliano in his foreword to Pasolini's *Poems*, a companion
volume simultaneously published with his own remarkable biography of
the Italian writer and film maker. Not since Gabriele D'Annunzio has an
Italian poet so captured the public imagination and turned his life into a
legend.

Even the circumstances of his death—he was found murdered in 1975 in a
deserted field near Rome at age 53—seemed to punctuate his controversial
life and reputation. (A homosexual prostitute, who was perhaps politically
motivated, was the slayer.)

Pasolini, a brilliant film maker, writer, actor, director and photographer,
became both famous and scandalous. His own cultural sensibilities often
clashed with public taste in such films as *Mamma Roma*, *Canterbury
Tales*, *Arabian Nights* and *The Gospel According to Saint Matthew*. He
was even brought to trial for several films, but he was eventually absolved
or he paid damages.

Pasolini wrote two experimental novels, one of which shared the coveted
Viareggio prize in 1955. These works focused on the working class and on
children in the Roman slums, themes he used in several films. A poet of
many paradoxes, he was a Catholic Communist who was eventually
expelled from the Communist party for his independent spirit.

He wrote his first poem at the age of seven. His early verse was in dialect,
but he soon began writing pure, eloquent Italian poems of rigorous rhythm
and structure. His later poetry became more meditative and religious.
Curiously, he often expressed radical ideas in classical and archaic forms.
Many of his poems, including "Gramsci's Ashes," which won him a share

of another Viareggio prize in 1957, are written in a three-line stanza adapted from the form of Dante's *Divine Comedy*.

Norman MacAfee's volume is the largest selection of Pasolini's poems in English, but other translations long have been available in magazines and anthologies. The poems have always presented problems to translators. For instance, William Weaver's version of "Appenine" in Carlo Golino's 20-year-old anthology, *Contemporary Italian Poetry* (California) is an excellent rendering, but the syntax and meaning in MacAfee's version are quite different.

Biographer Enzo Siciliano, who played the role of Simon in the film on St. Matthew, knew all aspects of Pasolini and presents them in detail, honestly and objectively it seems. He understands the poems particularly well, and how the poet's life corresponded with them.

In pursuing many arts Pasolini had remarkable powers of self-renewal. In 1954 he wrote stoically,

> It is a dim hum, life, and those lost
> in it serenely lose it,
> if their hearts are filled with it. . .
> But I with the conscious heart
> of one who can live only in history,
> will I ever again be able to act with pure passion
> when I know our history is over?

Siciliano observes that in 1960 "everything seems truly finished" for Pasolini, "the trial of the inner life has ended with no appeal." But in the decade of the sixties he embarked on his most productive career in the cinema.

"I love life fiercely, desperately," Pasolini told a French interviewer, "and I believe this fierceness, this desperation will carry me to the end." He took extreme measures—even, it was alleged, staging a fake holdup of a shopkeeper, to understand and document his era. That era, he felt, was "a time of total evil" as he described it in his 1957 poem, "The Religion of My Time." But in a later appendix to that poem, addressing his mother, Pasolini tempered that pessimism with "A Light" in these lines:

A CHARLES GUENTHER RETROSPECTIVE
Prose: Critical Reviews and Essays, 1983-1992

. . . if something pure and always young
remains, it will be your meek world. . .you'll be there;
in every place where once the impure living
laughed and once again will laugh, you'll bestow
the purity, the only judgment left us,
and it's terrible and sweet, for we never have
despair without some small hope.

Review of *Pasolini: A Biography*, by Enzo Siciliano, translated by John
Shepley (Random House) and *Poems*, by Pier Paolo Pasolini, translated by
Norman MacAfee with Luciano Martinengo (Random House).

St. Louis Post-Dispatch, January 23, 1983, p. 4B.

THREE FACES OF AUTUMN
Poetry, Prose, Translations

A stroll through the 'Galleries' of poetry

Like other arts and crafts, poetry increases in enjoyment the more it is understood or practiced. And like all other artists, poets need publicists, critics and interpreters to help an audience appreciate and enjoy the work.

The book of poems, or an anthology, is the "gallery" where a poet's work is brought to public view.

After World War I, writer-anthologists like Joseph Auslander, Max Eastman and Louis Untermeyer influenced tastes in verse. Eastman's *Enjoyment of Poetry* first appeared 70 years ago and is still in print with Scribner's in a "reproduced edition" ($20). Auslander's *Winged Horse* (1927) and its companion anthology nurtured my early boyhood interest in poetry. Such collections promoted hundreds of new and traditional poets up to the mid-century—a period when fresh treatment of new and old themes was the order of the day.

Originality still is an important element of poetry of the 1980s, but now it is more casual and less obtrusive than it seemed in the earlier poems of, say, Carl Sandburg, E. E. Cummings and Marianne Moore. There is a wealth of enjoyment in certain new books of 1983, by poets of widely differing styles and attitudes.

Amy Clampitt, for instance, strongly "possesses" and assimilates her subjects. She has published poems in magazines for about five years. Her first collection, *The Kingfisher* (Knopf), is astonishingly rich in language and insight. Like a few other new poets (Marilyn Hacker and Pamela White Hadas) she commands form with ease, yet subordinates technique to meaning. The form, in other words, follows the function. Whether in sapphics, a sonnet or in tough free verse, her style delights us. Her themes of nature, culture and customs are broadly appealing.

Nikki Giovanni's poetry has more aural appeal. This fact, as well as her own vibrant personality, accounts for her popularity as a reader well known to many U. S. audiences. Her latest book, *Those Who Ride the Night Winds* (Morrow), deals with people who have tried to make changes, or have gone against the tide and "are determined to push us into the next century, galaxy—possibility." There are poems on John Lennon, Lorraine Hansberry, Robert Kennedy and many others more or less

eminent—friends, lovers, mothers and the poet herself. Giovannni's style
is concrete, readable.

John Martone's voice is more soft and subtle. Even the titles of his poems
("the silences in me," "so fragile," "Singing the child to sleep") reflect the
quiet, tenuous style of his lyricism. In one poem, "this abandoned
structure," for instance, he observes "a harp / of shattered beams / splintering / that hymns to the wind's presence /in winter." Martone's new
book, *Ocean Vows* (Copper Beech Press) is exemplary in its purity and
elegance—sheer enjoyment.

Dave Smith treats a wide range of themes, from football to fishing and
crab-picking. But as his new book's title suggests, *In the House of the
Judge* (Harper & Row) also contains, besides the title poem, many poems
on old houses: a Vermont cabin, a turn-of-the-century house, a landlord's
house and others. Smith has a sharp eye and an expansive, sensitive
nature. He also has a wondrous power of articulating a tableau or incident
in precise, lovely language and fitting form. He is at once dreamer and
builder, a rare craftsman among the newer poets.

U. S. poets seldom have espoused Continental trends like surrealism and
Dadaism. But there are occasional talented poets like Arthur Vogelsang
for whom the light "overdrive" speed of surrealism seems just right.
Marvin Bell has called Vogelsang's verse "fizzy, zippy, smart, humane,
personable, comic, absurdly American"—and one could hardly choose a
better description. Vogelsang's latest book, *A Planet* (Holt, Rinehart and
Winston), is a four-part collection of lyrics of the here and now. A few
titles: "A Swollen Sonnet," "A Little Crazy," "Acting Simple" and
"Another Fake Love Poem." Vogelsang's forebears are Heine, Laforgue
and Stevie Smith. At least, Vogelsang adds a bright, light (and enjoyable)
dimension to U.S. poetry.

In a more conventional mode, *A Joy Proposed: Poems*, by the late novelist
T. H. White (1906-1964), is a fine coup for its publisher, the University of
Georgia Press. White began publishing verse as a Cambridge under-
graduate and continued writing poems throughout his life. This new
collection is enhanced by an introduction and notes by Kurth Sprague,
useful data for White's fans who have read *Farewell Victoria, The
Goshawk* and other works of the author. White was born in India and
educated in England, where he later taught, but his settings range from

Ireland and Scotland to Italy and France, and his subjects include Richard Burton and Julie Andrews.

Today, books by newer writers and by anthologists like Sandra Hochman and Kenneth Koch help readers and novice poets to appreciate and enjoy current verse. But there is, after all, no better starting point than the poetry itself.

St. Louis Post-Dispatch, August 21, 1983, p. 4C.

God in her typewriter

Just a few weeks before her suicide in 1974, in her 46th year, I sent Anne Sexton a copy of my plaquette of poems on death from the Spanish of Juan Ramón Jiménez. I was stunned by Sexton's death and even speculated on the effect of the simple, haunting lyrics of Jiménez, who had won the Nobel Prize 18 years earlier. But, friends reassured me, the poems could not have a depressing effect. As Dean Adele Starbird wrote, reviewing that little book a week after Sexton's death, the poems expressed "affirmation of life."

Anne Sexton's friends and many readers knew of her preoccupation with, and attempts at, suicide from 1957 to the spring of 1974. But those attempts began earlier. At age 25, in 1954, she was a victim of postpartum depression. After the birth of her second child the following year, she suffered a second crisis. Her first openly acknowledged suicide attempt was on her 18th birthday, November 9, 1956.

In her foreword to *The Complete Poems* Maxine Kumin credits two persons with keeping Sexton alive for the next 18 years. One was a young psychiatrist, Dr. Martin Orne,who urged Sexton to write poems as therapy. The other was an elderly Catholic priest who told her, "God is in your typewriter."

Indeed, as Maxine Kumin writes, the "rich, rescuing obsession" of making poems kept Sexton from succeeding in a dozen suicidal impulses during that period. In 1957 she enrolled with Kumin in John Holmes's poetry workshop in Boston. In 1958-59 she audited Robert Lowell's verse-writing course at Boston University, where she met Sylvia Plath. The medical and spiritual therapy worked. Both courses seem to have given Sexton just the right type and amount of impetus at the right time. Holmes, who decried her personal, confessional style, nevertheless gently encouraged her. Lowell, and especially W. D. Snodgrass, who won a Pulitzer Prize in 1960 for his searingly personal book *Heart's Needle*, became even more influential to her.

In 1961 James Dickey, reviewing Sexton's first book, *To Bedlam and Part Way Back* (1960), made several remarks which became increasingly true of all her work which followed. Her poems, he wrote, emerge from such "deep, painful sections of the author's life that one's literary opinions scarcely seem to matter. . . . The experiences she recounts are among the most harrowing that human beings can undergo: those of madness and near-madness." He found this "extremely painful subject . . . a major one for poetry, with a sickeningly frightening appropriateness to our time." Dickey did not review her second book, *All My Pretty Ones* (1962) so kindly. But by then her work had been widely published in magazines and she had received many honors and awards. Her third book of poems, *Live or Die* (1966) won a Pulitzer Prize.

The Complete Poems, like the recent collection of Sylvia Plath's poetry, is long overdue. It finally brings together all of Sexton's ten books including the posthumous *45 Mercy Street* (1976) and *Words for Dr. Y.* (1978). The other books, besides the titles mentioned, are *Love Poems* (1969), *Transformations* (1971), *The Book of Folly* (1972), *The Death Notebooks* (1974) and *The Awful Rowing Toward God* (1975). Six other poems are added under the title "Last Poems." A title index and a chronological contents are included along with Kumin's retrospective essay.

Taken as a whole, Sexton's work reveals startlingly broader and deeper dimensions than any single book she ever published. She knew and practiced formal verse, but she gradually developed new personal forms. But even these were insufficient to articulate her experience, and her verse became freer. Her voice also became stronger, and she improved her perceptions of love (as in *Love Poems*) and of collective human experience (as in *Transformations*).

Her later work shows a straining to the limits to express old themes of pain, isolation and mortality in new ways. Anne Sexton's life and work, like Sylvia Plath's, are already an interlocking legend. The work is a repository of the real and the imagined, with elements of truth, plausibility and surrealism. Nor is her poetry as barren and open as some critics suggest. Even such simple lines as these, from her poem "Words," are charged with many meanings:

> Be careful of words,
> even the miraculous ones.
> For the miraculous we do our best,
> sometimes they swarm like insects
> and leave not a sting but a kiss . . . .
> But I try to take care

and be gentle to them.
Words and eggs must be handled with care.
Once broken they are impossible
things to repair.

Sexton made three important contributions to writing and writers of our
time. As a poet, she both explored and exploited the confessional mode in
unique ways, giving new limits to personal lyricism. As a woman, she
also broke new ground, defining the problematic position of women—
"the neurotic reality of the time," as Maxine Kumin observes—despite her
inability to cope with her own problems. And in her very frankness, although she attracted a cult group during and after her life, she gave hope
and sustenance to others with similar problems. For she had a large and
caring heart:

> Big heart,
> wide as a watermelon,
> but wise as birth,
> there is so much abundance
> in the people I have . . . .
>
> They hear how
> the artery of my soul has been severed
> and soul is spurting out upon them,
> bleeding on them . . .
> and my heart,
> which is very big,
> I promise it is very large,
> a monster of sorts,
> takes it all in—
> and in comes the fury of love.

[Unpublished review of *The Complete Poems,* written in 1983.]

THREE FACES OF AUTUMN
Poetry, Prose, Translations

Examining writers, their lives and works

Many years ago, during a lull in a conversation with Ezra Pound, I asked him an offhanded question about James Joyce; he answered earnestly, quizzically, "Do you mean the man or the work?"

With some subjects (Gandhi, Schweitzer, Martin Luther King) the life *is* the work, or almost so. But with literary figures the lives and writings are intricately mingled, even confused. Thus, in the last 30 or 40 years the critical biography has evolved almost as a separate genre of writing. Still, many variations appear, depending on the biographer's (or critic's) skills and interests, ranging from the fictional biography to pure scholarly criticism.

Unique among recent books is Peter Brazeau's "oral biography" transcribed from interviews with about 90 different people on one subject, poet Wallace Stevens (1879-1955). *Parts of a World: Wallace Stevens Remembered* (Random House) deals with only a few of the poems, impressionistically, in passing. But criticism abounds on Stevens, and there has long been a need to humanize this poet whose work is often coldly objective. *Parts of a World* is warm, bright, intimate, dealing with Stevens's family, friends and co-workers. Three aspects of Stevens—as insurance executive, man of letters and family man—are recounted and woven together in this extraordinary biography.

Another humanizing, but perhaps, more controversial biography is *The Marriage of Emily Dickinson by* William H. Shurr (University Press of Kentucky), a life based on the arrangement and interpretation of hundreds of Dickinson's poems. By newly analyzing the poems in the order in which Dickinson herself arranged them, Shurr concludes that the poet had a "marriage in spirit" with a married clegyman with whom she finally agreed to a lifetime of painful separation. Shurr reads more intimate details in the poems, too, contradicting earlier biographers (Richard B. Sewall, for instance) who hold that Dickinson had no unifying, sustaining vision in her poetry.

Less familiar to readers is the English author Charles Williams (1886-1945), a former editor at the Oxford University Press and a friend of T. S. Eliot, C. S. Lewis and other writers of an earlier generation. *Charles Williams: An exploration of His Life and Work*, by Alice Mary Hadfield

236

(Oxford), although conventional in treatment, is admirably researched and documented. Mrs. Hadfield, a longtime friend of Williams, gained access to some 2,000 letters dating from 1911 to 1945 to complete this work. Her style, warm and detailed, is always clear in the chronology of Williams's life. Sidelights on writers like J.R.R. Tolkien and James Elroy Flecker are particularly interesting. Altogether, we can sense the quiet, strong impact of Williams—as poet, novelist, dramatist, critic and theologian—on the literary life of our century.

The Odes of John Keats by Helen Vendler (Harvard University Press) is a specialized but readable work of criticism and interpretation. Vendler quotes the six great odes of Keats, plus a selection from "The Fall of Hyperion," and she explores these poems as a unit. They are an aesthetic whole, she feels, in which Keats not only illustrates the purity of his poetry but also confronts questions of language and philosophy. Vendler's theory is plausible, and certainly takes off on a new track from earlier biographies by Amy Lowell, Walter Jackson Bate, Aileen Ward and others. Yet Vendler is as immersed in this segment of the poet's work, and as informed on Keats as those who have dealt with the complete life and work.

A great influence on John Keats was Edmund Spenser, whose long allegorical work is interpreted in *The Poetry of The Faerie Queene* by Paul J. Alpers (University of Missouri). Although much of Alpers's study is designed for the devoted Spenserian reader, the first three chapters of background information are a must for anyone attempting to read *The Faerie Queene* and to appreciate its richness.

Critical essays are also, at times, biographical. Such a collection is *The British Dissonance: Essays on Ten Contemporary Poets* by A. Kingsley Weatherhead (University of Missouri), which deals with certain poets who are still relatively little known. Among these are Charles Tomlinson, Ted Hughes, David Jones and Basil Bunting—many of whom have been writing and publishing for over 30 years. Bunting, especially, is a legendary figure praised by Pound and Tomlinson. Weatherhead's book is a useful introduction; it contains a short biography and a bibliography on each poet as well as the critical commentary.

Finally, many volumes of personal essays are good sources of unusual biographical and critical viewpoints. Two recent books, *Vectors and*

THREE FACES OF AUTUMN
Poetry, Prose, Translations

Smoothable Curves: Collected Essays, by William Bronk (North Point Press) and *The Gift* by Lewis Hyde (Random House), delve into a host of old and new ideas and personalities, mostly literary. Bronk is the more traditional, dealing with Thoreau, Whitman and Melville in a section called "Ideas of Friendship and Society in the United States," Hyde, younger and more offbeat, deals with Whitman too, among other literary, political and social figures. Two of his best essays are "The Commerce of the Creative Spirit" and "Ezra Pound and the Fate of Vegetable Money." Hyde's book is profusely annotated, with a bibliography and index. These are but a few of the many noteworthy recent books of lives and works—and ideas.

St. Louis Post-Dispatch, January 8, 1984, p. 4E.

Symbols and influence in T.S. Eliot's work

On a recent winter evening, tabby at my shoulder and away from the electronic tonic of the tube, I perused one of my poems and found no fewer than 40 possible symbolic meanings in it which I had not consciously intended. I thought of T. S. Eliot's responses to scholars who professed to find hidden meanings in his poems—and how he neither denied nor claimed such meanings but let readers interpret the work as they pleased.

For 60 years this analysis of Eliot's work as "literature" has progressed (or retrogressed), often at the expense of ignoring the poet's life and times. Sometimes scholars blunder far from the true historic context of a poem. At other times symbols and meanings are not a writer's original creation but belong to his age—a kind of "folk symbolism" of some class of society.

Eliot devotees know there are already scores of excellent biographies and studies of the poet, more than enough perhaps. But Peter Ackroyd's book offers something different: a simple but strong, logical realignment of Eliot's life, catching the mood and tempo of three generations. While other biographers deal with important themes or aspects of the life from beginning to end, or examine the life and work in objective detail, Ackroyd sets the tone of his book by opening with the simple sentence, "Eliot was born in St. Louis, Missouri, on 26 September 1888." This, and the bare date headings of the chapters, shows the author's serious "no frills" approach.

Even with this approach, Ackroyd's biography is detailed, as complex as the poet himself. Eliot's St. Louis background is of course mentioned, but sparingly—for his adult life rarely touched St. Louis and his work had far stronger influences.

Ackroyd's biography has several notable qualities. First are Eliot's important relationships with figures like Conrad Aiken, Wyndham Lewis, Lady Morrell, Bertrand Russell, Virginia and Leonard Woolf, and Ezra Pound—all introduced in their proper turn and given some depth in this book. Then there is Eliot's tragic and difficult first marriage to Vivien Haigh-Wood, which Ackroyd describes with admirable objectivity. (In a sense this biography has a "happy ending," focused on Eliot's second

239

marriage, 1957-65, with Valerie Fletcher.) Throughout the book, Eliot's work surfaces unobtrusively and is discussed as part of his life. We also get a clear view of Eliot in his job with the Fabers, London publishers, and of how he helped to establish writers like W. H, Auden, Djuna Barnes, George Barker and Lawrence Durrell. Finally, readers will appreciate the nearly 70 illustrations, and the 60-odd pages of notes, bibliography and index.

"In my beginning is my end," wrote Eliot, and "In my end is my beginning." Ackroyd appropriately ends this biography with a quotation from the poet: "We also understand the poetry better when we know more about the man."

Review of *T. S. Eliot: A Life*, by Peter Ackroyd (Simon & Schuster).

St. Louis Post Dispatch, February 28, 1984, p. 4B.

Entertaining with messages and craftsmanship

To the lover of words and wordcraft, poets are among the great entertainers. The secret of the game lies in matching reader and writer. Some readers, for instance, prefer a solid "message" while others enjoy the form, sound and texture of the poem. Despite flurries of styles and fads, American poetry still falls broadly into two categories — craftsmanship and social consciousness. As critic F. O. Matthiessen noted, the one stems from Poe, the other from Whitman. As we might suspect, it isn't the choice of these traditions or the poet's name but the force of the poetry itself which makes the work endure.

Again today, just as after World War II, many poets have returned to wordcraft, even to the point of "art for art's sake," subordinating the social meaning of their work. A century ago the French had a term to describe such poetry, "Parnassian." The term was discredited and disused after the Symbolists appeared on the scene; but just as we can appreciate some Victorian art, we can enjoy the new Parnassianism of certain poets. Charles Edward Eaton's *The Thing King* (Cornwall Books) is a brilliant synthesis of color, form, sound and sense. These qualities appear not only in the style but in the very themes and in titles like "Rose-colored Glasses," "Purple Lilacs, Blue Water," "White Clown," "The Blue Pajamas," "Chocolate Cake," "Red," "Sleeping Nude" and "The Woman in Black." In these poems, as in "Artists Anonymous" and "The Pointillist," some readers may accuse Eaton of "painting" his poetry. But human warmth radiates from the lines:

> The woman, too, like a lily in the sun,
> In her green dress and coil of yellow hair,
> Rich as a hive, honeycombed with amber,
> Has a pulse that is the same as sunlight.

Eaton's artistry would have made the Imagists of 60 years ago green with envy.

While Jean Cocteau in his poem "The Crucifixion" avoided the figure 13, John Hollander confronts the number repeatedly in his book *Powers of Thirteen* (Atheneum). The collection consists of 169 (what else? 13 times 13) stanzas or poems of 13 lines each, with each line in 13 syllables. Whether read as a loose single poem or as a sequence of many poems, the

241

work shows a remarkable range of themes, styles, diction and modes—
from allegory and anecdote to song and satire. Hollander approaches form
with gusto. But the form has only a superficial sameness. This book is like
a diary, and each entry is unique:

> Words we have exchanged keep playing out their low treasons
> Against the journals of the usual, the nocturnes
> Of the odd, falling into line once they are uttered.

Some readers may call these sonnets, but no matter. *Powers of Thirteen*
follows the best traditions of George Meredith, D.G. Rossetti and others
noted for such sequences.

"Who or what is 'Oby'?" one naturally asks, seeing George Macbeth's
Poems from Oby (Atheneum). Oby is an English parish, near the sea in
Norfolk, where the author bought an old rectory and several acres of land.
One of the highlights of the volume (Macbeth's 27th) is a series of 14
sonnets titled "Thoughts on a Box of Razors Bought at a Stalham sale."
"For two pounds they were mine," the poet begins, and his memory and
imagination turn commonplace objects into universal symbols:

> . . . . The Royal Hospital
> Had instruments laid out on moving trays,
> Like razors. Did they shave the nightly dead,
> And lay them empty in each well-made bed?
> . . . . What happens with the knife
> Behind those frills must happen to us all
> In years to come. And it's good cause for rage,
> That frictive rage against the dying light.

Despite such echoes from Dylan Thomas, Macbeth writes a freshly
sensitive, sensuous verse on themes ranging from the abstract (jealousy
and melancholy) to the natural (owls, hornets, cats) — all rooted in love of
man and nature.

Herbert Morris has published poems in magazines for 25 years, but *Peru*
(Harper & Row) is his first published collection. Although only 80 pages
long, the book shows a consummate craftsmanship reminiscent of the
finest post-World War II work of Wallace Stevens and Conrad Aiken.
Morris epitomizes the new Parnassianism. Still, along with the minute

description and ornate, slow-moving narrative of these 23 poems, one finds, as in "History of China," bright little homilies in lines like these:

> Desert, in China, was of vast importance.
> Father, what is the desert? Desert, child,
> is the length of the daylight we have traveled,
> is the measure of darkness still to come.

Donald Revell's poetry in *From the Abandoned Cities* (Harper & Row) is a kind of blending of Gotham and Gaul. Seven of the 32 titles are in French, and many of the poems deal with Central Park and other Manhattan scenes. Revell has an open, drifting lyricism, formal in style yet free in expression. There is enough variation in themes, and skill in treatment of those themes, to make this a promising early work. Among the stronger poems are "Near Life," "Graves in East Tennessee" and "Homage." There is fine, subtle emotion in lines like these from "Here to There":

> The biggest part of any story is rooms
> and the things inside them . . . .
>   Rooms
> fix an itinerary of still points
> at the two ends of memory and join them.

Roland Flint's poems have Gallic qualities too, but the influence is in style, not language. Flint's French heritage covers a whole century from Baudelaire to Alain Bosquet, in the prose poem and the short, familiar narrative. Flint is a master of both forms. The prose poem, which all French poets seem to write well, is often badly written in English. Flint has 13 excellent examples among the 48 poems in *Resuming Green: Selected Poems, 1965-1982* (Dial). Like Bosquet, Flint can do pirouettes with simple, familiar language. Flint's finest skill perhaps lies in the taut, self-analytic narrative, the first person narrative. In other poems he easily transforms the self into a symbolic third person—a lowly pigeon, for instance, one who does not pray for miracles or get lost in some delusion, but knows "He'll get out alive, or even (for long) survive / This ugly place he loves in rapt confusion."

The poetry of Hans Juergensen startles and tests us by its language and syntax. His twelfth book, *The Record of a Green Planet* (Linden Press) contains nearly 50 poems on a broad range of themes: rituals, legacies, asperity, awareness—and love. Juergensen exploits to the full an unusually rich experience and a broad cultural background. In the "Legacies" section, for instance, he deals with Orpheus, Chaucer and Leonardo along with Beethoven, Rouault and Anne Sexton, all with equal facility. The verse style, although free, is tight and precise, as in these lines on an injured locust:

> It hauls itself too slowly
> along a broad dagger of green;
> two of its legs dangle
> over the abyss . . . .
> The creature cannot bound,
> and therefore cannot live.

Juergensen is both cerebral and sensitive, a master of taut, free form.

Laurence Lieberman is perhaps the finest American poet writing in patterned free forms. These forms are hard to describe or explain, and must be read to be appreciated, like the great "versets" of certain French poets. Lieberman's work in *Eros at the World Kite Pageant: Poems 1978-1982* (Macmillan), as in his earlier book, *God's Measurements*, is eye-appealing, elegantly displayed on the page like ocean eddies and breakers. The style is sensuously narrative and descriptive, in lines as sweeping as Whitman's, but somewhat more controlled, more modulated, broken into syllabic patterns. But behind the form is substance and meaning. The style is not surreal but rather coherent, logical and minutely descriptive. It is even didactic at times. Mostly, however, it exudes joy and vitality. Lieberman is a true American original.

Whether we consider these poets "Parnassian" doesn't matter. Their work certainly does not lack a social message, but that message is subtle, muted, and perhaps more effective and enduring than the open message of other poets. The art form enclosing and bearing the message, when it occurs, has grace and power.

St. Louis Post-Dispatch, April 8, 1984, p. 4B.

Fresh vision of Whitman

Walt Whitman wrote three of the finest free form odes in our language. For six generations his work has had a major impact on the poetry of four continents. He led an almost exemplary adult life as a family man devoted to his parents and brothers, and as a humanitarian, notably during the Civil War years. Yet, ignoring these facts, some editors of recent college texts introduce Whitman to young readers by quoting obscure, insignificant lines out of context and snidely alluding to his alleged sexual preference. Nothing else.

By comparison, Paul Zweig's new biography of the poet is like a breath of Whitman's "mystical, moist night air," full, fresh and expansive. Zweig's scope at first seems narrow. The biography is not a full life in the usual sense, but focuses on a 20-year span, 1848-1868, during which Whitman planned, wrote and revised his best-known work, *Leaves of Grass* (1855).

In that period too, the most startling and productive years of his life, Whitman made two "leaps" affecting his entire career. The first leap occurred in 1848 when he agreed, almost impulsively, to go to New Orleans to work on Sam McClure's newspaper, *The Crescent*. A teacher, printer, carpenter and journalist, the 29-year-old poet had never been farther from New York than Long Island. He had just been fired as editor-in-chief of the *Brooklyn Eagle*, and he needed money. Although he stayed just a few months in New Orleans, he was in the thick of life there. His experiences and observations in that "populous city" matured him, tempered his view of the Civil War to come, and affected his writing from *Leaves* to the later *Democratic Vistas*.

The second "leap" 14 years later was a terrible renewal for him. In December, 1862, he left New York again, to look for his brother George who had been wounded in battle. Eventually he found George in a camp in southern Virginia. But for four or five years beginning in 1863 he roved as a kind of "healing spirit" among the dead and wounded, in the field and in hospitals, mostly in and around Washington, where he held various jobs.

The war, as Zweig points out, was the great event in Whitman's life. Sometimes he saved lives, but more often he watched the lives of youths slip away. There was no glory or excitement, only pain and exhaustion masked with love and compassion for those less fortunate.

245

THREE FACES OF AUTUMN
Poetry, Prose, Translations

The years in between, the 1850s, were important too. It was for Whitman a decade of unlimited possibility, nourished by oratory and such phenomena as New York's magnificent Crystal Palace. Mostly it was a period of stylistic development for the poet whose genius, as Zweig reminds us, lay in his ability to write as if literature had never existed.

Such a concentrated biography naturally omits certain details such as Whitman's relations with William Rossetti and other writers. But the most important contacts, with Emerson and other New England writers, are included. Altogether Zweig's *Whitman* is strong, compelling and true— perhaps the finest biography of the poet in 30 years, since Gay Wilson Allen's *The Solitary Singer*.

Review of *Walt Whitman: The Making of the Poet*, by Paul Zweig (Basic Books).

St. Louis Post-Dispatch, April 29, 1984, p.3B.

A CHARLES GUENTHER RETROSPECTIVE
Prose: Critical Reviews and Essays, 1983-1992

Panning for gold in a mountain of T.S. Eliot studies

The conventional, plodding author, no matter how talented, seldom elicits criticism, controversy or "studies" (as in masters' theses). Or even a rash of reviews, good or bad. For T. S. Eliot, the magic and sensation of *The Waste Land* still carry on after 60 years, and he is one of the most popular subjects of dissertations since Shakespeare. Thousands of books and essays have appeared on every conceivable aspect of Eliot as poet, essayist, classical scholar, playwright, political writer, translator—even as a Londoner—and on and on. It's a veritable wasteland, too.

Most such studies purport to be "new"—and while most are not, one cannot blame the plodding authors for riding Eliot's coattails. And it has a cumulative value if we can sift the gold from the dross.

Ronald Bush's *T. S. Eliot* also is hailed as "a major new study." Of course it has new viewpoints, but we must look for other qualities, too, and these are surprisingly fresh and sound. For instance, Bush draws from only the most reputable criticism on Eliot, from Ezra Pound to Hugh Kenner, and disregards the sloppy or frivolous studies. Next, he stays on course by relating Eliot's life and work to the strongest influences in the poet's life, from Dante and Shakespeare to Laforgue and Pound. And he shows a strong command and assimilation of his sources.

Best of all, however, Bush has planned and organized his work well and stuck to two aspects of Eliot, character and style. He relates these aspects to both Eliot's life and writing. The works covered range from early poems like "Gerontion" to "Ash Wednesday" (1930) and "Four Quartets" (1943). By dealing with the major poems only, chronologically, Bush attracts all readers of Eliot, novice and experienced. Bush's style is factual and discursive, not racy and sensational. So our attention is on Eliot, not Bush, and we are rewarded with a wealth of new insights on Eliot.

One of these is Eliot's tension between Romantic yearning and intellectual development. The poet sought to accommodate both of these forces in his personal life, and the "difficult honesty" that resulted in his writing set a new standard for our time.

Bush shows a rare appreciation of "Ash Wednesday" in particular, and recognizes the personal qualities of that poem in relation to Eliot's St.

247

THREE FACES OF AUTUMN
Poetry, Prose, Translations

Louis background. He quotes at length from Eliot's 1959 talk at Mary Institute, a touch some readers will like. Other touches are the extensive notes and index.

Perhaps after all *T. S. Eliot* is a major new study. It's certainly among the best since Hugh Kenner's study, *The Invisible Poet* (1959). At any rate, there's gold in this Eliot.

Review of *T.S. Eliot, a Study in Character and Style*, by Ronald Bush (Oxford).

St. Louis Post-Dispatch, July 10, 1984, p. 4B.

A CHARLES GUENTHER RETROSPECTIVE
Prose: Critical Reviews and Essays, 1983-1992

Literary criticism, writers' letters closely analyzed

Criticizing literary criticism is like doing a strip-down job on a $2,000 camera. After it's taken apart and examined or analyzed, it seems to have lost its main function, its practical use.

All we have left is a scattering of cleverly contrived components.

Still, without picking and carping, a reviewer can perceive certain works with wonder and appreciation. Usually the university presses underwrite such studies, and the books at hand are no exception.

The University of Missouri Press, for instance, has a growing reputation for its list of literary biographies and criticism, and this reputation is enhanced by two new books: *Secretary of Praise: The Poetic Vocation of George Herbert* by Diana Benét, and *Pope and Bolingbroke: A Study of Friendship and Influence* by Brean S. Hammond. The Benét volume is full of brilliant insights on the English mystical poet George Herbert (1593-1633), who appeals to a wide spectrum of Christian readers. With profuse quotations from the poet, Benét shows order and reconciliation in Herbert's troubled life and work. This is a satisfying, well documented study. Like his age a century later, Alexander Pope was more worldly, satirical and moralistic. Hammond deals with Pope in a practical way, detailing the political and philosophical ties between Pope and Lord Bolingbroke (even during the latter's exile to France), and Pope's debt to Bolingbroke in the "Essay on Man." Hammond is saturated, it seems, with the history of the times, and he sparks interest in that age which has much in common with ours.

Literary research may not be as glamorous as, say, medical research, but it has its rewards in discovery, too. In *Dear Brother Walt* (Kent State University), editors Dennis Berthold and Kenneth Price have turned up previously unpublished letters and new information about Thomas Jefferson Whitman, brother of the poet Walt. Of special interest are some 70 pages of letters to Walt from Jeff written between 1867 and 1888 when Jeff lived in St. Louis and was superintendent of waterworks. (One photo shows Henry Flad and Jeff Whitman in a St. Louis *biergarten* about 1870). These are strange, important and at times funny documents—and they have barely begun to show up in Whitman scholarship. This is a handsome, tastefully annotated edition.

249

THREE FACES OF AUTUMN
Poetry, Prose, Translations

Nearly 500 letters written by William Faulkner and his circle between 1924 and his death in 1962 make up a new volume, *Faulkner, A Comprehensive Guide to the Brodsky Collection*, edited by Louis D. Brodsky and Robert W. Hamblin (University Press of Mississippi). One needn't be a Faulkner devotee to find these letters illuminating. Anyone may be surprised at the personal and domestic problems Faulkner had between 1951 and 1957, his period of greatest public acclaim. This rich, revealing assortment of documents—which includes photos and facsimile letters—is made more useful with Hamblin's long introduction and a detailed index. Some of Faulkner's ideas on social, racial and literary issues may surprise a few readers. One such letter, from 1957, deals with black and white equality.

Another important but less obtrusive Southern writer is the subject of *Allen Tate and the Augustinian Imagination*, by Robert S. Dupree (Louisiana State University). One of the most brilliant but least understood poets of our time, Tate has never been "humanized" to American readers, and I'm afraid this study won't make him more popular. But Dupree has a rare, rich understanding of Tate's heritage going back 15 centuries to St. Augustine. Although Tate was not a religious poet like George Herbert, certain visionary poets, especially Dante, influenced his work published in *Collected Poems, 1919-1976*. Any reader might envy Dupree's full, deep understanding of Tate.

Finally, two new studies of more recent poets, both of the "Objectivist" school, have added to a much-needed understanding of their life and work. These are *Zukovsky's 'A'*, an introduction to Louis Zukovsky by Barry Ahearn (University of California), and *Gary Snyder's Vision* by Charles Molesworth (University of Missouri). Zukovsky's "poem of life" was 50 years in the making and remains one of the century's most neglected masterpieces. Snyder, too, has a strong, esoteric following as poet, prophet and social commentator. Molesworth treats him with both scholarly appreciation and objective criticism.

Such books are helpful reference tools, enabling readers to understand better some favorite author. A little patience and one can discover lodes (and loads) of personal insights and enjoyment.

St. Louis Post-Dispatch, August 4, 1984, p. 4B.

250

Genius of Edgar Allan Poe untarnished

In a 1945 Viking Portable selection of Poe's works, one of the poet's most
admiring critics, Philip Van Doren Stern, observed that "Poe wrote of
elemental things—of love and hate, of fear and death, of the mysteries beyond life, and of the mutability and brevity of human existence . . . . He
was ever the eager seeker, the innovator who . . . drove back some of the
darkness of man's understanding of himself." Yet Stern's very next words
describe Poe as a "charlatan, plagiarist, pathological liar, egomaniac,
whimpering child, braggart, and irresponsible drunkard"—terms now
largely refuted by Poe scholars.

For a century after his death in 1849 at age 40, Poe's reputation was
tainted by an obituary written by Rufus W. Griswold, an exaggerated
"memoir" accepted as fact by even the most sympathetic Poe devotees. In
friendlier days Poe had named Griswold his literary executor, but the two
later became rivals. Poe's executor not only became his "executioner," as
one critic notes, but was accused of forging letters depicting Poe as a
heavy drinker, a gambler and a reprobate.

Yet, the 50 pages of Poe's letters Stern included in that volume 40 years
ago are enough vindication of Poe's character. The letters are one-sided,
of course, but other evidence—including these two splendid new volumes
edited by G. R. Thompson and Patrick F. Quinn—shows the improbability
of Poe's writing so brilliantly and prolifically in a short life of debauchery.
Let's look at some facts. There was one instance, in 1848, when Poe took
a dose of drugs (laudanum). This was the year after his young invalid wife
had died, and just after his brief engagement to another woman had been
broken off. Earlier, at age 17, he had incurred $2,000 in gambling debts
trying to get money to pay his expenses at the University of Virginia—
only after his wealthy but stingy foster father, John Allan, sent Poe there
without even the minimum tuition and board money.

Four years later, only after Poe had enlisted in the Army and distinguished
himself as a sergeant major, Allan grudgingly secured an appointment for
him to the U.S. Military Academy at West Point.

As for his drinking habits, Poe occasionally drank sweet wine (and cider,
as he relates in a letter), for which he had a low tolerance. Poe scholar
John Ostrom insists that Poe did not drink to write, and that Poe couldn't

have afforded hard liquor because he was in poverty during 13 of his 14 working years.

Why, in a review of Poe's works—possibly the finest edition ever compiled—all this preoccupation with Poe's life and character? The answer is simple: we must understand the man to appreciate his work. These two superb volumes, 3,000 pages, are the soul of Poe's literary legacy. Although they omit Poe's letters, they include nearly everything else: scores of essays and reviews, from the famous "Philosophy of Composition" to evaluations of American, British and Continental authors of the time. Here too are 100 pages of sketches titled "The Literati of New York City," honest, admiring, but sometimes biting remarks on 38 writers, and articles on topics as widely varied as music, geography, phrenology and South Sea exploration. Throughout his prose, especially in the essays on Cooper, Coleridge, Dickens, Bryant, Longfellow, and the less eminent Morris Matson, Poe shows brilliance, wit and clear-headedness. His anonymous review of his own *Tales* (1845) is both amusing and revealing. Generally laudatory, the review describes Poe's style, aims and craft accurately and in detail.

As for the poetry and tales, how can a few paragraphs in a review "show and tell" the essence of this work which has so deeply affected Western culture for 150 years? From the haunting "The Raven" and "The Bells" to the poignant "For Annie" and the strange iambics of "To Helen," Poe's verse was sparse but powerful, as much admired by the French (even in prose translation) as by American readers. Poe was, and remains, the master of Gothic horror, in such stories as "The Pit and the Pendulum," "The Fall of the House of Usher" and "The Cask of Amontillado." His work foreshadowed modern science fiction, and he invented the detective story as we know it with "The Murders in the Rue Morgue."

Altogether these two volumes are beautifully produced. The texts were carefully chosen from many versions available, the editing is flawless, and the materials and typography are excellent. Best of all, this is Poe's work, undiluted by long introductions or commentaries. Yet the chronology, notes and indexes at the end are necessary, enhancing touches.

Today if you visit the Academy library at West Point, you may be impressed (as I was) by the chapel-like atmosphere of the Poe Room there, with its dark tables and woodwork polished to a fragrant lustre. It contains an extensive collection of Poe materials, and the official host's enthusiasm reflects a warm pride in Poe's association with West Point. What reverence for a former student who was court-martialed and expelled (at his own prodding) after only eight months' attendance! Poetic justice? Maybe not. But perhaps it shows that the pen, after all, is mightier than the sword.

(A brief afterword: one scholar, John Ostrom, suggests that Poe may have had diabetes. I suggest another possibility: porphyria, a rare disease about which little was known even up to the 1960s, and which usually was fatal to male patients. Poe's low tolerance for both drugs and alcohol, his self-drive to exhaustion, his illness during 1846-47, and the circumstances of his final, fatal attack in 1849 could be symptomatic of porphyria. Perhaps a layman shouldn't dabble in such speculation, but this is offered for further consideration.)

Review of *Essays and Reviews by Edgar Allan Poe*, edited by G. R. Thompson (The Library of America) and *Poetry and Tales by Edgar Allan Poe*, edited by Patrick F. Quinn (The Library of America).

St. Louis Post-Dispatch, September 23, 1984, p. 4B.

THREE FACES OF AUTUMN
Poetry, Prose, Translations

Black poets seek wider audiences

In an article titled "Bonsai" the poet Gloria Oden urged black writers to break away from traditional and stereotyped black styles and themes, to become more universal in expression. But while some writers like M. B. Tolson have practiced this advice, for generations such freedom was neither accepted nor appreciated.

The Missouri-born Tolson was among those black American writers of broad social, economic and scholarly outlook. Yet despite his honors and apparently broad acceptance in the American community, he was best appreciated by black audiences, as a speaker and activist with free, forceful opinions. For seven years he aired those opinions in a column, "Caviar and Cabbage," that he wrote for the *Washington Tribune*.

In his poetry Tolson's voice and themes knew no bounds. The full range of his knowledge, experience and scholarship came forth in brilliantly crafted verse in such books as *Rendezvous With America, Harlem Gallery* and *A Gallery of Harlem Portraits*. Robert Farnsworth's biography of Tolson is a full, detailed and well-documented life and commentary. It reveals Tolson, paradoxically, as a highly honored yet rather neglected figure, as much a prophet as a poet. Farnsworth's account surely foreshadows a greater understanding of Tolson's life and diverse talents.

Tolson is among 33 American poets represented in *3000 Years of Black Poetry*, a reissue of an anthology first published in 1970. The collection covers a broad range, nearly 50 nations from antiquity to the present, and is surprisingly fresh. Other American poets include the best known—Phillis Wheatley, Langston Hughes, Countee Cullen and Gwendolyn Brooks, for instance—and later poets like Leroi Jones, Mari Evans and Nikki Giovanni.

Still, the selections are brief and certain gifted U.S. poets (Michael Harper, Gloria Oden and others) are left out. Readers looking for more depth might supplement this anthology with Robert Hayden's old *Kaleidoscope* anthology (Harcourt, 1967) and even the *Ebony* magazine issue (March 1974) featuring black women poets.

Altogether the Lomax-Abdul volume is a fine introduction and an eye-opener. It may surprise some readers that the editors include Alexander

Pushkin, José Marti, Rubén Darío and certain Brazilians among "black" poets. But why not?—for no race has exclusive claim to their talents. And times and attitudes change, as Arna Bontemps suggests in "Southern Mansion":

> The years go back with an iron clank,
> A hand is on the gate,
> A dry leaf trembles on the wall.
> Ghosts are walking.
> They have broken roses down
> And poplars stand there still as death.

Review of *Melvin B. Tolson, 1898-1900, Plain Talk and Poetic Prophecy*, by Robert M. Farnsworth (University of Missouri) and *3000 Years of Black Poetry, An Anthology*, edited by Alan Lomax and Raoul Abdul (Dodd, Mead).

St. Louis Post-Dispatch, September 27, 1984, p. 1B.

Women, politics and poetry in Pound's life

In September 1972, a few weeks before his death at age 87, Ezra Pound confided to a friend: "I was wrong . . . ninety percent wrong . . . I lost my head in a storm." Pound was referring, no doubt, to the World War II period when to earn a living as an expatriate trapped in Italy he broadcast personal propaganda over Rome radio—strong anti-war speeches that he maintained were "In support of the U. S. Constitution." But the U.S. government thought otherwise.

When the Allies occupied Italy in 1945, he was detained by American authorities, then was transferred to the United States to stand trial for treason. But the trial never took place, for he was found mentally unfit and was confined to St Elizabeths Hospital in Washington, where he remained for 13 years.

Throughout his years of confinement at St Elizabeths, and during the last 15 years of freedom spent mostly in Italy, opinions of Pound were sharply divided. One camp admired him as a poet, perhaps the greatest influence on world poetry in our century. The other camp scorned and castigated him for his political and economic theories—views that infiltrated into his poetry, including his *Cantos*. Even Pound's death did not quell the controversy surrounding his life and writing. Few who knew Pound or his work did not take sides. But it was not always so.

Pound's life and work were in fact marked by dichotomies. His strongest early influences, into the 1920s, were from arts and letters, from the Greeks to his contemporaries. Afterwards the art persisted, but it showed the impact of Pound's readings of such economists and social historians as Clifford Douglas and Charles Beard. To some, Pound's espousal of unpopular ideas was his undoing. That and the fact that he was an expatriate from 1908 until his death, except for his 13 years of confinement at St Elizabeths. Unlike his friend T. S. Eliot, who became a British subject, Pound never renounced his American citizenship.

Two women were prominent in Pound's divided life. The first was Dorothy Shakespear (1886-1973), the English woman he married in 1914 and who 12 years later bore him a son, Omar. The other was an American concert violinist Olga Rudge, whom Pound met in 1922. She was the mother of the illegitimate child born in 1925 that Pound once referred to as his "egregious daughter Mary." For expediency during World War II, Ezra and Dorothy lived briefly with Olga at her home near Rapallo, Italy. But the letters collected in *Ezra Pound and Dorothy Shakespear* are, of course, not Olga's. The cloud of silence that hung between the two women still prevails in this volume, in which Olga is not even mentioned.

Reading this book was like opening a box of old treasures that I had heard of but never seen. While Pound scholars may find nothing startlingly new in this collection, it does shed light on much of the poet's life and work, early and late. An older edition of Pound's *Selected Letters 1907-1941* (Harcourt, 1950) includes only four letters from 1907-1909, none from 1910-1911, and a few dozen (mostly to editor Harriet Monroe of *Poetry* magazine) from 1912-1914.

This new volume contains the first publication of more than 200 letters and entries from Dorothy's notebook, which show Pound's formative development as a writer, editor and translator before his marriage in April 1914. It also reveals Dorothy (daughter of the novelist Olivia Shakespear) as eloquent, witty and solicitious. In her life with Ezra she possessed the necessary strength of an oak and the pliancy of a poplar.

In this era just before movements like Dadaism (1918) and Surrealism (1918), Pound was completing an energetic and brilliant apprenticeship in post-Romantic poets like Browning and Rossetti and the English Georgians (1911-12), and he was already breaking new ground.

He was immersed in the roots of Romance, from the troubadours to Dante, and he read and reviewed newer French poets like Charles Vildrac, Pierre-Jean Jouve and Emile Verhaeren. Judging by his correspondence with Dorothy and the copious notes and comments, Pound almost single-handedly shook English poets out of their post-Victorian lethargy.

During this period four poets and artists had a special impact on his work, and he on theirs: W. B. Yeats, a lifelong friend whom he served as a secretary from 1913 to 1917; Ford Madox Hueffer (who later changed his last name to Ford); Wyndham Lewis; and the sculptor Gaudier-Brzeska.

Pound's excursions into Vorticism, Futurism and particularly Imagism began to be seriously debated, followed or denounced on both sides of the Atlantic.

THREE FACES OF AUTUMN
Poetry, Prose, Translations

But the controversy in his life and the turmoil and wonder of his age had barely begun. The century was to be marred by two World Wars, a great Depression, a Holocaust, assassinations, famines and untold disasters. The marvels of space exploration, medicine, atomic power, agriculture and electronics could not make it more humane. Pound's anxieties, it seems, mounted with our age.

After his release from St Elizabeths, Pound received a few honors, notably the Harriet Monroe Prize of *Poetry* magazine (1962) and the Academy of American Poets $5,000 award (1963). But the controversy over the 1949 Bollingen Prize for his *Pisan Cantos* never seemed to stop. In 1972 he was denied the Emerson-Thoreau Medal of the American Academy of Arts and Sciences by a 13 to 9 vote of a council that could not separate the man and his politics from his work.

Was Pound "wrong" or was he indeed wronged by a society that confined him so long for his words? Our answer perhaps depends on how seriously we take his art and on whether we believe his political and economic ideas truly influenced others or endangered our society. Most of his biographers and scholars, I find, have treated the man primarily as an artist. These letters reveal the grace and breadth of the man as an artist and point to his influence and encouragement of three generations to follow.

As a friend of the Pounds during his postwar confinement at St. Elizabeths, I often visited them (Dorothy lived in a house nearby) to talk mostly of writers and writing, and the art of translation. I found that Pound's interest in "pure" poetry and in the roots of his own craft never waned. ("Rossetti," he told me, "was like a father and mother to me.") During those years I translated from many French poets—some from Pound's French poets essay in *Make It New* (1935)—and he had me send off some of these translations for publication here and abroad.

Sometimes for a poem or a well-turned translation I received his "complimenti," the same accolade he had given Eliot's *The Waste Land* 30 years earlier. The Romance language poets were the strongest bond between us, especially the poetry of Verhaeren, Jouve, Laforgue and Jean Cocteau. He knew I didn't want to talk politics, and in one letter he lightly called me a "bloomin' esthete." But I felt that I should never betray his trust and friendship by publishing details of my visits or by quoting him at length.

258

A CHARLES GUENTHER RETROSPECTIVE
Prose: Critical Reviews and Essays, 1983-1992

Returning from one such visit nearly 30 years ago, I pulled a briefcase from under my plane seat and shuffled through notes, official and unofficial. As a federal employee I had served under three presidents of two parties. I thought of Pound's own father, Homer, who had been an official at the Philadelphia Mint. But for an expatriate life which clouded his view of America, Ezra too might have served the country he never renounced. He might have held a high post, like Archibald MacLeish. Or like the revered Robert Frost, he might have read at some function for "the young Senator from Massachusetts" who Pound predicted to me, in 1958, would become our next president. Pound had remained a friend to both these poets, who were to help secure his release in 1958.

Among my scribbled notes I ran across a remark of his that he "would be remembered 30 years from now." It suddenly struck me that of course he would be remembered! The year was 1955—and the centennial of his birth would be 1985.

This volume of letters is a fitting memorial for Pound's centenary.

Review of *Ezra Pound and Dorothy Shakespear: Their Letters 1909-1914*, edited by Omar Pound and A. Walton Litz (New Directions).

St. Louis Post-Dispatch, November 11, 1984, p. 4E.

THREE FACES OF AUTUMN
Poetry, Prose, Translations

Poetry from the anguish of war

As a boy I bought an old remaindered copy of *The Valiant Muse*—
"poems by poets killed in the World War"—and could not foresee any
sequels to it, or the wars that would inspire them. Not the stately,
celebrated lines of Karl Shapiro and Henry Reed, or the brilliant, formal
pieces of Richard Eberhart and Howard Nemerov. And certainly not the
Lowenfels anthology, *Where Is Vietnam?* (1967). But war poetry, like war
itself, seems always with us, increasing like war in its range and intensity.

War poetry is about death and suffering, and sometimes about absence,
futility, fear and bravery. The lighter pieces, at best, are grimly light-
hearted and sardonic. While collections of war verse are typically narrow,
appealing to one generation, this new Oxford book has both breadth and
depth. It is a generous sampling taken from several cultures and traditions,
mostly British and American. It contains some 250 poems by more than
165 poets, from the Bible and Homer through Chaucer, Spenser, Dryden
and Shelley, to recent work by Seamus Heaney (b. 1939) and James
Fenton (b. 1949).   .

Editor Jon Stallworthy has included, too, a few women poets—Emily
Dickinson, Marianne Moore, Carolyn Forché and others—an appropriate
touch not typical of such anthologies. There are a few translations, mostly
from French poets like Victor Hugo, Apollinaire and Louis Aragon. Yet
most European poets who wrote powerfully of World War II are omitted.
(But so is Shakespeare for that matter.)

As a whole, however, Stallworthy's choices are well balanced. Although
we could suggest many additions, we get the feeling that something just as
good would have to make way for them. (That is a test of a good
anthology.) There is something for everyone here, from the precise, formal
lines of Wilfred Qwen and Siegfried Sassoon to the rough barracks idiom
of Rudyard Kipling and Lincoln Kirstein. All is resolved to that time
when, as Rupert Brooke writes, "the worst friend and enemy is but
Death."

Review of *The Oxford Book of War Poetry*, edited by Jon Stallworthy
(Oxford University Press).

St. Louis Post Dispatch, December 1, 1984, p. 2B.

Three creative artists in one mixed bag

Finding links among the arts is a pursuit as old as Aristotle. One of the classiest studies, now a classic, is Helmut Hatzfeld's *Literature Through Art* (Oxford, 1952), which compares French art and writing from the Middle Ages to Surrealism.

Three American Originals has a somewhat different approach. In it Joseph Reed compares both the artistic and personal character of three Americans —John Ford the film-maker, William Faulkner the novelist and Charles Ives the composer. He shows that they have certain affinities in their lives and their expression: Each is a regionalist working in American themes, each is preoccupied by the past, each has created a large body of work, and each is a conservative "in the manner of Edmund Burke."

Because Reed is the author of an earlier book on Faulkner, one might expect this study to be heavily weighed on that side; but I found the long section on Ford by far the most fascinating. It lists and discusses 42 Ford films covering a half century, from *The Tornado* (1917) to *Seven Women* (1966). I confess an ignorance of film directors—aside from a couple like John Huston and Nelo Risi—but it now seems most of my favorite films must have been directed by Ford.

Reed, incidentally, bypasses Huston, but a huge parade of other Hollywood personalities from Hoot Gibson to Donny Osmond make appearances here. As for Faulkner, there are stacks of books of greater interest to serious readers. Ives is the "sleeper" in this trio, the one whose work I'll be more attentive to in the future, the composer whose work, like Ford's, I've long appreciated but seldom identified.

On the whole, Reed shows adroitly that these three artists do have common traits. One may ask the purpose of such a comparison. Perhaps it is to show Reed's own versatility as an interpreter of several arts. Yet this exercise, or demonstration, directs the reader into new channels of comparative appreciation. It opens infinite possibilities.

Review of *Three American Originals: John Ford, William Faulkner, and Charles Ives*, by Joseph W. Reed (Wesleyan).

St. Louis Post-Dispatch, December 25, 1984, p. 4B.

THREE FACES OF AUTUMN
Poetry, Prose, Translations

Finding historical truths in poetry

Historical truth is just one of the truths poets seek, and profess to find. Many celebrated poets have dealt with their national history— Shakespeare, for instance, who borrowed heavily from Holinshead's *Chronicles*. To some poets, like Ezra Pound, history had an obsessive fascination. If this book's title seems ambiguous, think of it rather as "poetry about history" or "poets as historians." Author Joseph G. Kronick, fed by literary interests, has a strong overall view of American history. He applies his knowledge and instincts well to the writers he deals with: Emerson, Thoreau, Whitman; Henry Adams, Pound, William Carlos Williams, Hart Crane and Wallace Stevens.

Of these eight writers Kronick is much less concerned with Thoreau than with the rest—and in fact he gives more attention to writers like Melville, Poe and T. S, Eliot—perhaps because Thoreau's philosophy seems less complex. Thoreau, who wanted to be a "father of an American literature," became instead a "perpetual son" of the authentic father, Emerson.

Kronick stresses the language (mostly the metaphors) used by these writers. Thoreau's metaphors, for instance, came from building and farming, while Henry Adams considered universal force or energy as paramount. Kronick points out that Pound, more than any other modern poet, brought the intellectual heritage of the nineteenth century into the twentieth. Adams had much in common with Pound, whose predilection for dynamic force in both man and nature could be examined more closely by Kronick. But Pound's affinities with Emerson—in their common interests in history, economics and physics— are described well.

Readers who dislike both history and poetry may find this book doubly dull. But those who like either, especially poetry, will find it doubly rewarding. Kronick makes us understand not only the importance of the American heritage to American poetry, but also how many aspects of history affected these writers—who in turn have greatly influenced our times and attitudes.

Review of *American Poetics of History: From Emerson to the Moderns*, by Joseph Kronick (Louisiana State University).

St. Louis Post-Dispatch, January 19, 1985, p. 5B.

A CHARLES GUENTHER RETROSPECTIVE
Prose: Critical Reviews and Essays, 1983-1992

Eminent man of letters

Letter-writing is a dying art even among men of letters. (We exclude of course the huge body of commercial and junk mail, and the endless solicitations, whose volume numbs our sensibilities.) Fewer and fewer of our letters are answered in kind; the phone call and the post card do the job.

Die-hard letter-writers hold out, and John Crowe Ransom (1888-1974), poet and editor of *The Kenyon Review* in Gambier, Ohio, was among them. He was not only one of the most eminent writers and critics of his day, a leader of the Southern Fugitive group, but also an effective, sensitive editor and correspondent. He even had a gift for making a rejection sound like an acceptance, as in this note to poet Babette Deutsch in 1953:

> Your verse is always poetry. I believe my feeling is adverse on one point only, but pretty steadily—I miss formality in it. I think I'm probably prejudiced.
> Thank you for sending this, and the nice note too.

Ransom did not push friendships, but allowed them to develop deeply and durably. Several did, especially with Allen Tate and Robert Penn Warren. The letters to Warren from 1930-1968, and with Tate from 1922 to 1967, form the bulk of this volume, which contains more than 250 letters dated 1911 to 1968. Ransom had a growing esteem for the younger Tate, whose poetry he considered superior to most, equal in fact to T. S. Eliot's. ("You and Eliot are the unique poets of that period," he wrote Tate, "and your performance was much pithier than his, more memorable.")

During his 21 years editing the review at Kenyon College, Ransom was a potentate of American letters and tiny Gambier became a Mecca for younger writers who sought his counsel. He encouraged or promoted hundreds, including Robert Bly, Howard Nemerov, Flannery O'Connor, Mona Van Duyn and James Wright. (Nemerov was even a candidate to succeed Ransom as editor of the review, one 1957 letter to Tate reveals.) The *Selected Letters* also shed light on other members of the Fugitives, especially Tate, Warren, Merrill Moore and Laura Riding. One long letter to Tate (1926) deplores Riding's rumors of infighting and rivalry in the group. In a much later letter (1965) to Tate, Ransom reminisces about

Donald Davidson and regrets that the prolific Moore (who wrote 43,000 sonnets) remained unrecognized until his death. Yet in an earlier proposal to Tate (1936) for an "American Academy of Letters" Ransom excluded Moore and Riding from the 25 hypothetical candidates while including Davidson and Warren among seven others "nearly qualified."

Ransom once wrote of his "lamentable shortcomings as a correspondent." But he wrote bountifully and well, and this compact selection shows the best qualities of his character and writing: gentility, humility, sensibility and, above all, ability. In American writing today, all these add up to a rare nobility.

Of closely related interest is an unusual 370-page document, *Radical Conservatism:* The Southern Review (1935-1942), by Albert J. Montesi of Saint Louis University, just issued and on file at the university. This quotes many rare sources, some first-hand to Montesi, on the Fugitive movement.

Review of *Selected Letters of John Crowe Ransom*, edited by Thomas D. Young and George Core (Louisiana State).

St. Louis Post-Dispatch, February 14, 1985, p. 4B.

From *Howl* to now

Nearly 30 years ago Allen Ginsberg shook up American letters with a pamphlet called *Howl*, its title poem a raucous, exclamatory piece that to some read like a parody of Whitman or Sandburg. To others, Ginsberg was a reincarnation of some earlier mystic, Blake or Rimbaud perhaps. He was to poetry what Elvis was to rock music, and *Howl* was his theme song.

Today we can appreciate the spontaneous intensity of *Howl* in the light of hundreds of his earlier and later poems of many moods and themes. I have always had ambivalent impressions of Ginsberg's poetry. When it is bad, like much of the juvenilia, it is pure truck. When it is good, as *Howl* and many later poems are, it is very good indeed: fresh, moving, imaginative, clever.

In the *Collected Poems* we continually look for the "real" Allen G.—and we find him mostly in the longer poems, from "Kaddish" to "Ecologue" and "Friday the Thirteenth." Like Ezra Pound, Ginsberg was a disillusioned political activist. A major source for understanding the poet and his work is Lewis Hyde's collection of more than 70 essays on Ginsberg. The contributors are many and varied, from Marianne Moore and Richard Eberhart to Robert Ely, Timothy Leary and Czeslaw Milosz. They view Ginsberg from every imaginable aspect—from a demented, misguided youth to a surrealistic visionary, a prophet, and a cantor of a new age. The most enlightening of the essays are by his peers and his fellow Beat poets, especially Kenneth Rexroth, Lawrence Ferlinghetti and Louis Simpson.

One short piece, a poem, stands out among the essays. It is by one who knew Allen best: his father, the poet Louis Ginsberg, who observes his son's struggles:

> Almost like Theseus, you grope
> Through dank, subterranean passageways
> Of your different selves . . . .
> May you soon see
> The Ariadne-thread
> Of your true identity
> To find the sun-burst opening ahead.

THREE FACES OF AUTUMN
Poetry, Prose, Translations

The *Collected Poems* are certainly a "sun-burst" revelation, even to the most devoted Ginsberg readers. The volume, with all its faults and virtues, reveals the total personality of one of the most compelling and talented poets of his generation.

Review of *Collected Poems: 1947-1980*, by Allen Ginsberg (Harper & Row) and *On the Poetry of Allen Ginsberg*, edited by Lewis Hyde (University of Michigan).

St. Louis Post-Dispatch, February 17, 1985, p. 4B.

A CHARLES GUENTHER RETROSPECTIVE
Prose: Critical Reviews and Essays, 1983-1992

Poetry collections: mark of a professional

"There is no visible success for the poet," Jean Cocteau wrote—and perhaps this is true. Two of the poets with the most influence on our century, Gerard Manley Hopkins and Emily Dickinson, might be considered amateurs because they earned little or nothing from their craft.

Of today's professionals—those who publish and sell—thousands enter the annual "literary lotteries" with grant applications, but only a few hundred are rewarded with the most lucrative fellowships and prizes, up to $20,000 and more. Poetry readings bring honoraria to some, but the overemphasis on "names" by a public largely ignorant of poetry keeps many talented writers off the circuit.

One measure of success always has been the appearance of a collection covering the span of a poet's career. At least a half dozen notable collections are published each year, balancing the thousands of slim books of new verse. These collections reveal much about the poets' development. Alan Dugan, for instance, in *New and Collected Poems, 1961-1983* (Ecco Press/Norton) shows little deviation from the terse, biting style which brought him early success. That style is powerfully simple and honest:

> . . . I have to fear death and expect
> something else once in a while like everybody else
> although I'm bored or hurting or both
> most of the time except for those split seconds
> of ecstasy which might be meaningful
> and seem to be, no matter how infrequent
> they are and how impossible to understand.

Another poet of the same generation as Dugan is Louis Simpson, and his style is just as open, casual and accessible as Dugan's. "I write poems in order to express feelings I have had since I was a child," he writes in an afterword to his new book, *People Live Here: Selected Poems 1949-1988* (BOA Editions). The collection is uniquely arranged, not chronologically but in groups of themes and ideas. Still, while it is easy to spot Simpson's early debts to Whitman and Eliot here and there, the arrangement is pleasing. Simpson shows a fine breadth of forms and modes, from short, personal lyrics to long dramatic episodes, slices of the poet's life in World War II and after.

THREE FACES OF AUTUMN
Poetry, Prose, Translations

James Fenton, an English poet born in 1949, already has published a strong but relatively small collection of work from three early volumes. His *Children in Exile: Poems 1968-1984* (Random House) shows a brilliant range of forms, diction and subject matter. The long title poem on Cambodian children is especially moving. Many of the earlier poems deal with war and war's aftermath: "Cambodia," "In a Notebook" and "Dead Soldiers," for instance. Fenton's first book, *The Memory of War* (1982), based on his experiences as a journalist in Indochina and Germany, was acclaimed in Britain, but has not yet settled in on American audiences. Fenton has been compared with W. H. Auden, the Auden of *Poems* (1930). Few American poets have his range, his intellect and wit, or his craftsmanship.

Finally, another younger poet, Kenneth A. McClane, has published *A Tree Beyond Telling: Poems, Selected and New* (The Black Scholar Press), drawn from four earlier books. McClane was born in New York City in 1951 and now teaches at Cornell. In *A Tree Beyond Telling*, dedicated to Gwendolyn Brooks, he reveals a literary indebtedness not only to Ms. Brooks but also to such poets as Langston Hughes, Robert Hayden, Michael Harper and Mari Evans. But that is indeed fine company, and his poetry shows a steady growth of perception and expression. A brief example of his sensitive observation is "Meditation at Jones River":

> When the river swells, the loose
> soarings of loon betray
> how difficult the singing: but if one looks
> beyond the mist, how the willows keep
> it fast and upwind: how they bend
> disk-shaped, resonative, frantic that the song be heard:
> and even the inlet, a natural tuning fork,
> will not let the slightest voice suffer silent.

Perhaps a poet's success is, after all, just fleeting and inconsequential. Nothing about a poem can equal the pleasure or pain involved in making it—unless it be the realization that it is shared and appreciated by others.

St. Louis Post-Dispatch, April 7, 1985, p. 4B.

The poetry-politics mix

"Poetry and politics don't mix" was an adage I firmly believed in my teens. Political verse of the far left and right seemed too blatant, while that of the center seemed too bland. Besides, the burning issues of one age usually vanish in the next. Famous examples bore me out: Shakespeare's most lumbering plays are the histories, and only a few scholars appreciate the subtle references in Pope and Aristophanes. Still, as Walt Whitman insisted, no subject is out of the domain of poetry, and politics remains among the most appealing topics to a "now" generation. Richard Jones's collection of 22 essays by various poets shows a broad view of the subject. The essays range from T. S. Eliot's "The Social Function of Poetry" to Stanley Kunitz's "Poet and State" and Amiri Baraka's piece on revolution in Afro-American literature. Politics here deals not only with revolutionaries and reactionaries (Stephen Spender) but also with national conscience (Howard Nemerov) and ecological survival (Gary Snyder).

Jones's introduction and the many viewpoints he brings together make this the finest modern collection I've seen on the subject. He understands and reintroduces the ageless questions relating politics and poetry (for instance, should poetry please or persuade?), and he lets the reader form his own opinions. Yet he too recognizes that poetry and politics, when mixed, can be divisive rather than informative. But controversy does not (and need not) silence any writer on any level. The poet is free to raise his own voice. Curiously, Jones notes a scarcity of poems about "the bomb" in the second half of our century. But if he would research certain anthologies and little magazines he'd find plenty of examples from the '60s.

Poetry and Politics is a well-balanced choice for our time. Women's views, from Muriel Rukeyser to Carolyn Forché, are well represented, although certain figures like Genevieve Taggard and Barbara Howes are omitted. I cannot imagine any writer, or any reader, failing to find something fundamentally moving or provocative in this set of essays. My favorite is Lewis Hyde's "The Commerce of the Creative Spirit." I usually shun the word inspiring, but it fits here.

Review of *Poetry and Politics: An Anthology of Essays*, edited by Richard Jones (Morrow).

St. Louis Post-Dispatch, July 19, 1985, p. 4C.

THREE FACES OF AUTUMN
Poetry, Prose, Translations

Using biography for better understanding

"A book is a machine to think with," wrote critic I. A. Richards.

Yet some books are more charged with thought than others. Never popular, they may affect only a few other writers, and through them, later generations of readers.

Such were the books of William Empson (1906-1984), with titles like *Seven Types of Ambiguity* and *The Structure of Complex Words*—certainly not destined to displace in popularity writers like Louis L'Amour or Studs Terkel. (In fact, 50 years after Richards and Empson introduced their New Criticism, learned journals still carry articles on "how to read" their work.)

In *Using Biography*, a series of 11 essays gathered just before his death, Empson takes a different, more humanistic approach for a change, less coldly analytical of words and meanings. Here he "uses" authors' lives for a better understanding of their work.

The half-dozen he deals with, all British, are well established and dead, almost beyond controversy: Andrew Marvell, John Dryden, Henry Fielding, W.B. Yeats, T. S. Eliot and James Joyce.

Empson was a brilliant scholar, but a maverick, drawing from unusual sources and his own insights. Sometimes, however, he gets a bit imaginative, as when he describes T. S. Eliot's American background: ". . . the young Eliot had a good deal of simple old St. Louis brashness"; and "he was just saying what any decent man would say back home in St. Louis—if he was well heeled and had a bit of culture."

By and large, Empson's books are intricate thought machines. Even his *Collected Poems*, a sparse 90 pages, holds curious, dark gems. This example is titled "Let It Go":

> It is this deep blankness is the real thing strange.
> The more things happen to you the more you can't
> Tell or remember even what they were.
> The contradictions cover such a range.
> The talk would talk and go so far aslant.
> You don't want madhouse and the whole thing there.

What a great epigraph for a science-fiction novel! Think about *that*, dear readers.

Review of *Using Biography*, by William Empson (Harvard).

St. Louis Post-Dispatch, July 30, 1985, p. 4B.

THREE FACES OF AUTUMN
Poetry, Prose, Translations

Searching out new facets to Eliot's *The Waste Land*

> The world is full of passing fads
> As hawked upon our tubes:
> Like hula hoops and cabbage kids
> And even Rubik's cubes.

Literary scholars too have their fads, and one of the most puzzling of all is the continued popularity of interpreting T. S. Eliot's *The Waste Land* for an age which feels little of the poem's new thrill. After *The Waste Land* appeared more than 60 years ago it was blasted by English critics like I. A. Richards and the Keats scholar Middleton Murry. Richards, especially, found the poem lacking "any coherent intellectual thread" and questioned "whether the poem is worth the trouble it entails" to understand it.

Well, three generations later the compulsion to interpret Eliot remains like an occupational disease in American universities.

Harriet Davidson's new study, like most of the rest, I suspect, was done as a personal appreciation of Eliot, incidentally shared by publication. Just when we think that nothing more can be found in Eliot, critics like Davidson extract new meanings or shades of meaning from his poetry. For each critic's background differs, especially in philosophy, and each brings new insights to the poetry, especially *The Waste Land*.

With Davidson the concentration is on philosophers Francis Bradley and Martin Heidegger. She deals not only with *The Waste Land* but also with Eliot's prose—and she shows how consistent Eliot was in his critical and artistic thinking. She reveals one secret of Eliot's great popularity: his graceful, non-technical language and his wide-ranging, non-abstract interests. (The audience of *Cats* would certainly agree!) The philosophy of *The Waste Land* is "a ceaseless hermeneutic" (or interpretation) between desire and death, Davidson concludes. These fundamental themes alone make the poem timeless.

I have but one important point of dissension with Davidson: her light treatment of Ezra Pound's influence upon Eliot, especially upon *The Waste Land*. The facts are known and the documents bared, but the collaboration is almost ignored here. Yet her overall interpretation of the poem is powerfully developed.

Even I. A. Richards later conceded that "Mr. Eliot's *The Waste Land* is major poetry." The poem is perhaps the greatest literary kaleidoscope ever invented in American letters, for each viewer (or reader) rattles its pieces in different patterns. Yet how many wastelands have been created by felling forests to make the paper to comment on the poem? (Only Weyerhauser knows.) Not as many, at any rate, as those created by pulp Westerns and romance novels.

One cannot help but wonder what Eliot would have made of all of this.

Review of *T.S. Eliot and Hermeneutics: Absence and Interpretation in The Waste Land*, by Harriet Davidson (Louisiana State University).

St. Louis Post-Dispatch, November 9, 1985, p. 4B.

THREE FACES OF AUTUMN
Poetry, Prose, Translations

Mirrors of life

Letters are the clearest mirrors of a writer's life. An inferior art, perhaps, they lack the imaginative self-projection and higher expression of poetry and fiction. Yet they are the raw stuff, the main documents, of biography which is selective and (even as autobiography) often prejudiced.

Like other writers, Charles Baudelaire (1821-1867) and Dylan Thomas (1915-1953) used their letters as a simultaneous social and business tool. Their whole correspondence shows many facets of character, and their lives and characters were alike in many ways: in the banning of their work (Thomas's by the BBC, Baudelaire's by the French government), in certain artistic tastes (each liked Wagner, for instance), and in weaknesses that led to their early deaths. But their strongest similarities were in pursuit of love, money and major recognition—all of which largely eluded them, and which are, after all, the universal pursuits of others besides writers.

Money, for instance. What an obsessive, yet genuine need it appears in these letters: "I have a big, big favor to ask of you," Baudelaire began one letter to his publisher Calonne, asking for a third advance, in 1859, after his banned *Flowers of Evil* had put him in deeper debt. Earlier, to Poulet-Malassis (1853) he wrote, "I beg you—. . . I beg you simply—if that's possible—to send me by post as soon as you receive this letter—a sum of money, any amount." Yet debt seemed a way of life with him, from his 20th year when he ran up tailors' bills to his mid-40s when he still depended on his mother, Caroline Aupick. Even his resolution in a New Year's Day letter to Mme. Aupick (1865) was short-lived: "I promise you first that this year you won't be forced to accept any request for aid on my behalf," he began. But two paragraphs later he drops a strong hint: "You've no doubt guessed how much I stand in terror of going through Paris without any money. . . without being able to offer some guarantees to some of my creditors."

Thomas too was continually impoverished, but his need was increased by the dependency of his wife Caitlin and their children. Just a few weeks before his death he confided to Igor Stravinsky, "One of my chief troubles is, of course, money. I haven't any of my own, and most of the little I make seems to go to schools for my children." Yet even at age19 (1934), he wrote to Pamela Johnson, "Short stories of the sort I write hardly make anything . . . . And poetry wouldn't keep a goldfinch alive." From early on he made repeated urgent pleas to publishers: "So do have a shot to get me that quid" (1936) . . . "I must have some money" (1938) . . . "I need that other 50 pounds. So very desperately" (1948) . . . "When do I get the 125 dollars? Am in trouble" (1951). Sometimes he posted letters without stamps (to Henry Treece, for instance), explaining that he and Caitlin had "no food and no money at all" (1938). Two of Thomas's publishers, James Laughlin (U.S.) and Princess Caetani (Italy), were especially generous, sending him periodic advances. He was not ungrateful. To Mme. Caetani (1951): "Thank you, very deeply, for your forgiving letter and for the money which . . . saved my life again, or, rather, paid a horned and raging bill. Oh, how many times you've saved my lives now! I've as many, I suppose, as a Hallowe'en of cats."

And love. Baudelaire and Thomas longed for a calm, solvent domestic life sometimes, but their strange, effusive genius wouldn't allow it. Writing to his mother (1852), Baudelaire confessed that his mistress, Jeanne Duval, had become "an impediment not merely to my happiness . . . but also to the improvement of my mental faculties." After his stepfather's death (1857) he turned more and more to his strong-willed mother for consolation and understanding: "Oh, my dear mother, is there still enough time for us both to be happy? . . . I want to tell you something I don't tell you often enough . . . that is that the tenderness I feel for you increases constantly. It fills me with shame that this tenderness doesn't even give me the strength to pull myself together. I contemplate the years that have passed and spend my time reflecting on the brevity of life" (1861).

Thomas's life with Caitlin was broken by his long reading engagements in America, where she rarely accompanied him, but often remained ill in their "crumbling home" in Wales. Thomas wrote long, affectionate letters to "my love, my own, Caitlin my Cat," sometimes enclosing money, but nothing could assuage the separation. Without Caitlin he found even the posh homes of his generous hosts (who included Francis Biddle and Charlie Chaplin) "hell on earth." He wanted especially to bring Caitlin to California with him, but when he finally did (1952), the teaching jobs promised him never materialized.

Luckier in love than Baudelaire, Thomas (like Baudelaire) died too soon to get deserved recognition. Neither got awards of the sort heaped upon lesser writers nowadays, like munificent grants and fellowships, professorial chairs and major prizes. To Thomas it didn't seem to matter.

THREE FACES OF AUTUMN
Poetry, Prose, Translations

America showed its appreciation to him by its large audiences and publication of his works, but he dreaded the exhausting trips through "this devastating, insane, demoniacally loud, roaring continent."

Baudelaire, who at age 40 sought election to the French Academy, had few influential supporters. (These included the critic Sainte-Beuve and poet Alfred de Vigny.) He withdrew his application and never reapplied. Besides his writing he was able to get only a few lecture engagements in France and Belgium—and he hated Belgium as much as Thomas despised America. Thomas wanted "to write poems of happiness," and Baudelaire longed "to know some degree of security, of glory, of contentment" with himself, yet their lives were cut short—avoidably by today's standards—Baudelaire's by syphilis and drugs, Thomas's by alcoholism and an untimely injection of morphine by a well-meaning physician. (Thomas didn't die, as some said facetiously, of "being Dylan Thomas.")

Finally, perhaps their most important letters aren't about love or money or the pursuit of fame, but about the arts—Baudelaire's letters about Edgar Allan Poe, for instance, whose work he translated into French, and his correspondence with figures like Flaubert, Hugo, Wagner and Vigny. And Thomas's letters to fellow poets like Henry Treece, Vernon Watkins and James Laughlin.

Historians may record that such letter writing expired with the coming of the pushbutton phone and the personal computer. Whatever the modes of future communication, these letters are precious relics of two brief, brilliant lives. They are an important legacy, touchstones for new generations.

Review of *Dylan Thomas: The Collected Letters*, edited by Paul Ferris (Macmillan) and *Selected Letters of Charles Baudelaire: The Conquest of Solitude*, translated and edited by Rosemary Lloyd (University of Chicago).

St. Louis Post-Dispatch, May 4, 1986, p. 4B.

The riddle of Emily Dickinson still fascinates 100 years later

There are several ways to read a poem: "cold" or intuitively, understanding it from our own experience, or through the interpretation of scholars, and critics.

A third, better, way is to combine both of these methods, using others' explanations only after we try to understand the poem ourselves. Some verse is so simple, of course, that its meaning comes right through to us. Such verse isn't necessarily bad; it may be excellent light verse, for example.

Few poets can be more vexingly vague than the beloved Emily Dickinson (1830-1886), author of 1,775 staccato gems variously interpreted by hundreds of critics. E. Miller Budick is one of the most eloquent of these. She probes deeply into how Dickinson used symbols to illustrate links between life and language. She quotes and analyzes dozens of Dickinson's best poems, and her interpretations seem strong and plausible.

Through her verse Dickinson's critics have depicted her in many guises, ranging from an impish parodist to an overly pious, sequestered spinster. I had long relegated Dickinson to the place of America's earliest and best "confessional" poet. She is after all one of the purest introspective lyricists, with opening lines like these: "I died for Beauty," "I dwell in Possibility," "I felt a Cleaving in my Mind," "I felt a Funeral, in my Brain," "I found the words to every thought," "I heard a Fly buzz...," "I taste a liquor never brewed," and so on.

Well! I never imagined Dickinson "having some premeditated concern with the verbalization of symbolic consciousness" or having a "profound psychological and aesthetic necessity for . . . that part of cosmic experience that is eminently accessible to symbolic representation." Heavy stuff. I've preferred to get to the roots of the poet's vocabulary and metrics. Critics pay little attention, for instance, to Dickinson's use of common meter—one of the three most frequently used meters of Protestant hymns—and its impact on New England audiences.

One can't help but feel that now, just a century after her death (May 15, 1886), Dickinson would be astounded and amused at the interpretations and analyses of her poems. Despite the psychoanalyses of critics, Emily remains the Grand Riddle. But while this study is sometimes repetitive and unnecessarily dense, Budick does understand Dickinson's poetry and gives us fine perceptual impressions of the poems.

Like many scholars, Budick may be overly dedicated to her subject—an admirable trait. Anyone who wants both a true text and a close reading of some of Dickinson's best poetry will find this an arresting, satisfying study.

Review of *Emily Dickinson and the Life of Language, a Study in Symbolic Poetics*, by E. Miller Budick (Louisiana State).

St. Louis Post-Dispatch, May 17, 1986, p. 4B.

Stories forged in the agony of hard times

To the connoisseur, bums, tramps and hoboes are different breeds. The hobo is a migratory worker, the tramp is a migratory non-worker and the bum is a non-migratory non-worker. John Wesley (Jack) Conroy, a gandy dancer in his younger days, knows them all for he lived and worked with some of them in the most grueling jobs in the hardest times. Not just floaters but pipe line diggers, bricksetters in paving gangs, cement loaders, bridge riveters and coal miners. That was before and during the Depression when many job-seekers rode the freights through the Midwest, sometimes "dizzy, hungry and . . . sick of roaming—about to give up and sneak back home like a whipped pup."

Once in that mood Conroy found a job as a "banjo player" (shoveler) excavating and laying the basement of a slaughterhouse. "As it grew hotter," he recalls in his story "The Cement King," "we all became lean as wolves, and just as snarly. Our inner thighs and forearms were galled so cruelly that it was a task to walk, let alone work like beavers, with the salty sweat smarting our raw places as it poured over them. The drinking water was tepid as dishwater, and many of us cursed over a sick stomach all day long, even though thirst might drive us to the bucket time and again."

Now over a half century after such experience, on which his celebrated novel *The Disinherited* (1933) was based, 32 of Conroy's tales have been gathered into this varied, entertaining collection. They include humorous "Uncle Ollie" stories, tall folk narratives, tales of the Monkey Nest mine area near Moberly where Conroy was born and raised, and stories of workers of the Depression era. In time they span the first third of our century, and the settings range from rural Missouri to factories, mills, shops and construction sites throughout the Midwest. The life they describe was harsh by today's standards. The best transportation, for instance, might have been a spavined mare—or more often, just "shank's mare" (walking).

The most striking feature of Conroy's writing is its power and durability. But its power is simply the power of truth, told and retold as a Gorky, a Steinbeck or a Faulkner might have told it. Even the tall tales, the anecdotes and exaggerations, have elements of credibility—up to a point—which increase their effect. As for the workers stories, they seem

totally unembellished by imagination, and their stark experience pops
from the pages like old documentary photos in a Depression album.
Whoever lived through that period at once recognizes Conroy's America
as the "real" one—not the America of the celluloid flicks which were only
a panacea to millions.

And Conroy's truth is durable because it is not served up with propaganda.
Sure, a born laborite and son of a labor organizer, he played with liberal
and left-wing politics. But reading him we needn't swallow a mold of
overt propaganda found in novels like Gilfilan's *I Went to Pit College* and
other works of that period. While he contributed to *The New Masses* and
edited *The Anvil Magazine*, he also wrote for such respectable journals as
American Mercury.

Physically large, Conroy has also grown in literary stature. The writers he
published or associated with included Nelson Algren, Jesse Stuart, Frank
Yerby, William Carlos Williams and St. Louis poet Will Wharton (who
later parodied the left-wing causes the group once embraced). Through his
magazine he became a mentor to other novelists, including Harry Mark
Petrakis of Chicago. Just recently, Petrakis presented Conroy the Friends
of Midland Authors Award at the annual meeting of the Society of
Midland Authors in Chicago.

After many years in Chicago, Conroy, now 86, has retired to Moberly. Not
surprisingly, he has continued to write stories, some of which, written in
his eighties, appeared in the Kansas City magazine *New Letters*. On maps
of Missouri today, Moberly is shown as the boyhood home of Gen. Omar
Bradley. But decades before Bradley became famous, another native son
was celebrating the life and land of that community—not only of Monkey
Nest but of places like Walden Grove, Kimberly, Happy Hollow and
Skinner Bottoms. Surely there is a place for Jack Conroy's name there too.

Review of *The Weed King & Other Stories*, by Jack Conroy (Lawrence
Hill).

St. Louis Post-Dispatch, June 22, 1986, p. 4B.

Why some poets endure

Great poetry, as Keats once noted, is so rare and precious that—considering our busy, hectic lives—it's a. wonder any of it ever gets written.

Even the best poets know that only one great line comes for every thousand merely competent lines, plus every ten thousand mediocre lines that should be discarded.

There is something special, then, about poets like John Ashbery and Hayden Carruth who have doggedly practiced the craft rather successfully for 30 years or so. And regardless of how many "great" lines they've written, there is something very special about the cream of their craft, skimmed into these finely produced and edited selections.

Ashbery and Carruth are among the best and brightest of the generation of poets born in the 1920s. Each represents a synthesis of the two strong traditions of American poetry: the artfulness of Poe and the social consciousness of Whitman.

Carruth tends to write about people, directly; Ashbery is more impersonal.

Ashbery's poems like "Wooden Buildings" and "The Bungalows" are dense, charged with personal meanings and memories, with words like "caique" and "tergiversation" to obfuscate readers. On a similar theme, Carruth's poem "Meadow House" is unmistakably clear from its opening line, "This is a poem for you, Ann. Impromptu . . . ."

On the theme of love Ashbery is equally obscure, and his "A Love Poem" of 11 lines reads like an eloquent, private note.

Carruth's longer "Essay on Love," 76 lines, is concrete, colorful:

> And goldenrod,
> plumes of yellow
> where yellow bees mumble, and asters, blue
> and purple and white. New England asters
> that are our stars, and the small
> speckled asters, massed
> at the edge of the clearing.

THREE FACES OF AUTUMN
Poetry, Prose, Translations

Yet Ashbery can evoke precise imagery too. His "Into the Dusk-Charged Air," a litany of rivers of the world, is a tour de force, written no doubt with a descriptive gazetteer in hand. By comparison, Carruth has a shorter "list" poem titled "Another Catalogue" listing scores of products "manufactured from/ open hearth and bessemer steel"—a bit too detailed to quote out of context.

Many readers undeniably feel that new American poetry is aimless, formless, flat. Much of it is, of course, for even mediocrity sometimes gets into print. But take heart. There are a few good craftsmen like Ashbery and Carruth who keep both form and language alive. But there are few better.

Review of *Selected Poems*, by John Ashbery (Viking) and *The Selected Poems of Hayden Carruth* (Macmillan).

St. Louis Post-Dispatch, August 3, 1986, p. 4C.

The entertaining business of interpreting poetry

Poetry is unique because it has two meanings: a literal meaning of everyday speech and a symbolic meaning that some critics say comes from our collective consciousness. But because scholars and critics differ in interpreting poems—and many of their different opinions seem reasonable—we may wonder if there is indeed a uniform collective consciousness. Maybe there is no absolute answer to this question. Some poems will always remain ambiguous, for interpreting poetry is as old as song itself.

Eight centuries ago in Provence, for instance, there were two schools of poetry, "open" and "closed," or plain and obscure. The poets chided one another for their styles, and the most common complaint was, "I don't understand it." Sound familiar? Of course it does—and today droves of critics and scholars put their interpretations into print for all to share. Their manifold ideas may strike us as too broad or narrow, too simple or complex, or too bizarre or offbeat or bigoted—or right on the mark. Whatever the case, debating literature isn't like arguing politics or religion, where the destiny of life (or afterlife) hangs in the balance. It can be a lot more fun.

If criticism is meant both to entertain and to interpret, one of the most enjoyable recent studies I've read is *The Poetry and Poetics of Amiri Baraka* by William J. Harris (University of Missouri). Amiri Baraka (formerly LeRoi Jones), now 51, represents perhaps better than any American poet of his generation certain aspects of black life and culture during the last 25 years. Baraka began writing with the Beat generation of poetry read and written to jazz. Using the "jazz aesthetic" as a main influence on Baraka, Harris shows how the poet learned to write and think from white avant-garde poets but later transformed what he learned into the rhythms of black life and speech. Harris shows also Baraka's influence on younger black poets, and he defines words like "scatting" and "signifying." This is a splendidly written study, supplemented by two appendices—one an interview with the poet, the other a new long poem by Baraka.

A new volume by Stanley Kunitz, *Next-to-Last Things: New Poems and Essays* (The Atlantic Monthly Press) also contains an interview and new poetry. But most of the book consists of seven essays and a set of aphorisms. Kunitz's prose is rare and revealing. The subjects here include John Keats, Robert Lowell and Walt Whitman. Most revealing are the interview with Kunitz and an essay on his strong-spirited mother, an immigrant born of a Lithuanian Jewish family. The essays enhance our understanding of Kunitz's poetry. One of the new poems, a long piece titled "The Wellfleet Whale," is an especially brilliant addition to his work.

Charles Simic is one of those exceptional American poets whose work blends the best of both worlds, old and new. Born in Yugoslavia, he emigrated to the U.S. in his youth and became naturalized in 1971. He has written or translated more than a dozen books and won numerous awards. In *The Uncertain Certainty* (University of Michigan), Simic sheds light on his own and other poets' work in seven interviews and a dozen essays dated 1972-84. Simic has a phenomenal breadth of appreciation of poetry and poets—from Keats and Hawthorne and Emerson to modern writers like the French Surrealist Benjamin Péret and the Yugoslavian Vasko Popa. Simic is most revealing when interviewed by other poets or when writing about his peers. One of the clearest statements on his own poetic process emerges from a brief essay on William Carlos Williams, when Simic expands on his idea that "poetry is made out of words and time."

Certain poems like Edgar Allan Poe's "The Raven" are never sufficiently explained, it seems. That poem and others by Poe have profoundly influenced French writers for more than a century—first .in the French Symbolist movement, which lasted about 50 years, and since then in a host of other writers, including the Surrealists. A new volume, *Metamorphoses of the Raven* by Jefferson Humphries (Louisiana State University Press) describes and traces that influence. While some of Humphries's analogies—like Poe's raven and the various birds (hawk, bat, thrush) of later U.S. poets—may seem far-fetched, Poe's impact on the French cannot be denied. This complex but interesting study has a fine glossary and a bibliography.

Another specialized book on a single poem is Marilyn Kallet's *Honest Simplicity in William Carlos Williams's "Asphodel, That Greeny Flower"* (Louisiana State). Kallet's title reveals her theme, and she develops that theme well in one of the most dedicated studies of Williams's later work. Williams is still an enigma to many readers despite his simple language and style. Kallet shows how "Asphodel," written in 1952-53, was no longer "pure improvisation" but a formal summation of Williams's life and craft.

Finally, one of the most ambitious works is Peter Stitt's *The World's Hieroglyphic Beauty: Five American Poets* (University of Georgia Press). This study explores the work and ideas of five poets: Richard Wilbur, William Stafford, Louis Simpson, James Wright and Robert Penn Warren. It is unique because it includes both an essay about, and an interview with, each poet. All of these poets, Stitt shows, have searched for some hidden meaning in the physical universe. Wilbur, for instance, as in his book *Things of This World*, celebrates spiritual elements in the material world. Warren expresses, powerfully, the human capacity for evil. The other poets, Stitt feels, are less specific in their quest but no less passionate and dedicated. Altogether this is one of the best recent books on a group of modern U.S. poets.

Understanding poetry takes a bit more than the intuitive enjoyment of words read as everyday speech. Some may feel all a critic needs are a plausible idea, a few facts and an earnest, persuasive style. But it takes a deeper interest by the critic to kindle that deeper interest in us. Whether on or off the mark, a critic gives us a starting point to enhance our appreciation. For great poetry needs more than great audiences. It needs great interpreters too.

St. Louis Post-Dispatch, July 19, 1986, p. 4B.

285

The Black masses' main poetic man

As America's foremost blues poet, Langston Hughes (1902-1967) became celebrated for his lyrics of pain and isolation, of deeply felt anguish. The voice of his suffering spirit was early recognized as true, timeless and universal.

After completing high school in his native Joplin, Hughes lived a year in Mexico, studied a year at Columbia University, then worked his way through Europe for a year. He later won a scholarship to Lincoln University (Pennsylvania) where he graduated in 1929. Meanwhile, in 1925 he won a prize for his poem "The Weary Blues," "which became the title poem of his first book of verse published the next year. Thirty more books of poetry, plays, fiction and autobiography followed.

The Big Sea is a reprint of Hughes's earliest autobiography, first published in 1940 and long out of print. In it Hughes recounts his experiences in Paris and Harlem during the 1920s, his friendships with the New York literati and others, and how he wrote some of his early poems. Today this book is especially enlightening for Hughes's views and descriptions of the Black Renaissance during that period.

In a brief foreword, poet Amiri Baraka warmly describes Hughes as "the Black masses' main poetic man" and—as I've often regarded him—"one of the most neglected and underrated American poets of his time."

Review of *The Big Sea, an Autobiography*, by Langston Hughes (Thunder's Mouth Press).

St. Louis Post-Dispatch, July 27, 1986, p. 4B.

Another angle on Shakespeare

Some books, even scholarly works, are so newsworthy and sensational
that they become front-page or featured news even before publication.
Such a book was Charlton Ogburn's *The Mysterious William Shakespeare*
(Dodd, Mead, 1984)—that brilliantly researched, controversial study
questioning the Bard's identity.

In contrast, Germaine Greer's brief study draws well-established facts
from conventional sources in a lively, easy style. She presents six aspects
of the poet under separate chapters dealing with his life, politics, ethics,
and so on. The life is a short summary of the few facts known about
Shakespeare. The chapter on poetics has little to do with versification but
rather discusses Shakespeare's language and style in certain plays like
"Hamlet" and "The Tempest." The chapter on politics touches on
Shakespeare's use of Holinshed's *Chronicles* as source material, and
compares Shakespeare's and Bertolt Brecht's political commentary.

As a champion of women's causes, Greer might have commented
extravagantly on feminism in the plays. She didn't, and in fact she doesn't
discuss "feminism" at all. Instead she merely shows (in a chapter on
Shakespeare's sociology) how the poet created female characters who
were "passionate and pure, who gave their hearts spontaneously into the
keeping of the men they loved and remained true to the bargain in the face
of tremendous odds." Only one of the plays, she adds (*Troilus and
Cressida*), deals with female treachery.

Greer's *Shakespeare* concentrates on the poet's plays, not his identity. It
reveals Greer as a scholar sensitive to art, truth and high ethical standards.

Review of *Shakespeare*, by Germaine Greer (Oxford University Press).

St. Louis Post-Dispatch, August 30, 1986, p. 4B.

287

THREE FACES OF AUTUMN
Poetry, Prose, Translations

Shakespeare, master of the sonnet

Great poetry comes in many styles, formal and free, and students not exposed to them all are missing something. All poets cannot write sonnets, of course, but even many teachers cannot scan or identify the sonnet forms, one of which Shakespeare perfected and is named for him. Shakespeare, best known for his prolific dramatic output, excelled as a lyric and narrative poet too. Had he written only these 154 sonnets he'd still have a high place in English poetry. This fine new edition in large, readable type also includes the verse tale, "A Lover's Complaint," first printed with the sonnets in 1609.

Reading or re-reading the sonnets is a heady experience, like hearing a fine concerto. There are the great favorites: "When, in disgrace with fortune and men's eyes" (number 29), "Not marble nor the gilded monuments/ Of princes" (55), and "Let me not to the marriage of true minds/ Admit impediments" (116). But it's even more interesting to find new meanings in the lesser known pieces.

For five centuries poets have written sonnets, from Philip Sidney to Elizabeth Bishop and Howard Moss. Each put a unique stamp on the form. One American poet, Merrill Moore (1903-1957), wrote more than 43,000 sonnets and gave the form fresh, new expression. But no one, not even Moore, could beat the Bard at the sonnet game.

Review of *Shakespeare's Sonnets*, edited by Stanley Wells (Oxford).

St. Louis Post-Dispatch, August 16, 1986, p. 4B.

Edited Emerson notebooks are a treasure of research

> Born for success he seemed,
> With grace to win, with heart to hold,
> With shining gifts which took all eyes.

Ralph Waldo Emerson wrote these lines for his brother Edward who died in 1834, and for a half-century after, he himself fulfilled his brother's promise. As a poet, philosopher and a onetime pastor (who resigned because of his objection to formalism in religion), Emerson became the great secular oracle of hope and progress, admired for his exalted character and positive thinking.

For 40 years or so, Emerson has been rather lost in the mainstream of American life. As one critic notes, he is either enshrined as a sage or dismissed as a relic. He is in fact a kind of embarrassment to America's drug culture—and to the crime and greed and immorality some find rampant now but not a century ago.

Well, the United States is much larger and more populous, and of course communications are much improved. But in a sense America has embarrassed Emerson; despite its science and technology, it has failed in the spiritual promise he demanded. Now there is a growing scholarly interest in Emerson—in books like John McAleer's *Ralph Waldo Emerson: Days of Encounter* (Little, Brown) and Gertrude R. Hughes's *Emerson's Demanding Optimism* (Louisiana State), which have recovered and warmly humanized him as never before.

When he left the ministry at age 29, Emerson was beset with tragedies, including the death of his young wife. He toured Italy and England, he met Coleridge, Wordsworth and Carlyle, he returned to the United States and remarried, then he settled into the family home at Concord. Based there, he wrote and lectured all over the country until his death at age 79 (in 1882).

Emerson wrote an enormous amount of verse in his lifetime. Many of his poems are the opening lines or mottos for his essays and lectures on subjects like art, nature, character, compensation, heroism, friendship, politics and experience. If his stature as a poet has dimmed in the brilliance of newer poetry beginning with Walt Whitman (whom he hailed and encouraged), Emerson has left several dozen poems of unusual power and interest, still carried in anthologies. These include "Days," "Seashore," "Two Rivers," "Merlin" and many more. His poems "May-Day" and "The Adirondacs" (a narrative journal) have influenced poets up to our time.

Emerson left nine poetry notebooks containing more than 1,300 inscribed pages, which form this new volume, *The Poetry Notebooks*. Although scholars and editors have long "mined" this work for poems to use in various editions of Emerson's works, the notebooks have been little consulted and never published in full.

A team of four distinguished editors, led by Ralph Orth and Albert J. von Frank, now has reconstructed them with incredible devotion, even recovering some erased lines and versions of poems. The rough drafts, revised versions and fair copies have been faithfully transcribed, analyzed, introduced and indexed.

Obviously these notebooks will appeal only to true Emerson buffs and to scholars. But as a sourcebook it becomes all the more valuable to writers, editors and researchers. The kind of painstaking, sometimes discouraging efforts of these notebook editors is not unlike the arduous, often disappointing labor of a salvage crew recovering sunken treasure. For Emerson's work is a cultural treasure, an unsinkable part of our national heritage.

Even 35 years ago critic F.O. Matthiessen recognized that "Emerson was the first American to articulate an organic theory of art, opening with the functional proposition that 'Words are signs of natural facts.'"

And as Brooks Atkinson observed, "he was the teacher of America."

It is not strange that those of all faiths for 150 years have admired the gentle, kindly and righteous Emerson, who was among the earliest Americans to bridge the gap between Eastern and Western philosophy and religion.

His honesty and his singleminded pursuit of excellence in life and art are nowhere better reflected than in these lines from his poem "Self-Reliance":

Henceforth, please God, forever I forego
The yoke of men's opinions. I will be
Light-hearted as a bird, and live with God.
I find him in the bottom of my heart,
I hear continually his voice therein.

Review of *The Poetry Notebooks of Ralph Waldo* Emerson, edited by
Ralph H. Orth, Albert J. von Frank, Linda Allardt and David W. Hill
(University of Missouri Press).

St. Louis Post-Dispatch, August 19, 1986, p. 4B.

291

THREE FACES OF AUTUMN
Poetry, Prose, Translations

Essays of eloquence and incisive style

"I think the function of literature," Ralph Ellison once told a West Point audience, "is to remind us of our common humanity and the cost of that humanity. This is the abiding theme of great literature."

From West Point to the West Coast, Ellison's novel *Invisible Man* has been required reading in English, education and sociology classes since it won the National Book Award more than 30 years ago. And since then, Ellison has been called on to elucidate and interpret that novel for audiences everywhere. His essays, addresses and interviews, such as the 16 pieces in this new collection, are the brilliant sequel to that earlier work —an enrichment not only to American letters but to the cause of racial harmony and understanding.

Indeed, it isn't *Invisible Man* but what that novel generated in its author that now unravels, reveals and measures Ellison.

In the title essay of *Going to the Territory*, an address given at Brown University in 1979, Ellison is especially revealing, wise and authoritative.

He traces his early influences in his boyhood Oklahoma to figures like Inman Page (the first black graduate of Brown University), Johnson C. Whittaker, and Dr. Page's daughter, Zelia N. Breaux. Other essays and lectures here include a memoir of Richard Wright, articles in homage to Duke Ellington and the artist Romare Bearden, and several perspectives of literature and the novel.

Ellison's literary interests were many, ranging from Baudelaire and Malraux to Melville, Mark Twain, T.S. Eliot, Faulkner and Kenneth Burke. Black colleagues like Langston Hughes influenced his reading, but he disavowed "attempts to claim Pushkin and Dumas" as black authors. He has also rejected the teaching of "Black English": "No one," he writes, "suggested that standard American English was beyond us: how could they with such examples as Dr. Page before us? He could make the language of Shakespeare and the King James version of the Bible resound within us in such ways that its majesty and beauty seemed as natural and as normal coming from one of our own as an inspired jazz improvisation or an eloquently sung spiritual. By daily examples he made us aware that great poetry and fluent English were a part of our heritage."

292

Ellison's acceptance of standard English is just one example of his exercising what he feels is "one of the most precious American freedoms, which is our freedom to broaden our personal culture by absorbing the cultures of others."

One of the most honored Americans, Ellison has perhaps not yet achieved that high visibility he deserves in American society. Not all educators—of whatever race or ethnic background—agree with him on certain issues. One of these is his apparent repudiation of the idea of a "multicultural" society now being taught on many campuses. But by his eloquence, his gently incisive style and his rare insight, Ellison seems one of the most forceful and appealing social philosophers of our time.

Perhaps *Going to the Territory* will eventually be required reading too. This book could be highly influential in shaping American social history.

Review of *Going to the Territory*, by Ralph Ellison (Random House).

St. Louis Post-Dispatch, August 26, 1986, p. 3B.

THREE FACES OF AUTUMN
Poetry, Prose, Translations

Stylish insights of a reader

To some readers "literature" is an abominable ten-letter word, and the word "classic" is especially abhorrent. Strangely, even those readers may enjoy the late novelist Italo Calvino in these essays after a few suspicious dips and browsings into what they are about. Call it style or attitude, but Calvino never seems to lose a sense of values where writing is concerned.

Here is an example from his essay, "Why Read the Classics?"—a question he answers in 14 fresh, unexpected ways:

> I can never sufficiently highly recommend the direct reading of the (classic) text itself. . . . Schools and universities ought to help us understand that no book that talks about a book says more than the book in question. . . . There is a very widespread topsy-turviness of values whereby the introduction, critical apparatus and bibliography are used as a smokescreen to hide what the text has to say and, indeed, can say only if left to speak for itself without intermediaries who claim to know more than the text does.

A strong indictment of academia, perhaps; and if we took him too literally we might abandon the enjoyment the rest of his essays hold—his delightful comments on science and philosophy and literature, on sex and laughter, on comedy and fantasy, and on cinema and the novel. We'd miss especially his personal discoveries (not "criticism") of writers from Homer and Ovid to Voltaire, Balzac and Rostand—to poets of our time like Montale and Marianne Moore. What an astounding catalog of writers, all precious to him, Calvino shares with us in these 30 essays! Calvino simply enjoyed reading as well as writing. He died of a stroke recently, after lapsing into a coma. He was reading a newspaper when it happened.

Review of *The Uses of Literature, Essays*, by Italo Calvino, translated by Patrick Creagh (Harcourt Brace).

St. Louis Post-Dispatch, October 12, 1986, p. 4C.

Poet's essays display high critical standard

A poet friend once told me that he never read other poets' work for fear it would influence his own. Incredible as this phobia seems, it was only partly true, for as an editor he had to read some manuscripts by others. Yet it reflected a curiously barbaric attitude. For poetry, like other arts, is accretive, mutable, "evolving"—not always better from age to age, but different. We must bring its scope and meanings to us if we would understand it. It demands and deserves intense apprenticeship.

I almost never read current reviews of books I am reviewing, but for good reason. I prefer to confront the books directly, with references at hand, and not get sidetracked (or derailed) by others' opinions. I choose to address the author, not to answer other reviewers. But I always enjoy reading criticism on any author or subject. Criticism, if properly aged, is stimulating and enlightening.

Anthony Hecht, a fine poet who has worked in many forms, sets a high standard of criticism in this first collection of his essays. *Obbligati* (the title refers to Hecht's literary debts to others) contains only 10 pieces, all dealing with poets and their work, from Shakespeare to Richard Wilbur.

Hecht's style and method aren't much different from those of other fine critics—but he seems richer in his resources, more contemplative and more articulate than most writing today.

Hecht heaps on us layer upon layer of ideas that—if they seem disparate or to lead nowhere in particular—hold our interest and at the end are somehow tied together. He opens the collection with an essay on "The Pathetic Fallacy," quoting John Ruskin and Shakespeare—and Frost, Richard Wilbur and others. He closes the volume with an essay on "Houses as Metaphors," quoting (among others) Beaumont and Fletcher, Horace, Sidney, Marvell, Yeats, Milton—and Shakespeare and Ruskin. The longest essay is on "The Merchant of Venice," a sensitive, revealing and well-documented piece on Jewish-Christian relationships in the play. (This is recommended for all who read or see that play.)

Hecht makes other excursions into the poetry of W.H. Auden, Elizabeth Bishop, Richard Wilbur and others. Of major interest, besides the Shakespeare essays, is one on Emily Dickinson in which Hecht quotes and interprets 15 Dickinson poems. Altogether, *Obbligati* is a strong, useful book of criticism.

R.P, Blackmur once defined criticism as "the formal discourse of an amateur." But the "amateur" is simply one devoted to an art or craft and its practice by others. An artist who deliberately ignores all others breaks the faith by his insularity. The expression of that art becomes like a marvelous but unheard wind-music raging through a deserted forest.

Review of *Obbligati: Essays in Criticism*, by Anthony Hecht (Atheneum).

St. Louis Post-Dispatch, November 24, 1986, p. 4B.

John Donne at his 'livelyest' in essays, poems and sermons

"Of all Commentaries . . . Good Examples are the best and the livelyest," wrote the English poet John Donne (1572-1631). Although Donne was referring to Bible texts, his aphorism applies equally to his own writings and sermons.

Readers have long enjoyed Donne's poems, but his prose (until the Berkeley edition of 1953-62) has been hard to find. As a theologian, Donne wrote many sermons on language and Scripture. In the new Stanwood-Asals selection more than 40 of these sermons are organized into 10 major topics. Each topic is introduced and explained by the editors, who have added a main introduction, a glossary (defining terms used in Donne's time), a bibliography and detailed references of the Biblical texts Donne used.

Savored slowly, Donne's essays can be rewarding, and in their introductions Stanwood and Asals have made the examples of Donne's prose even better and livelier. Donne deserves both broad understanding and painstaking dedication, a combination apparent here. The Stanwood-Asals edition is probably the finest and most useful one-volume selection of Donne's prose available.

Yet even as a poet, Donne's reputation lay dormant for generations after his death, obscured in the shadow of Shakespeare and Milton. The English *Chambers's Cyclopaedia* (1858), for instance, gave him scant notice but recognized him as the "first satirist" and a "Metaphysical Poet," a term later popularized by T. S. Eliot. But Donne's range has extended far beyond that of the metaphysical who influenced several generations of U.S. poets from Edna Millay and Elinor Wylie to about 1950.

This wide range is well illustrated in *The Eagle and the Dove*, a series of 15 essays on Donne introduced by the editors, Claude Summers and Ted-Larry Pebworth.

Altogether, 17 scholars—all of whom except one teach in the U.S.—share their special interests in many aspects of Donne and his work: his love letters to Ann More, his epigrams, his divine poem "La Corona," his *Holy Sonnets* and Christian diatribes, and his poetry and sermons as a whole.

THREE FACES OF AUTUMN
Poetry, Prose, Translations

My favorite essays in this collection are by Stella P. Revard, Michael P. Parker and Paul L. Gaston. Revard links Donne with the Roman poet Propertius, showing how both poets dealt with anger, despair and contrariness in their love poems, and how similar their attitudes were on love and death. Parker describes Donne's special legacy to the English poets Thomas Carew and Henry King. And Gaston explores Donne's interest in music and shows how one modern composer, Benjamin Britten—in the setting of Donne's *Holy Sonnets*—successfully used the 17th-century poems in a work published in 1946.

If there is one important gap of scholarship in these new books, as well as in other works on Donne, it is the "Spanish Connection." The Anglican Donne (of the "middle way") was greatly influenced by St. Augustine and St. Jerome, and his essay "The Name of God" reminds us of a similar treatise by the Spanish Augustinian monk, Fray Luis de León (1527-91), a contemporary of Sir Philip Sidney. Understandably, warring rivals like England and Spain were reluctant to acknowledge each other's influences. But this is a minor footnote on two splendid books which add a wealth and variety of interest to Donne.

Review of *John Donne and the Theology of Language*, edited by P. G. Stanwood and Heather Ross Asals (University of Missouri) and *The Eagle and the Dove: Reassessing John Donne*, edited by Claude Summers and Ted-Larry Pebworth (University of Missouri).

St. Louis Post-Dispatch, October 30, 1986, p. 4B.

The plain, enduring voices of poetry

The most eloquent and moving poetry uses a plain language. It is not surprising that our finest living poets—many of whom once wrote graduate theses sodden with strange, ponderously twisted poly-syllables—have returned to plain speech and have honed it with new meanings. Also, the steadiest poets find and hold a single voice. . . .

Take, for instance, James Laughlin's *Selected Poems, 1935-1985* (City Lights Books), one of the most remarkable poetry books of the year. In a credo poem titled "Technical Notes" Laughlin writes:

> I prefer to build with plain brown bricks
> of common American talk then
> set 1 Roman stone among them for a key

—that keystone being the Roman poet Catullus, in whose "bowl" Laughlin mixes "a little acid and a bit of honey," with love ("& the lack of love") as his subjects. While Catullus, Williams, Cummings and Pound were among his teachers, Laughlin has a unique, finely crafted expression. And while he sometimes uses Italian, Greek, Latin and other foreign phrases (and even includes 17 poems in French), the reader seldom feels alienated, but rather drawn to the local color of the poem and its theme. The theme (usually love) speaks a universal language, but Laughlin adds notes explaining his sources and meanings. To Laughlin "a poem /is finally just / a natural thing," but he has two skills few can match: a way of seeing and a technique of transmitting his wit, vision and experience.

One of the strongest independent (non-academic) influences on current poetry is Robert Bly, whose *Selected Poems* (Harper & Row) is a model handbook, by example, of a major poet's progress in his craft. Bly has severely but effectively self-edited this volume, which contains nine sections, each prefaced by the poet's comments on a particular period or aspect of his writing. The range is remarkable, from the earliest "musical" poems, such as blank verse narrative, to lyric and narrative free verse and prose poetry. Bly's thematic range is equally broad: politics, love, war and pure fantasy. Describing his earliest poems, he notes that the lyric "I" in them "had no weight." But the power and mysticism of Yeats and Rilke pervade later lines like these, from his book *Sleepers Joining Hands* (1973):

THREE FACES OF AUTUMN
Poetry, Prose, Translations

> I was born during the night sea-journey.
> I love the whale with his warm organ pipes
> In the mouse-killing waters . . . .
> I call out my wateriness in magnificent words.
> That is the water man, but what of the land man?
> He lives in a half-fixed house, with plank floor,
> Where things are half-said, half-sung, half-danced.

Philip Booth's poetry is as subtle as Bly's but even more concrete, earthy. Earthy, that is, in his use of familiar language and imagery. There is less social message and more clear, clipped description. But like Bly's poems, Booth's take shape unobtrusively in the poet's own voice, with quiet discipline, as in these lines from his latest volume, *Relations: Selected Poems 1950-1985* (Viking/Penguin):

> No matter how I feel,
> I am of several minds.
> Nothing I think is as sure
> as my mind's several voices.

From the hard, brilliant opening poem, "Adam," to the closing title poem, "Relations," is an extraordinary chronicle of personal experience. Booth is a master of descriptive metaphor, one of the best writing today.

For "experimental" poetry, Michael McClure is one of the best examples of our time. Compared with Booth's quiet voice, McClure's at times seems blatant: "LISTEN, LAWRENCE, THERE ARE CERTAIN OF US / INTENSELY COMMITTED / TO / a / real, / A REAL / REVOLT! . . . he begins one piece in his new *Selected Poems* (New Directions). But such lines, as poets know, are simply organic form—a form (and even a style and language) to fit a theme; in short, to make it poetry. In other poems like "Ode for Soft Voice," "Hummingbird Ode" and "Changer," McClure can be extremely low key. McClure's poetry radiates and at times explodes with sensual power (and even grace). McClure's style, his typographical distortions and his seemingly obsessive use of capitalized words may put off readers seeking the "quick fix" of cotton candy and marshmallow verse. But patient, probing readers will find McClure excitingly different and honest. He is one of the few authentic heirs to a tradition which has run for two centuries, from Blake to the Surrealist movement.

Another major work is Dave Smith's *The Roundhouse Voices: New and Selected Poems* (Harper & Row). Smith has a predilection for natural objects and creatures ("Rain Forest," "Tide Pools," "Goshawk, Antelope")—all with a strong, specific meaning. Like Bly, he has been a teacher and role model for many younger poets, and his voice is assertive, heady. His language is eloquently plain and familiar, a result of having lived and taught in many places. If the Midwest claims him (as it can), so can the West, the East and the South (he now teaches in Virginia). But the place doesn't matter, only the voice, which commands any setting the poet chooses. From "Cumberland Station," for instance:

> Gray brick, ash, hard-bent railings, steps so big
> it takes hours to mount them, polished oak
> pews holding the slim hafts of sun, and one
> splash of the Pittsburgh Post-Gazette.

Smith's poems are wondrously charged with word-music and today's imagery; and underlying these, the poet seems to hold "the world's unsayable secrets," like the wounded snow owl he lovingly commemorates in one poem.

In all these books of selected poems, not only the chosen contents but also details like arrangement, format and notes are important. But as the Symbolist Mallarmé said, "Poems are made of words," and language is fundamental.

St. Louis Post-Dispatch, November 30, 1986, p. 5D.

301

THREE FACES OF AUTUMN
Poetry, Prose, Translations

The Beats remembered

At the height of the Beat craze a generation ago, my students were fascinated by a poetry script Kenneth Rexroth sent me, which I described to my classes as showing "an authentic beer glass stain" from the Hungry Eye saloon in San Francisco. That strange totem, a mediocre poem on a long forgotten topic, now shows only how ephemeral certain aspects of the Beat movement were and remain today.

The Beat Generation was claimed by New York but became better known on the West Coast. It had hundreds of representatives—those who opposed what they felt was the materialistic, soulless society of the 1950s—writers like William Burroughs, Robert Creeley, Allen Ginsberg, Robert Duncan, Michael McClure, and others more or less famous then. Nearly 50 of these are portrayed in *Beats & Company*, a large handsome photo album which tries to recapture some of the spirit and energy of the movement.

Beats & Company is both striking and wanting: striking in its main purpose of photography, yet wanting as a fully representative document of the Beat Generation. (Such a document would certainly include many figures omitted here; for example, Robert Bly, Cid Corman and Leslie Woolf Hedley.) Still, Ann Charters manages to bring some of the more important writers here on film, with comments or salient extracts from their work. She obviously used her Rolleiflex, by the way, for her splendid low-angle shots of Gregory Corso, Gary Snyder, Charles Olson and Louis Zukofsky—a tribute both to her skills and to the royal Rollei, undeservedly maligned by some as an obsolete camera.

Although *Beats & Company* portrays only a few Beats, and one gets the feeling that it is a very closed company, it certainly beats beer glass stains for show-and-tell about the movement. Many if not most of the Beat poets, we should add, finally shucked that label to express themselves more independently.

Review of *Beats & Company: Portrait of a Literary Generation*, by Ann Charters (Doubleday).

St. Louis Post-Dispatch, January 4, 1987, p. 5D.

A CHARLES GUENTHER RETROSPECTIVE
Prose: Critical Reviews and Essays, 1983-1992

A critic's role is to learn, to propagate

Matthew Arnold defined criticism as "a disinterested endeavor to learn and propagate the best that is known and thought in the world." While skeptics may ask, "The best what?" Arnold's definition is intriguing. His broad view does not restrict criticism to mere scrutiny and appraisal but includes the critic's responsibility to "propagate" what he has learned or discovered to be the best.

And in the field of letters, few more talented appraisers and propagators have emerged in our time than an American and a Briton, R. P. Blackmur (1904-65) and V. S. Pritchett (b. 1900). Both were what I'd call creative critics. They came to criticism by well-traveled roads—Blackmur as a poet, editor and social-political essayist, and Pritchett as the author of 27 volumes of fiction, biography, memoirs and travel accounts, plus seven volumes of criticism.

Their two books of selected essays offer wondrous revelations and contrasts. For instance, they squelch the notion that all British writers are dense and all Americans are simple in style. Here the roles are reversed. Blackmur in his intricate, perceptive philosophizing on poetry (never on poets as persons but rather on their work and ideas) can digress from an apparently simple poem by Yeats to observe:

> Poetry is so little autonomous from the technical point of view that the greater part of a given work must be conceived as the manipulation of conventions that the reader will, or will not, take for granted; these being crowned, or animated, emotionally transformed, by what the poet actually represents, original or not, through his mastery of poetic language. Success is provisional, seldom complete, and never permanently complete.

And commenting on Henry James's *Critical Prefaces* Blackmur writes:

> The "story of a story" is not simple in its telling: it has many aspects that must be examined in turn, many developments that must be pursued, before its center in life is revealed as captured.

Indeed, every sentence Blackmur wrote seems to express or provoke or advance an idea—and all those ideas are constantly in process, in flux and change. His editor, Denis Donoghue, sums it up well by saying, "Black-mur thought the best kind of mind the most provisional." Perhaps no reader can rest comfortably in the atmosphere Blackmur created in these 14 "Selected Essays" that deal with writers like Stevens, Cummings, Hart Crane, Henry Adams and Thomas Mann. But they represent some of the most extraordinary, probing criticism of our time.

In a much lighter style, V. S. Pritchett's 46 selected essays— which include six on American and the rest on British and European writers, mostly novelists—run the gamut from serious analysis to chatty commentary. Of the minor 19th-century author Amelia Opie ("the Quaker coquette"), Pritchett writes:

> Being irresistible was not only an instinct but a business with Amelia Opie. She wrote frightful novels which made Sir Walter Scott weep, and awful verses which Sydney Smith quoted in his lectures—the bad taste of great men has a long history—but she had taken care, it might be observed, to get to know the great first. She asked Southey once to say a word to the reviewers. She was one of those women who, having addled a man's judgment by making herself physically desirable, like an ice on a hot day, then change about and insist on being admired for their minds.

Before feminists cry "Foul!" at this passage, I must add that Pritchett praised George Eliot, Virginia Woolf, Edith Wharton and George Sand, for instance—and in fact called George Eliot "the most formidable of the Victorian novelists." As for Opie, one can't help but admire her ingenuity in advertising and marketing her talents, however great or small.

Pritchett is as explicit, fast-paced and colloquial in his criticism as Blackmur is abstract, plodding and formal. Perhaps it's significant that neither Blackmur nor Pritchett belonged to the academic world, but remained or remain writers without institution. (This despite the fact that Blackmur, who had no earned degree, was for a while a professor of English at Princeton.) Still, academia may envy them for their unique legacies.

In their personal growth Blackmur and Pritchett are among the finer models of the culture of letters—in the broader culture Arnold once defined as "the pursuit of light and perfection, which made light and perfection consist, not in resting and being, but in growing and becoming, in a perpetual advance in beauty and wisdom."

Review of *Selected Essays of R.P. Blackmur*, edited by Denis Donoghue (Ecco) and *A Man of Letters: Selected Essays*, by V.S. Pritchett (Random House).

St. Louis Post-Dispatch, January 8, 1987, p. 3B.

THREE FACES OF AUTUMN
Poetry, Prose, Translations

Heroic Black voices—praise at last

Black poets have sung America from Colonial days, long before Walt Whitman and Emily Dickinson, yet recognition of their work has come slowly, sparingly even in recent years.

In his 1967 *Kaleidoscope* anthology of black poetry, for instance, the late Robert Hayden included only three poets representing the first century of our republic. These were the prodigy Phyllis Wheatley (c.1750-84); George Moses Horton (1797-c.1883), and Frances E. W. Harper (1825-1911).

Since Reconstruction days a host of talented poets has emerged—from Paul Lawrence Dunbar, Claude McKay, Jean Toomer, Arna Bontemps, Countee Cullen and Sterling A. Brown to more recent figures like Nikki Giovanni, Amiri Baraka and Gloria Oden. While some books and articles (*Ebony* magazine, March 1974, for instance) have featured black poets, critical recognition has been limited and hard-won, due in part perhaps to some poets' use of vernacular styles, or other language differences.

Despite such barriers two poets have achieved heroic status in our century: Gwendolyn Brooks (b. 1917; the first black woman to win a Puliltzer Prize (1950), and Langston Hughes (1902-67), whose poem "The Weary Blues," written at age 21, brought him immediate acclaim in white literary circles in the 1920s.

D. H. Melhem's study of Brooks is biographical, critical and analytical. After a short chapter on the poet's life, Melhem deals with nine of Brooks's volumes in chronological order from *A Street in Bronzeville* (1945) and the prize-winning *Annie Allen* (1949) to later works like *Family Pictures* (1970), *Aloneness* (1971) and *Beckonings* (1975).

More recent publications like *Primer for Blacks* (1980) and two books under her own imprint (Brooks Press), *Young Poet's Primer* (1980) and *Very Young Poets* (1983), are also discussed.

Brooks relates well to young writers of all tastes and talents. She is one of a vanishing breed of craftsmen who can use the "contours" of a grand heroic style—with fine techniques and forms of verse—in plain, informal and even vernacular language.

306

She shows a wide range of devices, from the romantic and ironic to the subtly didactic realism of this little piece titled "We Real Cool," once banned in Nebraska and West Virginia:

> We real cool We
> Left school. We
> Lurk late. We
> Strike straight. We
> Sing sin. We
> Thin Gin. We
> Jazz June. We
> Die soon.

Melhem's study is timely, enjoyable and useful. Other writers will be interested in the detailed accounts of Brooks's correspondence and relationships with her editors and publishers. One could wish that every major writer were the subject of a study as finely arranged and executed as this.

Though rather neglected since his death, Langston Hughes is still the main exemplar of modern black poets of social expression. His autobiography, *I Wonder as I Wander*, first published in 1956, is now reprinted with a new foreword by his longtime friend, Margaret Walker. The book takes its title from an old folk-song or spiritual, and begins about 1930, where his earlier journal, *The Big Sea*, leaves off. In his poetry Hughes had a genius for pithy messages in vernacular language. His journals are written in a crisp, plain style any journalist might admire. And his world travels are something anyone (including business travelers) might envy. In Japan, for instance, a half century ago. Hughes writes, "At the Imperial Hotel I was given a cream and beige room with deep rugs, a wide soft bed and a big bath. It was on the first floor just off the lobby and, at the rate of exchange then, did not cost very much." (How times have changed!)

I Wonder as I Wander is filled with wondrous revelations, confessions, descriptions. Some of the most fascinating parts deal with his journeys to the Soviet Union and Central Asia. Others deal with "Writing for a Living" and the production of his play, *Mulatto* in 1935-36 (a play banned in Philadelphia). Scores of eminent world writers, from Asia to Civil War Spain, befriended Hughes along with artists of all expressions. As Walker points out, these vignettes show Hughes's kaleidoscopic mind and

307

experiences; and, however briefly, give us "the exhilarating pleasure of his presence."

Review of *Gwendolyn Brooks: Poetry and the Heroic Voice*, by D. H. Melhem (University of Kentucky) and *I Wonder as I Wander: An Autobiographical Journal*, by Langston Hughes (Thunder's Mouth Press).

St. Louis Post-Dispatch, February 1, 1987 p. 5D.

A CHARLES GUENTHER RETROSPECTIVE
Prose: Critical Reviews and Essays, 1983-1992

Master of both the poetry and insurance games

Discussing professions with a friend, a Catholic nun, I mentioned that a cousin of mine worked for New York Life and his brother was a Presbyterian minister. "Oh," she beamed, "one sells insurance for the here and the other for the hereafter."

I thought of this remark while reading Joan Richardson's splendid new biography of the poet Wallace Stevens (1879-1955). As a youth I considered some occupations, like the spiritual and actuarial, wholly incompatible. Soon it became a revelation and a consolation to me (because I then worked as a factory hand and a salesman) to learn that a poet of Stevens's stature was in "the insurance game"—and he had worked his way up to a vice-presidency at Hartford Accident and Indemnity Company.

Outside of literary circles, however, only Stevens's family and several close business associates appreciated his growing reputation as a poet. He kept each "game" separate, and was successful at both. A graduate of Harvard, where he wrote stories and poems and formed literary friendships with Witter Bynner and others, Stevens was early influenced by the philosophies of William James and George Santayana. Others who had an impact on his work before he was 25 were Shakespeare, Keats and Matthew Arnold. Later there was Freud.

Richardson's biography covers Stevens's life up to the publication of his first book, *Harmonium* (1923). It stresses the literary aspects of the poet's life, and includes extensive quotations and derivations of the early poems. But it also covers rather fully his personal life: his parents' death, his courtship and marriage with Elsie, his relationships with her and other family members, including his daughter Holly; and above all, his own personal preoccupations and prejudices. Richardson gives a particularly brilliant account of Stevens's various concerns and friendships from 1913, when he began publishing his better poems, to the early '20s when art and letters began an exciting era.

Stevens's "real double life" had begun in that period. Yet it was not only a separation of his personal and artistic lives but a dichotomy of his literary expressions. He was still seeking, it seemed, a commitment to one or the other century-old traditions of American poetry: social message or craftsmanship. To Harriet Monroe's canonic *Poetry* magazine he contributed poems on moral issues (war and belief), but to the avant-garde group of *Others*, edited by Alfred Kreymbourg, he sent poems on human problems (death and sex). Like other younger poets (Eliot, Pound, Amy Lowell, John Gould Fletcher) he was fascinated by new French poetry and its rhythms and imagery. But he formed few close literary friendships— even with Kreymbourg and the latter's reclusive protégée, Mina Loy—and his relations with Pound were simply frosty.

Stevens once wrote that poetry was his "way of making the world palatable, acceptable." Louis Untermeyer called him a poet's poet, one who "fashioned a poetry of tangents, of elisions and startling sequiturs." He delighted in making "the visible a little hard," even for the most literate readers. Yet he could write haunting, tantalizing lines like these, from the coda of "Peter Quince":

> Beauty is momentary in the mind—
> the fitful tracing of a portal;
> But in the flesh it is immortal . . . .

This first volume of a planned two-volume life of Stevens is a superb product of research and analysis. Richardson draws heavily from the poet's journals and letters, and from reminiscences of his friends and family. There are hundreds of references to Stevens's contemporaries, from Walter Arensberg to William Carlos Williams, and several sections of photos and holographs. But throughout, as in the themes of her sections, Richardson is dedicated to tracing Stevens's poetic development and expelling certain myths which have grown around him even today.

This is one of the finest biographies I've read in decades. It compares favorably with Newman I. White's *Shelley* and similar works on major poets. By its single major figure it expands our understanding of a half century of American art and letters.

Review of *Wallace Stevens: The Early Years, 1879-1923*, by Joan Richardson (Beach Tree/Morrow).

St. Louis Post-Dispatch, April 4, 1987, p. 5D.

Mystical poets of 17th-Century England

England has a rich heritage of mystical poetry, from Richard Rolle (1290-1349) to poets like Francis Thompson, Evelyn Underhill and (more recently), Charles Causley and Derek Walcott. One early mystical work was so popular that it was said to have "run across England like a deere."

The 17th century golden age of mysticism produced such lyricists as John Donne, George Herbert, Richard Crashaw, Andrew Marvell and John Milton. These poets particularly are discussed in the 12 essays by various authors in *"Bright Shootes of Everlastingnesse."*

This book takes its title from a quotation by Henry Vaughan, another mystic who, with several others of equal stature, is treated to a lesser extent in these essays that originated as submissions to a Renaissance conference in Michigan in 1984. The essays range from examinations of single authors and poems to broad discussions of the religious ode and lyric by William A. Sessions, Stella P. Revard and Joseph Wittreich.

In *The Opacity of Signs* Richard Todd examines George Herbert's sacred poems, *The Temple*. Todd tries to reconcile the positions of two earlier critics (William Empson and Rosemond Tuve), one of whom stressed a subjective "participation" in Herbert's work, the other an objective "reading" of that work. Beginning with St. Augustine's theory of divine signs as "visible words," Todd recounts how Herbert "deciphered" God's signs through poetic expression.

By far the most readable and fascinating part of Todd's study is the long concluding chapter on "The Lyric Form." In this he deals with the structure of Herbert's poetry, and the correspondence of form and content.

One is amazed at the amount of current scholarship and interest in the late Renaissance religious lyric, as revealed in the extensive bibliographies and indexes. These are but two of a number of volumes the University of Missouri has published on Donne, Herbert and others in recent years. But what is the key to this interest?

"Herbert was a musician, and sang his own hymns to the lute or viol," according to one account in a century-old *Chambers's Cyclopaedia* I have

311

at hand. But the petty politics of Herbert's era seems more important to the encyclopedist than the poet's musical talents or spiritual growth. We must kindle our interest in such poets through an awareness of their interests. Perhaps simple, straightforward biographies are easier reading—but to the true devotee such studies as these are far more rewarding.

Review of *"Bright Shootes of Everlastingnesse," The Seventeenth Century Religious Lyric*, edited by Claude J. Summers and Ted-Larry Pebworth, (University of Missouri) and *The Opacity of Signs: Acts of Interpretation in George Herbert's* The Temple, by Richard Todd (University of Missouri).

St. Louis Post-Dispatch, May 23, 1987, p. 4D.

Italo Calvino's man of silences, of special visions

Reading *Mr. Palomar*, I thought of another fictional "Mister" — Mr. Chips (but who now remembers him!)—and was struck by the differences between them. Mr. Palomar is really a symbolic character, both a visionary (as his telescopic name implies) and a doer. But his life seems clogged with surreal and symbolic situations.

Mr. Palomar is not so much a novel as a perceptive social commentary in narrative form, and the late Italian novelist Italo Calvino organizes his character's life well. First, Mr. P is seen on vacation, roaming the beach and the garden, and scanning the sky. Then he is in the city, on a terrace, or shopping, or visiting the zoo. Finally, his "silences" are described, when he is traveling or in society or just meditating. These three divisions, Calvino tells us, represent the visual, cultural and speculative experiences of Palomar.

But we are struck, shaken, fascinated and amused by these experiences and by what Palomar encounters. Among other things, he sees tortoises, an albino gorilla and colliding starlings. He glimpses the planets, the shining sword of the sun, the moon in the afternoon. And finally, he perceives a sense of death.

Mr. Palomar is highly original and almost entirely without dialogue. Thus it will appeal to readers who like something novel, not the novel-by-formula—to readers who prefer contemplation to action.

Review of *Mr. Palomar*, by Italo Calvino, translated by William Weaver (Harcourt).

St. Louis Post-Dispatch, May 24, 1987, p. 5C.

THREE FACES OF AUTUMN
Poetry, Prose, Translations

A gift that prevails

This large, elegant selection shows the full range of Gwendolyn Brooks's poetry from *A Street in Bronzeville* (1945) and her Pulitzer Prize volume *Annie Allen* (1949) to her more recent poems of *The Near-Johannesburg Boy*. The breadth of Brooks's themes and styles will doubtless surprise most readers acquainted only with a few of her anthology pieces.

It may not be far-fetched to say that Brooks has become a kind of literary Mother Theresa to the Chicago black community—enlightening, inspiring, moving and perhaps even healing (psychologically, at least) an ever-growing audience. She is one of the steadiest and most appealing voices in American poetry. Even the 15 poems in *The Near-Johannesburg Boy* show wide-ranging insights and an ability to deal with current issues powerfully and eloquently, as in these lines "Of the Young Dead":

> The loss is level.
> But our grieving rises
> and plunges. It prevails. . . .
> Keeping those gifts of self, beyond the changes,
> we keep the living light of our
> young dead.

Blacks really transcends black themes. It is a major enrichment to U.S. and universal poetry.

Review of *Blacks*, by Gwendolyn Brooks (The David Company).

St. Louis Post-Dispatch, May 24, 1987, p. 5C.

Day by day in the life of Edgar Allan Poe

In mountain climbing, sometimes an anonymous sherpa reaches the
summit long before the famous explorer who reaps all the glory. So it is in
literary scholarship where certain basic reference books let other authors
take great strides. There are concordances and bibliographies, for instance.
There is also the literary log, even rarer. This is a day-to-day account that
(if it rises above the "laundry list" type of compilation) can be as
engrossing as the finest biography and of enduring use to all scholars in its
field.

The Poe Log is the ultimate reference work on Poe. There are
fascinating squibs, snips, quotes, summaries, reviews, correspondence and
comments taken from a wealth of documents, reports and records. But
among the peppering of extracts are also long, detailed entries and some
70 illustrations—making this huge volume a fine, monumental biography
in itself. The obvious advantage of this log is its omission of distracting
flashbacks. The log method imparts an authentic sense of the poet's life
from his birth in Boston to Elizabeth Arnold and David Poe Jr., both
actors, to his ignoble (and greatly misunderstood) death in a Baltimore
hospital 40 years later.

Two features of this book are especially outstanding. The first is a 36-page
introductory section of biographical notes outlining, alphabetically, the
lives of some 260 persons mentioned in the log. Such a list seems
rudimentary but, unaccountably, many major biographies lack similar
notes. It must have been an arduous "dog-job" to prepare these notes, but
they simply show how well the authors had the reader's needs in mind.
The other fine feature is more subtly extended through nearly a thousand
pages. This is the authors' extraordinary sense of balance, through 11
finely plotted chapters, of Poe's life and work. Each chapter covers a
major period in the poet's life and opens with a short summary. Other
brief summaries—and quotes from letters, poems and newspaper accounts
—record the progress of Poe's life and labors. But some events are given
longer, more detailed treatment. For instance, there is the $50 prize Poe
won from the *Baltimore Saturday Visitor* for his story "MS. Found in a
Bottle" in 1833. This early prize encouraged Poe and nudged him toward
developing certain themes in a highly imaginative style. There are also extensive accounts, in the 1835-37 period, of Poe's writing and editing for
the *Southern Literary Messenger* in Richmond, and of numerous later

episodes like the "Plagiarism" flap (1845) over Longfellow's poem "The Waif." The "Final Journey"—Poe's death in October 1849—is especially well covered. It is noteworthy that both Dwight Thomas and David Jackson are independent researchers, not academicians. The book was a 10-year full-time project for Thomas, who lived with his parents, and Jackson, a retired insurance agent. (Their situation is uncommon but not unique. The finest biographer of the French poet Apollinaire was a wholesale potato dealer!) Both have the finest credentials and have written extensively on Poe. With *The Poe Log* they have humanized the poet and made him more accessible as an American genius.

Besides the illustrations (daguerreotypes, photos, engravings and paintings of people and places), *The Poe Log* has a 20-page list of sources and is meticulously indexed. Altogether, this book is equal to the finest conventional biographies of Poe—and in one respect, organization, is superior to any of them.

As a footnote or coda to this review, a further comment on Poe's death should be added. In an earlier review of Poe's works I suggested that Poe might have died of a rare disease, porphyria. This opinion was based on many graphic descriptions of Poe's illness and death—and on Poe's habits of consuming drugs and alcohol, both deadly to porphyria patients. Even a generation ago porphyria (which is usually more fatal to men than to women) was little known, and only a half dozen or so cases were isolated in this country. Having long known of this disease, and its causes and effects, I believe that the possibility that Poe died of porphyria should be seriously explored.

Review of *The Poe Log, a Documentary Life of Edgar Allan Poe, 1809-1849*, by Dwight Thomas and David K. Jackson (G.K. Hall).

St. Louis Post-Dispatch, July 18, 1987, p. 3B.

316

Remembering Carl Sandburg, "The Old Troubador"

I last saw Carl Sandburg at one of his guitar performances several years before he died at age 89 in 1967, Even then he still struck audiences with awe and admiration. A school dropout (by necessity) at 13, Sandburg had taken many jobs and had fought in the Spanish-American War before he entered Lombard College in Galesburg, where he edited the school paper and was captain of the basketball team. Later he became one of the most honored American poets as well as a biographer, folklorist and songwriter—and a Pulitzer Prize historian for his incomparable works on Lincoln.

It was easy to relate to Sandburg, for I had read and loved his poems since I too was editor of my college paper, after which I also briefly dropped out to take any job I could get. But Sandburg had a stronger appeal than common experience. He had an uncommon zest for life in a present stabilized by the past. In 1948, at 70, he made a remarkable debut as a fiction writer with his huge panoramic novel *Remembrance Rock*, a still neglected classic. That same year he met and befriended Gregory d'Alessio, a noted cartoonist who was then secretary of the New York Classical Guitar Society. The fun-loving coterie included Andres Segovia, Edward Steichen, June Havoc, Tallulah Bankhead and other actors, artists, writers and publishers. *Old Troubadour* (a sobriquet bestowed on Sandburg by Frank Lloyd Wright) is d'Alessio's affectionate memoir of the last two decades of the poet's visits to New York. It contains nearly 30 short prose pieces on various subjects and events, from Sandburg on art to Sandburg getting a haircut. The book is interspersed with songs, poems, quotations and three sections of photos of Sandburg and his guitar-playing friends.

While this book lacks the breadth of a full biography, it has extraordinary detail and immediacy. D'Alessio's artist's eye and enthusiastic style draw us engagingly into a rather restricted phase and period of Sandburg's life. Altogether *Old Troubadour* reminds us how much poorer in spirit our present generation is without the living example of Sandburg among us.

Review of *Old Troubadour: Carl Sandburg with his Guitar Friends*, by Gregory d'Alessio (Walker).

St. Louis Post-Dispatch, October 31, 1987, p. 3B.

THREE FACES OF AUTUMN
Poetry, Prose, Translations

René Char

Critics admonish one another never to use superlatives, or else to use them sparingly. But René Char was a poet long accustomed to superlatives, especially in the decade after World War II when his exploits as "*Capitaine Alexandre*," a leader of the *Céreste maquis* in the French resistance, grew from legend into fact. In his preface to Char in the *Poètes d'aujourd'hui* series (1951), Pierre Berger wrote of Char's wartime diary *Feuillets d'Hypnos* that, written in France's darkest hour, "it arose and awakened us, calling us to the reality of Revolt."

But others were more direct. Albert Camus called him "our greatest living poet. . . the poet for whom we have been waiting." Jean Paulhan saw him as "the light bearer." Louise Bogan and William Carlos Williams recognized him as the most important living French poet, and Williams added, "I don't know of a poet in my own language to equal him."
Yet poets and artists must live up to superlatives, and sometimes live them down. With Char it was rather different. He easily deserved the enthusiastic accolades for *Feuillets d'Hypnos* (*Leaves of Hypnos*), written in 1943-44 and dedicated to Camus, and for such earlier volumes as *Le Marteau sans maître* (1934) and *Moulin premier* (1936).

Born June 14, 1907, at L'Isle-sur-Sorgue in the Vaucluse, Char spent most of his life in his native Provence. He began writing poetry at seventeen, joined the Surrealists in 1929, with Reverdy, Eluard and others, but broke with the group in 1937. Only after the war, in which his feats as an officer in charge of a parachute reception unit became known, was his poetry well known also outside of France. As Robert Greene has pointed out, Char's early alliance with the Surrealists was quite complete [1]. Char's first volume, *Arsenal*, appeared in 1929, and in the next five years he published three works under the imprint of the Editions Surrealistes; another work, *Ralentir travaux*, was written in collaboration with Eluard and Breton. In *LeMarteau sans maître*, containing all his poems up to 1934, he was just beginning to show the firm, aphoristic statement representing a departure from the diffuse, automatic writing of the Surrealists; from 1937 to 1939 he published four more volumes showing a further growth of his poetic identity.

Whether Char's involvement with the Surrealists was more a liberating experience for him than one that shaped his direction in poetry is still debated among critics. It has long been recognized, however, that Char's three basic forms (prose poetry, free verse and the aphorism) were inherent in his work before he had aligned himself with the Surrealists.

After his wartime books, *Seuls demeurent* (1945), poems that survived the war period, and *Feuillets d'Hypnos* (1946), Char produced a steady stream of new poetry that continued to the 1980s.

This work included *Les Matinaux* (1950), *La parole en archipel* (1962) and *Retour amont* (1966). This last book was reprinted in a further collection, *Le Nu perdu*, 1964-1970, published in 1971; and the next year *La nuit talismanique . . .* was first published by Skira (Geneva), and later (1978) republished by Gallimard (Paris).

During the 1970s Gallimard also published three more significant collections of Char's poems written between 1972 and 1979. *Aromates chasseurs* (1975), *Chants de la Balandrane* (1977) and *Fenêtres dormantes et porte sur le toit* (1979). More recently, Gallimard produced a fine, 1,400-page volume of Char's complete works (*Oeuvres complètes*) in the classic Pleiade Editions (1983), and followed that with another volume, *Les voisinages de Van Gogh*, in 1985.

René Char died in Paris on February 19, 1988.

Now, sixty years after Char's earliest work, we can discern how far he developed beyond his origins, and see how he remained faithful to them—to his obscurity, for example.

His was not the narcissistic obscurity of a cult or a school, but rather the obscurity of a poet expressing complexities of the world around him, and its intensities of feeling. The war, of course, was the great maturing experience which catalyzed his writing from craft to social concern.

Despite (or perhaps because of) his aphoristic breadth, René Char cannot be pinned down in his evolving thought and philosophy, which leap out and spark again and again like high voltage wires downed by a storm.

But surely among the many key aphorisms we may segregate in his work is this passage from *A une sérénité crispée* (*To a Tensed Serenity*, 1952), which opens with these thoughts:

Produce (work) according to the laws of utility, but let that
utility serve through everything but the medium of poetry.
(Valuable to one, to another, and still another, and one alone. . . .
Don't try to be new in it, or famous, but to retouch the same iron to
insure yourself a healing aftergrowth.)

Introduction to "René Char: 12 poems translated by Charles Guenther,"
The American Poetry Review, May/June 1988, p. 23.

[1] First published in *Six French Poets of Our Time* (Princeton University
Press, 1979), p. 105.

The search for clarity in Tudor and Romantic poetry

As our language and lifestyles change, the power and beauty of English Tudor and Romantic poetry become stranger and more remote. Once it was possible for students to go trippingly through Shakespeare or Shelley, for instance, but today such poets need the bridge of critical interpretation. Books like these serve that purpose.

This might be all we'd need to say about *Mind in Character* and *Romantic Texts and Contexts* if their authors weren't so uncommonly cross-grained. They bring logic and reason to the poets and works they interpret: Shakespeare's *Sonnets* in the case of David Weiser, and with Donald Reiman, a host of others—Byron, Coleridge, Wordsworth, Keats, Shelley and Browning.

Weiser's thesis is that the *Sonnets* are meant to be understood and appreciated, not lost in theory and speculation full of history and philosophy. He classifies and explains the poems by their modes of address, including soliloquy and dialogue. In a long closing chapter he discusses Shakespeare's last 28 sonnets, numbered 127-154 (the controversial "Dark Lady" sonnets), comparing them with their earlier poems. While Weiser quotes many passages, the reader needs the full text of the *Sonnets* at hand. Using Stanley Wells's edition of *Shakespeare's Sonnets* (Oxford, 1985). I found Weiser's comments do indeed restore "ordinary comprehension" to the poems, especially the soliloquies. Although the index lacks references to specific sonnet numbers, Weiser's extraordinary command of the music, style and structure of the poems, and his running comparisons, hold our interest.

Reiman's *Romantic Texts and Contexts* grew out of its author's early studies in Shelley, and six of the 19 essays or chapters deal predominantly with Shelley and his work. But generally, anyone interested in the Romantic poets from Wordsworth to Browning will enjoy Reiman's lively, tasteful style.

The most readable chapter is "Poetry of Familiarity," dealing with Wordsworth's life and affections. But even the "core" chapters on editing the Romantics are prefaced, like the rest of the essays, with the author's revealing personal comments. And Reiman's afterword (which should be read first) is a sterling manifesto urging "a respect for the intelligence of

the ordinary men and women" by (among others) "some graduate
professors in Ivy League schools."

In their search for clarity, both Weiser and Reiman are against the grain of
overblown scholarship. Perhaps they signal a new breed of academics
who, rather than "publish or perish," must communicate or be terminated.
In any case this brace of studies is a fitting appearance in this 30th
anniversary of the founding of the University of Missouri Press. Look for
many more titles from this press in fields of biography, poetry, criticism,
history and even fiction. It has emerged as one of the finest among scores
of university presses in the country.

Review of *Mind in Character: Shakespeare's Speaker in the* Sonnets, by
David K. Weiser (University of Missouri) and *Romantic Texts and
Contexts*, by Donald H. Reiman (University of Missouri).

St. Louis Post-Dispatch, June 14, 1988, p. 5D.

The evolution of a poet's style

In poetry as in other literature, "schools" and trends are often indistinct and sometimes artificial. Modernism, for instance, began 75 years ago and tapered off 50 years later as its leading figures expired (or retired) and it splintered into other expressions like Beat poetry and "confessionalism" in the '60s. Today we might expect Modernism to be understood, soaked into our culture, but it's as remote now to readers under 30 as are the older Classical and Romantic movements. The reason is that some Modernists like Wallace Stevens, Ezra Pound and Hart Crane were never popular and are still considered difficult. Pound's puzzlements we can understand (or understand that they're not understood); but the fine aesthetics, the word-magic of Crane and Stevens are another matter. Any reader who appreciates the texture and nuances of language should be able to enjoy their poems.

Besides biographies of Wallace Stevens (1879-1955) there are scores of books analyzing his life and work. These two critical studies by Joseph Carroll and George Lensing deal almost exclusively with his poetry, tracing its evolution of style and influences— especially Romantic influences like Keats, Wordsworth and Emerson.

Joseph Carroll, who teaches at the University of Missouri-St. Louis, interprets Stevens's poetry as a "supreme fiction" deeply rooted in the Romantic and Transcendental traditions. He deals with the poet in terms of life, death, imagination and reality—in philosophical concepts—and discusses in some detail poets like Shelley, Tennyson and Whitman, who are only briefly mentioned in Lensing's volume.

Carroll's detailed scrutiny of Stevens—a poet of concrete expression and abstract undercurrents—is perhaps the finest revelation of Stevens's metaphysical side I've seen. If Carroll's style is heavy, complex and at times tedious, how else could a writer discuss (as he does) ideas of God, spirit and paradise, for instance? Indeed, though we've often heard the term "pure poetry," I've never found it better described and illustrated than in Carroll's treatment of Stevens.

George Lensing's *Wallace Stevens*, like the Carroll volume, is not an "introductory study" but it is more readable, for it recounts Stevens's early growth as a poet and mentions hundreds of persons and events (some not indexed) touching Stevens's life and work. There is good coverage of his years at Harvard (1897-1900) and his influence there, and his contributions to the Harvard *Advocate*.

Lensing also gives a fascinating running discussion (and a full chapter) on that seminal journal of Modernism, *Poetry* magazine (Chicago) and its founder Harriet Monroe. Another chapter (35 pages) contains a listing and discussion of all 361 entries in Stevens's notebook titled "From Pieces of Paper," about a fourth of which Stevens eventually used in his poetry and prose. But Lensing, like Carroll, serves readers best by discussing and interpreting hundreds of Stevens's poems, quoting some in full.

Despite their scholarly tone, both of these books may be used selectively as primers for understanding Stevens's poems. The formula—take any poem of Stevens that appeals to you, immerse yourself in the lines, then look up the poem in Carroll or Lensing to find deeper, different interpretations. Why not start with "Sunday Morning":

> Complacencies of the peignoir, and late
> Coffee and oranges in a sunny chair,
> And the green freedom of a cockatoo
> Upon a rug mingle to dissipate
> The holy hush of ancient sacrifice. . .

—not a typical passage of Stevens but one of the best known.

Even now, a generation after his death, Stevens is not for the fainthearted but for the adventurous reader. In his unique way he made "extraordinary texts and memorable music" out of what "great numbers of people. . . feel and know."

Review of *Wallace Stevens's Supreme Fiction: A New Romanticism*, by Joseph Carroll (Louisiana State), and *Wallace Stevens: A Poet's Growth*, by George S. Lensing (Louisiana State).

St. Louis Post-Dispatch, July 12, 1988, p. 5D.

Poetry of blood and broken bones

> Shaken from sleep, and numbed and scarce awake,
> Out in the trench with three hours' watch to take,
> I blunder through the splashing murk: and then
> Hear the gruff muttering voices of the men
> Crouching in cabins candle-chinked with light. . . .

These lines from the poem "Trench Duty," by Siegfried Sassoon (1886-1967), are only a bland, peaceful prelude to the horrors of World War I, described by Sassoon and more than 60 other poets in Robert Biddings' powerful chronology of "the war to end wars." But first, an obvious question: why do "the" war poets represent only that first World War? The Great War was more than a sentimental tragedy. It was the first mechanized, mobilized war on a global scale. It was the first to use aircraft, trucks, submarines and automatic weapons together with the swords (bayonets) and cavalry of all wars since Alexander the Great. It was the unfinished war, which festered on its survivors and their immediate heirs.

Indeed, both World Wars may be blurred into one by future historians.

The War Poets is a simply but movingly planned summary of that war from its first year (1914) until its aftermath in 1919. It is a book by and about its soldiers — of their blood and broken bones, of shattered lives and landscapes. The war's great commanders and strategists (and bunglers) have been glorified and documented enough elsewhere, in books like Barbara Tuchman's *The Guns of August*. But only the poets and artists, it seems, can communicate war's sardonic realism.

Giddings's collection is unique in several ways. It traces the war's events and their meanings in poems, prose commentaries and illustrations (photos, paintings and drawings). While most of the poets are British—Rupert Brooke, Robert Graves, Wilfred Owen, Edmund Blunden, Sassoon and others—a dozen or more American, Canadian, French, German and Italian poets are also represented.

And unlike much earlier anthologies like *The Valiant Muse* (Putnam, 1936), which carried 60 poets killed in the war, Giddings's 60 poets include only 17 killed in the war and only a dozen from *The Valiant Muse*.

325

THREE FACES OF AUTUMN
Poetry, Prose, Translations

If Giddings seems to neglect those scores of poets killed in action, he compensates by his rich, rare choice of poems, many little known or read today — poems like Blunden's "Third Ypres," Owen's "Spring Offensive" and "Disabled," and nightmarish lines like these from "Dead Man's Dump," by the brilliant Isaac Rosenberg (1890-1918):

> The wheels lurched over sprawled dead
> But pained them not, though their bones crunched,
> Their shut mouths made no moan.
> They lie there huddled, friend and foeman,
> Man born of man, and born of woman,
> And shells go crying over them
> From night till night and now.

Besides a useful bibliography and an index, Giddings includes short biographies of all his poets. The illustrations, many in color or sepia tone, are skillfully coordinated with the text. Altogether, Giddings has compiled a powerfully effective book whose theme may be summed up in words from a preface Wilfred Owen wrote for his own first book, a book he would never live to see published:

> My subject is War, and the pity of War.
> The Poetry is in the pity.

Review of *The War Poets*, by Robert Giddings, (Orion Books).

St. Louis Post-Dispatch, August 14, 1988, p. 2B.

Petrarch as poetic touchstone

It is hard to imagine our civilization today without that small band of early Renaissance scholars and poets, among whom was a Francesco Petrarca (1304-1374). Petrarch is one of those "touchstones" Matthew Arnold wrote about—those standards without which our age would revert to barbarism.

Petrarch's scattered rhymes, *Canzoniere*, is the subject of this unique study. Here Sara Sturm-Maddox traces the "strategy" of the famous love poems to Laura, and shows how they evolved from the pagan imagery of poets like Ovid and Horace to the Christian imagery of Dante and St. Augustine. But she also knows Petrarch as a player of roles. In his Ovidian role, for instance, he reveals a vulnerable, alienated self encountering an object of erotic desire impossible of fulfillment.

Unlike Dante's poems in the *Vita Nuova* (*New Life*), Petrarch's *Canzoniere* contains no prose narrative commentary. It is up to scholars to supply interpretations for us, and they are abundant. In English one of the best books remains Ruth Shepard Phelps's *The Earlier and later Forms of Petrarch's* Canzoniere (Chicago, 1925), long out of print. Now Sturm-Maddox gives us new insights on Petrarch's work in a comparably brilliant, well-documented study.

Poets have imitated, plundered and borrowed from Petrarch for six centuries. It's refreshing to savor and understand the source in a study like this.

Review of *Petrarch's Metamorphoses,* by Sara Sturm-Maddox, (University of Missouri).

St. Louis Post-Dispatch, October 5, 1988, p. 4F.

THREE FACES OF AUTUMN
Poetry, Prose, Translations

Poetry of Donne and his era captured in print

Mark Twain was perhaps the first major author to use a typewriter a century ago, and since then the nature of "facsimile editions" has never been the same. One wonders indeed whether such editions will continue with today's authors who use word processors. Probably not, but meanwhile the manuscripts of thousands of earlier world authors remain to be gleaned from archives and reproduced.

The English poet John Donne (1572-1631) was a brilliant contemporary of Shakespeare, and his "word processor" consisted of quill pens and strong knuckles. This beautiful, large-format edition contains not only 70 manuscripts by Donne but scores of poems and prose selections by other famous writers of the English Renaissance, including Sir Walter Raleigh, Edward de Vere, Thomas Campion and Francis Beaumont. There are many poems by Sir Thomas Overbury (1581-1613), who was the victim of one of the most sensational crimes in English history, a murder conspiracy by the countess of Essex.

Editor Ernest Sullivan has added a 12-page introduction, a bibliography, several indices and other detailed, scholarly references to the poems.

The most striking feature of this book is the fine, large-type transcription of the poems side by side with the sometimes vexingly illegible manuscript reproductions. Readers seeking "pure" versions of the poems will find them here in the original text—as in these lines on earthly love from "The Triple Fools" by the testy, cynical Donne:

> I am two fooles I know
> for loving and for saying soe
>   In whyneing poetrie
> But wheeres that wyse man that wold not be I
>   if shee wold not deny . . .
> Greefe brought to numbers cannot be so fierce
> for hee teames (tames) itt that fetters it in verse

Another poet here is Joshua Sylvester (1563-1618), whose verse the great John Dryden once derided as "abominable fustian." Yet such lines as these from his poem "The Fruites of a cleer Conscience" have a timeless, popular appeal:

To shine in silks and glister all in gold
To shewe in wealth and feed on daintie fare
To build vs houses statelie to behold
The Princes fauour and the peoples care
Although theis guifts be great and very rare
The groaning gout the collicke & the stone
Will marre their mirth & turne itt all to moane

Donne scholars especially will admire Sullivan's patient, meticulous editing of this work, which is only the latest of many University of Missouri Press volumes on Donne and other poets of his period. Earlier titles include finely produced works of bibliography and criticisms. As for this facsimile edition, it's a pity that it wears a drab, gray jacket. It deserves a colorful, glossy wrapper and display space in bookstores. Few scholarly books like this reach a mass market, but great poetry needs wider audiences. It grows on the reader.

Review of *The First and Second Dalhousie Manuscripts, Poems and Prose by John Donne and Others, A Facsimile Edition*, edited by Ernest W. Sullivan II (University of Missouri Press).

St. Louis Post-Dispatch, November 13, 1988, p. 5F.

THREE FACES OF AUTUMN
Poetry, Prose, Translations

The controversial life of poet Ezra Pound

"If Ezra Pound had not existed, it would be hard to invent him," Humphrey Carpenter observes at the opening of his comprehensive, 1000-page life of the poet.

Perhaps no poet in history led a more controversial life than Pound, who was born in Hailey, Idaho, in 1885 and died in Venice 87 years later. Pound was a man of many masks and moods, a mover and shaker, a mentor to some of the century's finest poets from T. S. Eliot to Allen Ginsberg. To research and recount such a life with balance and objectivity is one of the most challenging tasks of a writer, and Carpenter's book is the most complete, unbiased life of Pound published to date.

Even those who knew and worked with Pound (as I worked with him in translating poetry during his years of confinement at St. Elizabeths Hospital in Washington) find it hard not to overemphasize some aspects of this poet. Carpenter has no ax to grind, and his book has all the elements of a classic biography: symmetrical treatment of Pound's life and work, a wealth of quotations and illustrations, and the appearance of most of Pound's friends and influences.

Yet there are a few gaps among the influences; for example, Missouri Senator Thomas Hart Benton is not mentioned at all. Benton's memoirs, *A Thirty Years' View* (1821-1851), had a positive impact on Pound in the 1950s during his 13-year confinement (1945-1958) for his wartime broadcasts in Italy.

Like Eliot, Pound was an expatriate most of his adult life, and Carpenter catches the "agile and slippery" (and disordered) life—in America, England, France and Italy—in 79 orderly chapters under five chronological parts.

He treats fully Pound's important relationships, from Eliot and Richard Aldington to William Carlos Williams and W. B. Yeats. His attention to Pound's friends—Conrad Aiken, Margaret Anderson, Allen Ginsberg and Archibald MacLeish—is especially noteworthy, for these figures are given little or no mention in earlier works on Pound, such as Hugh Kenner's *The Pound Era* (California, 1971). Carpenter also treats candidly, yet sensitively, Pound's family relationships: his life with Dorothy Pound and

Olga Rudge (and the love and pain of those women who shared that life), his son, Omar, and daughter, Mary, and his grandchildren.

Almost like family perhaps was one special figure, the American poet and publisher James Laughlin, who understood Pound's temperament and foibles as well as anyone. After his first meeting with Pound in 1933 until the poet's death, Laughlin published scores of books by or about Pound and became one of his truest friends and mentors. At first influenced by Pound, Laughlin later gently remonstrated him. (In 1940, for instance, Laughlin asked Ezra "that there should be no anti-Semitic material in the Cantos"—a suggestion which at least temporarily gave Pound second thoughts about such "habits of language.") Laughlin's name runs profusely through Carpenter's impressively documented biography.

Laughlin's own memoirs, *Pound as Wuz*, are a necessary adjunct to any full-scale biography of Pound. They consist of nine illustrated essays and lectures offering unique insights, not only on the friendship of Pound and "Jaz" (as Ezra called Laughlin) but also on Pound's poetry. In a succinct, rich style Laughlin deals with topics like Pound's pedagogy, his "Propertius" poem, and his translation style and sources. Laughlin's two essays on Pound's *Cantos*—the epic he published for Pound as sections were completed —are perhaps the most informative brief introduction to this poem available.

Laughlin writes also about Pound's economic theories (far out to most readers perhaps) and about the lighter side of Pound's nature.

As for Pound's anti-Semitism, Laughlin admits that it put a severe strain on his affection for the poet. But Laughlin came to understand this obsession when the head psychiatrist at St. Elizabeths told him, "You mustn't judge Pound morally, you must judge him medically." For Pound could not control his own paranoia. Paradoxically, in his own personal relationships with Jewish writers and artists—the sculptor Henghes, for instance—Pound often showed warmth and respect.

Laughlin knew Pound "in his best years, in his prime." As Hugh Kenner writes, in introducing *Pound as Wuz*, this included Pound's great creative period of the early and mid-thirties. To learn about the world and history, not only about versecraft, he adds, Laughlin came in at exactly the right moment.

331

THREE FACES OF AUTUMN
Poetry, Prose, Translations

Yet Kenner's introduction is as much a tribute to Laughlin as to Pound. As a publisher, Laughlin kept every book by Pound, and by poet William Carlos Williams too, in print whether it sold or not. Without Laughlin, Kenner asks, "what literature would America have to show for this century?"

In these strong, self-effacing memoirs, Laughlin shows a broad understanding of Pound's many friends, influences and sources, and of Pound's evolving ideas. *Pound as Wuz* is unusually revealing. Laughlin continues to show, in this and his recent books of poetry, an extraordinary brilliance. As Pound might have said, "He knows how to use the language."

Review of *A Serious Character: The Life of Ezra Pound*, by Humphrey Carpenter (Houghton Mifflin) and *Pound as Wuz: Essays and Lectures on Ezra Pound*, by James Laughlin (Graywolf Press).

St. Louis Post-Dispatch, January 1, 1989, p. 3B.

A literary correspondence

Books of letters dealing with people, events and ideas help us understand with extraordinary intimacy the lives and times and motives of others. Such is the correspondence of two honored American men of letters, Kenneth Burke (born 1897) and Malcolm Cowley (born 1898).

Their lifelong friendship began when they were eighth-grade classmates in Pittsburgh, and 75 years ago they started exchanging letters. This selection opens with a letter to Cowley in 1915 in which Burke describes his meeting with author Theodore Dreiser, and ends with a note from Cowley (1981) congratulating Burke for receiving the National Medal for Literature. (Cowley himself won a national award soon afterwards.)

Throughout these letters is a sharing of detailed experience and broad ideas, but the viewpoints differed as the writers' experiences differed. Cowley, for instance, served in France in World War I, and during World War II worked for the poet Archibald MacLeish as a chief information analyst in Washington, when MacLeish was head of the Office of Facts and Figures. Burke took his first trip abroad in 1969, visiting France and Italy soon after his wife's death. But Cowley's studies in France during the 1920s, and .his friendship with noted French authors of that decade, added a new dimension to the work of both Cowley and Burke.

Yet the exchange was not always bland or agreeable. The pages bristle with literary allusions, straight talk and occasional ethnic epithets. In an early letter Cowley berated Burke for the latter's anti-Semitism, which understandably waned with World War II. In September 1938 Cowley deplored "the big sellout in Munich" as a step towards war, a prophetic observation. In the same letter he added, "We haven't been seeing enough of each other, and it's a very bad idea to let friendships lapse through taking them for granted."

Without divulging the "plot" of this book, we conclude that two facts or values clearly emerge from this correspondence. One is the value of a long, compatible marriage—Burke a 35-year marriage to Elizabeth ("Libbie") and Cowley a marriage (1932) to Muriel. Significantly, Burke's loss of Libbie affected his writing ("she helped so much by my being so crazy about her, I was driven to prove, prove, prove . . . every day and night to her I was appealing"). While Cowley continued to produce during the 1970s as Burke's published work diminished, the second value of their friendship, its sustaining power, took hold and became more apparent after Burke's loss.

Burke was foremost a poet and critic, and Cowley a critic and literary historian. Still, both may become best known as makers of ideas, as literary philosophers who influenced new generations of young writers, as a different duo—Cleanth Brooks and Robert Penn Warren—had taught the same generations to understand poetry. Their letters offer a wealth of experience and insight on literary and non-literary matters alike.

Review of *The Selected Correspondence of Kenneth Burke and Malcolm Cowley, 1915-1981*, edited by Paul Jay (Viking).

St. Louis Post-Dispatch, March 26, 1989, p. 3B.

A daughter's view of poet Carl Sandburg

We could fill a column with a hundred names of once-prominent
American poets, now unremembered, who wrote and published since
1900, but the name and works of Carl Sandburg (1878-1967) will not soon
be forgotten. Sandburg stands like a rock of remembrance, a character and
a symbol that certain regional poets (like Robert Frost and Robinson
Jeffers) never outshone.

This second partial biography of Sandburg by his youngest daughter,
Helga, covers the last 45 years of his life. Sandburg hobnobbed with all,
from the poor and obscure to the rich and famous, including presidents
Kennedy and Johnson. Helga's account of Carl and his family is as much
autobiography as biography. The style is curious, elliptical, sometimes
patchy, but fast-moving and enjoyable, shifting when necessary from first
to third person and back again. While Helga and Carl are the central
characters, Helga's mother, Paula, and the latter's brother, photographer
Edward Steichen (Uncle Ed), and a host of others are remembered in
words and photos. There are tensions of course between the strong-willed
Helga and her famous father. A talented author in her own right, Helga felt
the hamperings of Carl's complex, exciting, yet unfathomable personality.
There were rifts with her father ("The Grizzly," "the household Bear") and
wrath for her husbands. (After two tumultuous marriages, Helga is now
married to a Cleveland, Ohio, surgeon.)

But the whole family situation between the Steichens and the Sandburgs,
and their combined circles of friends, brought experiences and advantages
to Helga. She came to realize this, and a reconciliation with Sandburg was
inevitable. And aloof from the rifts, it seems, stood Carl's lifetime mate,
Paula, the great mediator. ("Dad is proud of your poems. You are the
author in the family now.") Helga has been doubly blessed: first, with
such a father and, second, to have shared much of his life and experience.
Well, perhaps a third "blessing" should be added: a talent to write such a
fascinating book about her family whose generations may long be
renewed.

Review of *"Where Love Begins," a Portrait of Carl Sandburg*, by Helga
Sandburg (Fine).

St. Louis Post-Dispatch, June 11, 1989, p. 5F.

THREE FACES OF AUTUMN
Poetry, Prose, Translations

Edgar Allan Poe in words and images

What a perfect wedding of word and image! Some pictures may be worth a thousand words, but Simon Marsden's are worth ten thousand. Take a few stories and poems by Edgar Allan Poe, the best mood-maker in our language, and mix them with the powerful, eerie photographic art of a lensman dedicated to Poe—and the result is the finest abridged edition of this classic writer now in print.

Marsden's photos, about 40 of them, accompany 23 of Poe's writings ranging from poems like "The Raven" and "The Bells" to stories like "The Masque of the Red Death," "The Black Cat" and "The Premature Burial." The pictorial subjects are mostly from England, France, Scotland and Ireland and exude death and desolation: houses and castles, crumbling and deserted; pitiful old tombs and statuary, weird and weathered; and bleak, unpeopled landscapes. Marsden's technique is the crowning touch. The photos, in black and white, are meticulously dodged, cropped and focused, with soft or sharp or grainy treatment. Each photo seems wedded, or even welded, to the words it faces.

And what can we say of Poe? We smugly assume we know all about him —how he died ("of drink and drugs") at age 40 just 140 years ago. Most of us have read a little, but few of us have read most of his voluminous poems, stories, essays and criticism. He gave us the first modern detective story ("The Murders in the Rue Morgue") and shocks of the macabre and the magnificent. The shocks were felt almost at once in Europe, through the translations of the French poet Baudelaire, and eventually almost worldwide. Back and forth, the aftershocks continued from Jules Verne to the symbolist and surrealist poets and painters, and more recently in Dali and De Chirico, for instance.

But after Poe died, his jealous "friend" Rufus Griswold betrayed him by describing him as a weak, disreputable alcoholic—a myth carried down to our time in recent writings on alcoholic authors. In most accounts, Poe drank wine and sometimes took opiates commonly prescribed in his day. But no author dead drunk or spaced out could have written so much and so well as Poe. New interpretations of Poe's life and death support the idea that, even in small amounts, drugs and alcohol perhaps provoked a more serious illness in him such as diabetes or lead poisoning—or, as I believe, the rare disease porphyria. (The circumstances of his death indicate this.)

A CHARLES GUENTHER RETROSPECTIVE
Prose: Critical Reviews and Essays, 1983-1992

Read the details of his short, tragic life—then marvel at the legacy of letters he left us. The outpouring of that life of pain and devotion, and sensitivity and mystery, is a unique American gift. It too may pass, as Poe predicted, but it still reverberates in *Visions of Poe*:

> And, around about his home, the glory
> That blushed and bloomed
> Is but a dim-remembered story
> Of the old time entombed.

Review of *Visions of Poe*, with photographs and Introduction by Simon Marsden (Knopf).

St. Louis Post-Dispatch, June 25, 1989, p. 5C.

THREE FACES OF AUTUMN
Poetry, Prose, Translations

A 'No' to faddish poetry

At last! A band of critics with the courage to declare that the Emperor of certain new poetry—namely, the hackneyed "confessional" lyric—wears no clothes. In 13 essays plus an introduction, 13 critics, poets themselves, make a strong case for repudiating as "poetry" the short free verse autobiographical imagist lyric, a verse craze that has flourished since the early '60s. Editor Frederick Feirstein and his colleagues—Dana Gioia, Richard Moore, Dick Allen, Mark Jarman and others—urge that formal poetry and longer narrative verse be recognized instead.

This book is an important manifesto to poets, and eventually to readers, for an excess of meaningless verse still abounds. As Moore points out, "It is now possible to become a Ph.D. in our literature and not have the foggiest notion of the few simple rules that Milton used in composing his lines; and poets busy collecting government grants to go on mystifying one another need not trouble to learn them either." Indeed, many poets have alleged a scandalous inability of the National Endowment for the Arts to distinguish talent from mediocrity in granting fellowships to writers. Noting also how certain poets read their inflated diction, Feirstein describes their artificial oratory as they go "incanting banalities in sonorous, haranguing voices." A reaction to the "swinging prose" of the confessional poets was bound to happen, and perhaps this book by highly respected poets will clear the air. Yet, as explosive and controversial as "Expansive Poetry" may seem, its ideas and expression have appeared for more than a decade. Many literary magazines have published the new narrative and formal poetry, and essays supporting such poetry.

Finally, Feirstein and the others don't want their ideas turned into a "new conformism." Rather, they want narrative and meter and rhyme "to open worlds of reality and imagination" to other poets. And—free verse and confessional poets, take note—Feirstein adds that if "Expansive Poetry" is taken up as a dogma, "we expect we will remain true to our natures and attack it."

Review of *Expansive Poetry, Essays on the New Narrative & The New Formalism* (Story Line Press).

St. Louis Post-Dispatch, August 13, 1989, p. 5C.

William Carlos Williams's legacy to young poets

In May 1955, as a young poet on a panel with William Carlos Williams, I thanked him for his longtime encouragement to new and unknown writers, especially by his contributions of work to obscure little literary magazines. Years earlier one such magazine, *Palisade* (Iowa), had published my first poem (outside of campus journals) along with a Williams poem a few pages away. What illustrious company, I felt! Now as we look back at the generation of great Modernist poets born between 1875 and 1900—from Robert Frost to Hart Crane—we are hard pressed to find any of them whose influence prevails more than that of Williams. Not Frost or T. S. Eliot or even Ezra Pound was more responsive and supportive to younger poets, and today his impact is seen in scores of those poets from A. R. Ammons and Robert Creeley to Byron Vazakas and Louis Zukofsky.

Williams's *Collected Poems* have appeared in various editions since 1934, including a "complete" collection in 1938 and *The Collected Earlier Poems* in 1951. But this new, superbly edited two-volume set encompasses all of them, and it is likely to stand as a definitive edition for many years. The collection includes all of Williams's published poetry except the narrative *Paterson*, and some sections of that, too, are included.

Williams was born in 1883 in Rutherford, N, J., where he lived and practiced medicine most of his life. His father, whose mother's name was Emily Dickinson (no relation to the American poet), was born in England. His mother was born in Puerto Rico of Basque-Dutch-Spanish-Jewish descent. In 1897-99 the young Williams was sent to study in Geneva and Paris, and three years later he graduated from Horace Mann School in New York City. After studying dentistry he switched to medicine and interned in various hospitals from 1906 to 1909.

He then studied pediatrics in Leipzig (1909-1910), was appointed public schools physician in Rutherford, and later took up private practice.

Williams's first book, *Poems* (1909), was published in Rutherford and contained sonnets and formal lyrics. In 1913 his second book, *The Tempers*, was published in London by Pound's publisher, Elkin Mathews, and showed strong stylistic influences of Pound and the Imagist group. From then until his death in 1963 he published 20 more books of poetry plus other works of fiction, essays, letters and memoirs. Recognition gradually came with a Dial Award (1926), a National Book Award (1950), a Bollingen prize (1953) and a posthumous Pulitzer Prize (1963).

The most striking aspect of Williams's poetry as it evolves through these two volumes is its early and consistent use of a conversational idiom.

Although Williams considered 1939, the year the first volume breaks off, as the turning point of his poetic life, he had already written the forerunner of the *Paterson* series (published in the late 1940s) in the 1920s.

Yet that early period, he said, showed all he "had gone through technically to learn about the making of a poem."

While many of the poems up to the mid-1920s were clearly imitative (of Pound, Cummings, H.D. and others), Williams had already progressed toward an original idiom laced with color and movement, as in these lines from "Winter" (1928):

> This is winter—
> rosettes of
> leather-green leaves
> by the old fence
> and bare trees
> marking the sky . . .

Still, there were hints of the poet's strong social consciousness too, as in "The Men":

> Wherein is Moscow's dignity
> more than Passaic's dignity?
> A few men have added color better
> to the canvas, that's all . . .
> Violet smoke rises
> from the mill chimneys—Only,
> the men are different who see it
> draw it down in their minds
> or might be different

And with imagery echoing even into his final volume, *Pictures from Breughel* (1962):

A CHARLES GUENTHER RETROSPECTIVE
Prose: Critical Reviews and Essays, 1983-1992

> The metal smokestack
> of my neighbor's chimney
> greets me among the new leaves . . .

Whether we read Williams in bits or gobs, we are struck by his vigorous American rhetoric, his fine detail and subtle emotion, his ability to find poetry in the most common themes—in poem after poem like "The Yachts," "Gulls," "Death," "Drink," "The pure products of America" and "The crowd at the ball game":

> The crowd at the ball game
> is moved uniformly
> by a spirit of uselessness
> which delights them . . . .

At the risk of oversimplifying Williams, here is another of his early poems, "The Red Wheelbarrow" (1923), which I've often quoted in conferences and classes to students aged 4 to 94, wringing every meaning from its form and imagery:

> so much depends
> upon
> a red wheel
> barrow
> glazed with rain
> water
> beside the white
> chickens

—a seemingly artless piece which, closely examined, reveals classic elements of poetry: a formal structure (of syllables) in lines and stanzas, suggestion and colorful, crisp imagery. (I must add that I long insisted this could not be a poem without the first two lines, charged with suggestion—until I realized that, from an Oriental viewpoint, the last six lines alone may be more subtly suggestive.)

Still, Williams must not be judged by such "bits." Although the second of these two volumes is obviously stronger than the first, the earlier experimental poems and prose poems have a fascination of their own. But finally readers must go to the later and longer poem—in *Paterson*

341

(especially Episode 17), *The Desert Music* (1954), *Journey to Love* (1955) and *Pictures from Breughel*—to appreciate the full range and impact of Williams's work. And there is no finer sourcebook of Williams than this new set, laboriously annotated, indexed, edited and compiled with the encouragement of his longtime publisher, James Laughlin.

In 1951 Williams suffered the first of several strokes, yet he valiantly continued writing until 1961. On his last extensive reading tour, in 1955, he read his new four-part poem, "Asphodel, That Greeny Flower":

> . . . We lived long together
> a life filled,
> if you will,
> with flowers. . .

—perhaps one of the finest love poems in our language. His audiences on campuses throughout the country were overwhelmingly moved. And I was equally moved by his delight at my few words of gratitude to him for his living legacy of encouragement to younger poets.

Review of *The Collected Poems of William Carlos Williams: Volume I, 1909-1939*, edited by A. Walton Litz and Christopher MacGowan (New Directions), and *Volume II, 1939-1962,* edited by Christopher MacGowan (New Directions).

St. Louis Post-Dispatch, September 2, 1989, p. 5D.

A CHARLES GUENTHER RETROSPECTIVE
Prose: Critical Reviews and Essays, 1983-1992

Interviews with 16 modern poets

The poet and anthologist Louis Untermeyer (1885-1977) once told me "We have to steal time to write"—an idea his friend Robert Frost had endorsed in a 1961 interview for *The Paris Review*. Asked by an audience how he found leisure to write, Frost replied, "Like a sneak I stole some of it, like a man I seized some of it—and I had a little in my tin cup."

Frost is one of 16 modern poets interviewed in *Poets at Work*, a collection of *Paris Review* articles chosen from eight previous volumes of *Writers at Work*. That whole series, which contained interviews of 113 world writers in many fields, is a nearly forgotten classic of its type.

But the reader can't approach *Poets at Work* or any of the other volumes as a manual on "how to write."

The work habits of all the writers are as diverse as their lives and experiences. Yet the interviews provide some fascinating insights. Archibald MacLeish, for instance (as poet and playwright) felt that "all art begins and ends with discipline." His discipline, he adds, is in chipping away at his poems like a stonemason, but with "delight in the chipping." T. S. Eliot delves into his early sources and influences, especially French, and he explains the different "voices" of dramatic and lyric poetry. Anne Sexton reveals that her Pulitzer Prize (1967) gave her renewed impetus to write: Inspired by the recognition given her, she finished an 18-section poem in two weeks.

Other poets reveal specific work habits. Elizabeth Bishop said that she wrote prose on a typewriter, but used a pen for poetry. She was aware too that William Carlos Williams wrote entirely on the typewriter, and that "Robert Lowell printed—he never learned to write. He printed everything."

The 16 poets include also Conrad Aiken, W. H. Auden, Allen Ginsberg, Marianne Moore and several others. (Louis Untermeyer, Richard Wilbur and scores of other modern poets are not among those interviewed.) But one common aspect of these interviews is the frequent mention of other poets, living and dead, by the interviewees. Frost, Pound, Williams, Eliot and MacLeish, particularly, pay tribute—subtly or openly—to a host of world writers whose work affected their own.

343

There's also an occasional bit of sniping among the poets and their peers. But generally this only betrays a healthy respect for fundamental differences. Donald Hall's introduction and the notes on the interviewers give further enlightening insights on *Poets at Work*.

Review of *Poets at Work: The Paris Review Interviews*, edited by George Plimpton (Viking).

St. Louis Post-Dispatch, December 12, 1989, p. 6D.

To the heart of America

Biographies are written about the rich and famous, not the poor and
obscure. But the most fascinating and appealing books, it seems, deal with
those who became well-to-do and recognized through their own efforts—
the slave who became a scientist, the farmer or haberdasher who became
president, for instance.

Carl Sandburg (1878-1967) was born in Illinois of Swedish immigrants
and had little time or money for education. At 13 he worked on a milk
wagon, and before age 20 he had held jobs as a barber shop porter, a
scene-shifter in a decrepit theater, a turner-apprentice in a pottery, a truck-
handler in a brickyard, a dishwasher in Denver and a
harvest hand in Kansas. At 20 he fought in the Spanish-American War,
and on returning to his native Galesburg, he enrolled in college for several
years, but without a high school diploma. After college he worked in
advertising and journalism (a profession he entered, free lance, during his
war years).

Sandburg's first book of verse (1904) appeared with little notice, and not
until his Chicago poems were published, when he was 36, did he become
recognized. By the time he was 70 he was the author of eight books of poems, a novel, an autobiography, a collection of folksongs, several books of
stories for young people—and a magnificent six-volume biography of
Abraham Lincoln, for which he won a 1939 Pulitzer Prize.

As Penelope Niven shows in this magnificently detailed and documented
life of Sandburg, the poet spoke "to and from the heart of American life."
As his friend Louis Untermeyer observed, Sandburg sought an authentic
expression for all people, urban and rural, and ranged over America "more
volubly than any poet since Whitman."

I met Carl Sandburg in his last years, but even then (as in my youth) I
thrilled to the wisdom and warmth of his octogenarian minstrelsy. His
unique voice and style, as Niven observes, were hard-won during his years
of dogged struggle, and he never compromised or changed them for the
critics.

Pain and heartbreak, and once an unfounded bit of scandal, touched
Sandburg's life—but he never used (or misused) his fame for gain.

Penelope Niven writes powerfully and sympathetically, yet honestly, of her subject, as Sandburg wrote of his lifelong idol, Lincoln. And as Sandburg wrote of his Lincoln work, it was a book that "walks up to you and makes you write it." The reader feels that way about Niven's Sandburg, to whom she devoted 14 years of painstaking research and writing.

This is an extraordinarily fine biography.

Review of *Carl Sandburg: A Biography*, by Penelope Niven (Scribners).

St. Louis Post-Dispatch, September 15, 1991, p. 5G.

A timeless voice

Interpretation is the key to the fame or notoriety of an author's work, and it's not surprising that works of dense expression or meaning seldom appeal to a mass audience. Some writers, especially poets, produce work having many interpretations. Blas de Otero (1916-1979) is among the most eminent modern Spanish poets—and in fact one critic called him "the best poet to appear in Spain since the end of the Spanish Civil War." Otero's style is not dense, but rather direct, concrete and even colorful, yet his poetry has been subject to various readings. In this distinctive study, Geoffrey Barrow of Purdue University rejects the usual ways of examining the poet—as a member of a movement or a generation—and treats Otero on a "less topical and more long-range basis." In short, as a literary satirist.

Early writings on Otero, by the Spanish poet-critic Dámaso Alonso and others, focused on Otero's religious existentialism and compared him with other religious poets like St. John of the Cross and Gerard M. Hopkins. But this aspect of Otero's poetry was followed by two later periods of his writing—one of social-political commitment, the other of self-conscious reflection. Barrow covers all of these periods and shows how undercurrents of satire pervade Otero's work. He gives examples of satire in separate chapters dealing with hypocrisy, women, arts and letters, and political and social dissent. The study is well-annotated, with a long bibliography and several indexes added.

Despite the fact that several Spanish poets (Juan Ramón Jiménez and Vicente Aleixandre) have won the Nobel Prize for literature since the 1950s, modern Spanish poetry is still relatively neglected in the U.S. Barrow's study, which quotes and carries literal translations of scores of Otero's poems, is sound, useful and enlightening. As Barrow points out, readers aren't indoctrinated by Otero but rather amused by his wit. But this wit, Barrow concludes, emanates from a deeper, timeless voice that "bears constant and fascinating testimony to the indestructible continuity of the human spirit."

Review of *The Satiric Vision of Blas de Otero*, by Geoffrey R. Barrow (University of Missouri).

St. Louis Post-Dispatch, January 5, 1990 p. 8F.

THREE FACES OF AUTUMN
Poetry, Prose, Translations

Trials of Russia's 'greatest woman poet'

It was a curious, touching story. On September 4, 1946, Anna Akhmatova, then 57 and the greatest woman poet in Russian history, had just been expelled from the Union of Soviet Writers. She had not yet been told of her expulsion. As she left her Leningrad apartment and visited the Union office, she was surprised that everyone avoided her. On her way home she bought some herring and met a colleague, Zoshchenko, who also had been expelled. His brief, anxious remark, "What can we do?" puzzled her, and she passed it off with a comment that "everything will be all right."

Only when she unwrapped the fish from the newspaper did she read the resolution and learn of her banishment from the powerful Union. A few of her less talented colleagues, envious and resentful of her popularity, brought about her expulsion for "poisoning the minds of Soviet youth." (Her friend Boris Pasternak helped and consoled her with a gift of a thousand rubles.) It was not the first or the last of life's misfortunes for Akhmatova, who seemed to thrive on adversity. Born Anna A. Gorenko in the Ukraine in 1889, she adopted the pen name Akhmatova, and at age 20 she married a longtime friend and fellow poet, Nikolay Gumilyov, who founded the Acmeist group of poets in 1911. (It was the first of her three marriages.) Their son Lev was born the following year when her first book of poems, *Evening*, appeared.

Her second book, *Rosary* (1914), was enormously popular, and it was followed by other collections, *White Flock* (1917) and *Plantain* (1921). Meanwhile the Russian Revolution took place (1917) and civil war broke out in 1919. During the terror that followed, Akhmatova was increasingly regarded as pre-revolutionary and her works were denounced by Mayakovsky and other writers. In 1921 Gumilyov, whom she had divorced, was executed for conspiracy.

Akhmatova's poetry was suppressed in the Soviet Union from 1925 to 1940. Even her great cycle *Requiem*, written from 1935 to 1940 and memorized by her friends, was not published until 1963, in Munich. In spite of her patriotic poetry and her wartime example of courage to Russian women (in Leningrad during 1941, for instance), her life became a daily struggle to live with dignity under a regime determined to humiliate and dishonor her. Although she received an Italian literary prize (1964) and an honorary degree from Oxford (1965), her poems, including her final book, *The Flight of Time* (1965), were severely censored until her death in 1966. A further indignity was the frequent arrest and long imprisonment, on political grounds, of her son Lev who had fought in the Russian air force.

Eventually Akhmatova regained membership in the Union of Soviet Writers and even became its president in 1964. But two years earlier when Robert Frost came to visit her, she was not allowed to receive the American poet privately. In a monitored meeting with Frost, who was impressed by her grandeur and sadness, she thought of her own long humiliation and grief: her poverty, fear, prison lines, burnt poems, and poems created only in memory. In contrast, she knew Frost was honored by his President, taught in schools, and praised and openly published. Yet there she felt they were just "two old people in wicker chairs" awaiting a single end.

Translations of Akhmatova's poetry long have appeared in many languages—in English by C. M. Bowra, Frances Cornford, Babette Deutsch and others—but often piecemeal, in magazines and anthologies, for instance. One recent volume (1989), *Poem Without a Hero and Selected Poems* (Oberlin College Press) contains an excellent selection of free verse translations by Lenore Mayhew and William McNaughton. But it remained for Judith Hemschemeyer and her colleagues to produce *The Complete Poems*, numbering more than 700, in an incomparable bilingual (Russian and English) two-volume set.

Indeed, *The Complete Poems* is an extraordinary collaboration of scholars, editors, translators and friends of the late Akhmatova. Hemschemeyer's preface describes the development of Akhmatova's craft and her place in Russian poetry. Editor Roberta Reeder has added a long biographical and critical introduction. Three other authors, including Akhmatova's longtime friend Isaiah Berlin, contribute memoirs and accounts of visits with the poet. Each volume contains a chronology and an index of poems by source. There are other indexes, notes and bibliographies, plus 80 illustrations. But the essence of this work, and Akhmatova's life, is her poetry.

Poetry doesn't turn itself into poetry in other languages, nor is poetry necessarily lost in translation. It takes a dedicated, adept translator to restore the tone of the text, to make it sing again. Hemschemeyer's

349

translations are not formal and interpolative, but rather precise and communicative. Keeping Akhmatova's line breaks, she turns the poems into a fine English free verse, sometimes using direct or slant rhymes. She keeps the "look" of the Russian poems, an important point especially in the sonnets and short lyrics. The technique is highly successful in the open lines of "Incantation" (1936), for instance, resembling the style of American Imagist poet H.D.:

> Through the high gates,
> From beyond the Okhta swamps,
> By the untraveled path,
> Through the unmown meadow,
> Across the cordon of night,
> To.the sound of Easter bells,
> Uninvited,
> Unbetrothed—
> Come have supper with me.

The Acmeist poets had much in common with the American Imagist movement—but Akhmatova (in common with other great poets) transcended schools, movements and labels.

She was not as dense or mystical as certain Symbolists who preceded her, but like them her verse is often melancholy. From her earliest poems to her last, she sang a deeply intimate language of objects. In 1911:

> The willow spreads its transparent fan
> Against the empty sky.
> Perhaps I should not have become
> Your wife.

For many years readers and critics were unaware of Akhmatova's full range, considering her only as a poet of brief pieces and overlooking her sonnets and longer lyrics. Yet she also wrote longer poems in epic, dramatic and narrative form, including the extraordinary *Poem Without a Hero*, a triptych of Leningrad, Tashkent and Moscow written between 1940 and 1962. It has been compared with the major works of American Modernist poets, including Pound's *Cantos*. It is a poem of vague allusions and few specific objects, events and characters—a work the poet insisted on neither changing nor explaining.

Akhmatova, as Hemschemeyer writes, was "the poet of encounters, the diagnostician of love." And another kind of poetry, the poetry of witness of the terrible times during which, as Berlin observed, "she behaved with heroism." (Why then, we may ask, was her life oppressed?) Addressing some lines "To Poetry," Akhmatova wrote,

> You led me where there were no roads
> Through darkness like a falling star.
> You were bitterness and falsehood,
> But comfort—never.

Yet we are impressed not with her bitterness and regret, but with her supreme resilience, her ability to survive:

> . . . I never experienced crueler pain.
> It went away and its footsteps led
> Up to the very edge of the edge,
> And I, without it . . . I will die.

Irony and compassion marked her life and work, and sometimes even humor:

> I taught women to speak . . .
> But Lord, how to make them cease!

In 1988 the Communist Party finally annulled the decree that had condemned Akhmatova and Zoshchenko, and stated that their works "have taken their rightful place in the enrichment of the world of the spirit, and the shaping of man's civic position." It added that their works were restored "in their true greatness and significance."

The Complete Poems of Anna Akhmatova is an important and magnificent collection, one of the finest works of its kind produced in English over the last decade.

Review of *The Complete Poems of Anna Akhmatova*, translated by Judith Hemschemeyer. Edited and with an introduction by Roberta Reeder (Zephyr Press).

St. Louis Post-Dispatch, August 26, 1990, p. 5C.

THREE FACES OF AUTUMN
Poetry, Prose, Translations

A poet and her places, Kirkwood to New York

In the 1880s St. Louis was the birthplace of three eminent poets: Sara Teasdale, Marianne Moore and T. S. Eliot. Of these, only Eliot perhaps was sufficiently honored here on his centenary, although he had left the city in his youth and became a British citizen. Other, "urgent" circumstances—as Marianne Moore told me by letter nearly 30 years ago—led Moore (like Teasdale) to move East. Both spent their last years in Manhattan, where Teasdale took her own life in 1933 and Moore died at age 84 in 1972.

Charles Molesworth's *Marianne Moore* features the places of the poet's life and work: her birth and early childhood in Kirkwood, her college years and youth at Bryn Mawr and Carlisle, Pennsylvania, her several residences in New York City—and especially in Brooklyn from 1929 to 1966. Moore herself wrote a poem on the subject, "People's Surroundings," in which she recognizes the "usefulness" of the environment. Molesworth skillfully uses places as a background for the most important events in Moore's life, in describing her growth as a poet and public figure. He shows Moore's affection for English traditions (and authors like the Sitwells and George Saintsbury), despite her own new, distinctly American style. And he describes Moore's broad interests in the arts, natural science—and baseball. (Moore's 1968 essay, "One Poet's Pitch for the Cardinals to Win the World Series," proved accurate. She predicted that pitcher Bob Gibson would win at least two games. He won three for the Cardinals.)

Moore's celebrity status at times interfered with her serious work. In 1955, when the Ford Motor Company asked her help in naming a new car, she suggested a host of elegant, exotic terms—but Ford chose its own name, Edsel. So much for that.

Biographies by nature have errors and omissions. *Marianne Moore* has a few, mostly minor: several misspellings, an incomplete index, and a description of St. Louis as "west" of Kirkwood.

No matter, for Molesworth knows and describes Moore's literary life in Brooklyn and Manhattan incomparably well. But because no biographer has used (or had access to) all the poet's correspondence and sources, no exhaustive, definitive life of Moore is yet available.

Molesworth's study, though, is outstanding in several ways. It has a fascinating folio of photos of Moore at all stages of her life. She is pictured in later years with a variety of personalities: Muhammad Ali, David Rockefeller, Casey Stengel and others. One poignant photo shows her meeting her old literary friend and mentor, Ezra Pound, for the last time at the New York Public Library in 1969. (Moore's celebrated life, rich in major prizes and honors, sharply contrasted with Pound's life of controversy, confinement and public misunderstanding.)

Altogether, Molesworth's research and commentary show a strong, unbiased appreciation of Moore's life and work. And his comments on nearly 150 Moore poems make his biography an excellent background study of Moore's *Complete Poems*.

As for her "place," several cities may claim Marianne Moore, but she was at home in many. It bears repeating, however, that she wrote me long ago that there was "no city more cultured than St. Louis."

Review of *Marianne Moore, A Literary Life,* by Charles Molesworth (Atheneum).

St. Louis Post-Dispatch, October 14, 1990, p. 5C.

THREE FACES OF AUTUMN
Poetry, Prose, Translations

Wizards of Tin Pan Alley

One day in 1909 Irving Berlin peddled a lyric to a Tin Pan Alley publisher who assumed that Berlin also had music for the words. Led to a staff pianist where he was to "hum the music," Berlin, in the moments it took to cross the hall, concocted a melody. From then on, he became one of the few Alley songwriters who wrote both words and music.

This is but one of many anecdotes in the fascinating history of the popular lyricists—including Ira Gershwin, Lorenz Hart, Cole Porter, Oscar Hammerstein, Johnny Mercer and others who flourished on Broadway and in Hollywood in the first 65 years of our century. Their golden age spanned several wars and the Depression, from the mid-1920s era of the Harlem Cotton Club (and its great jazz composer Duke Ellington) to the 1950s when big bands began breaking up.

Philip Furia, a sophisticated, learned professor of English and author of a book on Ezra Pound, describes the lyricists as poets while analyzing the complex mystery and magic of their craft. His references to poets from Shakespeare to T. S. Eliot and his sharp dissection of the rhyme effect in works from W. C. Handy's "St. Louis Blues" (1914) to Johnny Mercer's "Satin Doll" (1958) are extraordinary. The creative genius of these lyricists was as genuine as that of popular poets like Frost, Sandburg and Eliot.

Hart's "Manhattan" (1925) is an example of the wondrously contrived verbal "ragging" that Furia compares with Imagistic poetry. Even the title of Hoagy Carmichael's "Star Dust" (1927), a song for which Mitchell Parish wrote the lyrics, was suggested by a suite of Emily Dickinson poems published under that title in *Poetry* magazine.

Together with tunesmiths, the wordsmiths cranked out song after song for vaudeville, Broadway, record and sheet music markets, and especially for Hollywood. The great musical films, starting with Astaire and Rogers in *Flying Down to Rio* (1933), brought out new talents like Vincent Youmans and Gus Kahn. Composer Youmans had an earlier hit in "Tea for Two" (1924), and Furia describes how Youmans got his lyricist, Irving Caesar, out of bed late one night to write the words. Caesar tossed off a "dummy lyric" just to get back to sleep—but the lyric stuck and became one of the most popular songs of the 1920s.

Furia includes tributes to the women lyricists who had to compete in the "old boy network" of Tin Pan Alley. Among these were Ann Ronell, who sold "Willow Weep for Me" (1932) to Paul Whiteman, and Dorothy Fields, who wrote "I Can't Give You Anything But Love" (1928) and "I Won't Dance" (1935).

Slangy, brassy, swingy, romantic and carnivalesque, the age also had its songs of vernacular elegance (especially Mercer's) and is still imbued in our American culture. Furia's history, with its quotes from hundreds of songs—and with 17 pages of credits alone—is a triumph worth trumpeting.

Review of *The Poets of Tin Pan Alley: A History of America's Great Lyricists,* by Philip Furia (Oxford).

St. Louis Post-Dispatch, October 28, 1990, p. 5C.

THREE FACES OF AUTUMN
Poetry, Prose, Translations

Critical reviewing

Critical reviewing has a valid, important place in the writing of every period because it reflects how other work, written and performed, is accepted or rejected. A slow song may be quickened or drastically changed in orchestration and arrangement; a play may be severely edited or adapted or "modernized." But the written word, in its original text, remains as it has always been—in Chaucer, Dante, Milton, Shakespeare, Poe. Only our attitudes, sometimes influenced or mirrored by critics, change in every generation.

I'm sure many book reviewers feel as I do that reviewing is a creative response to others' creative works. In book reviewing specifically, I have no "formula," no predetermined method of creating my response. There are as many different approaches perhaps as there are reviewers; certainly there are different approaches to reviewing different genres: fiction, biography, poetry, how-to books, political and historical works, etc.

My comments apply only to my specific fields, mostly belle lettres; poetry; criticism; translation, sometimes biography and fiction.

Reviewers expose themselves as wise or foolish or somewhere in between. One must have a certain bravado or confidence to review any author's work, for a book may be a sacred thing to its author. I've known authors and editors who took ten years or more to write or compile a book; their efforts deserve to be treated with respect and understanding.

Two of the hardest tasks any reviewer has are to admit that an author writes better than he does and (on the other hand) to contain his enthusiasm about an author—that is, not to praise each author reviewed as a new Shakespeare or Tolstoi. Still, it's perfectly logical and acceptable to compare elements of a work with the elements of works of any author, great or obscure. A reviewer must be skilled in making comparisons, in making valid comparisons, be they favorable or unfavorable.

For instance, one may write that a novelist is as long-winded and rambling as Faulkner but this doesn't mean the novelist is another Faulkner. Certain critics like Clarence Olson know of a broad range of writings, of all elements of fiction and of how they come into play in the novels they write about. His ability to recognize the strengths and weaknesses of a book, candidly and impartially, makes Olson, and others like him, first order critics.

There's not time or space to review every one of the tens of thousands of titles published yearly. In the field of poetry alone, with several thousand titles issued by small and large presses, a reviewer feels frustrated in his wish to bring good poetry to public attention. I compare the poetry reviewer to a geologist at the rim of the Grand Canyon: how much beauty and substance there is to be scrutinized but how little time and opportunity we have to review everything that deserves attention.

Reviewers understand that they neither have time nor space to devote 2,000 words to a deserving book, that 200 words may have to do, that it may be that or nothing for the book. Authors must realize that the reviewer also may be an author; his own creative work (outside of reviewing) always suffers with reviewing. New authors may not understand; dissatisfied, they lament that the reviewer "didn't give enough space."

Certain reviewing principles come to mind. 1) Know or find out some-thing about the author. Try to deal with the author as another person by knowing something of his/her background/experiences. 2) Know the field of the book under review—its finest authors and works—and use them as touchstones. 3) READ the book. This may seem elementary, but many a cursory review has been written using only "blurbs." 4) Describe the physical book; this is done sometimes near the end of a review. A potential book buyer needs to know if the book is well documented (indexes, appendices), illustrated (color, halftone), if the type is too small, the format size, page count, etc. 5) Criticize important elements of the book in perspective; do not lay stress on a few typos. Do stress errors if they reflect the book's shortcomings. 6) Imagine the book as your own; try to imagine yourself in the author's place. 7) Look for the author's purpose (often revealed in foreword, preface, introduction). Sometimes an author sets a limited goal and achieves it; it's better received than an author who strives for broader scope and misses. 8) Praise or blame with restraint. 9) Do look for good facets as well as the bad or repugnant points of the book. 10) Know the market for your review. Send scholarly reviews, well researched, to learned journals, for instance [as opposed to general newspapers]. 11) Write with interest (if possible, enthusiasm) about the book. Adapt style, vocabulary, length to audience. Connect ending with the lead, perhaps. And finally, 12) work with your editor or editors

357

cooperatively and constructively. Meet deadlines and respect your editor's wishes and preferences. Remember, editors must satisfy many demands and requirements—and loyalties.

—————————

"Critical reviewing" I define as serious, evaluative reviewing for a relatively wide range of newspapers and magazines.

The Missouri Writers' Guild News, Vol. 66, No. 1, Fall 1990, p. 3.

A CHARLES GUENTHER RETROSPECTIVE
Prose: Critical Reviews and Essays, 1983-1992

The capstone of an illustrious life

> It's not the dying kills us, but each breath,
> Each thought, which executes its own small share
> —It's not the death-blow, but the pilfering
> That wears your house, the mean activity
> Of pests that merely aggravate the air
> And multiply annoyance up to death.

Nearly 50 years ago, a young Royal Canadian Air Force pilot named Howard Nemerov published these lines in *Fantasy*, a literary quarterly with new writing by U.S. and Latin American authors such as Richard Eberhart, Herman Salinger, Nicolás Guillén and Pablo Neruda. Just out of Harvard and on his way to recognition as a poet, Nemerov had not yet stirred readers' interest like another RCAF pilot, John Magee, who was killed over England at 19. Nemerov was luckier. In fact, for a half century after Pearl Harbor, he was lucky—in life and love and in a dual career of writing and teaching heaped with honors to match an enormous talent.

Trying Conclusions is the culling of some of the best work that Nemerov produced between 1961 and his death in July at the age of 71. It contains selections from eight of his 12 books of poems, including many favorite pieces from his *Collected Poems* (1977), which won both the Pulitzer Prize and the National Book Award.

The book opens with "To Clio, Muse of History," in which the poet observes how "History has given/And taken away; murders become memories,/And memories become the beautiful obligations." In another early poem, "Sarajevo," Nemerov uses the sestina form to recall World War I: "In the summer when the Archduke dies," in stately, ominous measures; "Europe divides and fuses, side by side,/Ranging the human filings on the field/Of force . . ."

From *Gnomes and Occasions* (1973), the choices are more epigrammatic: "Zander on God," "Of Experience," and this quatrain titled "Epitaph":

> Of the Great World he knew not much,
> But his Muse let little in language escape her.
> Friends sigh and say of him, poor wretch,
> He was a good writer, on paper.

359

But there are also poignant, moving pieces including "To D - - -, Dead by Her Own Hand," in which Nemerov meditates on the life and death of his sister, the noted photographer Diane Arbus:

> You jumped because you feared to fall, and thought
> For only an instant: That was when I died.

The poems from *The Western Approaches* (1975) are a bit lighter, like "Ozymandias II" describing the life and times of a rusty old '57 Cadillac, and "Waiting Rooms," in which the poet asks, "What great genius invented the waiting room?" A particular setting leads to a general observation:

> Think how even in heaven where they wait
> The Resurrection, even in the graves
> Of heaven with the harps, this law applies;
> One waiting room will get you to the next.

There are later selections from *Sentences* (1980), *Inside the Onion* (1984) and *War Stories* (1987). The final 25 poems, *Trying Conclusions* (1987-91) comprise Nemerov's last work and give the title to the entire volume.

Altogether, this new volume contains nearly 170 poems, half of them from books published in the last decade.

Howard Nemerov was a great commentator—on past and present, on life and destiny. For his wry, witty style, I once compared him with W. B. Yeats (no mean comparison), but Yeats was not among his favorite poets.

His poetic lineage may be traced perceptibly from Lucretius to Shakespeare, and from Pope and Dryden to Browning and Allen Tate. He wrote with equal ease and humor of Ann Landers, of housewives, of pornography and postal clerks, of calendars and Adam and Eve—and these are but a few of the themes in one of his score of books of poems, essays and fiction.

Only in his final years did Nemerov publish his war recollections in *War Stories* (1987), recalling the few joys and the grinding griefs of the air war. Some of the pilots were confused, and many of them "did for themselves in folly and misfortune":

A CHARLES GUENTHER RETROSPECTIVE
Prose: Critical Reviews and Essays, 1983-1992

> Some hit our own barrage balloons, and some
> Tripped over power lines, coming in low:
> Some swung on takeoff, others overshot,
> And two or three forgot to lower the wheels,

Throughout the long postwar period, only a few other American poets (Richard Wilbur is one) seemed to match Nemerov's skill in the classic forms of verse. In the most powerful later lines of *Trying Conclusions*, Nemerov returns once more to his Shakespearean roots and echoes in poems like "Soundings," "The Forbidden City" and "Witnessing the Launch of the Shuttle Atlantis." In the last of these, he observes:

> So much of life in the world is memory
> That the moment of the happening itself...
> Appeared no more, against the void in aim,
> Than the flare of a match in sunlight, quickly snuffed.

A master of closure, Nemerov wrote poems with adroit, forceful conclusions. It is only fitting that *Trying Conclusions* is the capstone of a long, illustrious life. As he meditates in the closing lines of his title poem:

> What rational being, after seventy years,
> When Scripture says he's running out of rope,
> Would want more of the only world he knows?
> No rational being, he while he endures
> Holds on to the inveterate infantile hope
> That the road ends but as the runway does.

Review of *Trying Conclusions, New and Selected Poems, 1961-1991*, by Howard Nemerov (University of Chicago).

St. Louis Post-Dispatch, December 1, 1991, p. 5D.

Renaissance of black American poetry

In decades of writing for magazines, befriending poets and editors whose race, color or politics happened to differ from mine, I was either unaware of these differences or considered them irrelevant. The art or the impact of a poem, the truth of an idea—these were paramount in our relationships.

But I realized also that it is important to identify some cultural superstars of the black community. D. H. Melhem, poet and biographer, is herself a "superstar" in understanding and interpreting modern black American poetry.

In an earlier book on the life and works of Gwendolyn Brooks, Melhem presented Brooks as a dedicated, dynamic poet-hero of our time. Brooks was the first black to win a Pulitzer Prize (1946) and the first black woman to serve as Consultant in Poetry to the Library of Congress (now the post of American poet laureate). She has since received many other honors.

In *Heroism in the New Black Poetry*, Melhem places Brooks at the forefront of what (as Melhem suggests) may be a second Black Renaissance of literature—the first having occurred after World War I. She again shows how Brooks, a poet of enormous vitality, overcame many personal difficulties, emerging as an extraordinary example of courage and talent. But here Melhem doesn't simply summarize or restate her earlier writings on Brooks. She updates Brooks's achievements, and relates her life and works to those of other prominent black poets.

In narrative and interviews Melhem deals with five modern black poets: Dudley Randall, Haki R. Madhubuti, Sonia Sanchez, Jayne Cortez and Amiri Baraka.

Randall, (born 1914), a brilliant poet of formal expression, has been a publisher and editor in Detroit. While Melhem doesn't mention Ralph Ellison, Dudley Randall seems the epitome of Ellison's philosophy; that is, Randall has assimilated well both black and traditional European literatures. Melhem's labeling Randall as a humanist fits well.

If Madhubuti may be the least known of Melhem's poets, his work is strong and exciting. A younger follower and protégé of Brooks, Madhubuti (born 1942) was once known as Don L. Lee. He has published 15 books and several recordings since 1967. Melhem describes his "revolutionary" aspects and her interview brings out his strong realism and his clarity of purpose, as in his lines on the status for the black male:

> We walk in cleanliness
> the newness of it all
> becomes us
> our women listen to us
> and learn.
> We teach our children thru
> our actions.

Sonia Sanchez (born 1934) studied poetry under Louise Bogan and has taught at many universities, most recently at Temple. Since 1968 she has published a score of books—poetry, plays and works for children. Her work is clear, colloquial—and its main thrust is often political. (As an activist she helped introduce the first black studies programs in the U.S. in San Francisco.) Melhem in her interview compares Sanchez with Madhubuti, and stresses her rich voice and her dynamic life and work.

Jayne Cortez (born 1936) came to poetry from acting, and her works since 1969 include nine books plus recordings, films and videos. Melhem describes Cortez as a "supersurrealist" visionary, and her lines are at times charged with surreal, even ambiguous imagery. She lends her fine lyrical voice to a variety of social concerns, especially those of Africa. As Melhem writes, "Africa nurtures her; Cortez reciprocates." Her "African Night Suite" begins,

> Africa
> take my hands from the newspaper shacks of
> rotten existence and let my cataracts
> flow into the red clay of your loyalty.

Finally, Amiri Baraka (LeRoi Jones), perhaps best known of Melhem's group after Brooks, is also among the most prolific. In less than 30 years he has published nearly 50 books of poetry, plays, fiction and nonfiction. Now 56, he too has supported many social causes with his extraordinary talents, influenced by poets like Langston Hughes, Charles Olson and Allen Ginsberg.

THREE FACES OF AUTUMN
Poetry, Prose, Translations

Melhem's book is an excellent introduction to these particular poets. Black writing, rich and diverse, is enriched by other writers like Margaret Danner, Etheridge Knight, Gloria Oden, Audre Lorde and Eugene Redmond, to name a few. Since Colonial times, African-American poetry has sounded loud and clear (but it has not always been heard). Now with the profusion of such new talent there seems, indeed, to be another renaissance of black literature.

Review of *Heroism in the New Black Poetry: Introductions & Interviews*, by D. H. Melhem (University Press of Kentucky).

St. Louis Post-Dispatch, February 3, 1991, p. 5C.

A CHARLES GUENTHER RETROSPECTIVE
Prose: Critical Reviews and Essays, 1983-1992

Poetic words of war

As our century ends, so gradually does the living memory of its two World
Wars, fought only 21 years apart. Some historians consider those wars
together, one the outgrowth of the other. This unique anthology includes
poetry of both wars and the years between.

Yet the attitudes of the poets, as Michael Foss points out, differed with the
types of warfare. While many who wrote and died in the trenches had a
universal message of hope of a better world, the poets of the Second
World War sang of private griefs and sometimes ultimate despair.
Mankind became capable of self-annihilation.

Poetry of the World Wars contains about 150 poems by 65 poets, many of
whom (like Wilfred Owen and Charles Hamilton Sorley) were killed in
action. While Foss omits scores of other poets who died, like Alan Seeger
and the Grenfell brothers—and noted survivors like Edmund Blunden,
Archibald MacLeish and Karl Shapiro — he has mustered an unusual
group of old and new names. Besides Owen and Sorley, the Great War
poets include Edward Thomas, Isaac Rosenberg and Siegfried Sassoon,
along with more famous names: Hardy, Kipling and Yeats.

Two poets are represented by the most celebrated sonnets to come out of
each war: "The Soldier" by Rupert Brooke, who died with a British expe-
dition in 1915, and "High Flight" by John Magee, who was killed over
England at 19 a few days after Pearl Harbor. With calm patriotism Brooke
could foresee his own death as he sang of "hearts at peace under an
English heaven," and Magee, slipping "the surly bonds of earth," climbed
sunward and "touched the face of God." But other poets sang more grimly
of waste and pain and death, of fear and discomfort, of lost love and
ruined lives, and even of boredom: Alun Lewis, Roy Fuller, Sidney Keyes.
Randall Jarrell's most famous piece, "The Death of the Ball Turret
Gunner," is here with a half dozen of his other poems, including "The
Dead Wingman" and "A Pilot from the Carrier" in which a pilot, his craft
shot down, struggles free and dangles alone in his parachute to an
uncertain fate. While Owen, Rosenberg and others wrote powerfully and
poignantly of an earlier war, later and lesser-known poets—John Bayliss,
Charles Causley, Keith Douglas and Bernard Gutteridge—wrote moving
lines on World War II. Gutteridge, for instance, writes in "The Enemy
Dead" how the dead are always searched impersonally: "not a man, the

365

blood-soaked/ Mess of rice and flesh and bones/ Whose pockets you flip open."

One aches to toll the roster of their names, these war poets, but may the reader discover them. For there are many others we've seldom or never seen in anthologies: Hamish Henderson, Max Plowman, Edgell Rickwood. . . . Finally, the humanity of all, even the enemy, must be recognized personally, as Gutteridge writes at the close of his poem:

> . . . the man dies.
> And only what he has seen
> And felt, loved and feared
> Stays as a hill, a soldier, a girl:
> Are printed in the skeleton
> Whose white bones divide and float away
> Like nervous birds in the sky.

Review of *Poetry of the World Wars,* edited by Michael Foss (Peter Bedrick Books).

St. Louis Post Dispatch, March 3, 1991, p. 2B.

A CHARLES GUENTHER RETROSPECTIVE
Prose: Critical Reviews and Essays, 1983-1992

Why can't poetry and lyrics sing the same songs?

If "music and sweet poetry agree," as English poet Richard Barnfield wrote, we wouldn't know it today. Except for the impact of blues and jazz on poets like Langston Hughes and Charles Simic, musical lyrics—especially rock, pop and rap—and serious poetry seem wholly apart. A great divide falls between what is considered "literary" and what is written for a popular audience and becomes a commercial success. Serious (or literary) poets seem resigned to small audiences—in the "little"magazines.

So in spite of our long traditions of pairing music and poetry—from Ben Jonson's "Song to Celia" to the great hymns of Dryden, Watts and others —have the two, poetry and the song lyric, become unreconciled?

This debate was rekindled in my mind with the appearance of two books: *Jimmy's Blues: Selected Poems* by James Baldwin (St. Martin's) and *A Box of Rain*, the collected lyrics of Robert Hunter (Viking).

Baldwin's poetry, in his only book of verse, is spare, direct and charged with emotion. "Death is easy," he writes, "when, if, love dies, /Anguish is the no-man's-land focused in the eyes." Baldwin's blues poems are true poetry in the style of the late Langston Hughes. Yet they are also words without music, potent and plain-spoken, in deft rhythm and rhyme.

Robert Hunter, an offstage member of the Grateful Dead, has written lyrics for that group for 25 years, as well as lyrics for Bob Dylan, Jefferson Starship and others. His voluminous, finely produced volume collects, in alphabetical order, hundreds of these lyrics that have long moved popular audiences. Yet the pace and style of these lyrics seem little different at times from Baldwin's poems.

Meanwhile, scores of outstanding books by American poets have appeared in the past year with scarcely a ripple among readers, reviewers and booksellers.

First, there is *The Continuous Life* by the current U. S. Poet Laureate Mark Strand (Knopf), issued concurrently with the release of his *Selected Poems* (Knopf) in a fine paperback. Strand, Canadian born, is one of the most versatile poets, as an anthologist, translator and author of children's books as well. His *Selected Poems* contains work from six earlier volumes dating back to 1964—lyrics and narratives in free forms on many subjects. In *The Continuous Life* Strand shows a wider range of forms, from prose poems to loosely structured lines and formal epigrams. The imagery is often exotic, even fantastic, as in "One Winter Night" where the poet dreams a two-part dream of a Hollywood star and a bull in a snowy field. Colorful and imaginative, Strand is a singer of universal experience, as in "The End":

> Not every man knows what is waiting for him,
> or what he shall sing
> when the ship he is on slips into darkness,
> there at the end.

Stephen Dobyns also speculates about a doomsday in his poem "The Day the World Ends," in his book *Body Traffic* (Viking), describing human activities—indeed, how all life and nature may be caught in that final moment. Dobyns' casual style, at its best in his blank verse meditations and narratives, belies the precision of his imagery and observation. At least 15 poems of the 75 in *Body Traffic* are sonnets on the life and art of Paul Cézanne whom Dobyns introduces in commenting on aspects of the body — its journey, its curse (from Adam), its hope, its repose and discontent, its joy, its strength and its weight. Dobyns' book is brilliantly organized and strongly presented.

Brad Leithauser's *The Mail from Anywhere, Poems* (Knopf) opens with an epigraph from Paul Gauguin and contains 23 poems with widely varied settings — "mail from anywhere." Yet the settings never intrude on the theme or message of his poems. They are, as the poet suggests in "Rain & Snow" (from Kyoto, Japan), "as free-running as the sea," enforcing his universal outlook. Leithauser's lines have strong musicality in delicate forms (as in "The Candle") and subtle music in rhymed pentameters (as in "Old Bachelor Brother"). Altogether his poems show the breadth of nature in its peopled world, in fine vistas of organic poetry.

In *The Rest of the Way, Poems* (Knopf) J. D. McClatchy displays an unusual range of forms, fitting the tone and themes of his work. Sometimes, as in "Irish Prospects" which contains blank and rhymed verse and Sapphics, the forms vary within the poem itself. He can reconcile or juxtapose old and new, as in "Medea in Tokyo," or cast old tales (of Herakles and Zion, for instance) into new lines. Sometimes he deals with basic themes like anger and friendship, but with ever-present reminders of love and death. McClatchy's masterpiece here is a sequence of 15 sonnets, "Kilim," about terrorist violence in the Middle East.

A recent Devins Award volume, *Thirst Like This* (University of Missouri) contains 42 poems by John Repp on a wide variety of subjects, from watering the garden and trapping minnows to musings on baseball and depression photographs. But Repp sings equally well of basic emotions like love and loneliness. One lovely piece is "In the Absence," in quatrains with fine interior word-music, ending with the phrase, "dreamer of llamas/in low sun, under the moving limbs of oaks." Repp's form unfolds subtly, whether in the sestina or in a villanelle like "When Love Sharpens Its Knives" ("even Sappho's harp couldn't teach our lives"). Repp's voice is strong, deeply personal.

Peter Sacks, who was born in South Africa and now teaches at Johns Hopkins, writes mostly of places and seasons in his poems, *Promised Lands* (Viking). The 29 poems are generally cogent and upbeat. After a series of memorials to his birthplace, Sacks proceeds with a section of pieces on ancient settings including Galilee, Capernaum and Jerusalem. Yet his vision is particularly sharp in the poems on American States, in South and Southwest settings, such as a Confederate graveyard in Tennessee. Sacks brings fresh, crisp views of the America and its seasons which so many readers (and even writers) take for granted.

James Seay is thoroughly contemporary in *The Light As They Found It* (Morrow), whether writing on Tiffany's, Chuck Berry or Elvis. But he delves also into recent history and pop culture, with references from Scott Fitzgerald and Thomas Wolfe to Lenin and John F. Kennedy. Working in free forms, Seay challenges the reader to drink in his score of poems and absorb the meaning of his message—of love, life and the passing of time. Seay's "light" is the life of modern man given energy by recent generations.

Finally, Charles Wright presents a major collection of new and recent work in *The World of the Ten Thousand Things: Poems 1980-1990* (Farrar, Straus & Giroux, including his two notable earlier books, *The Southern Cross* and *The Other Side of the River*. The other half of this book consists of two sets of "journal" poems—ten "Zone Journals," long, meditative pieces, and 15 closing journal poems, shorter and more aphoristic. Wright's skill lies in his precise, intense observation, with a "trust in visible things," amid death and the enduring world. ("And soon enough the world will forget us," he adds.) His poems show, too, the fine impact of such Italian poets as Montale and Dino Campana whose work he has translated.

As for new poetry in music, some readers may contend that the open forms of Charles Wright, Mark Strand and others are not adaptable to the strong rhythms of popular melodies. Yet while modern music doesn't lack some fine poetry ("Where Have All the Flowers Gone?" is an example), composers continue to spurn the formal works of talented American poets. But we must remember that great poetry is expressed not only in lyrics but in dramatic and narrative forms as well. Today's serious poets are also singers, but their music doesn't intrude on the reader or listener. Some organizations offer special prizes for poems suitable for setting to music; but generally, poetry and music go their separate ways. Ours is an age in which the greatest poets write to the airs of a silent musician.

St. Louis Post-Dispatch, May 19, 1991, p. 5C.

Chester Himes prepared a feast of good reading

Oddly in our age of fast food, compact discs and "micro" everything, the short story has declined in popularity. Family magazines favor personal advice, "how to" articles and true experience stories. But the works of the great storytellers always have been around, and are being rediscovered.

Novelist Chester Himes (1909-1984) had an extraordinary bent for storytelling. He was born in Jefferson City and later moved with his family to Ohio where he attended the state university at Columbus. But at age 19 he fell into the company of racketeers and was arrested and imprisoned for jewel theft. At 23, while in prison, Himes published his first article in *Esquire* magazine. Released at age 27, he worked as a writer and journalist and wrote novels of black experience. But he wrote his most famous novels—about black detectives—in France and Spain where he lived from 1953 until his death. Three movies, including *A Rage in Harlem* (1991), were based on Himes's crime novels.

Himes's short stories, while realistic, are not mere personal ramblings or bland (or gamy) episodes. Plot and character are well developed in very few pages. Some stories are marked also by abrupt transitions and poignant or brutal surprise endings. (Compare Himes's "Christmas Gift," for instance, with 0. Henry's "The Gift of the Magi.") Many of the early stories, especially, like "Prison Mass" and "Friends," deal with stark, boring or violent details of prison life.

Other stories have distinct racial themes. There is a young married couple (in "Dirty Deceivers") who deceive each other about their black heritage. When they discover the truth, they are disillusioned—not about their race but about their own duplicity. In another story ("Two Soldiers") a white soldier learns a remorseful lesson when a brave black soldier, whom he had taunted and maligned, gives his life to save his white brothers. And in "Daydream" the author fantasizes an episode illustrating the "sickness" of racial prejudice. Altogether Himes's 60 stories are gems of dramatic suspense touched with humor and pathos.

Teaching a college fiction course a few years ago, I was dismayed that native Missouri writers Chester Himes and Jack Conroy were not among the scores of authors in our text. Once considered "radical" (but moderate by today's standards), both Himes and Conroy seemed to have lost their popularity. Yet this book represents only one of the genres of Himes's prolific genius, including autobiography, a score of novels, and uncollected poems and articles.

Come, let's abandon our addiction, our appetite for the "short fiction" of supermarket tabloids. Himes's stories are a full course (college or table) by themselves—a fat feast, a glorious glut.

Review of *The Collected Stories of Chester Himes* (Thunder's Mouth Press).

St. Louis Post-Dispatch, June 2, 1991, p. 5C.

Fine diamonds: poems from Mona Van Duyn

When Mona Van Duyn was named United States poet laureate in 1992, she broke several traditions. She became not only America's first woman poet laureate but also the first woman to become a national laureate in either this country or England in the three centuries since John Dryden became the first official English-language laureate in 1668.

Some of Dryden's score of male successors are little remembered— Thomas Shadwell, Colley Cibber, Henry Pye and others—but Mona Van Duyn's name as poet and laureate will not soon be forgotten. Now, two new books—*If It Be Not I*, her collected poems, and *Firefall*, her newer work—affirm her major status among modern American poets.

If It Be Not I is a solid, impressive gathering of 127 poems from six earlier volumes, from *Valentines to the Wide World* (1959) to *Letters From a Father, and Other Poems* (1982). It does not include Van Duyn's more recent book *Near Changes* (1990), which won a Pulitzer Prize in 1991 and is still in print.

As with other such works, *If It Be Not I* is not (and seems not meant to be) a final statement or offering, but its appearance at this time does provide several advantages. It allows us to compare and contrast her poems with the work of earlier poets of our century, from Léonie Adams and Conrad Aiken to Elinor Wylie and W.B. Yeats, and with that of later poets, both modern and postmodern. It also enables us to evaluate Van Duyn's strengthening place in American poetry and to examine her achievements (not simply her many, deserved titles and honors) as a major poet.

It is ironic that one prominent handbook of American poetry (published in 1973) failed even to mention Van Duyn in its discussion of latter 20th century poets, while including others who are now little known or even forgotten. If we were asked to describe Mona Van Duyn as poet and person, we might use terms such as resilient, durable and enormously talented.

If It Be Not I presents the pleasant dilemma of choosing the "best" of Van Duyn. Each of the six books in the collection is represented by from 16 to 36 poems with widely ranging topics, settings, scenes and situations, in many forms of expression. Like Yeats, Van Duyn is a poet of many masks, and it would be difficult to divine the impact of certain poems on all readers. Among the earlier poems, for instance, anthologists have chosen to reprint "The Gardener to His God," "Recovery," "Homework," "Into Mexico," "The Twins" and others showing a wide diversity, not of quality but of style and theme, for the quality is consistently high. Unlike writers whose work is drably uniform, Van Duyn's wears a coat of many colors—or, to mix metaphors, it is sparkling and multi-faceted.

The settings move from Maine and the Ozarks to Madrid and the Old Country, and include even "A Quiet Afternoon at Home." The voices range from dialect ("Bedtime Stories") to wit and whimsy ("Economics" and "Eros to Howard Nemerov"), and there is a fine, existentialist logic in "Causes" and "The Wish to Be Believed." Underlying all, particularly in poems such as "Along the Road," is the universal, for Van Duyn is steeped in the work of her great forebears: Donne, Arnold, Hopkins, Yeats.

And what can we say of *Firefall*—a magnificent coda to the collected poems? It contains nearly 50 poems, many gathered from magazines. Some are poems on persons—friends, fellow poets, politicians. Here too are commentaries whimsical ("We Are in Your Area") and urbane ("The Marriage Sculptor") and meditative ("Passing Thought"). Most moving are the personal glimpses of friends who have died: "Sondra" (to Sondra Stang) and "Endings" (for Howard Nemerov), with its closing lines:

> . . . I'll follow, past each universe in its spangled
> ballgown who waits for the slow-dance of life to start,
> past vacancies of darkness whose vainglory
> is endless as death's, to find the end of the story.

Firefall also contains some of Van Duyn's wittiest and most adroit compositions, in her "minimalist sonnets," for instance, which "translate" or encapsulate longer poems by a half dozen modernist poets, including Auden, Eliot and Frost.

Without making an issue of forms, Van Duyn has been an active, unique practitioner of forms, as her recent poems in *The Formalist* magazine (reprinted in *Firefall*) show. Perhaps her most revealing comments on use of rhyme and meter appear in her notes to "The Ballad of Blossom," a delightful piece that was published in a 1987 anthology edited by David Lehman. This ballad, incidentally, is the concluding poem in *If It Be Not I.*

Whether working in sonnets, sestinas, villanelles and other fixed forms or in free verse (or even prose poetry), Van Duyn writes "organically," with a firm control on tone, theme and expression. But she realizes, as she describes her ballad for Lehman, the intense concentration that formal composition demands of the poet.

As for "schools" and movements, Van Duyn has wisely bypassed the mine fields of the Beat, Projectivist, Confessional and "language" poetries of a generation ago, but her voice and vision have remained (as a reviewer wrote of *To See, to Take* more than 20 years ago) "personal, tartly eloquent, at rest in the modern vernacular."

Mona Van Duyn has now published nine books of poems since 1959. If, to some readers, even this lifetime production seems sparse, that of other noted poets is much less abundant: Poe, Dickinson, Hopkins, Joyce, Owen. If we treasure fine things, we must cherish these "nine fine diamonds" of Mona Van Duyn. Cut with clean, fine craft, they impinge enduringly on our mind and sensibilities.

Review of *If It Be Not I, Collected Poems 1959-1982*, by Mona Van Duyn (Knopf) and *Firefall*, by Mona Van Duyn (Knopf).

St. Louis Post-Dispatch, December 20, 1992, p. 5G.

Critical Reviews and Essays

1993-2004

An appreciation of nature's gifts: Stafford's best work

The poet William Stafford (1914-1993), who was born in Kansas and later lived and taught in Oregon, had a particularly strong impact on Midwest writers.

One of these is Robert Bly (b. 1926), whose own career of writing, editing and male counseling is legendary. In *The Darkness Around Us Is Deep* the poet Bly pays extraordinary tribute to Stafford's memory and has gleaned some of the best of Stafford's verse for readers new and old.

Stafford's poetry has been described as "a continual dialogue between the natural world and man's impact on it." His best known poem, "Traveling Through the Dark," from the book of that name that won the 1953 National Book Award, is typical. In it the poet encounters a dead doe (with a live unborn fawn) on a mountain road and decides, after he "thought hard for us all," to push the doe into the canyon below. To do otherwise "might make more dead."

Bly's selection contains this piece and nearly a hundred other poems grouped in sections on family and children, parents, memories of Kansas and Stafford's experiences as a conscientious objector in World War II. Some readers may remember how Stafford captured his St. Louis audiences, even decades ago, when reading his deceptively casual, low-key poems.

One of the longer sections, "Speaking the Native American Part in Him," deals with Stafford's part Indian background. Here especially we find, as one critic notes, Stafford's "almost apocalyptic longing" that civilization and nature might coincide. "Animals own a fur world," the poet writes; and in another poem, "In Fur," he elaborates:

> They hurt no one. They rove the North.
> Owning the wilderness, they're not lost.
> They couple in joy; in fear, they run.
> Old, their lives move still the same . . . .
> Winter bundles them close; their fur

bunches together in friendly storms.
Everything cold can teach, they learn.
They stand together. The future comes.

William Stafford wrote some of his finest poems at nearly 80, and as Bly points out, he is among our "national treasures."

Appropriately, BOA Editions, Ltd., (Brockport, N. Y.) has just published a small but attractive selection of 15 poems by Robert Bly titled *Gratitude to Old Teachers*. It includes poetic tributes to William Stafford and other American poets—Donald Hall, Wallace Stevens, William Carlos Williams, James Wright, and to the Chilean Pablo Neruda—and to Bly's father.

In both free and formal styles, the poems are highly personal, ingeniously metaphoric, and at times (as in "Waiting for the Stars") breathtaking in the poet's "thirst for the dark heavens."

Review of *The Darkness Around Us Is Deep, Selected Poems of William Stafford*, edited by Robert Bly (HarperCollins).

St. Louis Post-Dispatch, February 20, 1994, p. 3B

Kenneth Koch: both formal and free

On a long, lonely bus trip to western Kansas 25 years ago, when I first taught in poets-in-the-schools programs, I packed a copy of Kenneth Koch's new book, *Wishes, Lies, and Dreams,* on teaching children to write poetry. It was my crutch against failure. Although I had taught adults of all ages, I had little experience in teaching children (except as a father), and the prospect intimidated me. Kenneth Koch was and still is a fresh, inspiring poet whose imagination and creative energies have only improved with age and experience. It's fitting that an updated book of his selected poems spanning four decades now appears as a reminder of his impact on several generations of younger poets and writers.

Born in Cincinnati in 1925, Koch became one of the leading figures in the New York poets group that included John Ashbery and Frank O'Hara. A graduate of Harvard and Columbia, he still teaches at the latter university and lives in New York City. He is the author of 25 books, 15 of poetry and two of fiction plus four dramatic and four educational works. Throughout, Koch's works exude a sensation of "Fresh Air" (the title of a 1956 poem included in this latest selection). Unreal, surreal and even grotesque imagery abounds, especially in the early works.

On the Great Atlantic Rainway is a large assemblage of 62 titles (poems and excerpts from poems and plays). Only half of the book appeared in Koch's earlier *Selected Poems, 1950-1982* and the rest consists of work written since 1982, with some uncollected poems from the 1950s. It is the best overview of Koch's work published to date. Like Ashbery but more intensely perhaps, Koch can be formal and free, serious and light, even in the bounds of a single poem. His 14-page poem "In Bed," for instance, contains more than 100 subtitles of persons, objects, situations, flora, fauna and even "places" (Acapulco, Luxembourg) in bed. Serious readers may shun such poems that border on surrealism, but this and similar pieces exemplify Koch's genius as instructor to the young and very young. It may do the poet an injustice to quote the atypical, but here are squibs:

> She placed orchids in bed
> On that dark blue winter morning.

*

> The bantam hen frayed its passage through the soft clouds.

THREE FACES OF AUTUMN
Poetry, Prose, Translations

*

Ask them for the blue patience of lovers.

*

We saw the stars starting to come together
As we lay in bed.

To poets and writers, Koch as instructor may unfairly obscure Koch as one of the remarkable poets of our time. About 1950 the critic F.O. Matthiessen pointed out a "bifurcation" of American poetry in two traditions, craftsmanship (Poe, Longfellow) and social consciousness (Whitman, Langston Hughes). Kenneth Koch's strength is in following both traditions, sometimes even on facing pages; for example, some free variations on William Carlos Williams followed by a 22-page canto from Koch's epic "Ko, or A Season on Earth," in rhymed octaves Keats might have envied.

If Koch's greater strength lies in craftsmanship—as in "Ko" and the lovely long narrative "Seasons on Earth" that ends this collection—his social conscience runs subtly through a myriad of lines and settings (in "Pregnancy," "Impressions of Africa" and other pieces). The characters and situations are not as starkly drawn as, say, in Gwendolyn Brooks's poems. Yet we cannot deny his upbeat, imaginative stimulus on readers.

I still owe a debt to Kenneth Koch, who awakened me to teach Kansas schoolchildren to write of horses, mountains and red sunsets; and blind children to write of the sensory pleasures of flowers and hamburgers. It's a sheer delight to revel in the wide-ranging music, rhythms and imagery in *On the Great Atlantic Rainway*.

Review of *On the Great Atlantic Rainway, Selected Poems 1950-1986*, by Kenneth Koch (Knopf).

St. Louis Post-Dispatch, February 26, 1995, p. 5F.

A poet's essays

When a poet and visionary of Gary Snyder's stature speaks out in prose, the result is often uniquely astonishing.

Snyder's *A Place in Space* contains 29 new and selected essays spanning 40 years and includes 13 pieces written since 1990. The subjects range broadly, from the Beat Generation and the poetry renaissance to politics, ecology and philosophy. The longest essay is a 20-page tract on "The Politics of Ethnopoetics," drawing on Snyder's observations of ancient and modern societies.

At the heart of these personal essays is Snyder's sensible, practical view of language and culture. He is especially sensitive to the proper management of resources on our own planet and mindful of the indigenous people whose cultures and home jungles and forests have suffered and are disappearing—"even as we praise their songs." Yet the study of their cultures enriches our sense of human accomplishment "without stealing anything from anybody."

Gently but firmly, Snyder reminds us that we must begin to learn the "Old Ways" again, which are beyond history yet are forever new. Meditative and prophetic (but not pedantic), *A Place in Space* gives life and luster to the rather neglected genre of the personal essay.

Review of *A Place in Space*, by Gary Snyder (Counterpoint).

St. Louis Post-Dispatch, February 23, 1996, p. 6E.

THREE FACES OF AUTUMN
Poetry, Prose, Translations

The evolution of Rainer Maria Rilke

By most standards, Rainer Maria Rilke (1875-1926) was no role model. One of this century's greatest poets, he was born a sickly child of a broken family of Bohemian-Alsatian heritage. His own marriage with sculptor Clara Westhoff turned incompatible, leading to decades of separation from her and his daughter. He became a secretary to Auguste Rodin and later spent much of his life philandering around Europe with rich, talented friends. Conscripted at age 40 in World War I, a reluctant soldier in a baggy uniform, he served only six months in a cushy assignment to archival duties. He pulled strings and was discharged.

Throughout his life, Rilke knew or associated with the great spirits of Europe: writers like Tolstoy, Gide and Valéry, and artists too. He wrote in Russian and Italian and published several books of poems in French. He translated the sonnets of Michelangelo and Louise Labé into his native German. Above all, his fame as a German poet flourished.

The turmoil of Rilke's private life is recounted in sharp, honest detail in Ralph Freedman's profusely documented, illustrated biography. Freedman writes masterfully of the times and settings in which the poet produced such great works as the *Duino Elegies* and *Sonnets to Orpheus*. He describes Rilke's many moods and personalities, his restless nature and ambivalent politics; and most importantly, the evolution of a great poet. Rilke's *Uncollected Poems* is a selection of more than 100 of some 500 poems written between 1908 and the poet's death in 1926. Little known and neglected, these poems supplement the only two major volumes (the elegies and sonnets) Rilke published in German.

Like his earlier translation of Rilke's *The Book of Images* (North Point, 1991), Edward Snow's renderings of this new selection are pure, starkly communicative. If the poems lack the fixed form and frequent rhyme of the original texts (the German is included), Snow's free verse is wholly uncluttered by interpolations or forced effects. Even in English by Snow, Rilke's tight, powerful emotions emerge: "Everywhere joy in relation and nowhere any craving;/ world in excess and earth sufficient."

The publication of Rilke's *Book of Hours* (1905) was an early landmark in the poet's life. It consists of three books of "love poems to God," begun when the poet was 23 and inspired by French medieval devotional

384

breviaries. Now translated by Anita Barrows and Joanna Macy, with German titles (first lines) included, the 78 poems convey in English the austere, quiet power of the original German:

> So God, you are the one who comes after.
> It is sons who inherit, while fathers die
> Sons stand and bloom.
> You are my heir.

Barrows and Macy share well their experience of this book, a "cherished companion." Commentaries, notes and prefaces are included.

Review of *Life of a Poet: Rainer Maria Rilke*, by Ralph Freedman (Farrar Straus & Giroux), *Uncollected Poems*, by Rainer Maria Rilke, translated by Edward Snow (North Point Press) and *Rilke's Book of Hours*, translated by Anita Barrows and Joanna Macy (Riverhead Books).

St. Louis Post-Dispatch, June 23, 1996, p. 5C.

THREE FACES OF AUTUMN
Poetry, Prose, Translations

Early poems by T. S. Eliot show depth of sources

Twenty years ago the widow of a noted poet and editor asked my advice on whether his unpublished poems, many of them bawdy and scatological, were of a quality worth publishing. Although I appreciated their tone and cleverness, I simply couldn't decide, and I believe they remain unpublished.

The 40-odd poems T.S. Eliot wrote and kept in a notebook he titled "Inventions of the March Hare," from 1909 to 1917, offer a similar dilemma for readers. In this case, however, Valerie Eliot, the poet's widow, commissioned the publication of Eliot's early poems, doubtless in the interest of furthering Eliot scholarship. While they add little to Eliot's reputation, they reveal the strong depth of his influences and sources, particularly in French Symbolist and Parnassian poetry.

In the 80 years since Eliot's first volume, *Prufrock and Other Observations* appeared, followed by *The Waste Land* five years later, the "new thrill" and novelty of Eliot's poetry has diminished considerably. Three generations of modernist, post-modernist, beat, confessional, new formalist and other movements have worn the luster from his fresh, daring and even flippant lines, many of which (as in *The Waste Land*) his friend Ezra Pound revised or rewrote. Yet we can still marvel at and enjoy the skill and craft of these early "Inventions."

Eliot was among the earliest Americans (with Pound, Amy Lowell and John Gould Fletcher) to appreciate and assimilate the work of newer French poets after Baudelaire.

Eliot's "Suite Clownesque" reads like a parody of Paul Verlaine. Many other poems have French titles or (like "Tristan Corbière") are written in French and show profuse "borrowings" from Corbière, Jules Laforgue and Théophile Gautier.

Yet these poets often provided only a "take-off" for Eliot's imagination to invent new characters and settings in a newer idiom.

The result was a poetry—often slangy, surfeited in mood and outlook, bordering on parody, sometimes bawdy and suggestive—unlike any written before in our language. Its greatest influence can be traced to his disillusionment with women) affected Eliot's early days at Harvard and after.

Part of "Prufrock" is among these "Inventions." Other poems presaging Eliot's later work are "Suppressed Complex," "Afternoon," "Interlude: in a Bar," "Opera" and "The Little Passion."

Altogether the text of the poems forms only a fraction of this book, which is profusely annotated with appendices, plus a chronology and other material.

Of course, all such material is relevant to, and sheds light on, Eliot's later work. The "Inventions" is a useful, valuable source book.
But its general interest is only proportionate to readers' interest in delving into a figure still considered one of the great poets of our century.

Review of *Inventions of the March Hare, Poems 1909-1917*, by T.S. Eliot (Harcourt Brace).

St. Louis Post-Dispatch, March 23, 1997, p. 5D.

THREE FACES OF AUTUMN
Poetry, Prose, Translations

Powerful translation of Homer's *Odyssey*

One measure of an age's culture is its ability to interpret and appreciate the great works of preceding ages. Translation, especially of poetry, is a supreme example of appreciation—for the translator must assimilate the old and recast it in new, appealing language. Nowhere are the challenges and rewards greater than in great classics like *The Iliad* and *The Odyssey*. Robert Fagles of Princeton is one of the most eminent translators of our time. His translations of Aeschylus and Sophocles (including one nominated for a National Book Award), his prize-winning translation of Homer's *Iliad*, and his own poems are well-known among poets and scholars. Now with his masterly *Odyssey*, Fagles has joined a select company of poets who have brought Homer's complete works into current language.

In his *Iliad*, Fagles conveyed crisply and brilliantly the awe and horror of Homer's tale of war. Now in *The Odyssey*—the more romantic, adventurous epic—Fagles captures the precise, eloquent description and action of Odysseus's 10 years of wanderings after the fall of Troy. If *The Odyssey*'s settings and events seem limited by the geography (Greece and its surrounding lands and seas), the breadth of the narration is as fascinating as the odyssey of modern astronauts. The story uses roughly the same devices as today's most intricate novels: atmosphere, key moments, conflict, complications, climax and even flashbacks.

Atmosphere and excitement rise from Odysseus's incredible, tall tales ("Odysseus paused . . . . They all fell silent, hushed,/his story holding them spellbound down the shadowed halls"). Conflict occurs when Odysseus, disguised, returns home to Penelope and endures the arrogance of her suitors before he slays them; for her suitors

> . . . caught some godsent rumor
> of master's grisly death!. . . .
> Now, at their royal ease they devour all his goods,
> those brazen rascals never spare a scrap!

Fagles's dramatic sense and experience abound in his rendering of key moments in the narrative—as when Odysseus is reunited with his father, Laertes, and "father and son confirmed each other's spirits," at the denouement of Homer's tale. Fagles also, subtly yet powerfully, presents

Homer's women in true, mature and intelligent roles; Helen (in *The Iliad*) and now Circe, Calypso, Penelope and others in *The Odyssey*.

While we're awestruck by Fagles's painstaking scholarship and consummate craftsmanship, we appreciate most, as readers, his communicative skill. For generations the *The Odyssey* has wallowed in adequate but often uninspired renderings in florid, archaic prose or stately verse. Understandably, the prospect of translating Homer has intimidated many poets, including Matthew Arnold.

Without disparaging the brave, new verse translations by others (Ennis Rees, Robert Fitzgerald, Allen Mandelbaum), I find the fresh, precise poetry of Fagles's *Odyssey* the most appealing, even breathtaking. The rapid, direct and flowing style of Homer that Arnold admired is fully realized in this *Odyssey*—a book which long may be read and remembered.

Review of *Homer, the Odyssey,* translated by Robert Fagles (Viking).

St. Louis Post-Dispatch, March 30, 1997, p. 5C.

THREE FACES OF AUTUMN
Poetry, Prose, Translations

The art of writing letters

The art of casual, gracious letter-writing has almost disappeared, replaced by new phone and computer technology, e-mail, fax and even "Post-it" notes. Letter carriers are burdened instead by carefully honed, multi-page solicitations of all kinds; thus, our lands are deforested and landfills created.

Today trees grow in Brooklyn for St. Louis-born poet Marianne Moore (1887-1972), from saplings planted each year to commemorate her birthday on Nov. 15. They are a fitting memorial to one whose reputation has grown as her work has influenced other poets in the generation since her death.

Moore's first book, *Poems*, appeared in 1921, followed three years later by *Observations*, which won the Dial Award. After serving as acting, editor of *The Dial* (1925-1929), she moved to Brooklyn, where she lived for 36 years. Recognition came steadily. Her *Selected Poems* (1935), introduced by T.S. Eliot, was followed by four more books including her *Collected Poems* (1951), which won three major prizes.

Yet when Moore's *The Complete Poems* appeared in 1967, her 60-year output of 11 books seemed sparse—barely 250 pages. It was (and is) a masterpiece of selections, meticulously chosen and revised. It omits, for instance, nearly all of her project, *The Fables of La Fontaine* (1954), which showed incomparable originality in translation.

The Selected Letters of Marianne Moore shows similar selectivity by its editors. Although the letters cover a 65-year period, they represent only a fraction of Moore's lifetime correspondence. For instance, few poets understood Moore's work better than her friend Louise Bogan; they corresponded for 25 years and reviewed each other's books. Yet only one of Bogan's letters is included. Bogan was not the first, but one of the most eloquent critics who realized Moore's impact on modern poetry and how it related "the refreshing oddities of art to the shocking oddities of life."

Among other critics, the anthologist-poet Louis Untermeyer articulated and analyzed well Moore's daring but modest style and "highly dexterous kind of poetic montage." Yet Untermeyer is omitted, even as a reference, among hundreds of writers and other friends of Moore, in this book which includes a names glossary ranging the alphabet from Conrad Aiken to Louis Zukofsky. Despite the many necessary (and intentional) omissions, the book is splendidly edited, annotated and illustrated. The letters and a separate family glossary reveal Moore's close, faithful family ties, especially to her cousins, her brother John, and her mother. (Moore's mother, who had attended Mary Institute, died in 1947.) Moore, who had lived with her mother, never married; but from early on, she was not without a social life.

In one of the eight informative introductions to these letters, the editors mention that Moore had "seven suitors" while visiting Lake Placid in 1910, but considered them "has beens, wilted . . . . I am not changing my spots in regard to any of them." But Moore didn't evade the subject of love and marriage. In an intricate, 11-page poem titled "Marriage," she examined the institution of marriage ("perhaps one should say enterprise") in its many complexities, noting that "Psychology which explains everything/explains nothing/and we are still in doubt."

In a later poem titled "Love in America," she defined love as "a passion—/a benign dementia" and "a Midas of tenderness/from the heart," and concluded, "let it be without/affectation."

Elsewhere throughout these letters we are struck by Moore's expansive friendships and her active cultural life and influence. The names glossary alone reads like an abridged who's who in arts and letters, including Eliot, Ezra Pound, Virgil Thomson, Elizabeth Bishop and many others. Most fascinating to me, however, were Moore's letters and references to neglected poets such as Maxwell Bodenheim, Alfred Kreymborg, Leonora Speyer and similar figures of the 1920s.

While the letters are often intensely eloquent, Moore has bright, gossipy touches, as a passage in a 1924 letter to the British writer Bryher shows: "Elinor Wylie was married to William Rose Benét about this time last year. She is tall, spare, pale, with black shingled hair, rather wary and suspicious, with extreme intensity and energy of manner."

These selected letters are an important revelation of Moore's life. They help to break down any remnants of the "suspicious barriers" which some readers felt separated her from her audience. Marianne Moore "expanded the gamut of poetry," Untermeyer observed; and some of her greatest poems, such as "What Are Years?" and "In Distrust of Merits" are among the finest work of American poets. Her letters enlighten us and affirm her place among our most honored writers.

Review of *The Selected Letters of Marianne Moore*, edited by Bonnie Costello, Celeste Goodridge and Cristanne Miller (Knopf).

St. Louis Post-Dispatch, November 23, 1997, p. D5.

Birthday Letters shows caring between poet and troubled wife

The life and work of Britain's poet laureate Ted Hughes are inseparably linked with those of his wife Sylvia Plath, whose suicide at age 30 (1963) made her one of the great cult figures of the 60s.

For many years, Hughes's infidelity and other details of the couple's life were withheld by Hughes until biographies by Ronald Hayman (1991) and others explained the cruel circumstances of the final months of Plath's life. Understandably, in the sentimental fervor still surrounding the couple, U.S. magazines "jumped" the publication date of Hughes's book, *Birthday Letters*, a series of 88 poems in the form of letters addressed to Plath. Critics eager to replay the drama gushingly praised Hughes for producing his own confessional verse (some prosy, some poignant and incomparably eloquent) to document what "really" happened in their marriage. (One critic friend of Hughes even called him the first "major" laureate since Tennyson! That, as Ezra Pound once quipped to me, "leaves a lot of room for colonels and generals.")

Nevertheless, *Birthday Letters* is a fascinating document (Hughes' version anyway) of caring and sharing from their first meeting (1956), and their marriage four months later, until her death. It was a full, busy life of writing, teaching and traveling in Europe and the United States—a literary life "so wonderful," though not without quarrels, as Sylvia's first book was published and Hughes began garnering appointments and honors.

Their first child, a girl, was born in 1960; their second, a boy, in 1962. Hughes now writes (in his poem "The Owl"),

> I saw my world again through your eyes
> As I would see it again through your children's eyes.

Birthday Letters shows Hughes at his best in describing persons, places and events—his memories of the marriage before their separation in 1962.

Hughes, let's face it, still lives in Plath's shadow; that shadow, that talent, was so wide that it could accommodate the host of lesser "confessional" poets who followed her. Sylvia was a much finer craftsman, in free and formal verse, than Hughes. (Compare her poem, "Owl" in *The Collected Poems* published by Harper & Row, 1981.)

THREE FACES OF AUTUMN
Poetry, Prose, Translations

Hughes's strength in this tribute to Plath lies in his sensitive understanding
of her in their joy and the pain of her illness. "You caught something," he
writes:

> Had you caught something in me,
> Nocturnal and unknown to me? . . . Whichever,
> Those terrible, hypersensitive
> Fingers of your verse closed round it and
> Felt it alive. The poems, like smoking entrails,
> Came soft into your hands.

Review of *Birthday Letters: Poems*, by Ted Hughes (Farrar, Straus &
Giroux).

St. Louis Post-Dispatch, March 24, 1998 p. D3.

A CHARLES GUENTHER RETROSPECTIVE
Prose: Critical Reviews and Essays, 1993 - 2004

Nobel Prize poet discusses his Irish muse

Seamus Heaney, the 1995 Nobel Prize winner for literature, has been called the most important figure in modern Irish literature and a poet "whose pen has been the conscience of his country."

Such praise may seem high, but it may be inadequate. Indeed, Heaney, who is Ralph Waldo Emerson poet-in-residence at Harvard and has received numerous other awards and honors, is considered by some critics the successor to William Butler Yeats (1865-1939) as the greatest poet of our century.

The Associates of St. Louis University Libraries honored him last week with their annual St. Louis Literary Award at SLU's Busch Center, where in his warm, fluent Irish accent he addressed an overflow audience of about 500 people.

Having reviewed his work and corresponded with him long before he won the Nobel Prize, I was invited to interview him a few hours before his appearance at SLU. But it was more a genial, casual conversation than an interview. I was halting, deliberate, retrospective; he was pensive, eloquent, visionary.

Our discussion was light and serious, ranging widely from poetry to politics. I felt that, to understand and appreciate Heaney's life and work, readers should begin with his early poems and progress to his later writings. Two of his early poems that he read at Busch Center were "Digging" and "Follower," both from his book *Death of a Naturalist* (1966). These deal with his harsh, early experiences of working the farm with his father, and (in "Digging") his determination to "take the squat pen" between his finger and thumb and "dig with it." Predictably, Heaney, who was born near Belfast in 1939, turned to the craft of writing at age 11 when he won a state scholarship.

Heaney's literary interests, like his own writing, are universal and timeless. One of his early influences was Patrick Kavanagh (1905-67), whose poem "The Great Hunger" (on the Irish famine) left a mark on Heaney's own vocabulary. Kavanagh, Heaney observed, opened up the life of the common people and "still stands as a liberating voice for Ireland." Another example is Kavanagh's upbeat sonnet on the Iniskeen

Road, in which the poet on a lovely July evening declares himself "king/ of banks and stones and every blooming thing." Contrasting this with his own poem, "The Toome Road" (1979), Heaney pointed out that his poem was about "not being king." Kavanagh's road, he added, is in an independent Ireland, and "his poem is one of authority and possession." Heaney's "The Toome Road" is about "dispossesion." It is a "politically inhabited road" with British troops and armored cars. "I talk about them driving past, but they cannot shake the *omphalos*, which is the center of belonging for the Irish person."

In 1968, as a young university lecturer in Belfast, Heaney lived through the violent clashes that broke out, ending the next year with the British Army occupation of Derry. In 1972 he moved south to the Republic with his young family. He has since "served the people by serving their language," as he once wrote in an essay on the Russian poet Osip Mandelstam.

During a violent period, Heaney's second cousin, Colum McCartney, was shot and killed by a paramilitary gang who masqueraded as British soldiers. Heaney, who was with poet Robert Lowell at an arts festival in Kilkenny at that time, refers to this event in his poem "Station Island." Continuing our discussion, I referred to the two "roots" of American poetry—craft and social consciousness—one extending from Poe to the modern formalists, the other from Whitman and Sandburg to the Beat poets of the '60s and after. I remarked that Heaney blends both of these elements with fine, powerful style and language.

Taking a larger view of American and Irish histories, Heaney explained the differences between them, politically. White European experience in Northeastern America in the 1620s and for several centuries gradually led to the expulsion of Native Americans and the decline of their life and culture. In that same decade, he added, "people from London were also going to Ulster, and that's when the plantation of Ulster occurred," a time of English expansionism. While Native Americans "disappeared as a force," the Irish natives (the Catholics) remain as a resistance.

Heaney remarked, optimistically, "I think there will be new institutions which have been fought for politically and are on the verge of being successful. "It is also true that poetry and public life in Ireland are and have been linked," he continued. We discussed his long review of a recent

Yeats biography, and noted that poetry and politics were inseparable in Yeats's life. Heaney mentioned the case of Ezra Pound, with whom I had worked in translating French poetry during the 1950s, and noted that "Pound was very important to Yeats and vice versa." I confessed I had little interest in Pound's politics and economics, only in the poetry we both liked. (For this, Pound called me "a bloomin' esthete" in one of his letters.)

When asked whether he believed Roland Barthes' statement that "all poetry may be reduced to two themes, love and death," Heaney replied, "There's a lot to be said for that. As for the second half of your life, it's a preparation for exit, and the first half is a blind drive towards it." He preferred, however, Wordsworth's definition that "a poet is someone interested in the workings of his own spirit and the workings of the universe."

As for modern technology, Heaney dismissed the idea that (as Barthes wrote) poetry would become anonymous (by Internet or other means). That would not happen, Heaney said, for we live "in an age of Freudian ego rather than an abnegation of that."

Heaney's writing encompasses, powerfully, both freedom and com-mitment. I quoted the final stanza of his poem "Sibyl," charged with meaning, especially to his countrymen:

> The ground we kept our ear to for so long
> Is flayed or calloused, and its entrails
> Tented by an impious augury.
> Our island is full of comfortless noises.

The last line, he said, was "a spin on a line by Caliban in Shakespeare's *The Tempest*."

A decade ago I wrote (and still believe) that Heaney possesses one of the finest gifts of English song. In music, form and substance, he runs Irish fairy rings around other poets. No poet I've read or heard uses the language more richly and powerfully, or with more grace, skill and resonance than Seamus Heaney.

St. Louis Post-Dispatch, October 14, 1998, p. E3.

THREE FACES OF AUTUMN
Poetry, Prose, Translations

Gass's translation of Rilke retains the German poet's verbal music

"All in a few days it was a nameless storm, a hurricane in the spirit (like that time at Duino)," the poet Rainer Maria Rilke wrote in a letter describing the birth of his *Duino Elegies*. Begun in 1912 and completed in February 1922 in an "explosion" of poetry, the *Elegies* (along with Rilke's *Sonnets to Orpheus*) are among the masterpieces of German lyric poetry by a poet regarded among the greatest of our century.

A work rich in classical and personal allusions, but universal in its breadth of vision and insight, the *Elegies* are difficult to translate but have appeared in at least 19 English translations since 1931. Each translator doubtless felt (and must feel) that his or her version is the best and most meaningful. But William H. Gass, the prize-winning essayist, novelist and philosopher, had a strong purpose for making his own translation after a lifetime of reading Rilke in English. "The poet himself is as close to me as any human being has ever been," Gass writes, "because his work has taught me what real art ought to be" and "how it can matter to a life through its lifetime."

Translation, especially of poetry, is perhaps the most intimate and highest form of scholarship, for it forces an understanding on the translator. Yet while the translator's objectives are to learn, appreciate, and communicate by re-creation, the poet's purpose (as Gass points out) is, broadly, "to put the world into words and hold it steady for us."

Rilke's greatest works, the *Duino Elegies* and the *Sonnets to Orpheus*, are virtual symphonies of the universal *angst*—the realization of the transience of life and nature versus the relative permanence of art and nature's more enduring forms. The age-old themes of love, isolation, birth and death permeate the *Elegies* with a beauty and repetition comparable to the repetitive music of Hebrew scriptures.

The joy underlying some passages of Rilke impresses readers as an affirmation of life, yet the *Elegies* are also a sobering, cinematic meditation on a life filled with regrets and unfulfilled desires. Like Stephen Spender, one of his translators, Rilke keenly perceived the flux of urban society and the meaninglessness of war. Conscripted into the German army in World War I, Rilke was an ineffective soldier and soon was released. He died of leukemia at age 51 in 1926.

No poet's life is "typical" of the breed, but Rilke's was less than exemplary. Fidelity was not his forte; he lived beyond his means, often traveling around; and he was spoiled (even by today's standards). But his writing life was built on "great moments," as Gass points out. He was born in Prague and wrote fluently in both German and French. He also translated such poets as Paul Valéry and Elizabeth Browning.

William Gass's translations are brisk, often colloquial. *Reading Rilke* contains not only the 10 long "Elegies" but also 38 other Rilke poems translated in the text, including 10 "Sonnets to Orpheus."

The *Elegies* begin with a powerful expression of doubt: "Who, if I cried, would hear me among the Dominions/of Angels?" reminding us of the doubt (not of God but of Self) the great spiritual leaders Saint Paul and Martin Luther felt, and exhorting angels as Jean Cocteau did in his *Angel Heurtebise* (1925). But the despair is transformed into a recognition of the Here and Now ("even Sorrow, in the midst of lamenting, is determined to alter").

Gass's style in Rilke's poems is fluid, organic, highly sensitive. Rhyme and the march of meter are sparse, but when used, flow naturally. He has a strong appreciation of the poet's verbal music—the "hissies," the "lovely liquids," the "undulating beauties" of words. And his comments on other translations are equally strong and frank: *sappy, insipid, bizarre, jarring, ludicrous, pretty awful* (Gass's terms). He has little patience with one translator who "bungles things badly" and another whose version seems to be poor prose, "badly bollixing the meaning."

Let's consider a couple of examples. In "The Seventh Elegy," for instance, one translator writes, flatly, "Being here is 'glorious.'" Gass writes, giving us greater time to reflect, "It is breathtaking simply to be here." In another line, the first translator writes, awkwardly, "World will be nowhere, beloved, but inward." Gass's translation: "My love, the world exists nowhere but within us."

So attentive to Rilke's senses is Gass that he discovers that Rilke makes breathing itself one of our sensory organs. "The air we inhale—night air particularly—is the materiality of space itself" and we alter that space to "serve our inner world." Gass's "problems of translation," then, are broad—semantic, literary and philosophical—and often lie in his differences from other translators. But the difficulty of the text of the *Elegies*, especially in the most abstract passages, presents the greatest problems.

Long ago an Italian poet, Franco Fortini, asked me to translate his abstruse "Poem of the Roses" into English, after his German translator gave up the German version. Regrettably, I never finished the job, but yielded to translating less ambiguous poems, many by so-called "name" poets. Gass's choice of the *Duino Elegies* for translation and commentary is a fortunate gift for his readers, who often ask, "What makes a great poem?" Although we may "feel" and recognize a great poem, we cannot fully understand or appreciate it by a cursory rending.

Altogether, Gass's close reading of Rilke, with translations, notes and a bibliography of nearly 100 translated works, is the most fascinating and enlightening fusion of Rilke's life and art that I've encountered.

Review of *Reading Rilke: Reflections on the Problems of Translation*, by William H. Gass (Knopf).

St. Louis Post-Dispatch, September 26, 1999, p. F10.

"Essential Rilke" takes a textbook approach

It is not unusual for several versions of the same (or similar) work of a poet to be translated and published simultaneously. Indeed, it's an embarrassment of riches—and it has happened in recent years with works by Homer, Dante, Baudelaire and, now, Rainer Maria Rilke (1875-1926).

The Essential Rilke is an attractive, compact selection of the German poet's work from the early *Book of Images* (1902) to the *Duino Elegies* and *The Sonnets to Orpheus* (1923). The bilingual text, with German and English on facing pages (a desirable feature), is prefaced by a 10-page introduction by the American poet Galway Kinnell. Many of the poems, including the "Elegies" and five of the "Sonnets," appear also in William H. Gass's "Reading Rilke," but the two books are markedly different in other aspects.

Kinnell and Hannah Liebmann take a textbook approach, with a literal (almost line-by-line) but competent translation that challenges the reader to interpret its obscurities. Gass's strong, personal interpretation produces sheer poetry. For instance, in "The Third Elegy": "Listen the night troughs and hollows itself" (Kinnell-Liebmann); compare that to Gass's "Hear how the night grows hollow as a cave." In short, Kinnell and Liebmann have produced a commendably basic sampling from Rilke, 34 poems (compared with nearly 50 in Gass's more discursive *Reading Rilke*). While many obscurities remain, left, as Kinnell writes, "to the reader to puzzle out," the editors' devotion to Rilke is apparent. Their book seems more than a potboiler in an "Essential" series. It will find an appreciative audience.

Review of *The Essential Rilke*, translated by Galway Kinnell and Hannah Liebmann (Ecco Press).

St. Louis Post-Dispatch, September 26, 1999, p. F10.

THREE FACES OF AUTUMN
Poetry, Prose, Translations

Translation provides an eloquent version of an ancient epic

There's a story about how two scholars argued for years over an obscure word in the ancient manuscript of *Beowulf*, which had been damaged by fire in 1731. The argument persisted until another scholar pointed out that there was no word at all, only a spot in the parchment.

Orally composed about the eighth century and surviving in a manuscript written in England about the year 1000, *Beowulf* (although of Scandinavian background and form) is considered the first poem of English literature and among the oldest epics of modern Europe.

First printed in 1815, the Old English text has since become a classic and translated (but not as often as Homer or Dante), most recently by Nobel laureate Seamus Heaney.

Compared with many medieval epics, *Beowulf* is complex in its plot, settings, characters and action, part historical and part fictional. But its history is subordinate to Beowulf's fabulous deeds. The genealogy alone involves three tribes—Danes, Swedes and Geats (a Swedish tribe). Heaney's *Beowulf* contains a table of the family trees and a helpful note on names.

Beowulf, a Dane, is a typical superhero who encounters and kills two monsters who invade the palace of his king, Hrothgar. Eventually Beowulf succeeds to the throne and reigns in peace for 50 years. But the kingdom is again invaded, this time by a dragon; and Beowulf, with 11 men, arms himself and goes in pursuit. Deserted by all but one of his warriors, Beowulf finds and kills the dragon, only to be mortally wounded himself.

This sketchy, partial synopsis cannot convey the style, tone and flow of this remarkable epic of 3,181 lines and nearly 100 proper names, with its strong allegorical contrasts of good and evil. But is another *Beowulf* needed? Any student plagued by some turgid translation will welcome Heaney's spirited, direct, eloquent version.

A translator, unlike scholars who dwell on spots in a manuscript, is forced to make decisions and move on with the story. While nearly every translator strives for perfection, readers may find some versions of any work too literal or simply prosaic (even in verse form).

A CHARLES GUENTHER RETROSPECTIVE
Prose: Critical Reviews and Essays, 1993 - 2004

In a 1998 interview with this reviewer, describing his work in progress on *Beowulf*, Heaney offered some early insights. The four-stress Anglo-Saxon line of *Beowulf* was a natural vehicle for him, resembling the meter of his early poem, "Digging." This was also the meter of Ezra Pound's translation of "The Seafarer," whose "texture and intensity" Heaney long admired. Heaney describes these and other aspects of his work in a revealing 22-page introduction. Poet G. M. Hopkins, for instance, was another influence.

Understandably, Heaney hesitated to take on such a time-consuming project. (He once remarked, "I consider myself slow"—an attribute of many poets.) But the editors asked, "Who else do you think can do it?" Indeed, who else? No other major English poet has translated *Beowulf* since William Morris collaborated in a version with A. J. Wyatt in 1895. Other translations include those by C. K. Scott Moncrief (admirably literal, but dense), John R. Clark-Hall (1950), David Wright (1957), Kevin Crosssley-Holland (1965) and Howell D. Chickering Jr. (1982).

Heaney's translation, which won the Whitbread Prize in Britain, is strikingly different, yet accurate in the tone and details of the story. No other poet, it seems, has conveyed as well the stark, spare, alliterative and subtly harmonious lines of *Beowulf*. Uncluttered by archaisms, inversions or strained language, the poem flows naturally in modern English, with helpful marginal glosses.

Eight years ago, Heaney wrote to an older poet recovering from heart surgery, "I hope . . . that your beat in the breast is as sound as your sense of the beat of a line"—a good wish we might extend to Heaney himself, just turned 60.

In his poem "The Ministry of Fear," Heaney, one of several Irish writers to win a Nobel Prize, observed, "Ulster was British, but with no rights on / The English lyric." Now with *Beowulf*, he has staked a convincing claim on the English epic as well.

Review of *Beowulf, a New Verse Translation,* by Seamus Heaney (Farrar, Straus and Giroux).

St. Louis Post-Dispatch, February 20, 2000, p. F10.

THREE FACES OF AUTUMN
Poetry, Prose, Translations

Hecht's poems focus on Bible, Holocaust

The Darkness and the Light is Anthony Hecht's eighth book of poetry since 1954. For his poems and other works in essays, criticism and translations, he has received many awards, including a Pulitzer Prize (1968), and he is one of the steadiest and most distinguished American poets.

The 44 poems in this latest volume reflect the distinct versatility and disciplined precision that have marked his craft, in both free and strictly formal verse, from the beginning. As in his earlier works, Hecht shows his continued mastery of sonnets, villanelles, quatrains and blank verse narrative. This varied collection includes nine fresh, elegant translations from Goethe, Baudelaire, Horace and other poets.

At least a half dozen other poems allude to the symbol of the garden found in Hecht's early poetry, in which the Brooklyn Botanic Garden is viewed as "a kind of Eden," as one critic observed. One poem describes "The Hanging Gardens of Tyburn." Another is titled simply "Public Gardens," where "An impoverished exile in his loneliest hours / Knows that not everybody makes the boat," and where, jobless and hungry himself, he is harried for food by "importunate pigeons."

But Hecht's real strength lies beyond the everyday world of people and events. The extraordinary events of history, from classical and biblical times to the horror and inhumanity of the Holocaust, lend greatest power to his lines. In this collection alone he has poems on Samson, Haman, Lot's wife, Judith, Saul and David, and the road to Damascus.

One moving sequence is "Scripture," with sections titled "Abraham," "Isaac" and "1945." Hecht, who served as an infantryman in Europe in World War II, draws on his wartime experiences with parallels between the old and new, this time remembering how Isaac was spared from sacrifice. In "1945," he describes how the eldest son of a French family was spared assassination by a retreating German soldier, not out of charity but

> Perhaps mere prudence
> Saving a valuable round of ammunition
> For some more urgent crisis.

The drama of that incident affected the family for years:

> Through daily tasks, through all the family meals,
> In agonized, unviolated silence.

If certain poets are still regarded as prophets, gifted with extraordinary spiritual and moral insight, Anthony Hecht is surely a prince among the prophets.

Review of *The Darkness and the Light, Poems*, by Anthony Hecht (Knopf).

St. Louis Post-Dispatch, August 15, 2001, p. F11.

Van Duyn's poetry makes its case for immortality

Poets of the past, if remembered at all, are rarely remembered for more than one or two poems. Even brilliant works by Coleridge, Longfellow, Conrad Aiken and others are seldom read except by a few scholars. There's a reason for this, of course. Since the 1960s, with the advent of poets-in-the-schools programs, classes have emphasized the creation, not the appreciation of poetry. Students young and old have been urged to write their experiences and observations in lines defined as poetry, straying from traditional models.

Mona Van Duyn's career, fortunately, has embraced both periods. Raised in the era of the New Criticism, and as a co-founder and editor of the literary magazine *Perspective*, she learned early on the differences between the great and the commonplace, and to hone her own craft with utmost care and precision. In the 43 years since her first book, *Valentines to the Wide World* (1959), which won immediate acclaim, she has produced seven volumes of equally brilliant verse and is now among a very few most honored American poets.

Her new *Selected Poems* containing 93 poems from those eight earlier works is her most important volume to date. It's the capstone of an extraordinary devotion to the craft, and to the "traditional sanctity and loveliness" (as W.B. Yeats wrote) of this finest art of language. Whether in free verse or stately stanzas, many memorable lines fill these *Selected Poems*. Above all, Van Duyn is a formalist of the highest order, writing both free and metrical lines unobtrusively, organically. In her *Valentines* she observes,

> Hating is hard work, and the uncaring thought is hard;
> but loving is easy, love is that lovely play
> that makes us and keeps us.

And further on:

> Beauty is merciless and intemperate.
> Who, turning this way and that, by day, by night ...
> never will temper it,
> but against that rage slowly may learn to pit
> love and art, which are compassionate.

Van Duyn deals equally well with a variety of themes: nature, current events, classics, family and friends, love, change and death—in lines all charged with higher meaning. In fitting forms (quatrains, tercets, cinquains) her "Elementary Attitudes'' describes the four ancient elements of earth, air, fire, water. In one of her many sonnets, on Missouri earth tremors, she notes, "The earth, with others on it, turns in its course / as we turn toward each other, less than ourselves, gross, / mindless, more than we were." From her tour-de-force "Sestina for Warm Seasons": "Even the swollen heart can only make room / for one more self." Other lines too stand out in her longer narratives in couplets, blank verse, even rhymed quatrains ("The Ballad of Blossom"). And the free verse precision of "Leda Reconsidered" matches the finest style of the great Imagist poet Hilda Doolittle (H. D.). Van Duyn's poems "Photographs," "The Stream" and "Endings" (the last on poet Howard Nemerov) are both personally and universally appealing. Finally, no poet is more sharply observant of local color, whether in France or Missouri, for instance.

Van Duyn has avoided the pitfalls of transient "schools" and movements (literary, social, political) of earlier poets like Genevieve Taggard and Muriel Rukeyser, and even the confessionalism of the 1970s and '80s. Acutely sensitive and cerebral, her work has also been called a poetry that explores metaphysical changes; yet these changes are not "corrosive," as Coleridge once described metaphysics. Her enduring appeal is exemplified by a poet present at her November 1983 reading at the Library of Congress: "The audience occasionally gasped at eloquence and insights," he wrote. While we may list her many major awards and honors, including her 1992-93 appointment as poet laureate of the United States (the first such national post for a woman in the English-speaking world)—it is her poetry that gives luster and meaning to those honors. Mona Van Duyn, as person and poet, will surely not be forgotten.

Review of *Selected Poems* by Mona Van Duyn (Knopf).

St. Louis Post-Dispatch, April 7, 2002, p. F12.

407

THREE FACES OF AUTUMN
Poetry, Prose, Translations

Browsing poetry

Until about 60 years ago most poetry anthologies were pretty much the same. Standard (and sometimes new) poets of a single nationality, race or gender were lumped between covers—and the books sold well, especially as gifts. Perhaps the most sensational title was Selden Rodman's *A New Anthology of Modern Poetry* (1938), which broke the mold of convention and is still read. But as poets became more numerous and clustered, in and out of academia, anthology editors (mostly poets themselves) became more ingenious and imaginative. Today any subject (animate or inanimate) or group or theme may find an appreciative audience. Now it's good to see the Everyman's Library revived in poetry, with more than a score of finely edited titles. *Poems of New York*, edited by Elizabeth Schmidt (Knopf), contains work by 84 poets from Walt Whitman and Herman Melville to Nathaniel Bellows. The great range of poems on the city's periods, places and characters is wondrously caught and preserved. The poets, old and new, are well-chosen—and might even have been augmented by more famous names of the 1920s New York renaissance (Alfred Kreymborg, Maxwell Bodenheim, Louis Untermeyer). The Sept. 11 events are preserved too, of course. But one of the most eerie and poignant poems is David Lehman's "The World Trade Center 1993," written after the bombing that year. Lehman describes "the way / It comes into view as you reach Sixth Avenue" and "the towers dissolve into white skies"—the elegant towers now totally gone. The Everyman's Library series of pocket poets includes themed anthologies on war, gardens, animals, prayers, mourning, friendship, marriage and many aspects of love, among other subjects.

Another title, *Poems of the American West*, edited by Robert Mezey (Knopf) seems almost too broad for one volume. But Mezey has made a creditable selection of 75 poets, from Robert Frost (a native Californian despite his New England reputation) to Joe Bolton (1961-1990). Although the book includes four folk songs, like "The Streets of Laredo," and 15 American Indian tribal songs, it's not a collection of "cowboy poetry." Many names (Karl Shapiro, William Stafford, Weldon Kees) are nearly forgotten. Certain foreign poets, including Apollinaire and Bertolt Brecht, seem to lack the depth of experience with the West to write good poems about it. Other names (John Haines, for instance) are solid choices. One outstanding omission, however, is John G. Neihardt (1881-1973) whose "A Cycle of the West" and other poems are American classics.

A CHARLES GUENTHER RETROSPECTIVE
Prose: Critical Reviews and Essays, 1993 - 2004

A durable, elegant anthology in every classic sense is *Lyrics of the French Renaissance*, translated by Norman R. Shapiro with an introduction by Hope Glidden (Yale University). Shapiro's skill and, certainly, his prolific output as a translator of French poetry are unsurpassed in our time. His particular talent lies in form, fidelity and extraordinary immersion in the idiom of both English and French. For this collection he chose more than 150 poems by the three most important poets of 16th century France— Marot, Du Bellay and Ronsard—with the exception perhaps of Maurice Scève and several other poets already available in translation. Avoiding the grossly archaic, Shapiro gives their language, in English, a hint of antiquity in their songs, sonnets, elegies and other lyrics. Among the many delights of this book are Marot's epigrams including one titled "Stolen Kiss,"which ends: "That kiss I filched; without ado, / And kept; But I will tell you this: / Fain would I give it back to you."

Among the unique collections from smaller presses, one title of special interest is *St. Louis Muse: An Anthology of Regional Poetry*, edited by Chris Hayden (Urban League of Metropolitan St. Louis). It contains 86 poems and prose-poems of black experience by 10 poets of the Urban League's Vaughn Cultural Center. Written mostly in a spirited, colloquial style, these poems have a strong emotional appeal whether as performance poetry or read "holding the poem in your hand," as the Center Director Almetta Jordan writes in her preface. Vibrant and candid, all of these poets—who include Eugene Redmond and Darlene Roy—have a strong personal message. That message, whether of pride and pain or praise and protest, is, as Hayden notes, "in the tradition of St. Louis artists: a tradition of grit, persistence and dedication to the local voice and determination to make that voice heard." Hari Sky Campbell, who has nine poems in *St. Louis Muse*, also has a new collection of his own, *Shawmaul's House* (Back-Doe Publications). A former professional musician, Campbell has a crisp, perceptive vernacular style in haiku, prose-poems and other free forms. Sometimes rhymed, it resembles a syncopated verbalization of Miles Davis and Louis Armstrong, with concrete, familiar persons, places and events. His descriptive imagery (one example is "Pigeons") is fresh and original, and his vignettes of city life and characters are especially fascinating.

St. Louis Post-Dispatch, August 18, 2002, p. F10.

THREE FACES OF AUTUMN
Poetry, Prose, Translations

Keillor shares his standards for "good poems"

What makes a "good" poem? Some critics say "thought and form" (Emerson) or sound and sense. But these are just elements of an elusive impact on the reader.

One of Walt Whitman's finest short poems, seldom quoted, is about a "learn'd astronomer" lecturing, with charts and figures, in a crowded, stuffy room. The bored poet feels compelled to walk out by himself in the "mystical moist night-air" where he "Look'd up in perfect silence at the stars."

Whitman, represented by two passages, is one of more than 100 poets in an anthology of *Good Poems* chosen by the noted tale-spinner of North woods humor, Garrison Keillor. The host of two public radio programs and author of nine books, Keillor is as witty, informal and opinionated (yet engaging) as ever. *Good Poems* contains 287 poems read on his show called *The Writer's Almanac.*

Keillor's test of a good poem is "stickiness" and memorability. In a radio audience, "People listen to poems while they're frying eggs and sausage and reasoning with their offspring," he writes. "I read a truckload of poems to find the few thousand I've read on the radio." Yet, while observing that a "narrative line" makes a poem memorable, many of his choices are simply lyrical. And while many of his poets are new or unknown, most of the names, from Shakespeare to Marge Piercy and Dana Gioia, are quite familiar.

Keillor skillfully classifies his choices under 19 simple headings—music, scenes, lovers, language, beasts, snow, trips, lives, failure and so on—all appealing to a wide audience. If these themes seem simple, the poems (of many forms and styles) are generally good. A few, to some readers, may seem bad (downright awful), but these are outnumbered by superb lines by W.B. Yeats, Emily Dickinson, Seamus Heaney and others.
Several things make this anthology unique and quite appealing. One is his unusual selections (some little read or known) by well-known poets. The other is Keillor's own honest, uninhibited stamp on the project. His introduction is especially candid and engaging. He scorns terms like "confessional" and "regional" in poetry, and calls "women's lit" one of the "great dumb ideas" to come out of his generation.

Yet his assessment of poets and poetry is right on the mark. "Howard Nemerov seems larger and larger to me with each rereading, a kindly giant of great courage and elegance," he notes. And Robert Bly, writing at top form at 75, "gives hope to the rest of us." And though he "once cocked a snoot" at Raymond Carver, Keillor admits he was "dead wrong" and has high praise for that poet.

Altogether, *Good Poems*, despite its unconventional choices and incomplete "bio notes," can take its place beside any new or recent anthology of poetry in our language. It has pure entertainment as well.

Review of *Good Poems*, selected by Garrison Keillor (Viking).

St. Louis Post-Dispatch, October 13, 2002, p. H10.

THREE FACES OF AUTUMN
Poetry, Prose, Translations

A member of the tribe of Chaucer

For six decades after his first impulse to write poetry, Donald Finkel writes in his foreword, "I've been a maker—like an honest craftsman, an artificer, a carpenter of words, a member of the tribe of my beloved Chaucer." *Not So the Chairs* contains 29 new poems and 57 selections from eight of Finkel's previous books. A master of narrative observation like his late wife, the poet and novelist Constance Urdang, Finkel weaves persons, places and events with alternating clarity and intricacy.

Finkel studied sculpture and acquired early on a precise, inquisitive vision resembling Chaucer's sharp eye of the human procession. His unique and often subdued voice has long been recognized in American poetry. (I learned this 30 years ago, when one of my students at a Cape Cod writers conference described her enthusiasm for Finkel's early poems. And his reputation has only grown since.)

Love, death and human relationships are always the stuff of good (and great) poetry, and Finkel's books are replete with examples. His persons and settings merge or are juxtaposed sometimes startlingly, as in "Oedipus at San Francisco." In "Concerning the Transmission," he compares poetry to "tooling down freeways." Turning to nature, few poets sing more effectively than Finkel in poems like "Loosestrife Watch," which is brief but musically and colorfully eloquent, and "The Gardener," about the communion of man and nature. But there are human vignettes, too—of "The Husband," "The Father," "Piano Man" and, in the powerful metaphor of an early poem, "Letting Go," the acrobat Karl Wallenda.

A professor and poet-in-residence at Washington University for 41 years, Finkel has won several grants, including a Guggenheim fellowship. Two of his previous books of poems were nominated for the National Book Critics' Circle Award and another was a finalist for the National Book Award. *Not So the Chairs* is a fitting capstone to a distinguished career in poetry.

Review of *Not So the Chairs: Selected and New Poems*, by Donald Finkel (Mid-List Press).

St. Louis Post-Dispatch, June 29, 2003, p. F10.

A CHARLES GUENTHER RETROSPECTIVE
Prose: Critical Reviews and Essays, 1993 - 2004

A note on Jean Cocteau and "L'Ange Heurtebise"

Jean Cocteau (1889-1963) was among the most versatile, talented and prolific figures in twentieth century French arts and letters—yet one of the most enigmatic. He produced work in many fields, including nearly 30 books of poetry, plus works in the "poetry" (as he termed it) of fiction, criticism, drama, film, painting and illustration. His personality and his circle of famous friends and celebrants in all the arts were legendary.

Cocteau made his first public appearance in 1907, at age 17, in the entourage of the actor Edouard de Max. A longtime friend of Picasso, Cocteau worked with him and Eric Satie in 1917 on Diaghilev's ballet *Parade*, then considered scandalous. He became exposed to the most advanced artistic movements of his time, yet he remained uniquely independent of them, and in later life was alienated by passing fads and "isms." These included, as he wrote in his journals, Cubism, Futurism, Purism, Orphism, Expressionism, Dadaism, Surrealism, "and an avalanche of exposed secrets." He decided, he wrote, to put his secrets within himself and not to display them.

Having served honorably in the ambulance corps in Belgium during World War I, Cocteau chose to remain in Paris—where he was born and lived all his life—during the German occupation in World War II. Although somewhat alienated by poets of the new postwar generation, he continued to produce important work, especially poetry, criticism and memoirs, including the film *Orpheus* (1950), based on his earlier play (1927). Honors came to Cocteau late in life: in 1955, a seat in the Belgian Royal Academy of Arts and Letters; in 1956, an honorary doctorate of letters from Oxford; and in 1960 the title of Prince of Poets (an informal laureateship), succeeding Jules Supervielle, who died only two weeks after receiving that title. But the crowning point had been Cocteau's election to the French Academy in 1955.

Jean Cocteau was long best known for his plays, including *Les Enfants terribles* (1929), based on his novel, and for his films adapted from his novels and plays. But his poetry has received increased critical acclaim. As critic Wallace Fowlie observed, poetry to Cocteau was an "immemorial rite" as mysterious to the reader as religious mysteries appear obscure to the believer. Cocteau, he added, protected his speech with short, tense, and elliptical lines which formed a barrier between

413

himself and the reader. Yet Cocteau made "the noblest and most exalted claims" for poets, and the poet's immortality is very special and real.

*

In "L'Ange Heurtebise" both the character and the poem have been variously explained by critics, most notably perhaps by Jean-Pierre Millecam whose exegesis Jean Cocteau denounced in his journals. Any work, Cocteau notes, may have a thousand different allegories, and Millecam "attributes his own feelings to me." Cocteau explains the birth of the poem elsewhere in his journals.

Heurtebise originally appeared in Cocteau's play *Orphée* (*Orpheus*) in 1927, a play destined to be a story of the Virgin and Joseph. The angel was a carpenter's aid (a glazier); but the plot became so intricate that Cocteau substituted the Orphic theme in which "the inexplicable birth of poems would replace that of the Holy Child." But he didn't write the act until later, when he "felt free enough to disguise the angel with blue overalls and wings of pane-glass on his back." Even later, Cocteau adds, Heurtebise "stopped being an angel and became a nondescript young man who had died, a chauffeur of the Princess in my film," which appeared in 1950. But in 1928 Cocteau recalled how the angel appeared in the play (written in 1925).

Cocteau reveals that he found the name on the brass plate of a control lever in an elevator, "Elevator Heurtebise," one day when he visited Picasso. The elevator episode disturbed him day and night and the perturbation grew worse. "The angel was living in me without my realizing it, and I needed the name Heurtebise, which gradually grew into an obsession." For a week, the fabulous creature became unbearable, even diabolical, and forced the poet to write against his will.
At 7 p.m. on the seventh day, Cocteau adds, "Angel Heurtebise became a poem and freed me. I was still groggy and looked at the form he had assumed. He was distant, proud, totally indifferent to anything outside himself. A monster of egoism, a mass of invisibility."

Cocteau maintained that Heurtebise will always remain invisible, since his earthly form "did not have the same meaning for him as for us. Since then, people have written about him. But then he hides under the exegeses." Remarkably, to Cocteau, "the angel has me speak of him as if I had known him for a long time and in the first person. This proves that,

without my vehicle . . . he could only inhabit the vase of my body."
Heurtebise remained invisible and formless.

Long afterwards Cocteau described "L'Ange Heurtebise," with typical
wilful enthusiasm, as "a beautiful object, a flawless poem. It's so pure, so
beautiful that any thief intending to imitate it would simply circle it and
never find a way to get in. Not to be imitated, a miracle like that just can't
be imitated!"

Selected References

Brown, Frederick. *An Impersonation of Angels: A Biography of Jean Cocteau.* New York: Viking Press, 1968.
Cocteau, Jean. *Poèmes 1916-1955.* Paris: Librairie Gallimard, 1956.
Fowlie, Wallace, ed. and tr. *The Journals of Jean Cocteau.* New York: Criterion Books, 1956.
Howard, Richard, tr. *Past Tense, The Cocteau Diaries Vol. 1.* New York: Harcourt Brace Jovanovich,1957.
Knapp, Bettina L. *Jean Cocteau.* Updated Edition. Boston: Twayne Publishers, 1989.
Oxenhandler, Neal. *Scandal and Parade: The Theater of Jean Cocteau.* New Brunswick: Rutgers University Press, 1957.
These are but a few of hundreds of excellent sources on Cocteau's poetry, plays and films including *Orphée* and "L'Ange Heurtebise." Another recommended volume dealing with Cocteau's angelism is Lydia Crowson's *The Esthetic of Jean Cocteau* (University Press of New England, 1978).

The American Poetry Review, 33, No. 1 (2004), p. 23.

THREE FACES OF AUTUMN
Poetry, Prose, Translations

Voice of first female poet laureate "impinges enduringly"

Good writers abound; great writers are rare. Many good writers are deeply respected, widely read, highly honored. Mona Van Duyn was all these (even widely read, an unusual attribute for poets). But she also had qualities of greatness that set her apart: style and originality, and above all a unique perspective of life.

Perspective was the name she and her husband, Jarvis Thurston, gave their magazine, which they founded in 1947 and continued for 20 years in St. Louis. I first met them 50 years ago, when they accepted and used a couple of my poems in the Spring 1955 issue. It was through them that I first met William Carlos Williams, as a "young poet" on a panel with Williams, and afterward enjoyed an evening with Williams and other guests at the Thurstons' home. Meetings there with other poets continued for several years.

Through the following years, Ms. Van Duyn's poems appeared in many anthologies and magazines, and her reputation steadily grew. I was dismayed, however, that she was not represented in more collections. But many of her great forebears, including Emily Dickinson and G. M. Hopkins, had little or no publication during their lives.

In 1992, when Ms. Van Duyn was named United States poet laureate, she became the first woman in England and America to hold that title, a landmark for women. Until about 1900, women verse-writers were "female poets" and until the mid-20th century still called "poetesses." After being classed, too often, as "women poets," today their gender is simply among the "poets," of the rich "perspective" Mona envisioned.

Ms. Van Duyn spurned poetry "schools" and movements. She wrote equally well on many themes: nature, current events, the classics, family and friends and—the underlying themes of all great poetry—love, isolation, change and death. Her language is fine, fresh; her metaphors are sparkling, multifaceted, diamond-like in sharpness and density. Her poems were formed, "organically," fixed or free as appropriate.

Rereading Ms. Van Duyn's *Selected Poems* (Knopf, 2002), I wanted to choose a "best" poem to quote, but there are too many. Almost at random,

I chose "Sestina for Warm Seasons," in which she muses on her birthday (May 9) in that intricate sestina form, and I found these lines:

> Whoever believes the mirrored world, short-changes
> the world. Over and over again, our years
> let us reconsider, make the old molecules fall
> from out of our skins, make us go burning with birthdays . . . .
>
> For love is against birthdays, and locks its room
> of mirrors. If your heart changes it will let fall
> my face, to roll away in the defacing years.

In her last note to me that year (2002), thanking me for reviewing that book, Ms. Van Duyn advised me of her growing infirmity and her "trouble with handwriting." I was touched by that news, for I knew that she composed her poems by hand. But her voice was, and remains, strong. As a poet at one of her readings remarked, "The audience occasionally gasped at eloquence and insights." Whether in print or on one of her recordings, her voice, through her clean, fine craft, impinges enduringly on our mind and sensibilities.

St. Louis Post-Dispatch, December 12, 2004, p. C3.

Reflections & Partialities

Reflections

Remembering Ezra Pound

I first met Ezra Pound on February 21, 1951. More than a year earlier, I had sent one of my translations to Pound at St. Elizabeths Hospital, asking if he would comment on it. I received back, almost immediately, a post card with this scrawled message: "I don't write letters; I receive them." It was the start of a lively correspondence with this fascinating, obstinate poet who had put new vigor into America literature. Now, in Washington for a short stay, I boarded a bus to Congress Heights, where the broad grounds of the hospital adjoin the Naval Air Station, and walked to the Center Building, where Pound was confined.

I had to see several officials before my visit could be cleared. Then I was escorted to an outside stairway leading to a second floor hallway—one end of which was separated by a portable screen. Before I reached the top of the stairs, a tall husky figure in slacks and a brown open-collared sport shirt—and wearing a familiar ruddy beard—sprang from a chair behind the screen.

"Charles Guenther!" he said, and extended his hand.

Conversations with Ezra Pound, 1951 – 1955

Ezra Pound never had guests in his room; he always "held court," as it were, in the private area screened off for him in the hall, where there was more room. He had a chair and guests sat on a window bench. When weather was pleasant, Pound held conversations in the yard—Pound presiding from a chair and others sitting facing him on a bench under the large trees near his building.

THREE FACES OF AUTUMN
Poetry, Prose, Translations

On my first visit, I asked Pound about his treatment at the hospital. He said little, meaning much. "After 18 months, I've become resigned to life at St. Elizabeths."

But he added, "I'm always eager to keep in touch with my friends. I don't write at length, but I like to get news from the outside world."
At this point, there was a slight disturbance down the corridor. Pound shook his head. "Apologies for that. My colleagues who are here for various reasons and with various degrees of illness don't bother me. But I live for all the news I can get from outside."

On the subject of psychiatry, Pound said, "In 30 years or so psychiatry will decline. But poetry will be more alive than ever then—when its true value is realized."

During a discussion on techniques of translating, I gave him a copy of my translation of Valéry's *Cimetière marin* that I had completed in 1949 and remarked about the encouragement that Pound had given to T.S. Eliot and many other young poets and artists over the past 30 years. "I'd like to recommend a work program for you," he told me. "But not, of course, something like submarine anthropology."

He changed from the reading glasses he had been wearing to his ordinary viewing glasses and continued: "You'll learn much more—it's a thing the French have taught us—you'll learn much more by taking a limited area. Even so, there's an enormous amount of work to be done. I sometimes speculate, in my case, on what might have happened if I had gone to work on all the troubadours instead of just Arnaut Daniel."

I told him I had recently obtained a rare copy of an old French epic, *Raoul de Cambrai*, and intended to start translating it. This work was not at once familiar to him, but to my surprise, he told me correctly the name of its publisher. He said he had not worked on old French verse for some time. He was reading in other languages. "At present," he said, "I am telling everyone else to go to work on Greek and leave the Chinese to me."

Later: "The Chinese ideogram for progress is the head and feet."

A CHARLES GUENTHER RETROSPECTIVE
Prose: Reflections and Partialities

I asked Pound about "The Alchemist"—"one of the most beautiful poems in English," I told him. "I've often wondered where you get your ideas."

"That poem comes out of reading Rémy de Gourmont," he said.

"I've read Gourmont's poetry—but I would never have connected Gourmont with 'The Alchemist.'"

Pound smiled. "Until you see an elephant you may not think of writing a poem about an elephant."

"This 'new criticism'—what do you think about it?" Pound asked.

"It probably opens up some interesting ideas," I said, slowly. "But I think it's a barren method of making good literature."

"Yes. The idea is important, of course. But," he added, "it must find its expression in some form—such as poetry."

"Grandpa," Pound said, "is getting more and more interested in music."

He was looking at the booklet of music scores—a rare collection of some 40 concerti of Vivaldi—that he had brought with him from Italy. He read me the introduction, translating from the Italian, "in case you don't read Italian."

He paged through the booklet. Then he looked up at me. "I don't believe that music and poetry are well adapted to each other—at least their techniques don't mix."

Pound on Cocteau: "The '90s in England got to where France was in 1830 . . . . After the last war there were no older men left whom the younger men respected. Cocteau was the one man there who was keeping up the best French tradition. . . . Cocteau writes better than the rest of them because he knows his Greek. . . . He thought he was among men of letters but looked up and saw he was among a gang of garage assistants— or garage mechanics. . . . "

❧

"If you do have literary tea parties, attempt to get some good writing. Read the Adams-Jefferson-Waterhouse correspondence. Or Agassiz— there's nothing better in Europe."

❧

During one of our conversations under the trees outside the building, Pound bent down, picked a sprig of clover from the yard, held it up for me to look at. "All that life in nature is the life blood of poetry," he said. "We see the intelligence of nature in Dante; he has that vitality. And in Heraclitus we're told that all things flow. Certainly all things flow, but they don't flow like water down a drain. They go somewhere, they progress."

❧

Ezra Pound on Translation

2935 Russell blvd.
St. Louis 4, Missouri
Aug. 2, 1954

Dear Mr. Pound,

A brace of poems from Tailhade, pgs. 194-195 of
MAKE IT NEW.

**

If you prefer, I can find a strict rhyme pattern
following the original, but the meaning may be blurred.
I'd appreciate having the carbon copies returned with
any appropriate comments.

I have written to Rev. George Griffith, among the
Kansas Citians of that name, and await a reply. No
source of my information was revealed to him of course.

Best wishes,

Charles Guenther

**by all means DO so / but do NOT blur the meaning / AND more
important , DO observe the usage of the murkn langwidg/

AND search for precision of meaning/ I hv/ not french text , but
vague memory of" douche ascendante"/ which shd/ be TECHNICALLY
nailed down as to whether it is internal or external (or in
some other poEM)
    ALZO . greater liberty and nacherlness of lang/ can be
obtained IF by getting funny rhymes you put 'em where they
 FIT , not necessarily every tenth syllable /

hidalgo's helment

            family resemblance to The Florentine

                it is the bloody MEANING / get the bloody
meaning . and to hell with literality word by word

        not ad VERbuMMM , but ad sensum.

Florentine/ Alighieri , dirty fairy /
    the bard of Florence / whence / dispense.

alzo SYNcopate/   Translation: Charles Guenther
                                        2935 Russell blvd.
                                        St. Louis 4, Mo.

gornoze Mauberley eggsploitz the back smakkk. and reverse
to tighten. Hawas nearly rimes with segarz.
             or cigahhhs.

YOU can enliven by kakography or disorthographikz.
          and Tailhade was not afflicted with decorum /

forget which " Willy" novel uses /him, caricature, Think it is

" La MMMMM Maitresse des Aestetes "

and L.T. the pharmacien.   HYDROTHERAPY   but aint sure.

                 (From the French of Laurent Tailhade)

          The old gentleman, to take a Turkish bath,

          Has crowned his head with the helmet of an hidalgo

          Which, despite his full paunch and his lumbago,

          Gives him a certain air akin to Dante.

          So his numb limbs and backbone in the nick

          Of time run through the gear of shafts and spears

          While insolent masseurs with horsehair gloves

          Rub down his back where acne pimples prick.

          Oh good cold water, singular remedy

          Which alone can restore the worn-out frame

          And protoplasm of sluggish senators!

          Now in the street, emerging from the steam,

          The old fellow known as a surly magistrate

          Plies little 12-year-old girls with some lewd scheme.

                     guess Paris. Cremorne
                                             london

Vauxhall , celebrated music hall / whether in London or Paris or
BOTH , I dunno /
             For Kansas readers / Vauxhall stage
       rage, corsage ,

Translation: Charles Guenther
2935 Russell blvd.
St. Louis 4, Mo.

old buggars saw her on the Vauxhall stage
and still retain
nor synonyms for the dignity
she still displays / washing the sink
and pushing a petty sale.

LATIN QUARTER

(From the French of Laurent Tailhade)

In the barroom where the odor of cigars

Never dispels the piercing smell of vomit

The charms of Mother Cadavre are triumphant

Whose name is known as far away as the Howes'.

Dark, she was long glorified among brunettes

While the memory of her stayed at Vauxhall.

And with a gesture of grand dignity

She washes down the bar or sells her plums.

Because of this, her tavern's filled at night

With future lawyers eager to postpone

Some time on foolish study of the Digests;

Boys from Valais and the banks of the Amur

Are captivated by crude chemists' clerks

Who go there to be trained in the art of love.

Gawddammit the THING / the what L.T. wd/ say NOW in describing
presenting the OBJECT.

Get a PARTICULAR female into yr/ mind's eye/ cross , say, between
May West and Eleanor Roosevelt/ May to have got on , and
enough May to have kept her as far up as bar, not all the
way down to street lavatory.

T.L. cert had INDIVIDUAL
in his mind.

Partialities

The teacher Zarathustra once said of poets, "They all muddy the water that it may seem deep." Indeed, much of the magic and mystery of certain poetry lies not only in its curious remoteness to our daily lives—in its exotic language, of course, and the connotations of words—but also in its word-music, and rhythm and meter, and the evoking of emotions. Examples abound from all ages, from Homer to Dante to Spenser's "The Faerie Queene"—and from "Kubla Khan" and "The Raven" to Masefield's "Cargoes" and Pound's "The Alchemist." Such poetry celebrates "things counter, original, spare, strange," as G.M. Hopkins wrote in "Pied Beauty." To some it is the purest form of poetry. The charm upon one reader may not fall upon another, perhaps. Some poets, like the Lettrists in France 40 years ago and the Dadaists a generation earlier, tried to communicate in gibberish, but they failed. They were great experimenters. But who can surpass the magic of:

> In Xanadu did Kubla Khan
> A stately pleasure-dome decree:
> Where Alph, the sacred river, ran
> Through caverns measureless to man
> Down to a sunless sea. . . . .

St. Louis Post-Dispatch, September 28, 1985, p. 4B.

428

A CHARLES GUENTHER RETROSPECTIVE
Prose: Reflections and Partialities

Will the poets of today be quoted tomorrow?

There is no pat answer to this question, and we must begin by asking other questions. First, is new poetry really being read; and if so, is it understood and appreciated? How much of it applies to us, personally and universally? And finally, are we naive to seek out, perhaps futilely, quotations which (if they exist and are timeless) should eventually surface on their own?

It is not an awesome task to look for memorable or quotable lines. Everyone to his own taste. . . .

To answer our original question—is new poetry quotable?—of course it is. The older American masters (Bryant, Emerson, Thoreau . . .) stay very much in our heritage. But there is room to expand that heritage, to include a newer heritage too. New poetry mirrors our complex society, and in many ways today's poets are even more subtle and sensitive than their forebears. Much of this poetry is worthy of being enjoyed and long remembered.

St. Louis Post-Dispatch, January 9, 1983, p. 4C.

Each year hundreds of notable poetry books slip into oblivion or appear unnoticed. Even their authors are scarcely remembered.

Who now recalls Pulitzer Prize winners Audrey Wurdemann (1935) or Leonard Bacon (1941)? These and a host of other prize poets, from Léonie Adams to Marya Zaturenska, seem unduly forgotten. One living poet, Karl Shapiro, even had to go to court to prove that he was alive and well, and hadn't taken his own life! The experience was documented in his recent book, *Reports of My Death.*

St. Louis Post-Dispatch Magazine, November 25, 1990, p. 16.

THREE FACES OF AUTUMN
Poetry, Prose, Translations

Free verse and prose poetry, practiced by American poets for more than 150 years, have ancient traditions in world writing. But some devotees of formal verse still don't accept them as "poetry" in the elusive definitions of the term.

Yet some of the finest poems in our language—Walt Whitman's elegy on Lincoln, "When Lilacs Last in the Dooryard Bloom'd," for instance—are in free verse. And Edgar Allan Poe, in the preface to his 100-page romance, *Eureka* (subtitled *A Prose Poem*) wrote that "it is as a Poem only that I wish this work to be judged after I am dead."

Since the Imagist movement (1910 and after) free verse has taken an equal, if not predominant, place in our literature; and in fact even many New Formalist poets (since 1985) occasionally write in free verse. The standard is simple: Form should fit function, as in other arts and crafts.

St. Louis Post-Dispatch, August 13, 2000, p. F10.

Some forms of poetry never change. The Japanese haiku and the Italian sonnet, for instance, are more than 700 years old. Poets still find their voice in these forms, but in new and different styles and expressions, in English and other languages. Similarly, free verse, ageless in its infinite forms, no longer has Walt Whitman's rhetorical punch or the Imagists' polyphonic melody.

Now poetry is often expressed in terse lines of prose in which imagination and fantasy have given way to experience and reality. Even in forms, poetry often downplays "music" (lyricism) and meter favoring subtler rhythms and plain narration.

St. Louis Post-Dispatch, December 30, 2001, p. G10.

A CHARLES GUENTHER RETROSPECTIVE
Prose: Reflections and Partialities

The earliest poetry anthology in English was probably *Tottel's Miscellany* (1557), a small collection of songs and sonnets compiled by a printer, Richard Tottel. But the forerunner of the modern anthology was a volume titled *The Poets*, published in Edinburgh in 1777.

Many writers dislike the idea of "packaging" poetry. Reed Whittemore once called anthologies "a bad circus," in which poets, like clowns, "all crowd into one tiny car, and sit mysteriously inside."

St. Louis Post-Dispatch, December 30, 2001, p. G10.

"Most Americans do not like poetry," critic Gilbert Highet wrote 40 years ago. But he also observed that readers might appreciate poetry in our new century, just as audiences grew to appreciate complex classical music in the 20th century.

He was right, but the change came sooner than he predicted, for in 1970 a landmark volume appeared. Kenneth Koch's *Wishes, Lies, and Dreams* was instantly popular for its unique examples of how children create their own poems. It has since spawned scores of similar manuals, and today most poets under 35 have been influenced by the new approach to teaching by writing. Whatever its influences, the new poetry is surprisingly strong. Its strength derives from the skillful use of forms and the fresh treatment of age-old themes.

St. Louis Post-Dispatch, April 14, 2002, p. C10.

THREE FACES OF AUTUMN
Poetry, Prose, Translations

Although poetry has always been taught and enjoyed (or suffered through), it is now 30 years since the poets-in-the-schools program began with a new approach to bringing poetry into the classrooms. Today, despite our society's many distractions, poetry flourishes as never before in the United States.

"Movements" persist, of course. After modernism came post-modernism, with Beat and confessional poetry. More recently, since the 1980s, the New Formalists and Expansive poetry movements have revived traditional rhyme, meter and narrative with extraordinary skill and freshness. Browsing through . . . recent publications, however, one finds that few of them reveal alliances with movements, but rather reflect individual experiences, expressions and influences.

St. Louis Post-Dispatch, July 18, 1999, p. C12.

If poetry were baseball, the trade of the century would have been Auden for Eliot—when Wystan Hugh Auden (1907-1973) emigrated to the United States in 1939, a generation after T.S. Eliot left America to settle in England. Perhaps it's facetious to call it a "trade," but for more than 30 years Auden's cultural presence was felt in the U.S., not only in poetry and prose but in music, film and the theater. . . . After World War II, Auden gained U.S. citizenship (1946) and his reputation soared in both America and England, where he wrote, taught, and lectured. . . . Auden's poems, plays and essays . . . comprised some 40 books published between 1928 and 1973. Of particular note was the long dramatic eclogue, *The Age of Anxiety* (1947), which became as famous as Eliot's *The Cocktail Party* (1950). Among other dramatic works, Auden wrote a script, *Paul Bunyan*, for Benjamin Britten's music, and a libretto, *The Rake's Progress*, for Igor Stravinsky.

St. Louis Post-Dispatch, March 25, 1990, p. 5C.

432

A CHARLES GUENTHER RETROSPECTIVE
Prose: Reflections and Partialities

T.S. Eliot has always been "good copy" for the St. Louis media, especially after he won the Nobel Prize in 1949. But except for the circumstances of his birth and early education, his ties to St. Louis are remote and tenuous. He left the city in his teens to attend Harvard, and after graduating he became an expatriate in France and England. He lived and worked in England—as a schoolmaster, bank clerk and partner in a publishing house—from his twenties on and became a naturalized British subject. Having said this, we find it hard to "place" Eliot in any context except that of a Briton with an occasional American voice. . . . Eliot's use of "voices" preoccupied the poet in all of his best work. . . . One of Eliot's key works is a lecture he delivered in England in 1953, published as "The Three Voices of Poetry" (1954) Some readers may simplify these voices as grammatical "persons" (I, you, he, etc.) . . . . But Eliot's idea and use of them was far more complex and creative. Just think, for instance, of . . . the characters in *Cats* and how [Eliot's] original narrative, "Rhapsody on a Windy Night,"

> Along the reaches of the street
> Held in a lunar synthesis,
> Whispering lunar incantations
> Dissolve the floors of memory . . .

differs from the lyric "Memory," written by Trevor Nunn:

> Memory. All alone in the moonlight
> I can smile at the old days.
> I was beautiful then . . .

Finally, whether we consider Eliot an American or a Briton perhaps doesn't matter. He really "used the language," as his friend Pound might have said as a compliment, and we know him by our language. Although younger poets tend to neglect him now, Eliot was certainly a fine "English" poet in his time.

St. Louis Post-Dispatch, October 13, 1991, p. 5C.

THREE FACES OF AUTUMN
Poetry, Prose, Translations

More than 2,500 years ago when the Greek poet Sappho wrote enduring love lyrics, she was an anomaly in a field dominated by men. Indeed, as late as 1872 Frederick Rowton in his *Cyclopaedia of Female Poets* (J.B. Lippincott) asked, "Where are the memorials of the Female mind?" and added that "Poetesses . . . are either left unnoticed altogether or mentioned with a flippant carelessness which is even more contemptuous than total silence."

. . . . Rowton's *Cyclopaedia* was progressive, even radical for its time. It contained more than 300 poems by 103 British and American "poetesses" of two centuries. Eventually it helped to pave the way for poets such as Harriet Monroe, who founded *Poetry* magazine in 1912, and Edna St. Vincent Millay and Sara Teasdale.

Until the 20th Century, women wrote mostly lyrical poetry on conventional themes in traditional forms. [Now, however] . . . in language, themes, and treatment of those themes, the work of today's poets is in sharp contrast to the poem-making of Léonie Adams, Elizabeth Bishop, Louis Bogan, Marianne Moore and others of the mid-century 25 years ago. . . .

Interestingly, Sappho's quatrain form (Sapphics) is still used, but often with adaptations. It is seldom lyrical now, but rather narrative, discursive.

St. Louis Post-Dispatch, October 24, 1999, p. F10.

When I was editing an anthology of women's poetry, one of my correspondents, a distinguished poet, told me that she abhorred the term "women poets." I too dislike the term. It smacks of discrimination. . . . But realistically, I justified using "women poets" to emphasize achievements in a field where talented women often remain unrecognized.

I chose at random a group of recent anthologies, published since 1976, and perused them to get an idea of the number of women represented. The results were sometimes shocking. For instance, one selection of contemporary world poetry contains 12 poets in its English language

section but only two of these are women—Sylvia Plath and Anne Sexton,
both dead. Women fare no better, in fact worse, in other sections of the
book. In still another anthology only one woman is included among 27
poets. It made me feel the need for much more equal representation—of
work from such well-known and recognized poets as Erica Jong, Maxine
Kumin, Audre Lord, Joyce Carol Oates, Marge Piercy, Adrienne Rich,
Judith Sherwin, Mona Van Duyn and Diane Wakoski. Somewhat older
and longer established poets like Léonie Adams, Elizabeth Bishop, Laura
Riding and Muriel Rukeyser are sometimes unduly neglected despite the
depth and brilliance of their work. . . . Margaret Lee Johnson puts it this
way:

> Observe
> the woman freed from parentheses
> and the crippling comma—
> she walks certain in the sun.

St. Louis Post-Dispatch, July 30, 1978, p. 4D.

"There is no visible success for the poet," Jean Cocteau wrote—and
perhaps this is true. Two of the poets with the most influence on our
century, Gerard Manley Hopkins and Emily Dickinson, might be
considered amateurs because they earned little or nothing from their craft.
Of today's professionals—those who publish and sell—thousands enter
the annual "literary lotteries" with grant applications but only a few
hundred are rewarded with the most lucrative fellowships and prizes, up to
$20,000 and more. Poetry readings bring honoraria to some, but the over-
emphasis on "names" by a public largely ignorant of poetry keeps many
talented writers off the circuit. . . .

Perhaps a poet's success is, after all, just fleeting and inconsequential.
Nothing about a poem can equal the pleasure or pain involved in making
it—unless it be the realization that it is shared and appreciated by others.

St. Louis Post-Dispatch, April 7, 1985, p. 4B.

III. Translations

1937 – 2004

Writers and scholars at least since the Romans—who brought Greek writing into Latin—have engaged in translation: in bringing into their own language works written in a foreign language. Today, however, there is still much writing, especially poetry, which remains untranslated, or inadequately translated, and which needs to be brought into our language. I maintain that translation is the highest form of scholarship, for the translator must assimilate completely the meaning and purpose of the writer of the work which he/she is translating. This is the most authentic form of communicating: to bring into English a work by a foreign language author.

In addition I think of the process/skill of translation as an important part of my own writing: as a means of making new poems, or recasting old poems into new languages. In a great poem, there is something magic, a haunting spirit. It's so rare that you keep looking for it. When I was 15, a junior in high school, I spent hours in the library reading poetry—especially European poetry, in translation at first and later in the original language. That was when I first started doing my own translations, buying copies of Petrarch and Dante, struggling with the Italian, reading the words, looking them up in a dictionary and writing the definitions above the words and in the margins. If you want to translate, or "reform," a poem you must first have a love of language, infinite patience, and a willingness to work arduously, word by word, phrase by phrase, with other languages. And then you have to be able to look at the whole result and, if it doesn't seem right, throw it out and try again.

The art of translation still remains popularly misunderstood and embedded with fallacies: for example, the notion that poetry cannot be translated. It is erroneous to assume that all translations are inferior to the originals. To experience a poem by reading it in an unfamiliar language seems ineffective unless the poem is a harmonious chant like Victor Hugo's *"Les Djinns"* (The Genies). Reading or reciting a different and unfamiliar word order, one cannot possibly understand or appreciate the emotive value of foreign words. A skillful idiomatic translation would be far better.

This leads to interesting questions: Should the translator, when dealing with early texts, keep a balance between the period language and contemporary idiom? Or, should the translator bring a sense of the life of the poet's times to carry an early text to today's readers? Further, there are many degrees of translations, from strictly literal to broadly creative. Thus, translation presents problems, or choices, of form, style and language. One of the more interesting translators, for example, was the English poet Humbert Wolfe (1885-1940) who created bright, inimitable versions of Ronsard sonnets in the idiom of London barristers and brokers. But my own tastes have been both evolutionary and eclectic. I can appreciate both the most formal, archaic renderings of Louise Labé by Robert Bridges, for example, and the free, impressionistic paraphrasing of Labé sonnets in the more recent "translitics" of Sibyl James.

Although most of my translations are "reformations" (reformation = to recast a foreign poem into its original formal or free verse form), my earliest work—if faithful in forms—was often imitative, interpolative. But I abandoned this practice soon after Jules Supervielle wrote me—I took it as a compliment at the time—that I was doing a "polishing job" on his poems. I then realized that Supervielle's strength lies in his simplicity, the powerful undercurrent of his lines. However, other early work (from Verhaeren and Saint-Pol-Roux, for instance) drew encouraging comments from critics including Wallace Fowlie, foreign editor of *Poetry* magazine.

While this selection, made from thousands of poems and hundreds of poets, omits the most brash and carefree verse (of Corbière, Laforgue and Tailhade, for instance), it includes a broad choice of poets (ten of whom are Nobel Prize winners) all well known in their native languages. Omitted also are the uncontrolled inventions of Dada and Surrealist poets (Breton, Eluard, Picasso and Reverdy, among others) which I translated for magazines during the Beat period, 1955-75.

Finally, we may extend the idea of "translating" to recasting, in modern terms, the experiences and emotions of earlier poets in our own language: Chaucer, Donne, Bryant, even Shakespeare. Despite my appreciation of such "translitics" and imitations, my own practice when translating early poets is to place them in their own time, with a hint of antiquity, avoiding the grossly archaic language of their contemporaries. My purpose is to make a poem from a poem.

To illustrate my "translating/recasting" of poems from other languages into English, I present, on the following six pages, three Renaissance poems. The first poem is *"Soneto XXIII,"* by Garcilaso de la Vega, with a literal draft version appended and my translation facing. The second poem is sonnet CCLXXII, by Francesco Petrarca, with my translation, "For Laura in Death," facing. The third poem is *"À sa Maîtresse,"* from Pierre de Ronsard's *Livre, I, Ode XVII,* with my translation, "Ode (*Mignonne, allons voir si la rose . . .),*" facing.

Soneto XXIII

En tanto que de rosa y de açucena
Se muestra la color en vuestro gesto,
Y que vuestro mirar ardiente, honesto
Con clara luz la tempestad serena;
   Y en tanto quel cabello, que en la vena
Del oro se escogio, con buelo presto
Por el hermoso cuello blanco, enhiesto
El viento mueve, esparze y desordena;

   Coged de vuestra alegre primavera
El dulce fruto, antes que el tiempo ayrado
Cubra de nieve la hermosa cumbre.
   Marchitara la rosa el viento elado.
Todo lo mudara la edad ligera,
Por no hazer mudança en su costumbre.

—Garcilaso de la Vega (1501-1536)

[Literal translation]

While the color(s) of the rose and lily
are shown in your face,
and your ardent (burning), modest (fair) look
kindles and restrains the (my) heart,
and while your hair which was gathered
into a vein (lode) of gold, quickly (freely) flying,
by (on) your beautiful neck, white, erect (upright),
the wind moves, scatters and disarranges (puts in disarray)

gather from your joyful spring
the sweet fruit, before angry (furious) time
covers your beautiful top (summit) with snow.
The frozen wind will wither (fade) the rose,
swift (fleeting) age will change everything,
by not making a change in its customs.

Sonnet 23

While colors of the lily and the rose
are delicately tinted in your face,
and while your modest glance which holds a trace
of fire restrains me though my passion grows,
   and while your hair, tossed by the wind, still glows
in twisted strands of gold that softly race
along your throat that's poised in lovely grace,
and heedlessly entangles as it blows;

   gather the ripe fruit of your joyful spring
and taste its sweetness now with full delight
before age wreathes you with a crown of white;
   for even the rose will wither in its prime
when icy winds arrive, and everything
is mutable to swift, relentless time.

—*from the Spanish of Garcilaso de la Vega (1501-1536)*

CCLXXII

La vita fugge, e non s'arresta una ora,
E la morte vien dietro a gran giornate,
E le cose presenti, e le passate
Mi dánno guerra, e le future ancóra

E 'l rimembrare e l'aspettar m'accora
Or quinci or quindi, sí che 'n veritate,
Se non ch'i' ho di me stesso pietate,
I' sarei giá di questi pensier fòra.

Tornami avanti s'alcun dolce mai
Ebbe 'l cor tristo; e poi da l' altra parte
Veggio al mio navigar turbati i vènti;

Veggio fortuna in porto, e stanco omai
Il mio nocchier, e rotte arbore e sarte,
E i lumi bei, che mirar soglio, spenti.

—*Francesco Petrarca (1304-1374)*

For Laura in Death

Life hurtles forward with a steady speed
And close behind it death comes following fast,
And all wells up in me, present and past,
And wars with everything that's to succeed.
Now and again, so pitifully indeed,
Such hordes of hopes and memories are massed
That if my melancholy thoughts should last
I'd surely go where their reflections lead.

My sad heart once knew joy and how it mattered,
But now it turns to find, troubled and tossed,
Happiness blown to port with broken spars;
I see my once proud sails and rigging tattered,
My pilot tired, my fairest guide-lights lost—
Those eyes extinguished that were once my stars.

—*from the Italian of Francesco Petrarca (1304-1374)*

THREE FACES OF AUTUMN
Poetry, Prose, Translations

À sa Maîtresse

Livre I, Ode XVII

Mignonne, allons voir si la rose
Qui ce matin avoit desclose
Sa robe de pourpre au Soleil,
A point perdu ceste vesprée
Les plis de sa robe pourprée,
Et son teint au vostre pareil.

Las! voyez comme en peu d'espace,
Mignonne, elle a dessus la place
Las! las! ses beautez laissé cheoir!
O vrayment marastre Nature,
Puis qu'une telle fleur ne dure
Que du matin jusques au soir!

Donc, si vous me croyez, mignonne,
Tandis que vostre âge fleuronne
En sa plus verte nouveauté,
Cueillez, cueillez vostre jeunesse:
Comme à ceste fleur la vieillesse
Fera ternir vostre beauté.

—*Pierre de Ronsard (1524-1585)*

Ode

(Mignonne, allons voir si la rose. . .)

Come, darling, let's see if the rose
Which just this morning did disclose
Her dark red garment to the sun,
Has lost already at this late hour
The petalled folds of her bright flower
In tints of your comparison.

Alas, see how in such short space,
My dear, she holds the highest place
And yet her beauty falls so fast!
Nature in its marauding way
Allows that but a single day
Her flowering loveliness will last.

So then if you believe me, dear,
As you have grown to flourish here
In all your greenness, young and new,
Gather the joys of your brief prime,
For soon just like that flower, time
Will make your beauty wither too.

—from the French of Pierre de Ronsard (1524-1585)

Joachim du Bellay, born at Liré in 1525, was studying law in Poitiers when, about 1548, he met Pierre de Ronsard and became actively interested in poetry. In 1550, with the publication of his first book of verse, *Olive*, he was already established as the most important poet of the *Pléiade* next to Ronsard. He died in 1560, after publishing several more books (mostly sonnets), of which *Antiquités de Rome* and *Regrets* are best known.

Although I had translated other poems (mostly French) earlier, Joachim du Bellay's famous "Sonnet," from *Regrets*, was the first I had published. It appeared in the Jefferson College *Campus* (November 1937), a paper the faculty had just appointed me to edit. I used the poem as filler copy with two of my original poems, one (on a cliff dwelling) in free verse, the other (on a sea voyage) in prose poetry. The sonnet has been reprinted twice: in *Poet Lore* (Boston), Spring 1945, with a group of my other translations from French and Spanish; and in *The Formalist,* Issue 2, 1997. The following text differs from my 1937 version in two lines: in line 4, "dear" has been emended to "loved"; in line 14, "gentleness more than sea air" has been emended to "sweetness more than salt sea air."

Sonnet

—from *Les Regrets*

Happy who like Ulysses traveled free,
Or like that prince who won the Fleece of Gold,
And then returned, experienced yet not old,
To live among his loved ones peacefully.

But when shall I in my own village see
The hearth aflame to dull the bitter cold
Or in the kingdom of my house behold
The garden I once tended carefully?

I love far more the home my fathers made
Than any Roman court with proud façade,
Prefer thin slate to marble hard and fair;

More than the Tiber I love my native Loire,
Better than Palatine, Liré afar,
And Anjou's sweetness more than salt sea air.

—from the French of Joachim du Bellay (1525-1560)

From the Eskimo and from the Piute

In the late 1940s, early 1950s—partly because of reading through Mark
Van Doren's *Anthology of World Poetry*, with its wealth of translations
from Sanskrit to more modern languages—I became interested in
translating, or "transforming," native American songs. In a collection of
folk songs translated from their original languages into French, I found
these songs—one from the Eskimo and one from the Piute (a dialect of the
Northern Shoshone language). Here are my "transformations" of them
into English.

My Whisper

Eskimo Song

I'll sing a little song,
a song about myself.
I've been sick since last fall
and I'm weak as a boy.

Unaya, Unaya

I want my woman
to go off to another hut
with another man
who'd take care of her,
hard and sure as winter ice.

Sadly I want her gone
with a better protector
since I haven't the strength
to get out of bed.

Unaya, Unaya

Do you know what'll happen to you
now that I'm weak and can't get up
and only my memories are strong?

Song for His Young Son

(Piute lament)

My son, my son.
I'll climb the mountain
and build a fire
to the spirit of my son,
and grieve for him.
I'll say,
my son, my son,
what is life to me now
without you?

My son, my son,
we dropped you gently
into the earth;
we wrapped you in a chief's robe
and gave you a brave's new weapons,
and in that spirit country
the fame of your deeds
is already known.

The corn will ripen again,
but here
I am the stalk which the reapers
see barren on the prairie.

My son, my son
what is life to me now
without you?

From the Greek

Literary translation is its own reward, as most translators realize or they soon quit the game. I started in my teens, when relatively few translators were active. I dreamed of attacking several languages, singlehandedly, and a host of editors nourished that illusion—Willis Barnstone, Robert Creeley, Sheila Cudahy, Wallace Fowlie, James Laughlin, Sonia Raiziss and Theodore Weiss. I vowed to stop when I turned 25; but how can one forsake this craft on discovering its infinite nuances and needs—and knowing that so much old and new remains to be translated? For world poetry like civilization itself is marked by growth and change. The new poets arrive.

Fivos Delfis (or Phoebus Delphis) was the pen name of the Greek poet George Canellos (b. 27 July 1909), author of at least ten books of verse and recipient of major awards. I corresponded with him beginning in the 1950s. Although my manuscript of his poems, *Dog Barks at Moon*, for which Mark Van Doren wrote a preface, was never published, my translations of his poems were published in about a dozen American magazines, including *Athene* (Chicago), Vol. XIX, Summer 1958.

A CHARLES GUENTHER RETROSPECTIVE
Translations

Aegean

Numberless blue waves
under the transparent sky,
I dream of your voyage to Colchis,
of your voyage to the legendary
and fair Helen.

Aegean: lovely as a dream
in your fresh dawn,
you open like a rose,
your wind is scented
and you make our lyrical Argos scud along.

Sappho's tender sobs
still resound on your shores
like soft melodies
carried off by the wind
on gulls' white wings.

The warlike rhapsodies still roar
and the rough nights and shipwrecks
of your seafarers.

War and love for the elements
are the Venus rising from your foam,
your blue blood's Aphrodite.

You are the Ionic Idea laying out
the sacred road of Delphi.

Today Apollo's dolphins
lead the new god again
and hands shake in the wind,
and lovers' wet handkerchiefs float away.

—*from the Greek of Fivos Delfis (George Canellos, b. 1909)*

457

Measurements

We measure all with our meter
and we are beyond every dimension
of truth which is dream.
Shadow of a reflection morning flower
world's desire
in your room.
A window always
open to the view.
An all purple moon
that wheels around the universe.
Shadow of flowers
that burns doubly in the cold spring water.
The east.
Thought has pierced my heart.
My thought has taken wing
and travels.
Seas
bitter seas.
Drops and fragments of my pain
fluid automatic images.
What more do we wait for now
to hear Tiresias?

—from the Greek of Fivos Delfis (George Canellos, b. 1909)

A CHARLES GUENTHER RETROSPECTIVE
Translations

On the Hundred-Voiced
Deserted Shore

Throw your stick in the sea
traveler.
The wind lifts your worn tunic
and your legs stagger.
Everything travels,
you alone are motionless
as a stone.
Everything changes shape.
God's face
is an endless face
that you still don't know:
his soul is this wind
with a hundred voices
on the lonely crossroads
of pain,
it's this countenance
with a hundred masks.
Throw your stick in the sea.
What do you wait for, alone
on the deserted shore?

For some Ulysses to appear
who would bring you
the tempest of his dead heart?
The day grows light.
The clouds roll,
the waves roll,
white flocks.
Metamorphoses of the moment
which hides and engulfs death.

—*from the Greek of Fivos Delfis (George Canellos, b. 1909)*

From the Provençal

"Lo Ferm Voler Qu'el Cor M'intra," an Arnaut Daniel sestina which I
translated in the late 1940s, was published in *Civ/n* (Montreal), No. 5,
1954. The magazine had on its masthead a quotation from Ezra Pound:
"Civilization—not a one-man job."

Ezra Pound had translated Arnaut Daniel's complete poems in 1911, but
that book went unpublished; one of Pound's publishers went bankrupt and
another kept the manuscript for three years before returning it in 1916.

Although I had read Pound's book, *Provença, Poems* (Boston, 1910), *The
Cantos* and most of his other works, I had never seen Pound's version of
this sestina until 2004, when I found it in his complete *Poems and
Translations* (New York, 2003). Pound's translation is appropriately
archaic. Except for "uncle," his line-ending words are quite different:
"ingress," "nail-tip," "hope," "osier" and "bower." I have been told that
the following version is "more understandable." But I leave that to the
reader. After all, Pound's translation is nearly a century old.

A CHARLES GUENTHER RETROSPECTIVE
Translations

Sestina

The strong will that in my heart enters
Cannot be slashed apart by tooth and nail
Of the hypocrite who by lies corrupts his spirit;
Since I dare not flog him with bough or switch,
At least by stealth, not spied on by my uncle,
I'll revel in joy in orchard or chamber.

When I remember her chamber
Where I know by my lady no man enters,
Where all is more to me than brother or uncle,
No limb of me but trembles to the nail,
As an unruly child before the switch,
So fear I she may be filled with my spirit.

May she take body and not spirit,
Allowing me admittance to her chamber,
For my heart breaks more than blows of a switch;
Wherever she is, not by her he enters;
Always I'll be with her as flesh and nail
And will not be rebuked by friend or uncle.

Never was sister of my uncle
More friend to me or closer to my spirit!
And we are kindred as finger and nail;
If it please her I'd belong to her chamber:
Better the will of love that my heart enters
Than that of a strong man with a fragile switch.

Not since there blossomed a dry switch
Or since from Adam came nephew and uncle
So fine a love as now in my heart enters
Has ever been, I think, in body or spirit.
My heart, where she may go, on the square or in her chamber,
No farther is than the reach of her nail.

So my heart clings and sinks its nail,
Holding fast to her as bark upon a switch;

THREE FACES OF AUTUMN
Poetry, Prose, Translations

To me she's the joy of tower, palace and chamber,
And I love her more than brother, parent or uncle:
And I'll not have this great joy in my spirit
If into heaven by good love no man enters.

Arnaut sends forth this song on nail and uncle
By grace of her (a rigid switch her spirit),
Her lover who freely a chamber enters.

—*from the Provençal of Arnaut Daniel (1180-1210)*

From the Italian

The selections following offer a representative sampling from four poets of the Italian Renaissance on the theme of love:

Guido Cavalcanti—contemporary with Dante—wrote poems that mirrored his strong, temperamental personality with a directness of diction characteristic of the *dolce stil nuovo* of the thirteenth century. He left about 50 poems, mostly on the theme of love that causes deep suffering. Dante Gabriel Rossetti translated many of Cavalcanti's poems in *The Early Italian Poets* (1861).

 Dante Alighieri—best known for his monumental epic *Commedia*—had, by the time he was 18, already taught himself "the art of making verse." The sonnet, "Beyond the Sphere," and "Sestina for Ms. Stone" reveal aspects of Dante's art that a reader familiar only with *The Divine Comedy*, might find interesting.

Petrarca's "For Laura in Life," is a companion sonnet to his moving "For Laura in Death." (p. 445).

Neapolitan poet Jacopo Sannazzaro became court poet of the house of Aragon at the age of 20. His *Arcadia* (1504), a prose narrative interspersed with short poems, partly allegorical and partly autobiographical, was the first pastoral romance. In addition to *Arcadia*, Sannazzaro wrote lyric poems, like Sonnet XXIII "*O gelosia, d'amanti orribil freno,*" in Petrarchan style.

466

A CHARLES GUENTHER RETROSPECTIVE
Translations

Sonnet: *Perché non fuoro a me. . .*

Now why, I wonder, was I not struck blind
Or moved with feeling that my eyes would start
With such emotion to possess my mind
To ask, "Do you not hear me in your heart?"

For then new torments came before my eyes,
So sharp and cruel they filled me with such fright
My soul called out for help in desperate cries,
"Lady, I beg you, don't destroy my sight!"

You left my eyes so weakened, Love appeared
Pitifully weeping for them at their loss
That presently a profound voice was heard

Saying, "Whoever feels such agony
Should find his own heart in that man and see
Death holding it in her hand, carved like a cross."

—*from the Italian of Guido Cavalcanti (1250-1301)*

Beyond the Sphere. . .

Beyond the sphere that circles the farthest skies
The sigh that flows out of my heart has gone;
A new perception which sad Love supplies
Within himself draws him still farther on.
Reaching at last the place desired, he
Beholds a lady honored on that site
And shining so, that in her brilliancy
The wandering spirit is dazzled by her light.

He sees her in such a state that when he says
These things, I don't understand: he speaks so low
To the grieving heart which makes him talk like this.
But I'm sure he speaks of one who has gentle ways,
For often he recalls my Beatrice:
So I know whom he must mean, dear hearts, I know.

—*from the Italian of Dante Alighieri (1265-1321)*

Sestina for Ms. Stone

I've come to the dim light and the wide arc of shade
and at last to the whitening of the hills
where color disappears from the grass.
But my desire doesn't change its green;
it's rooted in the hard stone
that speaks and hears as if it were a girl.

Even so this young girl
stays frozen like snow in the shade
for she's not moved, except like a stone,
by the fair weather that warms the hills
and makes them turn from white to green
so it may cover them with flowers and grass.

When she crowns her head with a wreath of grass
she reminds me of no other girl
for she blends the curled yellow and green
so well that Love comes to stand there in the shade,
Love who sealed me in among low hills
more firmly than limestone.

She's more beautiful than a precious stone,
and the wound she gives no medicine made of grass
can heal; so I've run through plains and hills
trying to escape such a girl;
and in her light nothing can give me shade,
no hill, no wall, nothing green.

One time I saw her dressed in green,
so fashioned she'd have stirred a stone
with the love I have for her very shade;

469

then I summoned her in a field of grass,
as much in love as any girl
and hidden all around by the highest hills.

But rivers will surely flow up hills
before this wet green
wood catches fire, as a pretty girl
usually does for me; I'd pack off and sleep on a stone
all my life and go feeding on grass
only to see where her clothing gives shade.

No matter how darkly the hills throw their shade,
under her fine green a young girl
covers it as a man hides a stone under grass.

—*from the Italian of Dante Alighieri (1265-1321)*

For Laura in Life

Two roses newly plucked in paradise
The first of May, that is but recently,
A fine gift from a lover old and wise
To a younger pair divided equally,

With such sweet talk and with a smile so bright
Even the most barbaric heart would move,
And shining with a brilliant, amorous light,
Transforming both expressions into love.

"The sun has never seen such a loving pair,"
Laughing and sighing in one breath, he said;
Then hugging both of them, he turned away.

So he divided the words and roses there,
And the weary heart is touched with joy and dread.
0 happy eloquence, delightful day!

—*from the Italian of Francesco Petrarca (1304-1374)*

THREE FACES OF AUTUMN
Poetry, Prose, Translations

Sonnet XXIII

O gelosia, d'amanti orribil freno

0 jealousy, my love's tight, terrible rein
which turns me back and stops me in my course;
0 sister of cruel death and cause of pain,
breaking the peace of heaven with your force!
  0 snake conceived and brought to infancy
from a womb of lovely flowers, my hope lies still;
after a lucky start, adversity,
after a tasty meal, a poison pill.
  From what infernal pit did you appear,
0 plague of mortal men, 0 vicious beast
who fill my days with bleak unhappiness?
  Since you returned, my misery hasn't ceased;
what do you want now, bitter grievous fear?
Wasn't love enough with its burdens of distress?

—*from the Italian of Jacopo Sannazzaro (1456-1530)*

By the time he was 16, Giacomo Leopardi had mastered Greek, Latin, and several modern languages; had translated many classical works; and had written two tragedies and many poems in Italian. Forced by illness to suspend his studies for long periods, wounded by his parents' neglect, disappointed in love, he developed a doctrine of despair which his poem "To Himself," seems to embody.

Umberto Saba established his reputation as a poet with the publication of *Il canzoniere* (1921). Influenced primarily by Petrarca, D'Annunzio, and Leopardi, he became noted for his simple, lyrical, autobiographical poems. The poetry of his final, reflective phase is perhaps represented best by "Ulysses."

To Himself

Now rest forever,
My tired heart. The last illusion's dead
Which I had thought eternal. Dead. I feel
How the hope and desire
Of fond illusions in us has gone out.
Now rest forever. You have throbbed
Enough. Your motions are worth nothing,
Nothing at all, nor does the earth deserve
A single sigh. Life's bitter
And tedious, nothing else: and the world is dirt.
Calm yourself now. Despair
For the last time. To our kind, destiny
Gave only death; therefore despise
Nature, the ugly power
Which rules unseen for the common detriment
And the infinite vanity of everything.

—from the Italian of Giacomo Leopardi (1798-1837)

A CHARLES GUENTHER RETROSPECTIVE
Translations

Ulysses

When I was young I sailed along the shores
off the Dalmatian coast. Small islands there
rose from the waves where a solitary bird
intent on seeking prey sometimes would pause;
covered with seaweed, slippery underfoot,
those islands shone like emeralds in the sun;
and when high tide and night shrouded the land,
vessels swerved leeward, listing, and stood clear
to escape the treacherous reefs.
                        My kingdom now
is only that no-man's-land. The harbor lights
are lit for others; and I stand out to sea,
my indomitable spirit still impelled
by melancholy love and love for life.

—from the Italian of Umberto Saba (1883-1957)

The modernist poetry movement, *Ermetismo* (Hermeticism)—rooted in the poetry and poetic theory of Novalis and Poe (as well as linked with the poetry and poetic theory of Baudelaire, Mallarmé, Valéry, and Rimbaud)—produced, in early 20th century Italy, works characterized by highly subjective language, unorthodox structure, and illogical sequences. Guiseppi Ungaretti (whose education in Paris had introduced him to French Symbolism) was the group's primary exponent and leader. During the fascist regime and through World War II, Ungaretti, together with Salvatore Quasimodo and Eugenio Montale, wrote poetry whose cryptic brevity, obscurity and involution both baffled fascist censors and gained them international repute. Ungaretti's first volume of poems, *Il porto sepolto* (1916), illustrated the major technique of Hermeticism which all three poets employed: brief, intense lyrics which eliminated punctuation, syntax, and structure in order to focus on the evocative power of individual words.

After World War II, the three Hermetic poets developed their own individual styles— Ungaretti incorporating more structure, Montale moving in the direction of greater simplicity, and Quasimodo turning to more socially committed themes. Quasimodo's poems, like those of the residually Surrealist French poet René Char, are stylistically dense—often enough, at least, to terrify some translators. I had tried for book rights to a Quasimodo collection right after Quasimodo received the Nobel Prize for Literature in 1959. I lost out to Allen Mandelbaum, who really deserved the rights and who did a marvelous job with Quasimodo in his *Selected Writings of Salvatore Quasimodo* (1960). Montale received the Nobel in 1975.

The early poetry of both Mario Luzi and Pier Paolo Pasolini displayed elements of Hermeticism. However, the later verse of each, particularly of Mario Luzi (as typified in his 1963 collection *Nel Magma*), seems to be characterized more by direct language.

A CHARLES GUENTHER RETROSPECTIVE
Translations

Watch

A whole night
lying next
to a slain
comrade
with his twisted
mouth
turned to the full moon
with the convulsion
of his hands
penetrated
my silence
I've been writing
love letters

I've never been
more
attached to life

—from the Italian of Giuseppe Ungaretti (1888-1970)

THREE FACES OF AUTUMN
Poetry, Prose, Translations

Day and Night

Even a flying feather can sketch
your figure, or the ray which plays hide-and-seek
among the furniture, the mirror's image
of a child, from the roofs. On the circle of walls
trails of smoke prolong the spires
of poplars and down on the rickety truck the knife grinder's parrot
ruffles its feathers. Then the sultry night
on the little square, and the footsteps, and always this hard
labor of sinking to rise just the same again
for centuries or moments, from nightmares which can't
recover the light of your eyes in the luminous
cave—and still the same cries and the long
weeping on the veranda
if suddenly a shot resounds which reddens
your throat and breaks you wings, O perilous
messenger of dawn
and the cloisters and hospitals awake
at a tearing of trumpets. . .

—from the Italian of Eugenio Montale (1896-1981)

On an Unwritten Letter

Is it for tingling sunrises, for a few
strands on which the tuft
of life is tangled and strung out
in hours and years that dolphins somersault
in pairs with their young today? Oh that I'd hear
nothing of you, that I could escape the flash
of your eyes. There are other things on earth.

I can't disappear or reappear; the vermilion
furnace of night is late
and evening lingers on;
prayer is torture and not yet
among the rising rocks has the bottle
reached you from the sea. The waves
break emptily on the cape at Finisterre.

—*from the Italian of Eugenio Montale (1896-1981)*

THREE FACES OF AUTUMN
Poetry, Prose, Translations

Seascape

The wind rises, the dark is torn to shreds,
and the shadow you cast on the fragile
railing bristles. Too late

if you want to be yourself! The mouse
drops from the palm tree, the lightning's on the fuse,
on the long, long lashes of your gaze.

—from the Italian of Eugenio Montale (1896-1981)

The Shade of the Magnolia

The shade of the Japanese magnolia
is scattered now that the purple buds
have fallen. A cicada whirrs
at intervals on the summit. It's no longer
the time of voices' harmony,
Clizia, the time of the boundless deity
who devours his believers and reincarnates them.
It was easier to spend oneself, to die
at the first wingbeat, at the first encounter
with the enemy, a game. Now the harder way
begins: but not you, consumed
by the sun and rooted, and yet a downy
thrush flying high above the cold
wharves of your river—the shivering of frost
doesn't bend you, frail fugitive
to whom zenith nadir Cancer Capricorn
remained indistinct so that war
might be in you and in who adores in you
the prizes of your Husband . . . The others withdraw
and fall back. The lime which subtly
engraves will pass over in silence, the empty husk
of him who sang will soon be dust
of glass underfoot, the shade is livid—
it's autumn, it's winter, it's the sky beyond
which leads you and in which I throw myself, a mullet
leaping in the dry wind under the new moon.
                              Good-by.

—from the Italian of Eugenio Montale (1896-1981)

THREE FACES OF AUTUMN
Poetry, Prose, Translations

The Incomparable Earth

For a long time I've owed you words of love
or perhaps they're the words which quickly fall
every day when they're scarcely uttered
and memory is afraid of them, transforming
the inevitable signs into a dialogue
fallen in the hands of a hostile enemy. Maybe
my words of love are immersed in my plunging mind
and they go unheard or the fear
of the arbitrary echo which comes
from the slightest image of an affectionate sound;
or maybe they touch the invisible
irony, with the sharpness of an axe,
or my life now overwhelmed, my love.
Or maybe the color blinds and dazzles them
if they clash with the light
of the time that will come to you
when my time can no longer call love obscure
love already lamenting
beauty, the impetuous break
with the incomparable earth, my love.

—*from the Italian of Salvatore Quasimodo (1901-1968)*

Where the Dead Stand
With Open Eyes

We'll follow along silent houses
where the dead stand with open eyes
and children already grown up
in the smile that makes them sad,
and boughs slap silent windows
in the middle of the night.

We'll also have voices of the dead
if we've been alive somehow
or the heart of the woods and mountains
that pushed us to the rivers
meant nothing but dreams to us.

—from the Italian of Salvatore Quasimodo (1901-1968)

THREE FACES OF AUTUMN
Poetry, Prose, Translations

Inscribed on a Gravestone, Perhaps

Here far from everyone the sun beats down
on your heads and rekindles the honey in you,
and already the last cicada of summer
recalls us alive from its shrub,
and the siren that wails its profound
alarm over the Lombard plain.
0 burnt voices of the wind, what do you want?
Tedium still rises from the earth.

—from the Italian of Salvatore Quasimodo (1901-1968)

A CHARLES GUENTHER RETROSPECTIVE
Translations

As You Wish

The north wind cracks the clay,
it presses, it hardens the farmlands,
it disturbs the water in the basins; it leaves
hoes fixed, ploughs inert
in the field. If someone goes out for wood,
or changes places with difficulty or stops a while
shrunk up in cowl and cape,
he clenches his teeth. What prevails in the room
is the silence of the testimony
of the snow, the rain, the smoke,
of the immobility of change.

Here I put pine logs
on the fire, I listen
to the shuddering windows, I'm neither calm
nor anxious. You who come
through long promise and occupy the place
left by suffering
not to despair either of me or you,
search in the nearness of the house,
the grey door-frames.
Little by little the measure is filled,
little by little, little by little, as
you wish, the solitude overflows,
you come and enter, draw with downward hands.

It's a day of this year's winter,
one day, one day of our life.

—from the Italian of Mario Luzi (1914-2005)

485

The Holiday Ended

The holiday ended over a Rome
deaf to every simple expectation, night fell;
like trash caught on the wind, footsteps
return home, voices and whistles
die away far and wide through the streets
with their vacant alleys. It's supper time.
But where the city's chaos is congealed
in open fields and constellated lights
along the avenues walled within a peace
of death, the night's already old;
and sunk as in a tranquil
tomb, the city's chaos is congealed
on the mud the cyclist burns up lost
in his desolate race—a song
that echoes tenuously on the dirty wet
pavements . . . Then on the river road
dazzling crowns of headlights,
a star beside the clouds—
around the outskirts, from Monteverde
to Monte Testaccio, stagnating damp and exhausted.
a droning of workers' voices
and motors—a paper crust
of our world over the naked universe.

—*from the Italian of Pier Paolo Pasolini (1922-1975)*

From the Spanish

On a graduate fellowship at Saint Louis University, during which I took 45 hours of Hispanic language and literature courses, I became interested in Garcilaso de la Vega, the first great poet of Spain's Golden Age. Amazed that his work was long neglected, and his complete sonnets never translated, I translated several long eclogues and many of his sonnets and songs by 1978. I completed the 40 sonnets later, for my long collection of his poems for Garcilaso's 500th anniversary (2001). Pedro Salinas has called Garcilaso Spain's "greatest writer of lyrics in his time," and Garcilaso's *Eclogue I* "the purest and clearest love elegy that has ever resounded in the Spanish language."

Fernando de Herrera (bynamed "El Divino") elaborated on Garcilaso's style and, in his later poetry, moved toward even more ornate and affected verse.

Francisco de Quevedo y Villegas, both poet and virtuoso of rhetoric, won the esteem of his elder contemporaries, Miguel de Cervantes and Lope de Vega, for his poetry; he became a master of the then-new Baroque style of *conceptismo*—a complicated form of expression depending on puns and elaborate conceits.

Sor Juana is only one of two or three women among more than 90 poets in the first Spanish anthology I had, which was published in Chile in 1938. I soon realized that, until the 20th century, few women poets were given any prominence in most cultures, even in the United States. As late as 1976 another Spanish anthology included only one woman among 27 poets from 1900 to 1975. Sor Juana's sonnet, "To a Red Linnet," has a special meaning for me. The day after I translated it a red linnet (or its Midwest U.S. species, a purple finch) alighted on my shoulder and remained there a long time as I was filling a bird bath in a back yard patio.

A CHARLES GUENTHER RETROSPECTIVE
Translations

Sonnet 1

When I begin to think about my state
and see those steps which brought me to this place,
I find, knowing how lost I was of late,
they might have led me into more evil ways.

Yet when I forget the road I've traveled on
I don't know why I've such adversity;
I only know I'm dying, and when I'm gone
my love and all my cares will die with me.

My life will end, and all that life was given
to her who can outwit me if she's driven
to strike me down, and she will want that too.

If I can take my life by my own will,
hers, which cares less for me, can also kill,
it has that power—so what else would it do?

—from the Spanish of Garcilaso de la Vega (1501-1536)

Sonnet 6

I've come by rugged pathways to a place
from which I'm now afraid to move, and where
if I should stir or take a single pace
I'd only be drawn backward by my hair.

I'm just a fatalist whose life is cursed
to seek the best advice but never take it;
I know what's best for me but choose the worst,
and choosing the worst of habits, never break it.

Besides, in whatever time is left for me
and in the misguided progress of my days
from earliest youth to full maturity,

my habits which I stubbornly maintain,
the certainty of death and the end of pain
make me not care to change or mend my ways.

—*from the Spanish of Garcilaso de la Vega (1501-1536)*

A CHARLES GUENTHER RETROSPECTIVE
Translations

Alone on a sunlit road . . .

Alone on a sunlit road where steadily
in a wayside overgrown with thorns and weeds
my journey slowly, wearily proceeds,
and my return is blocked by a restless sea.

Sad silence lives on this deserted road
and silence suits the pain which I feel here,
and musing as I ride I see appear
a longer way, the sureness of my load.

On one side are the mountain peaks with high
close-gathering cliffs that soar into the sky,
and on the other side a deep abyss;

I don't know whom to turn to now in this
predicament to free me from my plight
unless it be your hope, my love, my light.

—from the Spanish of Fernando de Herrera (1534-1597)

THREE FACES OF AUTUMN
Poetry, Prose, Translations

Everything's stolen away . . .

Everything's stolen away by our brief hours
Of mortal life which ridicules all we hold
Timeless as steel or marble hard and cold
In the test of time defeated by its powers.

Before our feet can walk, their course must be
The road of mortality over which I bring
My gloomy life: a poor and muddled spring
Swallowed by the breaking waves of a dark sea.

Every short moment is a long step I take
Along this road, regretting each moment spent
As I plod on, whether I sleep or wake.

But if it's the law and not a punishment
Why then lament this brief and final breath,
My bitter destined heritage of death?

—from the Spanish of Francisco de Quevedo y Villegas (1580-1645)

A CHARLES GUENTHER RETROSPECTIVE
Translations

To a Red Linnet

Little red linnet which at early light
Mourned your beloved mate in your sad cry
And, plucking at the amber rose's bright
Stamens, colored your beak with coral dye;

Sweet mournful linnet, innocent little bird,
Who scarcely seeing daylight and were gone
Before the measure of your song was heard,
Found death there in the beauty of the dawn.

In life we never know when death draws near,
For now the hunter, hearing you, is lying
In wait, takes aim and shoots unerringly.

Oh fortune which, at once, we seek and fear!
Who would have thought your lovely melody
Itself might be the accomplice of your dying?

—from the Spanish of Sor Juana Inés de la Cruz (1651-1695)

Antonio Machado was the first Spanish poet I read, during my teens, and I
deeply admired his work. In 1940-41 I translated 125 poems from his
posthumous *Obras* (Mexico: Editorial Seneca, 1940). The translated ms.
was never submitted for publication, but some of the poems were printed
in magazines and anthologies. "Springtime," on the Spanish Civil War
(1936-39), appeared in *talaria* (1946) and has been reprinted several
times, most recently in *Romantics Quarterly* (Autumn 2003). "This Light
of old Seville . . ." and "Rose of Fire" first appeared in *The Formalist.*

A CHARLES GUENTHER RETROSPECTIVE
Translations

Springtime

More violent than war, the awe and fright
when like a giant hawk hovering aloof
the ominous bomber pauses in its flight,
then dips and plunges toward the helpless roof.

Now in the wind the meadow grasses bend
and the black poplar sprouts its vivid green,
and melting snow drops from the boughs to blend
with ashen earth, and sunlight may be seen.

As sea and mountain rumble and one hears
the sirens shriek, and sees the aircraft's wild
swift streak against the blue, above that din

how keenly penetrates into our ears,
immortal goddess, persevering child,
the piercing sweetness of your violin!

—*from the Spanish of Antonio Machado (1875-1939)*

This light of old Seville . . .

This light of old Seville . . . . Here's the residence where
I was born, with its courtyard fountain's bubbling brim.
My father in his study. His thinning hair,
his imperial beard, his moustache curved and trim.

My father is still young. He reads, writes, flips
the pages of his books, meditates, then springs
from his chair, goes to the garden gate; he slips
out for a walk; he talks to himself or sings.

His wide eyes seem to wander aimlessly,
then become fixed in space where he can see
to contemplate on how the years have fled.

Now back to tomorrow from his yesterdays,
my father looks through time and turns his gaze
mercifully, kindly on my own gray head.

—from the Spanish of Antonio Machado (1875-1939)

A CHARLES GUENTHER RETROSPECTIVE
Translations

Rose of Fire

Lovers, you are the simple stuff of spring,
the stuff of earth and water and sun and skies,
with mountains in your breasts that heave and sing
and fertile, blooming prairies in your eyes:

So walk together in this spring you share
and boldly drink the sweet milk without delay
which the slippery panther offers to you there
before he cruelly seizes you on your way.

Go, when the planet's axis rises high,
inclining where the summer solstice stands,
when the violet fades and the almond tree turns green,

thirsty and with the source of springs nearby,
into the dusk of love where you have been
and carry the rose of fire in your hands.

—from the Spanish of Antonio Machado (1875-1939)

I found Juan Ramón Jiménez's early Modernist poem "Retreat Among the Roses," in my 1938 Chilean anthology. My translation of this colorful nocturne appeared in *The Kansas Magazine* (1959). I have never seen this poem in other translations.

The two short free-verse poems following "Retreat Among the Roses" have another story. In the early 1950s a guest brought a visitor to our apartment—Suzanne Jiménez, a young niece of Juan Ramón. She told me that her brother in Spain was a poet as well, and that I would hear from him. After Juan Ramón died (May 29, 1958), and for many years thereafter, I received commemorative cards from Don Francisco Hernández-Pinzón Jiménez of Madrid. Each card contained a poem or poems, some in holograph, none of which I had found in translation. I translated a dozen of these "poems of death and resurrection" in memory of the poet and his wife Zenobia; the translations were distributed to American poets. "Life Isn't What Makes Us Fear . . ." and "A Tongue of Fire, Poets at Last?" are from that collection (1974).

A CHARLES GUENTHER RETROSPECTIVE
Translations

Retreat Among the Roses

Large red lanterns of the summerhouse
Among the nocturnal trees . . .
The silence of roses is hardly disturbed
Under the great full moon.
A sharp martial air echoes
In the luxuriance of the quiet shadows . . .
The magic mumbling of time is effaced:
Crickets, leaves, water and moss.
There is a moving festival of colored fires
In the glass of the restless river,
The dark, deep river beautified by phantasmal boats
Unmanned, closed and silent.
And in the clatter of drums and bugles
A musical weeping sobs indistinctly,
An adolescent waterlogged bassoon
In the warm romantic July night . . .
Echoes are wakened through the distant woods,
And the wet, broken windows
Sorrowfully adorn the wild obscure retreat
With imaginary eyes . . .
The retreat vanishes . . . The white roses return
To perfume the moonlight . . .
Then full of azure, sleep and foreboding
Come the uncertain winds of other worlds . . .

—*from the Spanish of Juan Ramón Jiménez (1881-1958)*

THREE FACES OF AUTUMN
Poetry, Prose, Translations

Life Isn't What Makes Us Fear . . .

Life isn't what makes us fear
death, just death.

Life gone by isn't gone,
as the day we were born isn't gone
or the dream we dreamed or the rose
we breathed or the clasp of arms
around us or the book we read.

The past isn't dead,
the ruin still lives,
and dead we'll live as dead,
if we live,
while life lives.

Our life isn't something that dies,
for what has been doesn't die.
Death is what dies.

—from the Spanish of Juan Ramón Jiménez (1881-1958)

A Tongue of Fire, Poets at Last ?

Our death isn't underground,
for it kills us in the light;
we die here in this light,
in the gold wineglasses of light.

We'll revive deep down more alive;
death will give us life
in the rich ponderous dark
of the fresh roots of trees.

We weren't what we are for a day,
nor was that day the best;
from the dark we came and to dark
we'll return; our home is the dark.

A seed opened for us and we're another,
and this is only once;
creating more like us doesn't come from us,
an unexpected tongue springs from us.

A tongue of ours to change us mythically
into spring, a tongue
of our miraculous fulfillment.
A tongue of fire, poets at last?

—*from the Spanish of Juan Ramón Jiménez (1881-1958)*

Chilean poet Gabriela Mistral was the first Latin American woman to win the Nobel Prize for Literature (1945). Her countryman Pablo Neruda was awarded the prize in 1971. Other Nobel laureates of the Spanish language were Juan Ramón Jiménez (1956), Vicente Aleixandre (1977) and Octavio Paz (1990).

The Melancholy Mother

Sleep, sleep, my little master,
without care or trembling,
though my soul may never sleep,
though I may never rest.

Sleep, sleep, and at night
may you be more silent
than a blade of grass
or a strand of silken fleece.

Let my body sleep in you,
my care, my trembling.
Let my eyes close in you,
my heart sleep in you!

—from the Spanish of Gabriela Mistral (1889-1957)

Rocking

The sea, the divine sea
rocks its countless waves.
As I hear the lover sea,
I rock my son.

The vagabond wind at night
rocks the wheat.
As I hear the lover wind,
I rock my son.

God the Father noiselessly rocks
His countless worlds.
As I feel his hand in the shade
I rock my son.

—from the Spanish of Gabriela Mistral (1889-1957)

A CHARLES GUENTHER RETROSPECTIVE
Translations

Gentleness

When I sing to you,
all evil ends on earth:
your head is completely smooth:
the ravine, the thorn.

When I sing to you,
all cruelty ends for me:
the lion and the jackal
are gentle as your eyelids!

—from the Spanish of Gabriela Mistral (1889-1957)

The "Generation of 1927"—a group of Spanish writers who rose to prominence in the late 1920s—derived its name from the year in which several of the group produced editions of the poetry of Luis de Góngora (1561-1627) in commemoration of the tercentenary of his death. Generally speaking, the members of the "Generation" were influenced by Symbolism, Futurism, and Surrealism; they rejected the use of traditional meter and rhyme; they coined new words; and they introduced elaborate or symbolic metaphors and images into their poems.

Although the six "Generation of 1927" poets I've chosen to translate (Pedro Salinas, Jorge Guillén, Vicente Aleixandre, Dámaso Alonso, Luis Cernuda, and Rafael Alberti) often differed in individual styles and concerns, their work presents an interesting sampling of what might be considered the dominant trend of cultivated aestheticism in Spanish poetry between 1920 – 1945.

506

I Don't See You, but I Know

I don't see you, but I know
you are here, behind
a frail wall
of brick and mortar, well within range
of my voice if I'd call.
But I won't call.
I'll call you tomorrow
when, not seeing you any more,
I imagine you following
close to me here, beside me,
and the voice I wouldn't give
yesterday is enough today.
Tomorrow . . . when you're
there behind a
frail wall of winds,
skies and years.

—from the Spanish of Pedro Salinas (1891-1951)

City Life

Streets, a garden,
A plot of ground—and its corpses.
To die—no, to live.
How urbane, that eternity!

Upright marble stone.
The names of other people.
Immortality
Preserves its aftermath.

And what about that grief?
A plot of ground knows nothing
Of partings.
Where is death?

The city seethes
All around the graves.
A similar peace
Floats far and wide.

Now joined
By a common neglect,
The living and the dead
Crowd together.

—from the Spanish of Jorge Guillén (1893-1984)

My Voice

I was born on a summer night
between two pauses. Speak to me: I am listening.
I was born. If you could only see
how the moon suffers without trying to reveal it.
I was born. Your name was happiness.
Under a brilliant light a hope, a bird.
Arriving, arriving. The sea was a pulse,
the hollow of a hand, a lukewarm medal.
Then these become possible: light, caresses, skin,
the horizon, speaking meaningless words
that roll like ears, seashells,
like an open lobe dawning
(listen, listen) among the trampled light.

—from the Spanish of Vicente Aleixandre (1898-1984)

Epitaph

To cross out your name,
burning body waiting on earth
as a god waits for oblivion, I name you here,
boundary of a life; here, necessary
body that blazed. No tomb: free earth.

Leave at once the lingering gaze
which a hard stone will demand of you,
or a tree without birds requires,
pure in the night, in its naked vigilance.

The sound of a river is never heard here.
Death lives in the deep earth
like absolute earth.
                    Men, pass by:
your steps won't sound on a breast.

—from the Spanish of Vicente Aleixandre (1898-1984)

Insects

—To José Maria de Cossío

I get terribly annoyed by insects, I
absolutely distrust insects, I
get suspicious of all those signals, those heads and feet and those eyes,
especially those eyes
that keep me from warding off my fear at night,
in the awful dryness of night when insects
buzz around, on nights of insects
when I suddenly doubt they're around and I ask myself, are there really
    insects?
when insects buzz around and around and around,
when my soul completely aches with insects,
with all those feet and eyes, with all those little worlds of my life
where I've been suffering in the insects
when they buzz around and fly and dive in the water, when . . .
oh whenever insects.

At night the insects come out of the earth and out of my insect flesh
and gnaw on ashes and nibble away on me.
Dried insects, dried and mounted insects!
Item: dried insects that used to buzz around and nibble and dive in the
    water.
Oh, on creation, on creation day,
when they nibbled on the leaves of the insects, of the trees of the insects
and nobody anywhere saw the insects that nibbled and nibbled away on
    the world,
the world of my flesh (and the flesh of insects),
the insects of the world of nibbling insects.

They came in many colors, those insects: green, yellow, the color of the
    date, the color of dry clay,
hidden, buried—outside the insects and inside my flesh, inside the insects
    and outside my soul—
disguised as insects.
And with laughing eyes and laughing faces and feet
(The feet didn't laugh) the metallic insects nibbled and
nibbled and nibbled and nibbled on my poor soul,

511

buzzing and nibbling the corpse of my soul that didn't nibble and buzz,
nibbling and buzzing around my poor soul that didn't buzz, no, but finally
    nibbled, feebly nibbled,
nibbling and nibbling this metal world and these metallic insects that
    nibble my world of little insects,
that nibble my world and my soul,
that nibble my soul made of little metallic insects,
that keep nibbling my world and my soul, my soul . . .
oh the insects,
those wretched insects!

—*from the Spanish of Dámaso Alonso (1898-1991)*

A CHARLES GUENTHER RETROSPECTIVE
Translations

An Old Springtime

Now in the darkening purple of the west
At evening, when magnolias wet with dew
Are still in flower, I'd walk across those streets
And daydream as the moon grows in the sky.

Proclamations of swallows will enlarge that sky
With their complaint; the rising fountain spray
Will purify and free the earth's deep voice;
And then the earth and sky are left in silence.

In the corner of some spot a ghost appears,
Alone and with its head between its hands,
And meditating there you would lament
How beautiful and useless life had been.

—from the Spanish of Luis Cernuda (1902-1963)

THREE FACES OF AUTUMN
Poetry, Prose, Translations

The Harp

Cage of an invisible bird,
of the kindred water and air,
whose voice the stroking hand
slowly and softly calls.

As the water caught
in its fountain trembles, it rises
in a rainbow flight,
teaching our spirits.

Like wind through the leaves
the harp so vague, so clear,
speaks of things remembered
or forgotten, legends of time.

What fruits of paradise,
what heavenly fountains nourish
your voice? Tell me in song,
sing bird of the harp, O lyre.

—from the Spanish of Luis Cernuda (1902-1963)

A CHARLES GUENTHER RETROSPECTIVE
Translations

Poem from Exile

Who are you, voiceless, who now summon me
from far away with such a fearful mind
and on the soundless and destructive wind
utter my name, calling me silently?

Who are you, what do you ask in your hushed tones
and what in such remote a distance dies;
who are you, who with your strange silent cries
enter my skin and tear it from my bones?

My teeth taste like a word that turns to frost,
my tongue tastes like a death of what I feared,
my heart feels like a pulse whose beat is lost.

The bull's skin flows continually in blood,
the sea flows in a weeping dried up flood . . .
and those who called me now have disappeared.

—*from the Spanish of Rafael Alberti (1902-1999)*

Chilean poet, diplomat, and Marxist, Pablo Neruda (Neftalí Ricardo
Reyes) began writing poetry when he was 10. But from 1927 until the late
1940s, he devoted more time to politics than he did to his poetry. When
the Chilean government turned to the right, Neruda was forced, along with
other leftists, into hiding. In February 1948, he left Chile and
subsequently traveled throughout Europe, the Soviet Union, and Mexico.
In 1952, after the order to arrest leftists was rescinded, he returned to
Chile. Neruda won the Lenin Prize for Peace in 1953 and the Nobel Prize
for Literature in 1971.

I had read Neruda's early (Whitmanesque) poems in 1942; but Neruda had
other translators, even then, and I preferred to translate the mss. that
Professor Louis G. Zelson brought me, new work, from other Central and
South American poets—Cuban, Mexican and Bolivian especially. Yet I
appreciated and translated some of Neruda's shorter poems for their
striking imagery. "A Flower Falls," "Reason" and "Animal" are
included here.

A Flower Falls

The seven petals of the sea
are joined in this corolla
with the diadem of love:
All happened in the valve
of a rose that fell in the water
when the river reached the sea.
So one spurt of scarlet
leaped from the beloved day
to countless lips of the waves
and a rose slipped in
toward the sun on the salt.

—from the Spanish of Pablo Neruda (1904-1973)

THREE FACES OF AUTUMN
Poetry, Prose, Translations

Reason

The bough's oblong reason
seems motionless but it hears
the sound of light in the sky
in the zither of its leaves
and if you lean over to learn
how water rises in the flower
you'll hear the moon singing
in the night of the roots.

—from the Spanish of Pablo Neruda (1904-1973)

Animal

The well-aimed beetle
flew with wings spread
toward the infrared cherry.

He devoured it not knowing
the chemistry of power
and when he returned to the foliage
turned into a firebrand.

His heart fell
like a comet saturated
by the delicious radiation
and he was scorched in the substance
of those burning electrons:

on dissolving he became
a symptom of rainbows.

—from the Spanish of Pablo Neruda (1904-1973)

Miguel Hernández was a goatherd in his childhood; he had little formal education but he read voraciously in school and public libraries and became well-grounded in Golden Age poetry and drama. In 1934 he met, and was influenced by, Aleixandre and Neruda; and he received early encouragement from Jiménez and Machado. He joined the Spanish Communists in 1936, fought in the Civil War, and was imprisoned in Alicante, where he died of tuberculosis at age 32. His best work—mostly sonnets of a pure, rich style—appears in *El rayo que no cesa* (*The Unending Lightning*), 1936. A posthumous collection (1958) contains poems written in prison for his wife and son.

520

A CHARLES GUENTHER RETROSPECTIVE
Translations

To smile with the olive tree . . .

To smile with the olive tree, both sombre and bright,
to wait, and not tire of waiting for joy to arrive.
Let's smile, let's paint each day with a golden light
in this sad and joyful futility of being alive.

Every day I feel much lighter and more taken hold
by this smile that's at once so dark and yet so fair.
The storms that drift and pass over your cold
mouth drift and pass over mine as the summer air.

A smile rises over the deep: it expands, amplifies
like a tremulous abyss, but with wings beating and driven.
A smile is always warm as it rises and flies.

Steadily it comes and it doesn't darken or fall.
You defy everything, love: you climb over all.
With a smile you have transcended earth and heaven.

—*from the Spanish of Miguel Hernández (1910-1942)*

Octavio Paz, born in Mexico City, became a leading literary figure and diplomat in Latin America; he published his first book of poetry, *Luna silvestre*, in 1933. In 1937, he visited Spain; his poems, *Bajo tu clara sombra y otros poemas* (1937) are reflections on that experience. *The Collected Poems of Octavio Paz, 1957-1987,* appeared in 1987. In 1990, he received the Nobel Prize for Literature.

Oblivion

Close your eyes and lose yourself in the dark
under the red foliage of your eyelids.

Sink in those spirals
of the sound that buzzes and falls
and echoes there, remote,
toward the place of the drum
like a deafened waterfall.

Submerge your being in the dark,
drown yourself in your flesh,
and even in your inmost depths;
let your bones, livid lightning,
dazzle and blind you,
and between abysses and gulfs of darkness
unfold their blue splendor and will-o'-the-wisp.

Soak your nudity
in that liquid shadow of dreams;
abandon your form, a spume
left on the shore anonymously;
lose yourself, infinite woman,
in your infinite being,
a sea lost in another sea:
forget yourself and forget me.
In that ageless, bottomless oblivion
love, kisses and lips are reborn:
the stars are daughters of the night.

—from the Spanish of Octavio Paz (1914-1998)

Although Blas de Otero's first book, *Cántico espiritual* (1942), with its sense of national pride, showed early influences of the Generation of '98—particularly of the poet Miguel de Unamuno—Blas de Otero gradually became in his next eight books (through 1970) the most important voice of social protest among poets of post-Civil War Spain. For many years, he was an expatriate, living in France, Cuba, and the Soviet Union. His books were published outside of Spain. It was not until 1964 that his work, heavily censored, was again published in Barcelona.

These Poems

It's to that vast majority who frown
with worried brows and heavy hearts, to those
who struggle against their God and are struck down
in His deep darkness by His mighty blows.

To you and you and you, and you, round wall
of the parching sun, to those starving lands now long
laid waste, are sent direct to one and all
these poems which are composed of flesh and song.

Hear them as you would hear the sea. They will
bite the hand of whoever strokes their burning skin;
there on the shore their sound comes crashing in,

and they topple over like a leaden sea.
Oh this mortal angel, trying valiantly,
rushes to save you but he lacks the skill.

—from the Spanish of Blas de Otero (1916-1979)

Carlos Bousoño, born in Boal (in the province of Asturias) is regarded as a
leading critic of Spanish literature. His early influences included Vicente
Aleixandre, on whose poetry he published a study in 1950; but his major
critical work is *Teoria de la expresión poetical* (1952), for which he
received the Fastenrath Prize of the Spanish Academy. Bousoño's own
poetry reflects a broad exposure to both traditional and modern
movements.

A CHARLES GUENTHER RETROSPECTIVE
Translations

Come In

Here the radiant fields of the landscape fill
our eyes, a life imprisoned in the stone,
in mountain, valley, moon, that distant hill
inclining gently, lazily sloping down.

Now free me, river, rippling, undulating,
fountains of the world, life flowing endlessly;
with your darkness or your captive sweetness waiting,
come in, dark sunset, rosy evening sky.

Come in, come in, the soul stirs from its sleep.
It longs for life with its certainty of night,
with its sure and terrible menaces, its deep

disillusions, loves, come in, half-light,
days, months and years, moonlight and the subdued
and unknown terror and black solitude!

—from the Spanish of Carlos Bousoño (b. 1923)

From the French

Charles d'Orléans, one of the last and greatest courtly poets, was taken prisoner at the Battle of Agincourt (1415) and was brought to England where he remained for 25 years. In prison he wrote many poems—in French, English and Latin—and after his liberation, he lived in his chateau in Blois where he held a kind of literary court. His poems remained unpublished until 1734. This well-known rondel by the Duke d'Orléans was among my earliest translations. It appeared in *Poet Lore* (Boston), Spring 1945.

Rondel

Winter sheds his coat of snow,
  Bitter winds and frost and rain;
  Spring has dressed herself again
With the sun's embroidered glow.

From all animals outflow
  Happy songs with this refrain:
  Winter sheds his coat of snow,
Bitter winds and frost and rain.

River, stream and fountain flow,
  Thaw and tint with silver stain
  Summit, valley, hill and plain,
Roots awaken deep below:
Winter sheds his coat of snow.

—from the French of Charles d'Orléans (1391-1465)

"Now take this rose . . . ," as well as two other sonnets and an ode by
Pierre de Ronsard, I translated expressly for a national convention of the
American Rose Society held in St. Louis in the early 1980s. A folder of
the poems was distributed to 500 members at a banquet where a rose was
named for the keynote speaker, Eva Gabor. For years thereafter I urged
rosarians to name a new rose for Ronsard. In 1987 a highly rated (8.1)
large climbing rose, pink blend, the Pierre de Ronsard, was listed in the
official ARS Handbook.

532

A CHARLES GUENTHER RETROSPECTIVE
Translations

Now take this rose . . .

Now take this rose, like you in loveliness
Who are the fairest of all roses grown,
The blossom of all blossoms newly blown,
The muse to muses and to me no less.

Now take this rose, and with it too possess
This constant heart of mine within your own;
With countless bitter wounds it dwells alone,
Stubbornly watchful of its faithfulness.

We differ in one thing, the rose and I:
In a day or two the rose will bloom and die;
A thousand suns have seen my love endure,

Reborn each day, remaining ever pure.
Would God my love, destined to grow and stay,
Just like the rose, had perished in one day.

—from the French of Pierre de Ronsard (1524—1585)

Although my earliest French-into-English verse included work by poets like Sully Prudhomme and François Coppée, I liked the French Romantics, too—especially Alfred de Vigny. Vigny, a count and infantry captain, was decommissioned in 1827 and retired to his "ivory tower" to write novels and plays and a very few poems. "The Parisian Spirit," reflecting his pessimism and isolation, is one of his rare sonnets.

A CHARLES GUENTHER RETROSPECTIVE
Translations

The Parisian Spirit

March 1836

The spirit of Paris—old Byzantium's curse!
Decrepit sophist, drinking every night,
Like a heady wine that dulls your cares by the light
Of the glorious day, for better or for worse.

Cold leveller, casting in clay when each departs
This life, the great man and murderer alike,
Measuring their skulls, when in their breast you strike
And sink your vampire teeth deep in their hearts.

Rejoice! for this happy month you gave by threes
The guillotined heads displayed in the public square.
Tonight proclaim your faith, your Christian vow.

Like other kings, king of evil, get on your knees!
Sweet Charity with her angelic fingers there
Makes a sign of the cross on your convicted brow.

—*from the French of Alfred de Vigny (1797-1863)*

Charles Baudelaire, at first considered a minor Romantic poet and
translator of Edgar Allan Poe, became probably the most popular and
frequently translated 19th century poet. Although I translated many of
Baudelaire's poems in rough form in the 1930s and '40s, I later turned to
little known or untranslated poets like Supervielle, Char, Apollinaire, and
others. In my translation of Baudelaire's "Cats," I have taken the liberty
of changing his plural to a singular.

A CHARLES GUENTHER RETROSPECTIVE
Translations

The Cat

Scholars and ardent lovers, when they grow old,
Admire the strong and gentle cat, for he
Like them enjoys the indoors and similarly
Is sedentary and sensitive to the cold.

A friend of learning with a sensual side,
The cat seeks silence and the darkness' spell.
He'd be the ideal funeral horse of hell
If such a task did not demean his pride.

Musing, he takes the noble attitude
Of some great desert Sphinx in solitude
Stretched out and slumbering in an endless dream.

His fertile loins have sparks of sorceries,
And bits of gold as fine as gold dust seem
Galaxies drifting in his mystic eyes.

—from the French of Charles Baudelaire (1821-1867)

"The Dancer" is one of at least ten sonnets by Degas who, like Picasso, Dali, Jean Arp, and other artists, wrote verse before or during the Surrealist movement.

Stephane Mallarmé ("You don't write sonnets with ideas, Degas, but with *words.*"), although linked with Verlaine as an "original" Symbolist, was rather an Impressionist poet. A teacher of English at the lycée Condorcet, he influenced scores of young poets at his Tuesday evening soirées in Paris; but his strongest impact came after 1907, with the Cubist and Surealist poets, like Apollinaire and Reverdy. Mallarmé's "The Tomb of Charles Baudelaire" is from a small plaquette of my Mallarmé translations, eleven of which appeared in *Weid,* Vol. X, June 1976 (Homestead, Florida). Unlike Dadaism, or random, irrational expression, Mallarmé's poems were wrought with meaning—but with strict etymology, fresh contexts, inverted syntax, and other technical devices. I tried to moderate Mallarmé's syntax, not by introducing soft "poetic" words as synonyms (a practice of some translators) but by trying to restore some order in the lines and minimizing inversions. Still, any lines of Mallarmé are likely to remain abstruse.

In the latter half of the 19th century, concurrently with the Symbolist movement, the Parnassian school of poets—who stressed technical perfection and objectivity—became equally important. While Paul Verlaine, whose name is linked with both schools, advocated "music above all," the most authentic Parnassian poet was undoubtedly J.-M. de Hérédia (a Cuban self-exiled to France). His only volume, *Les Trophées* (1893), is a collection of 118 brilliantly honed sonnets and several longer poems on Classical, Renaissance and historical themes. "The Prisoner," along with a group of other Hérédia sonnets I translated in 1939-40, first appeared published in *talaria* (Cincinnati), Vol. IX (Autumn 1944).

538

Dancer

She dances as she dies, as around a reed,
To a flute where the sad air of Weber plays:
The ribbon of her footsteps writhes and twists,
Her body sinks and drops like a falling bird.

The violins drone. Cool with the water's blue,
Sylvana comes and daintily flutters there.
The joy of coming alive and pure love play
over her eyes, her breast, her whole new being.

And her satin feet embroider, like a needle,
Patterns of pleasure; and the springing girl
Tires my poor eyes straining to follow her.

But always with a nod the lovely mystery stops:
She draws her legs far backward as she leaps;
It's a frog leaping in Cythera's pools.

—*from the French of Edgar Degas (1834—1917)*

The Tomb of Charles Baudelaire

The buried temple reveals by its sewer's
Sepulchral mouth dribbling mud and rubies
Abominably some idol of Anubis
Its whole mouth blazing like a savage bark

Or when the recent gas twists the dark wick
An endurer as we know of sustained disgraces
It wildly lights an immortal pubis
Whose flight stays awake according to the street lamp

What dried foliage in the cities without a votive
Evening could bless as his shade is seated
Vainly against Baudelaire's marble

With the trembling veil that circles its absence
This his own shade like a tutelary poison which will
Always be inhaled even if it should kill.

—from the French of Stephane Mallarmé (1842-1898)

The Prisoner

The muezzin at the mosque has hushed his voice:
Green skies turn burnished gold; a crocodile
Slips from the mud and plunges in the Nile,
And bank to bank resounds its rippling noise.

Legs crossed, lulled by soft smoke that he enjoys,
A chief dreams, drawing on his hashish while
There labors in the gleaming *cangie* a file
Of sweating oarsmen, half-bare native boys.

An Arnaut plucking out tunes wild and fierce,
Singing with grating *guzla* string a-quiver,
Casts from the stern derisive, savage jeers

At an old sheik who, heedless of the airs,
Lies on the boat in bloody chains and stares
At minarets that tremble in the river.

—*from the French of José-Maria de Hérédia (1842-1905)*

I began reading Paul Verlaine, with the Belgian Symbolists (Maeterlinck, Rodenbach and Verhaeren), when I was 18. I was fascinated by the poems in his early *Fêtes galantes*, based on the "pleasure parties" in Watteau's paintings. (Verlaine must have read Charles Blanc's book, *Les Peintres de Fêtes galantes,* published in 1854.) At about the same time, I found a W.B. Yeats essay in which Yeats mentioned that "young poets" were translating Verlaine and Verhaeren—and I felt reassured. Verlaine was a natural lyricist, with an easy, musical style (Two lines from his poem *"Art poétique"* are: "Music above all" and "Take eloquence and wring its neck"). Although he is classed among the Symbolists, he had much in common with the dying Romantic movement and the emerging Parnassians.

I have never seen another translation of "The Clown" (*"Le Pitre"*), but its music, rhymes and all, seemed to fall into place in English. My translation first appeared in *Driftwind* (Vermont), XX (November 1945) and was reprinted in *Civ/n* (Montreal), No. 5, 1954.

The Clown

The stage a lively band is shaking rumbles
Under the clumsy-footed clown who flouts
(Not without skill and haughtiness) the louts
Stomping the boards up front and whom he humbles.

His painted cheeks are marvelous! He mumbles,
Then stops as suddenly as he puffs and shouts,
And roguishly receives quick kicks and clouts,
Pecks at his plump companion's neck, then tumbles.

Let's heartily applaud his claptrap speech!
His short, flowered vest and nimble limbs that reach
And twist deceptively are worth the view;

But most of all we like that wig, perched high
Upon his head, with its long dangling queue
Trailed by a swiftly fluttering butterfly.

—from the French of Paul Verlaine (1844-1896)

Many eminent French-language poets were not, of course, aligned with "movements," and among these were Emile Verhaeren, Jules Laforgue, and Saint-Pol-Roux. My translation of Verhaeren's "Toward the Future," which appeared in *Driftwind* (Vermont) in 1946, drew the attention of Wallace Fowlie, who liked its formal style and fidelity to the original. Tart and sardonic, Laforgue was admired especially by Pound and Eliot. Saint-Pol-Roux (Paul Roux) created a catalog or dictionary of linguistic symbols and ingenious, harmonious, images. "I arrange the great flow of words musically," he wrote, "placing them on the orchestral staves: here and there strings and woods, there the brasses and percussion instruments." The word-music of "Larks," which also appeared in *Driftwind* (December 1944), is particularly effective.

Toward the Future

O human race bound to the golden stars.
Have you felt with what dreadful striking toil
Suddenly for a century
Your boundless power is shaken?
From the seas' depths, across the earth and skies,
Up to the wandering gold of the lost stars,
From night to night and over distances
Projects above the voyage of the eyes.
While down below the dismal years and ages,
Resting in tombs now stratified by time,
From continent to continent are explored,
Arising from their darkness bright and dusty.
The eagerness to weigh and know all things
Ransacks the dense and shifting wood of beings,
And yet despite the briars that check his progress
Man overcomes his law of rights and duties.
In ferment, in the atom, and in dust
Unbounded life is studied and appears.
All's trapped in an infinitude of snares
Gripped or distended by immortal matter.
Adventurer, apostle, hero, scholar,
Artist—each breaks the black mysterious wall;
And by those labors, single or in groups,
New man perceives the universe completely.
And now it's you, you cities
That stand
At distances, beyond, from end to end
Of plains and provinces
Who concentrate enough humanity,
Enough red power and enough new splendor
To kindle with a teeming rage and fever
The patient or the violent brains
Of those
Who find the law and in themselves resume
The world.
The spirit of the landscape was the spirit
Of God; he feared research and man's revolts.
He fell, and now he dies under the axles

545

THREE FACES OF AUTUMN
Poetry, Prose, Translations

And under fiery cars of new results.
Decay sets in and blows to the four corners
From where winds rise, across the finite plain,
While from a distance the great city draws
What heat is left it in its agony.
Red factories blaze where lonely fields once shone,
Black waves of smoke now raze the churches' spires,
Man's spirit advances and the setting sun
Is not the gold, divine and fruitful host.
And will the fields be reborn someday,
Freed from mistakes, from terror and from madness;
Gardens for weary labors and endeavors,
Cups full of health and pure transparency?
Will they remake with the good ancient sun,
With wind, with rain and with the servile beasts,
In moments of free enterprise and wakening
A world saved from the encroachment of the cities?
Or will they be the final paradise,
Purged of the gods and freed of their forebodings,
Where, dawn and noon, wise men will go to dream
Before they fall asleep in peaceful evenings?
Till then the full life satisfies itself
To be a human joy, wild and abundant;
The rights and duties? They are changing fancies
The world's youth dreams before each new-found hope.

—from the French of Emile Verhaeren (1855-1916)

A CHARLES GUENTHER RETROSPECTIVE
Translations

Apotheosis

Forever out in space silence is sown
With whirling golden stars that gather and seem
Gardens where scattered diamond pebbles teem,
Each flashing its desolate, solitary stone.
High in those heavens, glittering unknown
With rubies in its wake, a single beam
Gloomily flares out in a peaceful gleam:
A Patriarch scout who guides his tribe alone.

His tribe: spheres swarming, clumsy and vegetated.
One is the earth, the speck of Paris on it
Where a lamp is lit and a fool scribbles away;
A unique miracle of all things created,
He knows that he's the mirror of one brief day.
He dreams . . . then writes about it in a sonnet.

—from the French of Jules Laforgue (1860-1887)

Larks

The clipping of scissors snips the air.

Now the crepe of mystery twilight ghosts drape over the cool flesh of life, now the crepe of the dark has stolen over the town and countryside.

The clipping of scissors snips the air.

Do you hear the good Lord's low bell cajole with the firebrand of its tolling the eyes, those yellow asphodels, the eyes crouched under the ashes of night?

The clipping of scissors snips the air.

Then rise from the dream in which we seem to be dead, my love, and adorn your window with the lilies, peaches and raspberries of your being.

The clipping of scissors snips the air.

Come up on the hill where the windmills charter their linen wings, come up on the hill where you can watch the divine diamond of the sky's enormous alliance spraying eternal sparks.

The clipping of scissors snips the air.

From the summit scented with thyme, lavender and rosemary we'll attend, I the caress, you the flower, the light and dark festival of hours on the clock where destiny rests, and there we'll watch the smiling world pass by with its long mournful shadow.

The clipping of scissors snips the air.

—*from the French of Saint-Pol-Roux (1861-1944)*

Maurice Maeterlinck was awarded the Nobel Prize for Literature in 1911. In 1914, at the outbreak of World War I, at age 52, he tried to enlist in the Belgian army; however, his government turned him down, advising him that his "superb pen" made him as valuable as a "battery of artillery." Best known as a playwright, Maeterlinck wrote some of the earliest free verse published in France. I translated *Serres Chaudes* (1889), one of his two books of poems, in college during 1937-39, but the manuscript was never published.

My translation of Paul Valéry's "Helen" has been reprinted several times; it is from my book of translations of Valéry (Olivant Press, 1970).

THREE FACES OF AUTUMN
Poetry, Prose, Translations

Hothouse

0 greenhouse deep in the forest
With your doors forever closed!
And everything that's under your dome,
And under my soul as under you!
The thoughts of a hungry princess,
The anxiety of a sailor in the desert,
A brass band at the windows of incurables.

Go to the warmest corners!
We might say a woman fainted on a harvest day,
There are postillions in the hospital courtyard;
In the distance there's a deer hunter, now become a nurse.

Examine moonlight.
(There's nothing like it!)
It's like a madness before judges,
A gunboat at full speed on the canal,
Night birds on lilies,
A passing-bell at noon
(Down there under those bell-glasses!),
A halt of sick people on the prairie,
An odor of ether on a sunlit day.

My God, my God, when will we have rain
And snow and wind in the hothouse!

—*from the French of Maurice Maeterlinck (1862-1949)*

A CHARLES GUENTHER RETROSPECTIVE
Translations

Helen

Blue! Here I am, come out of the haunted caves
To hear the thundering surf break on the shores
And see those ships, when sunrise strikes the waves,
Emerge from the dark with banks of golden oars.

My lonely hands summon those majesties
Whose salty beards amused my soft, light fingers.
I cried. They sang of their nebulous victories
And of those bays where the wake of their warships lingers.

I hear the martial trumpets, the profound
Sea shells beat a rhythm for the flying blades;
The clear song of the oarsmen stills the storms,

And the gods on heroic prows where the rollers pound,
Their ancient smiles battered by foam cascades,
Stretch out to me their indulgent, sculptured arms.

—from the French of Paul Valéry (1871-1945)

Rainer Maria Rilke was fluent in many languages. Although his best poems are in German, he published many poems in French—the result of having spent 12 years in Paris. In 1949 I bought a newly published edition of his French poems, intending to translate them all; but I found it more delightful just to read them. "Interior Portrait," from Rilke's *Vergers*, 1925, appeared in *CIV/n* (Montreal) No. 5, 1954.

A CHARLES GUENTHER RETROSPECTIVE
Translations

Interior Portrait

In me there is no memory
conversing with you still;
through an exalted will
no more do you belong to me.

You are made present by
the ardent turning action
that's described in my
blood by a lingering attraction.

Now I don't possess
a need to see you come;
enough that I was born
to lose you somewhat less.

—from the French of Rainer Maria Rilke (1875-1926)

Born in Uruguay of French Basque parents, Jules Supervielle was educated in France; by the 1930s, some critics considered him the best living French poet. In 1960 he was given the title Prince of Poets (an informal laureateship), but he died only two weeks later. Jean Cocteau succeeded him in that title. Supervielle had two distinct styles: early (predominantly descriptive, narrative free verse—as in "The World Is Full of Voices of Lost Faces") and later (more formal and meditative). The translation of "Sonnet to Pilar" was first published in *Luna 4* (2001).

Jules Romains (Louis Farigoule), one of the founders of the Unanimist movement, wrote curious "modern age" poems early in the century; Romains was 18 when he became aware of "an elemental being emanating from and transcending the jostling crowds and traffic" of Paris. His "Propagations" (which appeared in *The University of Kansas City Review,* Summer 1953) recaptures, for a reader, some of the wonders of electricity in the early 1900s when it first lighted the boulevards of Paris.

The World Is Full of Voices
of Lost Faces

The world is full of voices of lost faces
That turn around day and night to ask for one.
I tell them, "Speak to me in a familiar way
For I'm less confident in a large crowd."
"Don't compare our lot with yours,"
A voice then answers. "I was called one such,
I no longer know my name, I have no more brain
And can only prevail on that of others.
Let me depend a little on your thoughts.
It's a great deal like a living ear
For someone like me who scarcely exists.
Believe me, I am nothing but a dead man.
I want to tell someone who weighs his words."

—from the French of Jules Supervielle   (1884-1960)

THREE FACES OF AUTUMN
Poetry, Prose, Translations

Sonnet to Pilar

So that I'll not forever be alone
I look forward to your future company
For when, in spirit, we'll play at the life we've known,
Entrusting our faith in its validity.

No seasons, summer or winter, will be there
Nor shall we die again full of memories
For, starting now, we'll labor in this life we share
Driving our slow oxen, pausing as we please.

See how we might replace in our new being
Our land, its fruit, our loved ones and the sun
And change to a lovely day a night of strife,

Without hands to touch and without eyes for seeing,
Speechless to speak without words when our voice is gone
And motionless, to move away from life.

—*from the French of Jules Supervielle (1884-1960)*

A CHARLES GUENTHER RETROSPECTIVE
Translations

Propagations

Over the boulevard the human dusk
Is crystallized in an electric arch.
A slight sound skips; the swiftly passing current,
Caught in molecular thickets, starts to bleed.
Ethereal chills go off with stamping feet.
The sidewalk crowd's recovered confidence.
Darkness has summoned hearts and led them dancing
On tunes of songs grown faded or obscene,
Far in the solitude and in memory.
And now the light has sketched a circus ring:
The rhythms whirl there an instant, subjugated;
Souls recently concealed are unsheathed
To dip their edges, parallel and bare,
In brightness.
                    But within the bodies, cells
Feel marvelous inner rivers flow to them.
The arch that crackles with a solar fire
Flings in each cell a chivalric desire;
And unseen glitterings quaver, raucous bugles.
The unity of the flesh begins to crack;
The captive globules rage about like wasps
Caught in a cobweb, and the air is filled
With liberties that new embraces bind.
The radiance helps a tree to wish for spring.
Brains think less in the body, and the branches
Desire less a soul and strive to grow.
The spirit yields its force to the electric
Infusion. Now the street resolves to play.
Couples coagulate upon the corners;
The seeds stir. Men have gone to sit and chat
In small round groups in taverns; while the crowd
Dreams of being a village in the sunlight.

—*from the French of Jules Romains (1885-1972)*

Saint-John Perse (Alexis St. Léger-Léger), winner of the Nobel Prize for Literature in 1960, was born near Guadeloupe, educated in France, and at 25 entered the Diplomatic Service. After service in China and the French Foreign Office, he came to the United States to work with Archibald MacLeish at the Library of Congress. The translation of "Song," from Perse's *Anabase* (Gallimard, 1924), first appeared in the *St. Louis Post-Dispatch* (Nov. 13, 1960).

A CHARLES GUENTHER RETROSPECTIVE
Translations

Song

Halting my horse under the tree of doves, I whistle a call so clear that it bids fair all the rivers will break over their banks. (Living leaves in the morning are the image of glory.)

And not that a man isn't sad, but rising before dawn and discreetly holding communion with an old tree, and resting his chin on the last morning star, he sees at the end of the fasting sky great pure things revolving at will.

Halting my horse under the cooing tree, I whistle a clearer call. And peace to those on the point of death who haven't seen this day. But we have had tidings of my brother the poet. He has written another delightful piece. And some are familiar with it.

—from the French of Saint-John Perse (1887-1975)

Jean Cocteau was perhaps the most versatile, talented and prolific figures in 20th century French arts and letters. Besides producing works in other fields, he wrote more than 25 books of poems, fiction, criticism, and drama. Ezra Pound commissioned me to translate Cocteau's poem, "The Crucifixion," in 1953; and by 1987 I completed a book ms. translation of Cocteau's selected poems, and long extracts appeared as special supplements in *The American Poetry Review* in the September/October 1991 and January/February 2004 issues. "The King of the World" and "Sometimes Cruel Time . . ." are from the 1991 selection in *APR*.

Tristan Dérême, one of the early 20th century *fantaisiste* poets, never seemed to leave the 19th century. He wrote graceful, formal elegies reminiscent of Keats. In one of my rare multimedia performances, I read my translation of his poem, "The Strawberries" (published in *Western Humanities Review,* 1958), accompanied by "La Vie en Rose," at the opening of The Stradivarius, a Clayton supper club.

Like Saint-John Perse, the Belgian poet Henri Michaux traveled widely. One of the most original French language poets, he became noted for his "inner journeys" in many media and his unorthodox technique in whatever form he worked. "On a Picture by a Chinese Painter" appeared in *The Pennsylvania Literary Review* in 1956.

Raymond Queneau, who joined the Surrealist movement in 1924, was considered a precursor of the Existentialists. This translation of "Little Man" (from *Chelsea 13*, June 1963), exemplifies Queneau's characteristic cynicism and mock-heroic attitude.

The King of the World

How you sicken me, old intellectual world.
Your unbelief has chilled me to the bone:
    There are some young men
    Who go from Tibet to the stars.
Loquacious Europe, deaf to the flutes of Tibet,
You've spoken too much, Tibet knows how to be silent.
Tibet knows how to walk above the earth . . .
If suddenly, Tibet, your mask should fall
Which covers your mysterious childish smile,
This babbling deaf woman would be so afraid,
So fearful curled up in her Voltaire chair,
    That a cry would shake her sleep,
    Would make her pale lips red.
Tibet, crack open her eyes and cut her tongue:
    Give us the treasure of your heart.

—from the French of Jean Cocteau (1889-1963)

THREE FACES OF AUTUMN
Poetry, Prose, Translations

Sometimes Cruel Time . . .

Sometimes cruel time you show your mechanism.
Our wrist nibbled by the insect of watches
Clasps far away from us its bright blue veins
Rivers of a land insensible to our fears
And under the deceptive skin where their bends are painted
Mixing a red ink with the salt of the sea.

The blood doesn't seek to understand its course
Its destiny is to run to rejoin its source
It frightens me and my pulse beats with my watch.
I dare not watch one or the other live . . .
Then lazily I wallow in you, sleep
I mount your broom and fly to the midnight revels.

—from the French of Jean Cocteau (1889-1963)

562

A CHARLES GUENTHER RETROSPECTIVE
Translations

The Strawberries

The strawberries on the white porcelain plate still yield
The chill, fresh smell of sunrise in the field,
Of boughs and moss and ice-encrusted streams.
I've laid upon the cloth your cluster of dreams,
And while you ponder with a thoughtful gaze
I watch among the leaves how the moon plays
As in old elegies on this somber night.
A pure warm breeze flickers the candlelight
Rocking the arbor where the vine-boughs weave
With the pale rose. Take strawberries. You perceive
Sugar dissolving in the golden wine;
Time on our brows spreads sugar powdered fine
And soon my hair will be thick, white and free.
What matter, if tonight you lean to me,
Fearless how red the leaf of autumn is,
And smother the lamplight reaching for my kiss.

Stay in your shell, then, snail-like and oppose
This moist perfume of apricot and rose;
Your solitude adorned with dreams may yet
Be sweet; it rains; your horns are getting wet.
The sod is crushed under the hot rain's lash,
The house is brightened by the thunder flash
Which lights the wall where you cling close behind
Cobwebs; the stars are blown out by the wind;
The moon, like fruit, has tumbled over the lawn.
Pull in your horns; with noise and lightning gone,
In self reflection gild your reveries.
Outside the storm crumples the grass and trees,
Rattles the slates and makes the roof resound.
Let the world fall to ruin all around!

—*from the French of Tristan Dérême   (1889-1943)*

On a Picture by a Chinese Painter

A flock of birds swoops over the valley
With a gust from the sky
   with a thick lenticular tumult
   the squadron rises
There's a vast whiteness
   above
   below
   sideways
   everywhere
   a mourning white
Busy trees search for their boughs torn off and
   splintering distracted trees
trees like bloody nervous systems
   but no human beings in this drama
The humble man doesn't say "I'm unfortunate"
the humble man doesn't say "We are suffering
our loved ones die
our people are homeless"
He says "Our trees are suffering"

—from the French of Henri Michaux {1899-1984)

A CHARLES GUENTHER RETROSPECTIVE
Translations

Little Man

Little man you haven't worked tonight
a fly falls in the paste pot
You pick it up and throw it in the air again
Little man you haven't worked tonight

Little man you haven't worked tonight
You confound the past the present and the dishwater
you've written a poem again or even only a few verses
Little man you haven't worked tonight

Little man you haven't worked tonight
Not a cent has fallen into your purse
All is deserted around you
Little man you haven't worked tonight

Little man you haven't worked tonight
Will it be like that until the day of your mortal death
Then who will pay for your funeral the casket and the need
       for a monstrance
Little man you haven't worked tonight.

—from the French of Raymond Queneau (1903-1976)

Léopold Sédar Senghor, although linked with the Surrealist movement, was more celebrated as a founder and influential advocate, in his native Africa, of Negritude—black African expression in art and literature. This translation of his "Song" for a native guitar appeared in *Focus/Midwest* in 1965. I had translated his poems since before he became the President of Senegal in 1960; selections from my book ms. of his work appeared in *Poetry* and *Ramparts* (among other U.S. magazines) from 1963 to 1965. Senghor, educated in France, was a teacher in French schools before World War II. Early in the war he was drafted and was captured by the Nazis. On his release in 1942, he joined the French Resistance. In 1980, in his fifth term as President of Senegal, he retired. He was elected to the French Academy in 1984.

Song

(for *khalam*, a four-stringed native guitar)

I was sitting on the prose of a bench at evening.
The guard duty hours lined up before me like the monotony of posts
    on a road
When I felt the bronze rays of your face on my warm cheek.

Where did I see that color before, the shade of a proud old fortress?
    It was in the days of Bour Sine Salmonn
And my great-grandfather read his darling's face on the tin of springs.
But what sweetness at day's end! And it's summer in the streets of my
    heart.
Trees of gold leaves, with their flowers in flame—is it spring now?
Women have the airy step of bathers on a beach
And their long leg muscles are harp strings under their platinum skin.
Servants of royal collar pass by, going to draw spring water at six o'clock
And the lamp posts are tall palms where the wind sings its laments
And the streets are white and peaceful as in childhood siestas.

O my Africa-colored love, prolong these hours of guard.
Those who are hungry carry off these treasures of Foresight!
Their smile is so sweet! It's the smile of our Dead who dance in the
    blue village.

—from the French of Léopold Sédar Senghor (1906-2001)

René Char joined the Surrealists in the 1920s, but he broke with the movement in 1938. A captain in the Resistance during World War II, he "arose and wakened" France in its darkest hour with his wartime diary. After the war he produced a steady stream of poetry into the 1980s. Albert Camus, among others, considered him the greatest living French poet. I first corresponded with Char in 1957, and learned that he liked the translations of his work to resemble the original text—that is, the English words to approximate the French in appearance. To keep my integrity (and sanity) as a translator, I found that I had to continually "negotiate" with Char, respecting his wishes as much as possible. (Char was nearly always right, I might add.) By 1967 I had translated and had published more than 50 of his poems; and for 50 years have compiled a book ms. of his work. "The Inventors" appeared in *Poetry* (Chicago), March 1957, and "Course of Clay" in *New Letters* (1985). After René Char's death in 1988, *The American Poetry Review*, in its May-June 1988 issue, featured a dozen more translations with a tribute.

A CHARLES GUENTHER RETROSPECTIVE
Translations

The Inventors

They came, the rangers of the other side, those unknown to us,
    the rebels to our customs.
They came in great numbers.
Their band appeared at the dividing line of the cedars
And from the field of ancient harvests hereafter watered and
    green.
The long march had overheated them.
Their caps broke over their eyes and their foundered feet were
    stuck in the waves.
They noticed us and stopped.
Obviously they didn't expect to find us there,
On fertile lands and well-enclosed fields,
Wholly indifferent to an audience.
We raised our brows and encouraged them.

The most eloquent one drew near, then a second one just as
    uprooted and cumbersome.
We came, they said, to warn you of the impending arrival of
    the hurricane, your implacable foe.
We don't know him any more than you do
Except by reports and ancestral secrets.
But why are we unaccountably happy before you and suddenly
    like children?

We thanked and dismissed them.
But earlier they drank and their hands trembled and their eyes
    laughed around the edges.
Men of trees and axes, able to resist some terror but unfit to direct
    water, lay out buildings or cover them with pleasant colors,
They would ignore the winter garden and the economy of joy.

Surely we could have persuaded them and conquered them,
For the hurricane's distress is moving.
Yes, the hurricane was going to come soon;
But was that worth the trouble they spoke of and which turned
    the future upside down?
There is no urgent fear here where we live.

—*from the French of René Char (1907-1988)*

THREE FACES OF AUTUMN
Poetry, Prose, Translations

Course of Clay

Notice, shrill bearer from morning to morning,
The long frenzied blackberries coiling their sprouts,
The earth closing in on us with its absent gaze,
A cricket's even song to lull our pain,
And a god showing up just to swell the thirst
Of those whose words are addressed to living waters.

Therefore rejoice, my dear, in the following fate:
This death doesn't close the memory of love.

—from the French of René Char (1907-1988)

Pierre Emmanuel, born in the Pyrenees, spent his early years in the United States with his parents. He studied engineering in Lyons, France; however, influenced by Valéry, he turned his interests to poetry and philosophy. Between 1940 and 1951 he published 15 books of poems, as well as criticism, journal articles and an autobiography. In 1949, I began translating his wartime poems and published at least 15 in various magazines by 1967. When I was hospitalized for ten weeks in 1961, Emmanuel sent me an inscribed copy of his *Selected Poems* and wrote to me—which both lifted my spirits and helped my recovery; for I set to work translating more than ever from his poetry and prose, and eventually got most of it in magazines like *The Literary Review* and *Poet Lore.* Emmanuel was inducted into the French Academy in 1969. "Pledges" is from my feature of his work in *Poet Lore* (1965).

Alain Bosquet was born in Odessa, Russia, and grew up in Belgium where he attended the University of Brussels. He served in both the French and U.S. armies during World War II, and became a U.S. citizen in 1943. After the war, he graduated from the Sorbonne, Paris (M.A., 1951). One of the leading figures in French poetry, he published more than 50 books of poetry, fiction, essays and translations. Part of my M.A. was earned by turning some 50 of his poems into English—one of the most practical uses of the craft in my life. In addition to collaborating on a translation of his *Selected Poems* (1963), I have continued to work on his poetry since. "Characters" was published in *Poetry* (Chicago) in April 2001 and was the French Embassy's website poem that month.

Rene Guy Cadou's first poems, written in college, appeared in 1937 and were followed by more than 20 small pamphlets. Influenced by other French poets, including Supervielle, Cadou preferred the rustic lifestyle and avoided the salons of Paris. My translations of his poetry were featured in *The Literary Review* (Spring 1961) and in *Chelsea 13* (Spring 1963). "Helen or the Vegetable Kingdom"is the title poem of his most important collection, published posthumously in 1952 by Pierre Seghers (Paris). My translation of this poem first appeared in the *Chelsea* issue.

Pledges

This blood will never dry up on the earth
And these slaughtered dead will stay unburied.
We'll grind our teeth by strength of being silent.
We'll not weep over those inverted crosses.

But we shall remember these dead without memory.
We shall count our dead as they have been counted.
Those who weigh so heavy in the balance of history
Are astonished tomorrow that they are considered light.

And those who were killed for fear of being understood,
Their silence will not be forgiven any more.
Those who stood up to argue and pretend
Will be condemned even by the least pious men.

These dead, these simple dead, are our whole heritage;
Their poor bloody corpses will remain undivided.
We shall not let their image lie fallow—
Orchards will flourish on the greening meadows.

Let them be naked under the sky like our earth,
And let their blood be mixed with the well-loved springs.
The eglantine will cover with angry roses
The fierce spring seasons roused by this blood.

Let these spring seasons be unspeakably gentle to them:
Full of birds, songs, and children on roads.
And like a forest sighing around them
May a great multitude pray softly, lifting their hands.

—*from the French of Pierre Emmanuel (1916-1984)*

A CHARLES GUENTHER RETROSPECTIVE
Translations

Characters

Early in the morning all the characters
leave the book where they were born to wander
no matter where in the ironic city streets
among real people of flesh and blood and sweat.

We recognize them by their nervous look,
their ink-stained hands, their faces carried off
like a tail end of speech. They aren't happy
in their sudden freedom. Do they dare to live

with proper intelligence in their phony fate
as heroes in manuscripts? They return at night,
ashamed but sensitive, to their home: those pages

between poetry and prose where their distress
takes shelter.   Now his anger gone, the author,
skeptical and generous, takes them back in his book.

- from the French of Alain Bosquet (1919-1998)

THREE FACES OF AUTUMN
Poetry, Prose, Translations

Helen or the Vegetable Kingdom

You're in a garden and you're on my lips
I don't know what bird will ever imitate you
Tonight I entrust my hands to you so you may tell
God to use them for his blue business

For you are heard by the angel your words
Stream in the wind like a tuft of wheat
And the children of heaven returned from school
Apprehend you with ecstatic faces

Bend your ear a bit lower than the clover
Inform the horses that the earth is saved
Tell them all's well with the hemlocks and the brambles
That your love has been enough for all to change

Helen I see you in the middle of the fields
Acquitting the rosy crimes of the orchards
Opening the high lifts of the world so man
May reach the luminous counters of the sun

When you're far away from me you're always present
You stay in the air like a smell of bread
I'll wait a hundred years for you but you're already mine
By all those prairies you carry inside you.

—from the French of René Guy Cadou (1920-1951)

From the German

Goethe's "Wanderer's Night Song," with its simple, universal message, was published in *The Cresset* (Valparaiso, Indiana) in September 1959.

Wanderer's Night Song

Over all the mountaintops
Is peace.
In all the treetops
You feel
Scarcely a breeze.
In the woods the little birds are still.
Just wait, soon
You too will rest.

—from the German of Johan Wolfgang von Goethe (1849-1832)

I first intended this metrical translation of Rainer Maria Rilke's "Wilder Rosenbusch" for use, with selections from Rilke's 24-poem suite, "Les Roses," in a series of poem cards ("Laura Cards")—nearly all on the theme of roses—that I began in 1983. Rilke's poetry, both in the French of his "Interior Portrait" (p. 551) and in the German of "Wilder Rosenbusch," is tightly constructed. The original "Wilder Rosenbusch" is in alternately 11- and 10-syllable lines (except for line 2 in the first stanza, which is 8 syllables); and the original rhyme scheme is abab, cdcd, efef, in the three stanzas—but I found it impractical to rhyme without making the poem sound strange. Well, that's the problem with many poems in all languages, I suppose.

A CHARLES GUENTHER RETROSPECTIVE
Translations

The Wild Rosebush

See how it's set against the gloomy landscape,
fresh and innocent in the rainy dusk
with petals folding down in wild abundance
and still preoccupied with being a rose

of buds and blossoms, some now in full bloom,
with each untended and with each unclaimed;
so infinitely outflowing from itself
and indescribably self-energized,

it calls the wanderer, who in contemplation
passes along the road when evening falls:
Oh, see me, see me here, safe and secure,
and though unguarded, having all I need.

—*from the German of Rainer Maria Rilke (1875-1926)*

Hermann Hesse, in his youth, entered a seminary but, unable to adjust, dropped out to work in a factory and, later, in a bookstore. During World War I, to avoid military service, he lived in neutral Switzerland and edited a journal for war prisoners. He was granted Swiss citizenship in 1923. He was awarded the Nobel Prize for Literature in 1946. Although best known as a novelist (*Steppenwolf*, 1927, and other works), Hesse produced an impressive body of poetry, reflecting his strong self-awareness. The translation "Sometimes" first appeared in *The Cresset* (Valparaiso, Indiana) in October 1956; "Over the Fields" is an unpublished translation.

A CHARLES GUENTHER RETROSPECTIVE
Translations

Sometimes

Sometimes when a bird calls out
Or the wind barrels through the trees
Or a dog howls on a farm far away,
I stop and listen.

My soul turns back again:
A thousand forgotten years ago
The bird and the blowing wind
Were like me, they were my brothers.

My soul becomes a tree,
An animal and a cloud.
Transformed, it comes home as a stranger
And questions me. How can I answer?

—from the German of Hermann Hesse (1877-1962)

THREE FACES OF AUTUMN
Poetry, Prose, Translations

Over the Fields

Clouds roll over the sky,
the wind blows over the fields,
and over the fields wanders
my mother's lost child.

Leaves blow over the street,
high over the trees birds cry;
far off, over the mountains,
my home must lie.

—from the German of Hermann Hesse (1877-1962)

From the Hungarian and Italian

In the 1950s I met the Hungarian poet and scholar, Leslie Konnyu, who had emigrated to the U.S. and become a citizen after World War II. A P.E.N. member and founder of the T.S. Eliot Society, he also founded and edited *The American Hungarian Review* which published poetry in both languages. Through him I became interested in Hungarian poets, especially those who wrote during the Hungarian revolution of 1956.

In the early 1960s Robert Bly sent me a copy of work by some of those poets, with Hungarian and Italian texts; he asked me to make English translations for an anthology to be edited by David Ray. The anthology was adapted from the Hungarian *Füveskert*, edited by Tibor Tollas. Six of my translations—among them, "Cut and Run"—appeared in *From the Hungarian Revolution* (Ithaca, New York: Cornell University Press, 1966). Meanwhile, most of my translations not used in the Cornell University Press anthology were published as "Twenty-One Hungarian Poems" in the Summer 1966 issue of *Poet Lore*, with a note on David Ray's anthology. "Where the Monastery Stood" and "Old Farmer" appeared in *Poet Lore*; and a revised version of "Old Farmer" appeared, most recently, in *River Styx 53* (1998).

About the Hungarian poets represented here: Tibor Tollas ("Where the Monastery Stood") edited a newspaper in Munich and lectured widely; Gábor Kocsis ("Old Farmer") left Hungary in 1956 to study in Vienna and later taught in Germany; Vince Sulyok ("Cut and Run") left Budapest, published two books of poems in Rome and Brussels, and later went to Norway and was a scholar at the University of Oslo.

584

Where the Monastery Stood

A century ago the yellow linden trees
Flowered in this courtyard where a monk in white,
Weeding the roses, whispered rosaries
And a murmuring fountain played in the dying light.

A century ago the humble, gentle fingers
With silent gestures left the mark of ages
Where the illumination of manuscripts still lingers
Indelibly on the yellow parchment pages.

But now the cloister is a moldy hell:
Chains mourn the loss of flesh, and mutilated hands
Scratch out defiance in the darkened cell

On walls that echo with men's tortured cries;
Take heart; beyond these crumbling stones all lands
Of Europe join to share their agonies.

Vac, 1955

—from the Hungarian and Italian of Tibor Tollas (b. 1920)

Old Farmer

With heavy steps down over the hill he strode
Where lines of grass between the hay rows died;
His pipe lit up his copper face which glowed
Through wisps of smoke, ghost-like and fiery-eyed.

Around him as he sat down the silence grew
Like plants spread out in the blue lake of night;
My mother's grandfather must have been like him too,
At ninety years, a coal still burning bright.

At times some words came through his moustache where
They fell to the earth in clods, broken and brown—
Tiborc's *Lament* . . .* sung on eternally,

While the moon's white disk plowed furrows in the air
And tiny astral particles newly sown
Sank slowly, slowly, slowly into the sky.

*Tiborc is the character of the oppressed peasant
    in Josef Katona's play *Bano Bank* (1815).

—*from the Hungarian and Italian of Gábor Kocsis (b. 1932)*

Cut and Run

Endlessly a strange joy shakes in me, as
Endlessly the sea runs thundering to land, scattering
Foam over the rocks.
                  The waves' anger spends
Its final energy at my feet. Like a man revived,
I tremble in the wind, and stare around
At the steel-blue sea, the tepid bay, the green skies with white sails,
And beyond, the lazy ships. Gradually I realize
Here are no guards or guns or barbed-wire fences. I've come
To a clean, cool world. I've come from wastelands,
I've run from nightmares, from the dark into light, I've come
By magic seas to the stone-laced Norwegian coast;
And it's sweet to lie on rocks in the sun, to pierce
The soft waves, to swim in the deep, to drink
The summer, the clamoring sea, and the view; and I know
Freedom, my life's meaning.

—*from the Hungarian and Italian of Vince Sulyok (b. 1932)*

Index

INDEX

I. Poetry

INDEX

II. Prose

INDEX

INDEX

INDEX

INDEX

599

INDEX

INDEX

601

INDEX

INDEX

Murry, John Middleton, 272
Mussolini, Benito, 154
My Sister, Life, 115
Mysterious William Shakespeare, The, 287
Myths and Texts, 193

1960 Nobel Laureate, The, 117-118
1984, 113
95 Poems, 106
Nash, Ogden, 216
Near Changes, 373
Near-Johannesburg Boy, The, 314
Negro Caravan, 198
Neiges, 106
Neihardt, John G., 408
Nemerov, Howard, 191, 196, 203, 204, 260, 263, 269, 359-361, 411
Neo Magazine, 138
Neruda, Pablo, 151-152, 180, 359, 380
Nerval, Gérard de, 187
Neva, 130
New & Selected Things Taking Place, 176
New and Collected Poems, 1961-1983 [Dugan], 267
New Anthology of Modern Poetry, A, Selden Rodman
New Birth, The, 139
New British Poets, 189
New Directions, 79
New Letters, 280
New Life, The, 164, 327
New Masses, The, 280
New Poems (1968-1970), 151-152
New York: Poems, 204
New Yorker, The, 157, 204, 216, 217
News of the Universe . . ., 203
Next to Last Things: New Poems and Esssays, 283-284
"Night of the Four Songs Unsung," 110
Nin, Anais, 174
Niven, Penelope, 345-346
No Thanks, 103
"Nobel Prize, The," 116
Not So the Chairs: Selected and New Poems, 412
nouville naissance, La, 139

Novalis, 187
Novy Mir, 130
Nu Perdu, Le, 319
Nunn, Trevor, 433

O'Hara, Frank, 381
Oates, Joyce Carol, 435
Obbligati: Essays in Criticism, 295-296
Observations, 390
Ocean Vows, 231
O'Connor, Flannery, 263
Oden, Gloria, 254, 364
Odes of John Keats, The, 239
Odets, Clifford, 201
Odyssey, The, 388-389
Oeuvres complete [Char], 319
Ogburn, Charlton, 287
Old Troubadour: Carl Sandburg with his Guitar Friends, 317
Olson, Charles, 302, 363
Olson, Clarence, 356
"On a Bicycle," 129
On English Poetry," 135
On Poetry and Poets, 105
On the Poetry of Allen Ginsberg, 265-260
One for the Rose, 219
On the Great American Rainway, Selected Poems, 1950-1986, 381-382
Opacity of Signs: Acts of Interpretation in George Herbert's The Temple, The, 311-312
Opie, Amelia, 304
Opium and Kubla Khan, 81-82
Opportunity, 109
Oresteia of Aeschylus, The, 178
Origin, 96
Orne, Martin, 233
Orphée, 413, 414
Orpheus (see *Orphée*)
Orpheus, 244
Osmond, Donny, 261
Ossian, 108
Ostrom, John, 251
Otero, Blas de, 161, 347
Other Side of the River, The, 369-370
Others, 195, 310

604

INDEX

INDEX

INDEX

INDEX

609

INDEX

INDEX

INDEX

INDEX

III. Translations

INDEX